Promises to Keep

PROMISES

TO

KEEP

Technology, Law,

and the

Future of Entertainment

William W. Fisher III

STANFORD LAW AND POLITICS
An imprint of Stanford University Press
Stanford, California

For Jess and Cricket

Stanford University Press
Stanford, California

© 2004 by William W. Fisher III.
All rights reserved.

Printed in the United States of America on acid-free, archival-quality paper.

Library of Congress Cataloging-in-Publication Data

Library of Congress Cataloging-in-Publication Data

Fisher III, William W.
   Promises to keep : technology, law, and the future of entertainment /
William W. Fisher.
      p.   cm.
   Includes index.
      ISBN 0-8047-5013-0 (cloth : alk. paper) -- ISBN 978-0-8047-5845-1 (pbk.: alk. paper)
      1. Copyright—Music—United States.   2. Piracy (Copyright)—
United States.   3. Internet entertainment industry—Law and
legislation—United States.   I. Title.
KF3035.F57   2004
346.7304'82—dc22   2004010000

Original Printing 2004

Last figure below indicates year of this printing:
13   12   11   10   09   08   07

Typeset by James P. Brommer in 10/13 Sabon and Stone Sans display.

Contents

Preface to the Paperback Edition

This book describes a crisis in the entertainment industry, explores its origins, and compares possible ways in which it might be resolved. It was originally published in the summer of 2004. Since then, distressingly little has changed.

A few things are different—or, rather, a few trends already underway in 2004 have continued. Perhaps the most important is that online sales of digital audio and video recordings have increased considerably. The best-known and most popular of the online sellers, Apple's iTunes MusicStore, continues to grow, and new businesses using similar strategies spring up weekly. But two forces are limiting their success. The first is that almost all of the online sellers wrap their products in technological protection measures (TPMs) in an effort to discourage purchasers from redistributing them. TPMs have several disadvantages (explored in Chapter 4 of this book) from the standpoint of overall social welfare. Partly as a result, most consumers dislike them and are reluctant to purchase recordings that are subject to them. The second force is the continued availability on the Internet of very large numbers of unauthorized copies of recordings. It remains difficult for the new businesses to "compete with free."

Another, related trend that has continued since 2004 is the tightening of the legal rules that seek to prevent the unauthorized reproduction and distribution of recordings. Chapter 3 of this book describes several ways in which copyright law was modified between 1990 and 2004 in order to strengthen the positions of copyright owners. Those reforms slowed but certainly did not stop unlawful trafficking in recordings. Consequently, in the past few years, copyright owners have sought—and sometimes obtained—additional legal protection. In the United States, the most important recent innovation was the decision by the Supreme Court in the *Grokster* case, which made it easier for copyright owners to bring suits against intermediaries who "induce" copyright infringement by others. Some European jurisdictions have increased the penalties for infringement. And in China, a group of entertainment companies prevailed, at least temporarily, in a high-profile copyright suit against Baidu, the operator of an enormously successful search engine that enabled users easily to locate on the Internet unauthorized copies of recordings. These changes undoubtedly have had an impact, but have done far less than their sponsors hoped. The net result: in the music industry, the traditional market in CDs and tapes is declining faster than the new market of online sales is growing. Copyright owners are justifiably worried that they are driving toward a cliff. The major players in the film industry fear that they will soon suffer the same fate.

A more encouraging recent development is an increase in the frequency with which consumers are making creative uses of the digital recordings that come into their hands. Chapter 1 of this book contains several examples of such creativity and argues that it should be celebrated and fertilized. Many more instances could be identified today. But TPMs and a justified fear of copyright infringement have curbed this trend as well.

In short, the crisis described in this book has deepened since 2004, and the need to resolve it has grown. Somewhat more specifically, we need to identify a combination of legal rules and business models that will enable us simultaneously to realize the huge potential social and economic benefits of the digital revolution and to provide the creators of the entertainment products from which we all benefit reliable sources of income.

How are we to accomplish that? I remain convinced that the best solution would be a state-sponsored alternative compensation system of the sort described in Chapter 6 of this book. Last year, France came close to adopting a system of that general sort, but in the end backed away. There is some hope that Germany would institute such a regime, but probably not quickly.

So what are we to do in the meantime? In the last section of Chapter 6, I suggest how, even in the absence of legal reform, one might construct a private enterprise that would have many of the advantages of a government-run alternative compensation system. Since the publication of the book, a group of us have been working to build such an enterprise. The fledgling venture was nurtured by a generous grant from the MacArthur Foundation, but now is on the verge of flying on its own. Known as Noank Media, it aspires to create a world in which all Internet users pay, through their access providers, small amounts of money into a pot, in return for unlimited access to unencrypted digital recordings. The money in the pot is then distributed to copyright owners in amounts proportional to the frequency with which their creations are watched or listened to. Companies seeking to implement these principles are now taking shape in both China and Canada. If successful there, similar enterprises may spring up in other countries. With luck, they may provide a solution to this increasingly serious problem.

William Fisher
May 2007

Acknowledgments

The foundation for this book was laid by an extraordinary group of research assistants. Gabriel Bell, Marcelo Guerra, Aaron Kotok, Kathy Kraig, Todd Larson, Cristine Reynaert, and Jeff Shih gathered and digested much of the data on which it rests.

During the four years in which I've wrestled with those materials, I've presented portions of my evolving argument in a variety of settings: at a workshop at the NYU Law School called "A Free Information Ecology"; at the Law School of the University of California at Davis; at an annual meeting of the International Society for Law and Technology; at the Queensland University of Technology; at the International Congress on the Law of Information Technology, held in Brasilia; at two of the annual conferences of the Future of Music Coalition; at the Stanford Center for Internet and Society; to the New England Copyright Society; at the South-by-Southwest Music and Film Festival; at the Summer Faculty Workshop and the Law-and-Economics Workshop at Harvard Law School; to the Yale Information Society Project; at Boston University Law School; at Nassau Community College; at Duke Law School; to a group of senior lawyers for the film industry at Warner Bros. Studio; to the legal staff of HBO, to the Stanford Law-and-Economics Seminar, at the Santa Fe Institute, and at the 2004 Canadian Music Week. The comments of the participants in those events have been invaluable.

In December of 2003, a group of scholars, activists, and businesspeople met for a one-day workshop at Harvard to discuss the creation of an alternative compensation system for digital media. The debates we had that day (and our continuing conversations online) have helped refine the argument of the final chapter of the book.

Several colleagues, friends, and strangers have generously commented on parts or all of the manuscript. Especially useful have been the suggestions of Harold Akselrad, Jack Balkin, Joseph Bankman, Yochai Benkler, Benoît de Boursetty, Oren Bracha, Paul Cappuccio, Anupam Chander, Steve Crandall, Peter Eckersley, John Gilmore, Louis Kaplow, Larry Lessig, Jim Logan, Ronaldo Lemos, Douglas Lichtman, Michael McGuire, Amar Mehta, Isaac Lidsky, Neil Netanel, Michael O'Hare, Dotan Oliar, Mikael Pawlo, Steven Shavell, Derek Slater, Tim Sullivan, Aaron Swartz, Gregory Teves, Siva Vaidhyanathan, and Fred von Lohmann.

Donald Passman, author of the appropriately titled *All You Need to Know About the Music Business*, kindly saved me from many errors in my description of the recording industry in Chapter 2. Jeremy Williams and Shelley Presser (of Warner Bros. Entertainment) and Jared Jussim (of Sony Pictures Entertainment) were similarly helpful critics of my description of the film industry.

My collaborators at the Berkman Center for Internet and Society—Charlie Nesson, John Palfrey, and Jonathan Zittrain—have provided both shrewd criticism and essential logistical support throughout the project. I hope to continue to work with them on the opportunities and problems associated with digital media for years to come.

Neeti Madan of Sterling Lord Literistic and Amanda Moran and Mariana Raykov of Stanford University Press helped me prepare the book for publication. David Horne's work as a copyeditor was terrific.

Most important of all have been the encouragement and guidance of my wife, Diane Rosenfeld.

Introduction

In August of 2000, *Napster* was a household word in the United States. Millions of Americans were using the Internet-based file-sharing system of that name to exchange "MP3" versions of copyrighted sound recordings. The major record companies had brought suit against Napster, arguing that, by enabling and encouraging this behavior, Napster had itself violated copyright law. In July, the federal judge before whom the case was tried had agreed with the record companies and ordered Napster to stop "facilitating" the illegal copying and distribution of musical compositions and recordings. An appellate court had temporarily suspended the trial judge's order, but most commentators in the United States expected that the original decision would eventually be upheld. Napster thus continued to operate, but a cloud hung over the company and its subscribers.

In the midst of this controversy, I was asked to give a lecture in Rio de Janeiro on the subject of the impact of the Internet on the law of intellectual property. The audience consisted of approximately 350 Brazilian lawyers, 150 judges, and 200 law students. Midway through my presentation, I began to discuss the Napster case and its likely outcome. Uncertain how many of the attendees would already be familiar with the way in which the system operated, I decided to ask, "How many of you have used Napster?" Approximately half raised their hands.

The response to my question illustrates several aspects of the crisis currently afflicting the music industry in the United States and elsewhere. The most obvious lesson of the story is that the business model upon which all record companies and many musicians depend is being threatened by new, Internet-based technologies. For many years, the primary way in which recorded music has been distributed throughout the world is through sales of objects ("singles," long-playing vinyl albums, cassette tapes, and, most recently, compact discs) containing sound recordings. If large numbers of consumers can easily obtain sound recordings for free over the Internet, demand for those objects sooner or later will decline. The extent to which the use of file-sharing systems has *already* corroded sales of recordings is a complex question we will address later in this book. But eventually, if use of those systems is as widespread as the Brazilians' response suggests, the market for authorized sound recordings is bound to deteriorate.

A somewhat less obvious lesson is the fact that the technologies that the record companies justifiably fear also have considerable social and economic benefits. The Brazilian lawyers and judges (as some explained to me after the lecture) were able by using Napster to obtain sound recordings much more cheaply, easily, and quickly than they could by purchasing compact discs. That the music obtained over the Internet is cheap is not necessarily socially beneficial. After all, its low cost reflects in large part the fact that the musicians and intermediaries who created it are not being compensated—which both seems unfair and threatens to reduce their incentives to produce more music in the future. But the speed and convenience of the Internet-based distribution system are surely socially beneficial. As we will see, those advantages represent only the tip of an iceberg of cultural and economic benefits that full deployment of currently available technologies could make possible. If, in hopes of protecting the record companies' traditional business model, the law suppressed those technologies, much would be lost.

A third lesson pertains to the character of the audience for the lecture. These were not teenagers and were not Americans. That half of them had used a music-distribution system first deployed in the United States less than a year before is testimony to the speed with which such technologies spread, virally, throughout the world. Even more significant, the audience was composed almost exclusively of lawyers, judges, and post-graduate law students hoping to become judges. Even before my lecture, most of them knew that an American court had declared the mode of copying and distributing sound recordings that Napster made possible to be copyright infringement. Brazilian copyright law is similar, in relevant respects, to American copyright law. There was thus a good chance that use of the Internet to share copyrighted musical files was also illegal in Brazil. Yet half of these legal sophisticates had engaged in that behavior and did not hesitate to acknowledge as much in public. How do we account for that behavior?

One possibility is that they had read the trial judge's opinion, found it unpersuasive, and expected it to be overturned by the Court of Appeals.

This is conceivable, I suppose. As we will see, the logic of the judge's treatment of Napster was far from airtight. An expert in copyright law might well conclude that it was inconsistent with the more tolerant way in which the United States Supreme Court had previously responded to the manufacture and marketing of videocassette recorders. But my conversations with members of the audience after the lecture suggested that few if any of them had explored the issue to this depth.

A more plausible explanation is that, although the attendees were (as yet) unaware of the details of copyright law, they did not regard file sharing as improper and assumed that the courts would eventually render a decision consistent with their moral intuitions. Two circumstances lend credence to this hypothesis. First, polls conducted in the United States during the summer of 2000 revealed that somewhere between 40 and 56 percent of all respondents (and higher percentages of Internet users) believed that it was not immoral to download music from the Internet. It would not be surprising if Brazilians felt the same. Second, most people in the United States and elsewhere assume that the law by and large tracks their sense of justice. It would thus be natural for the Brazilian listeners to assume that the courts shared their view that file sharing is benign and would eventually embody that view in judicial decrees.[1]

If this was indeed the reason that the attendees responded as they did, it's cause for concern. The widespread faith, just described, that the law by and large tracks our sense of morality is socially and economically very important. Enormous amounts of time and energy would be wasted if people lost that faith and felt obliged, before making major decisions, either to look up the relevant laws themselves or to consult with lawyers. When, ultimately, the courts defied the audience's moral intuitions and declared that the use of Napster constituted copyright infringement, the result may have been to corrode their willingness to trust their intuitions in analogous situations in the future.[2]

Yet another possible explanation is that the members of the audience knew that file sharing was illegal and did not expect the Brazilian courts to conclude otherwise, but were willing to engage in the activity anyway. This is perhaps both the most likely and the most troubling of the explanations. As Jonathan Zittrain has observed, one of the most remarkable features of the new technologies is that they have made it easy and natural for large numbers of people to violate the law. To be sure, popular lawbreaking is by no means new. Speed limits and prohibitions on the use of certain drugs are violated regularly. But the scale of the illegal behavior enabled by Napster and the brazenness with which it is acknowledged are striking. After all, the audience consisted almost exclusively of people upon whom we rely to interpret and enforce the law. Something is dangerously out of whack if half of them knowingly violate the law and, moreover, have no compunctions about admitting as much.

A final aspect of this vignette, though not new, is also troubling. It would have been possible for the members of the audience to have used the Napster system to share recordings of Brazilian music. But conversations after the lecture suggested that that was not the case. Rather, they were primarily interested in gaining quick access to American popular music. To some observers, that phenomenon is puzzling and worrisome. After all, the population of Brazil is three fifths that of the United States, speaks Portuguese, not English, and has a rich musical heritage. Against this backdrop, it's at least odd that they should be such avid consumers of American musical products. As we will see, Napster and other recent technological innovations are by no means the only source of the global power of American popular culture, but, at least as they have been deployed to date, have reinforced that power.

In the end, the Court of Appeals did indeed uphold the crucial portions of the trial judge's ruling. After a few months of procedural maneuvering, Napster was forced to shut down. The result was to halt file sharing by Napster's seventy million subscribers—including, of course, the subscribers in my audience. Had this been the end of the tale, there would have been no need for this book.

But Napster was not the last or the largest of the technological waves to wash over the music industry. (Nor, for that matter, was it the first.) It was followed, in short order, by the deployment of several new file-sharing systems, which were both legally differentiable from Napster and, perhaps more important, much less vulnerable to closure through judicial decree; by the widespread distribution of "CD burners" and a rapid increase in their use to copy sound recordings; and by the extraordinary proliferation of "Webcasters"—the Internet equivalent of small radio stations. Nor have the waves ceased; the next set, as we'll see, is on the horizon.

Thus far, the record companies have been less successful in meeting the challenges presented by the more recent technologies than they were in fighting off Napster. Legal proceedings against the innovators are unfolding more slowly and generating less consistent results. Partly because of this, the encroachments upon the traditional business models of the music industry are increasing. In 2001, over five billion sound recordings were exchanged over the Internet. At the same time, sales of blank compact discs—most of which are used to produce duplicates of commercial sound recordings—rose rapidly. Indeed, in the United States, sales of blank discs exceeded sales of prerecorded discs. Not surprisingly, the number of record albums sold in the United States declined by 9 percent. In 2002, these trends accelerated. The use of peer-to-peer copyright systems increased further. (For example, KaZaA became the sixth-most-heavily-used Internet application among Americans, attracting roughly thirty million active users per month.) Blank CDs again outsold prerecorded discs. And commercial record sales fell 9.9 percent— from 929.2 million to 837.4 million.[3]

So far, the film industry has not been hit as hard as the music industry. Indeed, box office receipts rose during both 2001 and 2002. This is partly because video files are much larger than musical files and thus harder to exchange over the Internet and store on one's computer. It's also partly attributable to the different ways in which movies and music conventionally have been consumed. Listening to a "pirated" MP3 file on a good home stereo is a nearly perfect substitute for listening to a commercial CD, but watching a "pirated" DivX file of a film on a home computer screen is far from a perfect substitute for seeing the film in a theatre. Recently, however, the executives of the major film studios have justifiably expressed growing anxiety concerning the viability of their traditional business models in the rapidly changing technological environment. Several converging developments have them deeply worried: the increasing availability of broadband Internet access; the increasing size of hard drives; the emergence of digital television; rising sales of personal video recorders; and proliferation of the hardware and software necessary to "burn" DVDs. In 2001, approximately five hundred thousand video files were exchanged over the Internet. With the new technologies, that number is likely to increase exponentially—with predictable adverse effects on the numbers of consumers who pay for access to films.[4]

As the crisis in the record industry has deepened—and has threatened to engulf the movie business—debates over who is responsible for it have become increasingly acrimonious. Representatives of the record companies and movie studios refer to the developers and users of the new file-sharing systems as "thieves." Consumers and their advocates increasingly describe the companies and studios as "greedy monopolists" and celebrate their impending extinction as a form of "creative destruction." Some musicians, actors, and directors associate themselves with the companies, others with consumers.

Divisions among the various industries that formerly had collaborated in the distribution of entertainment products have further complicated this debate. The record companies and film studios, for example, have accused such seemingly respectable enterprises as Intel, Apple Computers, and Gateway of deliberately designing equipment optimized for stealing and then encouraging consumers to use them to "rip, mix, burn" copyrighted recordings. The accused companies respond that they (like firearms manufacturers) are not responsible for the illegal use of their products and should not be forced to police the behavior of their customers. (Recently, the record companies and the leading hardware manufacturers agreed at least temporarily to bury the hatchet, but the Motion Picture Association of America pointedly refused to join the truce.) On a separate axis, the efforts by the record companies to develop copy-protected compact discs have angered Philips (the Dutch electronics giant that helped develop CD technology), which argues that the new discs don't meet the "Red Book" audio CD standard. In short, the companies that together have supplied us with recorded entertainment are not only fighting with consumers; increasingly, they are fighting among themselves.[5]

How did we get into this mess? And how are we to get out of it? The aspiration of this book is to answer those questions. The inquiry proceeds as follows.

Chapter 1 describes the technologies that are currently transforming the entertainment industry, and then assesses their social and economic implications. A seemingly technical change—from analog to digital format—in the manner in which entertainment products are stored and replayed, combined with the "communication revolution" associated with the Internet, has produced an extraordinary array of new ways in which music and movies can be created and distributed. As we will see, both the creators and the consumers of entertainment products stand to benefit enormously from those new systems. If available technologies were exploited fully, the costs of recordings would drop sharply, the incomes of artists would rise, many more artists could reach global audiences, the variety of music and films popularly available would increase sharply, and listeners and viewers would be able much more easily to participate actively in the (re)shaping of the entertainment they receive. We will see, however, that the new technologies also pose serious risks. A well-known danger is that they will corrode the traditional ways in which artists have made money from their creations. Less notorious but also worrisome are the threats they pose to the interests of artists in the "integrity" of their works and the interest of the general public in the stability of our cultural environment.

Plainly, it would be best if the entertainment industry and the legal system could be shaped to assist us in reaping the large potential benefits of the new technologies, while minimizing the concomitant problems. Chapters 2 and 3 explain why, unfortunately, we have thus far failed to strike that balance. Chapter 2 lays the groundwork for the explanation by describing how sound recordings and movies were made and marketed in 1990, just before the storm of technological innovations broke. We will examine how, in the music industry, a combination of legal rules and industry customs structured the complex relationships among composers, publishers, recording artists, record companies, radio stations, and various financial intermediaries. We will pay particularly close attention to who won and who lost when the interests of these players conflicted. Turning to the movie industry, we will study the ways in which law and custom made it possible to aggregate the creative energies of all of the people who participate in the making of a film —producers, screenwriters, directors, actors, musicians, cinematographers, editors, and so on—and how their collective products were traditionally marketed. Finally, we will consider the strengths and weaknesses of the systems in place in the two industries. In many respects, they were remarkably effective—as evidenced by the extraordinary outpouring, under their auspices, of commercial audio and video recordings and by the increasing power of American companies in foreign markets. However, the systems also had three drawbacks: they were unnecessarily expensive, they produced highly skewed income distributions among artists, and the range of the products they placed in mass circulation was disturbingly narrow.

Chapter 3 then examines what happened in the two industries between 1990 and the present. The narrative line resembles that of a country song. Each verse begins optimistically, with the introduction of a new service or device that, by exploiting in some way the new technologies, offers consumers significant benefits. Quickly, however, things go awry. Typically, companies that stand to lose from the innovation invoke either the law or technological countermeasures to curtail or eliminate it. Services and devices that have met (or are about to meet) this fate include digital audiotape recorders; "music lockers"; interactive and noninteractive Webcasting; encryption circumvention; centralized file sharing; decentralized file sharing; CD burning; and enhanced personal video recorders. In seeking to block these innovations, the companies that dominate the music and film industries have not been malicious; at worst they have been shortsighted in their efforts to protect their existing business models. But the net effect has been highly unfortunate. We have forfeited most of the potential benefits of the new technologies, while alienating consumers and incurring enormous legal costs.

The remainder of the book sets forth three alternative ways in which, through legal and institutional reform, the music and film industries could be remade. Each offers a way of reaping at least some of the potential advantages of the new technologies, while fairly compensating the creators of entertainment products.

The first of the proposals, examined in Chapter 4, takes seriously the long-standing claim of the record companies and movie studios that copyrights are property rights and should be treated as such. The right to control the use of a song or film, the companies argue, deserves the same scope and protection as the right to control the use of a piece of land. To test this proposition, we will first explore the legal principles that govern property rights in tangible objects and then consider what extension of those principles to musical compositions, sound recordings, and motion pictures would entail. For the most part, this exercise will point (as the companies have long insisted) toward significant strengthening of the rights of copyright owners. But it will also identify some less obvious ways in which those rights should be limited. The heart of the chapter then considers what would happen if we implemented this combination of reforms. Many good things, it suggests, would likely ensue. Effectively protected against unauthorized trafficking in digital files, the record and movie companies would more rapidly deploy subscription and "a-la-carte" systems for distributing entertainment products over the Internet, collaborate in the creation of flexible private organizations that would enable them efficiently to license their products to various intermediaries, and develop sophisticated price-discrimination schemes that would both increase their revenues and enhance the availability of entertainment products. Consumers, for their part, would gain legal access to music and films more easily and cheaply. Other effects, however, would be undesirable: increased concentration in the industries and associated price increases; impediments to the ability of consumers to reshape the entertainment products they receive; troublesome cultural repercussions of the price-discrimination schemes; and, perhaps most seriously, a brake on the pace and range of innovation in computer equipment and software. In short, though better than our current situation, the world generated by pursuit of this strategy would be seriously flawed.

Chapter 5 takes a different tack. It looks for guidance, not to the analogy between real property and intellectual property, but instead to the theory and practice of traditional regulated industries, such as telephone companies and railroads. Several aspects of the entertainment industry make this analogy apt, including its dominance by a few firms, the cultural importance of the commodity it controls, its dependence on governmentally created monopolies, and the notorious inequality in bargaining power between, on one hand, the dominant firms and, on the other, creators and consumers. What would happen if we treated the entertainment industry like a public utility?

Most important, we would require the record companies and movie studios to license their works to distributors, we would regulate the fees that they could charge, and we would prescribe the shares of those revenues that went to different groups of artists and intermediaries. Again, these and related reforms would have very considerable benefits, including a rapid increase in the Internet distribution of entertainment; greater diversity in the services available to the public; an increase in the incomes of creators and performers; and stabilization of the revenues of the record companies and studios. The drawbacks of this approach, however, would also be serious: high transaction costs; impediments to consumer creativity; and the distortions always associated with tight governmental control of private enterprise. Though not so serious as the disadvantages of the first approach, these drawbacks make this strategy less than ideal.

Chapter 6 outlines the best of the possible solutions to the crisis: an administrative compensation system that would provide an alternative to the increasingly creaky copyright regime. In brief, here's how such a system would work: The owner of the copyright in an audio or video recording who wished to be compensated when it was used by others would register it with the Copyright Office and would receive, in return, a unique file name, which then would be used to track its distribution, consumption, and modification. The government would raise the money necessary to compensate copyright owners through a tax—most likely, a tax on the devices and services that consumers use to gain access to digital entertainment. Using techniques pioneered by television rating services and performing rights organizations, a government agency would estimate the frequency with which each song and film was listened to or watched. The tax revenues would then be distributed to copyright owners in proportion to the rates with which their registered works were being consumed. Once this alternative regime were in place, copyright law would be reformed to eliminate most of the current prohibitions on the unauthorized reproduction and use of published recorded music and films. The social advantages of such a system, we will see, would be large: consumer convenience; radical expansion of the set of creators who could earn a livelihood from making their work available directly to the public; reduced transaction costs and associated cost savings; elimination of the economic inefficiency and social harms that result when intellectual products are priced above the costs of replicating them; reversal of the concentration of the entertainment industries; and a boost to consumer creativity caused by the abandonment of encryption. The system would certainly not be perfect. Some artists would try to manipulate it to their advantage, it would cause some distortions in consumer behavior, and the officials who administer it might abuse their power. But, on balance, it is the most promising solution of the three models. The chapter concludes with a brief discussion of how a variant of this approach might be implemented on a voluntary basis—as either a prelude to or as an alternative to its creation and management by the government.

In the course of our examination of these three models, we will take looks at several of the specific proposals for legislative change currently being debated inside and outside of Congress. Our focus will not be on the details of those bills, however. In the next few years, some will change, others will be cast aside, and some new ones undoubtedly will surface. The goal of this book is to provide a general framework for evaluating not just the current slate of legislative options, but also the iterations and substitutes that will arise in the future.

As suggested by the anecdote with which we began, the current crisis in the entertainment industry is not limited to the United States; most countries are now undergoing similar convulsions. Nor, for that matter, is the crisis confined to the production of recorded music and films. The markets in television programs, books, photographs, and video games will soon be transformed by the same technological and cultural forces. One book cannot address all aspects of the problem; by necessity, our attention in the following pages will be confined, for the most part, to the American music and film industries. Without undue difficulty, however, the proposals offered in Chapters 4, 5, and 6 could be adapted to other media and jurisdictions.

Many people and organizations would have to cooperate in order to implement any one of those proposals. The intensifying strife during the past dozen years between consumers, record and movie companies, technology manufacturers, and artists might suggest that such cooperation is unlikely. One characteristic shared by all three models, however, provides the basis for optimism. Under each one, almost everyone would fare better than under the current regime. If the representatives of each group of players could come to see that regimes beneficial to all parties are imaginable and feasible, we could work collectively to transform the world of recorded entertainment.

1 The Promise of the New Technology

In June 2001, I gave my younger daughter a new laptop computer as a high-school graduation present. My hope was that she would use it primarily as a tool for research and writing in college. The model that I selected came equipped with many features that would help her work: a fast microprocessor and considerable "random access memory" (to speed her writing and calculations and to enable her to operate several software programs simultaneously); an Ethernet card (to enable her, through her college's high-speed network, to communicate via email and to do online research); a large hard drive (to enable her to store her notes, essays, and the fruits of her research); a DVD drive (to enable her to use the growing amounts of data and software that are commonly stored in that format); and a large, high-resolution color screen (to ease eye strain).

The computer has so far served her well in exactly the ways I'd hoped. But it has also, to my mild surprise, come to function as her media center. The hard drive now houses (along with Abnormal Psychology notes and email archives) over three hundred sound recordings, all downloaded from the Internet. The computer also functions as a mini-theatre. On weekend evenings, a group of her friends will borrow it for a few hours, drop a DVD into the drive, and huddle together on a couch to watch the show. Finally, she was recently given a "CD burner," which, when connected to the computer, enables her to copy audio recordings either from her hard drive or from compact discs borrowed from her sister or her friends onto inexpensive blank discs. In short, my daughter, like most of her classmates, routinely employs her computer, not just to read, write, communicate, and calculate, but also to gain access to and then enjoy music and movies.

Watching the ways in which my daughter and her friends use their computers to obtain entertainment, I've been struck by four aspects in which their experience differs from how, thirty years ago, my college classmates and I experienced entertainment. Most are differences in degree, not kind, but in the aggregate they foreshadow a fundamental shift in our culture.

First, my daughter and her friends experience entertainment as inexpensive. Recorded music, in particular, they experience as free—easily obtained from a variety of Websites and peer-to-peer copying services for no charge.

To be sure, their attitude on this score could be challenged on a couple of grounds. Most obviously, it could be objected that recorded music seems to them free only because they are stealing it instead of buying it. That objection rests upon some assumptions concerning the shape of copyright law and the associated legal rights of the creators of the music—assumptions that will be examined in detail in Chapters 2 and 3. For the time being, it is sufficient to observe that legal constraints have thus far made little dent on either the behavior or the attitudes of my daughter and her friends.

It also could be objected that recorded music is far from free, even to my daughter, when one takes into account all of the costs associated with gaining access to it. After all, her computer (now supplemented by the CD burner) cost a good deal of money, as does a subscription to an Internet service provider, which enables her to download the music. As it happens, my daughter does not bear any of those costs. She received the computer and burner as gifts, and the cost of her ISP access is buried somewhere in the list of fees that accompany her college tuition. But surely they should be taken into account when determining the price of providing her access to recorded music. This well-founded objection points toward a refinement of the characterization with which we began. The *average* cost to her of each sound recording—taking into account the costs of the computer and the connection to the Internet—is surely positive. But the *marginal* cost—the cost of obtaining each additional recording—is near zero.

This helps to explain the second of the four ways in which my daughter's engagement with entertainment differs from mine. For her, entertainment is plentiful. Her collection of sound recordings (modest by the standards of her classmates) dwarfs my college record collection. And she has easy, casual access to a menu of movies for which there was no parallel in my experience.

This surfeit of material, in turn, partly explains the third feature: the culture of sharing. To be sure, my classmates and I sometimes shared music. We would occasionally loan our record albums—to selected friends whom we expected would take care of them and return them. And a few of my classmates had tape recorders that enabled them, at a relatively modest cost, to make and give away imperfect copies of albums. But these exchanges are trivial compared to the promiscuous sharing of the current generation.

Finally, my daughter and her friends expect that entertainment of all forms should be available anywhere anytime. The mobility of entertainment technology is of course not an altogether new phenomenon. Portable and car radios have been around since before I was in college. Portable cassette players and CD players are well-established features of the cultural land-scape. But until recently, these were experienced as exceptions to a pattern of sharp constraints on space and time. Movies were best seen in theatres, which operated on rigid schedules. Television programs were best watched at home, and (before the advent of the VCR) could only be watched at pre-determined times. Music was best heard through a stereo system, which was inconvenient to move around. These distribution channels—and the expec-tations they engendered—have not disappeared. But the ubiquity of devices that provide users more control over when and where they listen and watch have shifted the locus of normality. Now, temporal or spatial constraints on the availability of recorded or interactive entertainment are seen as excep-tions, in need of explanation or justification, not the rule. (Years ago, my daughter, watching broadcast television at home, rose to go to the bath-room. As she left the room, she called back, "Please pause the movie.")

In several ways, in short, the manner in which my daughter engages with recorded entertainment is different from the manner in which I did. Is it bet-ter? Yes. Not because she listens to more music or watches more movies, nor because the average quality of her fare is higher than that of mine. The im-provement, rather, lies in the diversity of the menu of material available to her, her ability to select the time and place with which she consumes it, and, most subtly, the communal, cooperative way in which she and her friends collect and enjoy audio and video recordings.

Is this revolution now complete? On the contrary, one of the central claims of this book is that we have only begun to tap the extraordinary power of the new technology. But the way in which my daughter and her friends are already using their machines suggests the direction in which we could move. The balance of this chapter tries to chart that course.

The Technology

The precondition for the entertainment revolution was the widespread use of digital technology. Until the mid-1980s, the dominant ways of storing and transmitting popular entertainment all relied upon "analog" technol-ogy, in which information is stored or represented in the form of some continuously variable quantity: the shape of a record groove, voltage, the position of magnetic particles on a tape, and so on. One after another, each analog system has been or is being replaced with digital means of representing information—in which complex messages (such as the sounds emitted by an orchestra or the pattern of colors in an image) are represented by combinations of electronic pulses and the spaces left between them.

The principal examples of this transformation are undoubtedly familiar to most readers. During the late 1980s and early 1990s, most "record" stores in the United States replaced their analog long-playing vinyl record albums with digital compact discs. Correspondingly, sales of turntables and cassette players plummeted, while sales of CD players skyrocketed. During the 1990s, sales of digital audio recording devices—digital audiotape (DAT) recorders, "minidisc" recorders, and, most important, CD burners—rose, at first slowly, then very rapidly. At the turn of the century, sales of analog videocassette recorders (VCRs) began to decline, displaced by digital versatile disc (DVD, formerly digital videodisc) players (for playing prerecorded movies) and digital personal video recorders (PVRs) (for recording broadcast signals). In 2002, sales and rentals of movies in DVD format for the first time exceeded sales and rentals in analog VHS format. Finally, radio and television stations are just now beginning to make the transition from analog over-the-air signals to digital signals, and studios are beginning to produce movies in digital format (rather than on 35mm film), forcing theatres to install digital projectors.[1]

In terms of the quality of the sounds and images they produce, not all of the digital systems are dramatically better than their predecessors. (Some audiophiles continue to insist that a good turntable, using an excellent cartridge to play an unblemished vinyl album, sounds better—"warmer," "fuller," "less brittle"—than a CD player playing a compact disc.) The digital systems do, however, have at least two characteristics that have proven crucial to the entertainment revolution. First, copies of digital recordings are identical to the originals, whereas copies of analog recordings are inferior to the originals. This means that digital recordings can be copied an unlimited number of times without degrading, whereas analog recordings cannot. Stephen Kramarsky provides the following illustration:

> [I]f I have a photograph of a sunrise that I want to send to you, I might photocopy it and mail you the copy. The photocopy would be less clear than the original photograph, and if you decided to send a copy to your friend, your photocopy would be even less clear and so on until, twenty friends down the line, even the best color copiers would have reduced the image to a red and orange blur. This is because photocopying is an analog process. If, on the other hand, I had a digital copy of the sunrise image saved on my computer, I could

email it to you, and you could email it to whomever you liked and so on down the line. The twentieth copy of the file would be identical to mine, and so would the twenty thousandth.[2]

Second, as this illustration suggests, digital recordings, unlike analog recordings, can be stored on and manipulated by general-purpose computers. One of the most important implications of that capacity is that they can be compressed. The digital media in which sound and video are most commonly stored contain unwieldy amounts of data. A typical compact disc contains over six hundred megabytes, while a typical movie stored on a DVD contains five gigabytes. During the 1980s and 1990s, compression standards were developed and popularized that made it possible to reduce those numbers dramatically—not by removing bits of information at random but, more cleverly, by identifying and removing bits that do not contribute significantly to the quality of the sound or image that a recording, when replayed, generates.

Currently, the most popular audio compression standard is the Moving Picture Experts Group's MPEG-1 audio layer 3 algorithm, popularly known as "MP3." Using freely available software, one can use the MP3 format to reduce the digital recording of a song on a CD by a ratio of up to twelve to one. To most ears, the compressed recording sounds virtually identical. The most popular family of video compression formats, known as DivX, enables one to shrink a recording of a movie by a factor of somewhere between seven and ten. Again, the compressed version is hard to tell from the original.[3]

Compression technologies continue to improve in ways that will affect the argument of this book. Already, audio compression systems substantially better than MP3 are available. For example, MP4 (short for MPEG-4 AAC) contains audio "codecs" (compression-decompression systems) that are substantially more efficient, scalable, and modular than MP3. Even more radical improvements are on the horizon. A compression system currently under development at the MIT Media Lab uses metadata to describe the content of music—in much the same way that modern graphics programs communicate with modern laser printers—to achieve extraordinary levels of compression with minimal loss of quality. Several companies are currently working hard to develop better video codecs. Meanwhile, consumers are being offered ever larger and ever cheaper hard drives suitable for use in home computers. The net result: with relative ease and at modest cost, consumers can already create large libraries of recorded entertainment, and soon they will be able to maintain enormous ones.[4]

The many advantages of these new technologies have fueled demand for the machines that embody them. The speed with which Americans have been buying the new devices is extraordinary. Currently, 54.4 percent of American households own stand-alone DVD players; 54.3 percent own computers with CD players; 28.1 percent own computers with CD burners; and 23.3 percent own computers with DVD players. Most of these numbers have increased sharply since 2002.[5]

The foregoing innovations, dramatic as they are, would have had only modest impact on the music and film industries if it were not for the creation and popularization of the Internet. A few statistics suggest the speed and importance of the emergence of this new communications system: in 2000, roughly 43.5 million households in the United States (41 percent of all households) had access to the Internet. In 2001, the numbers were 53.4 million (50 percent); in 2002, 58.2 million (54 percent). They are projected to rise to 65.0 million (59 percent) by the time this book appears. The foregoing numbers actually understate rates of Internet usage, because many Americans who do not have access to the system at home do so at school, at work, or in libraries.[6]

As one might expect, Internet usage is roughly correlated (inversely) with age, but not as much as one might think. As Figure 1.1 (prepared by the Department of Commerce) shows, teenagers use the system the most, but Americans between the ages of twenty and fifty also log on in large numbers—and that pattern has held true for the past several years.

Internet usage is also correlated (positively) with income, but again not as much as one might expect: over 25 percent of Americans living in households earning less than $15,000 per year use it. Finally, since 2000, Internet usage rates have ceased to vary with gender; women now use the system just as often as do men.[7]

In most other countries, Internet "penetration" is lower than in the United States, but is increasing fast. The total number of people worldwide who had access to the Internet was 388 million in 2000, 493 million in 2001, and 591 million in 2002. Although the annual growth rates in North America and Europe have slowed to 8.5 percent and 15.6 percent, respectively, the rates in other parts of the world remain extraordinarily high: 22 percent in Africa; 34 percent in Asia; and 36 percent in Latin America and the Caribbean. Already, the total number of Internet users in Asia exceeds the total number in North America, which, in turn, slightly exceeds the total number in Europe.[8]

The Internet has many uses, of course, but the most important for present purposes is that it enables people to transmit—easily, quickly, and inexpensively—digital audio and video recordings. Somewhat more specifically, it makes possible three different ways of delivering and enjoying recordings, which for the purposes of this book we will define as follows:

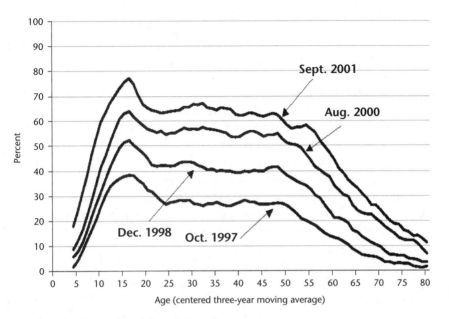

FIGURE 1.1. *Internet Use Age Distributions, 1997–2001.*

SOURCE: United States Department of Commerce, *A Nation Online: How Americans Are Expanding Their Use of the Internet* (2002), 14.

Downloading: The transmission over the Internet of a digital copy of an audio or video recording, followed by storage of that file on the recipient's computer, enabling the material to be replayed repeatedly on demand.

Interactive Streaming: At the request of the recipient, the transmission over the Internet of a digital copy of an audio or video recording, which is then "played" but not stored.

Noninteractive Streaming: The same process not at the request of the recipient.

Downloading is the most notorious of these activities, primarily because of its extensive use in the past few years as a way of distributing sound recordings. It encompasses both the delivery of permanent copies of recordings to personal computers from a centralized set of servers (such as MP3.com a few years ago and iTunes today) and the "sharing" of such copies by individual computer users (through "peer-to-peer" systems, such as KaZaA). To date, interactive streaming has been employed for the most part only to distribute video recordings—through various "pay per view" systems. Noninteractive streaming has recently become increasingly important as growing numbers of radio stations have begun to "simulcast" their programs over the Internet—and as dedicated "Webcasters," such as Spinner.com, have emerged to do the same.

Many examples of all three models—and many hybrids—will be considered in Chapter 3, when we review the series of technological innovations that have recently swept over the entertainment industry and the legal responses to them. For the time being, it is only necessary to keep in mind the essence of the three ideal types: *downloading* involves Internet delivery of permanent copies; *interactive streaming* enables recipients to view or hear recordings "on demand" but not to store them; and *noninteractive streaming* is the Internet equivalent of traditional radio or television broadcasts, in which the sender, rather than the recipient, determines what is transmitted when.

The technological developments reviewed in the preceding pages interlock, and in practice they have helped drive one another. The digitization of entertainment made possible the transmission of copies of recordings over the Internet. The development and improvement of compression systems have reduced the amount of time required to transmit files and the amount of disk space required to store them. Opportunities to gain access to entertainment over the Internet have helped fuel the increased popularity and use of the system. In the future, improvements in each of these technological dimensions are likely to continue to stimulate and reinforce one another.

The opening section of this chapter sketched a few of the economic and cultural effects that these innovations have had to date. Full exploitation of the opportunities presented by the new technology could lead to far more radical changes. To see the possibilities, it will be necessary to ignore the constraints that the legal system does or might exert. We will examine those constraints soon enough. For the time being, assume that neither copyright law nor any other system of legal rules interfered with the abilities of creators, intermediaries, and consumers to exploit the new technology. What might the world of entertainment look like?

Opportunities

Cost Savings

The most obvious and perhaps most important advantage of full exploitation of the new systems is that entertainment could be delivered far more efficiently. The potential benefits are most easily seen through an examination of the current mechanisms for distributing sound recordings (although analogous gains could be realized in other media).

At present, the primary way in which consumers obtain permanent copies of sound recordings is by buying prerecorded compact discs, either in traditional "brick and mortar" stores or through online stores such as Amazon.com. The undiscounted retail price of a CD purchased in this fashion is currently around $18. In the United States, that money is distributed roughly in the following way. (The data and methodology underlying these estimates are set forth in the Appendix.)

$7.00 (approximately 39 percent) goes to the retail store that sells the disc to the customer. $9.50 (approximately 53 percent) goes to the record company that produces the disc and typically owns the copyright in the sound recording. The record company's share, in turn, is subdivided as follows:

- $2.57 (approximately 14 percent) is allocated to the company's "overhead"—the salaries of its executives and employees, rent, maintenance, utilities, and so on.
- $.95 (approximately 5 percent) goes to cover the company's "Artist and Repertoire" expenses—consisting primarily of advances made to artists whose recordings later fail to sell enough copies to cover their costs.
- $1.52 (approximately 8 percent) is spent on marketing the disc.
- $1.42 (approximately 8 percent) is paid to the firms (typically quasi-independent companies) that manufacture the disc and the accompanying artwork and packaging.
- $2.09 (approximately 12 percent) is formally allocated to the recording artists who create the music.
- $.76 (approximately 4 percent) is paid to the music publishers that own the copyrights in the musical compositions performed on the disc.
- $.19 (approximately 1 percent) stays with the company in the form of profit.

(All of these numbers, it should be emphasized, are estimates. Don't be misled by the apparent precision of the dollar figures.) Finally, $1.50 (approximately 8 percent) goes to the distributor of the disc—often a subsidiary of the record company. (Early in the history of the music industry, record companies relied upon established distributors of other products, such as televisions or firearms, to do this job. In the 1970s, the major record companies, led by CBS, began developing their own, more efficient distribution systems. By the 1980s, the superiority of the new practice was sufficiently manifest that virtually all of the smaller record labels were obliged to contract with the majors to deliver their products.)[9]

In practice, the 12 percent allocated to the recording artists represents an outer limit, rarely achieved. It is customary for performers to agree by contract to pay out of their shares for studio costs or other expenses. Beau Brashares, a former musician (now lawyer) describes how the system works:

> There's a saying among musicians: before you sign a record deal, get out your dictionary and look up the word "recoupable." Recoupables have been a part of major label contracts forever, and they work like this: your band has paid its dues, generated a buzz, and potentially stands ready to reap the benefits of this work in the mainstream marketplace. A label approaches you and says, we'll spend maybe a hundred thousand on recording and releasing your record. We own the masters. You get roughly a tenth of the money we make from selling it, but all the money we spend on recording, on manufacturing, on promotion, on touring, on deli trays for the music writers is taken out of your tenth. If the record looks like a hit, the label will keep spending the band's small share on more pressing, promoting, and so on. Why not? Once the act is selling, it behooves a label to spend as much of the band's future income as possible and reap virtually all the returns. This is why a major release frequently needs to sell 500,000 copies—go gold—before sales proceeds begin reaching the band's pockets. And while the labels lack imagination in most respects, they are notoriously creative when it comes to accounting. All in all, the deal offered to artists by a major record label is, you get the glory, and we get the money.[10]

In Chapter 2, we'll examine in considerably more detail the character and magnitude of these various deductions. For the time being, it's sufficient to recognize that the recording artists' 12 percent share substantially overstates the amount that actually ends up in their pockets.[11]

Now indulge your imagination a bit. Suppose that sound recordings were distributed not through sales of compact discs but by downloading digital copies of songs onto personal computers through the Internet. There are many complex ways in which this might be achieved—some of which will be considered in subsequent chapters—but let's start with a simple scenario. A friend tells me that the latest recording by Joshua Redman is excellent. I go to my computer, start up my browser, type "Joshua Redman" into my favorite search engine, and find his homepage. A link takes me to a list of his recordings. I enter my credit-card number, after which I am permitted to download to my hard drive all eleven tracks of *Elastic*. I can then either replay the music using the sound card and speakers attached to my computer or burn the files onto a CD, enabling me to play the music through my stereo.

An immediate objection: the reason that Redman's Website does not currently contain such a link is that, if he supplied digital copies of his recordings (for a fee) to a few customers, those recordings would soon be recopied and redistributed (for free) to millions of other potential customers, destroying his ability to make money on his creations. Thus, the system sketched above could never work. Whether this is a decisive objection depends upon the shape of the legal system, the effectiveness with which the relevant legal rules are enforced, and the availability of encryption systems to prevent illicit traffic—all topics that, as promised, we will examine. For the time being, to repeat, assume that these difficulties are surmountable and concentrate on the potential benefits of such a system.

It should be apparent that an Internet distribution system of the sort sketched would save a lot of money. Under this system, there would be no need for a retailer, because I would be able to get the recording directly from the creator. Nor would there be any need for a CD manufacturer, because I would be able to "manufacture" a copy of the recordings on my own with virtually no effort. The costs associated with those activities—39 percent plus 8 percent, for a total of approximately $8.50—would thus be eliminated. Already, in other words, we've "saved" almost half the cost of the CD.

Other cost savings are also likely, though harder to measure. On one hand, in the Internet distribution system, there would be no need for a traditional "distributor." On the other hand, to make his music available for downloading, Redman would have to contract with an Internet service provider (ISP) capable of handling the resultant traffic and with an intermediary capable of collecting revenue through an online credit-card system. Would those costs total less than $1.50 per "album"? Almost certainly, but by how much it's hard to say.

What about the remaining $8.00, currently used by the record company to cover its various expenses? Does the Internet system enable us to save any of that money? That depends on what services record companies provide in exchange for that revenue—and whether, in the new technological environment, those services can be either dispensed with or obtained at lower cost. What, then, are the services record companies supply? Four things, they argue:

- *Locating Talent.* Record company employees scour the musical landscape (go to clubs, listen to "demo" tapes, and talk to personal managers), hunt for promising new artists, and negotiate contracts with them. Success in this endeavor is said to require "good ears"— a knack for identifying the kinds of sounds, personae, and performance styles that consumers will find attractive. (Before the advent of rock and roll, record company employees also often selected the songs the artists would play—that is, determined their "repertoires." This function atrophied when most rock musicians began writing or at least choosing most of their material.)[12]

- *Production.* The companies orchestrate the creation of commercially valuable sound recordings. At one time, record company executives were personally involved in this activity. For example, Clive Davis, then-president of Columbia Records, reportedly persuaded Janis Joplin to shorten her version of "Piece of My Heart" and to make it more memorable by repeating the title lyric more often. Nowadays, this activity is more often outsourced to semi-independent producers. Their job is to manage the many aspects of the process of generating an album—"hiring studios, [session] musicians, and engineers, getting the best performances out of those people, supervising the creative aspects of the recording and mixing process to get the best sound recording, supervising and approving the mastering and references—all with the goal of producing a recording that is marketable and at the same time is a good representation of the artist's abilities and any messages that the artist wishes to convey with the recording."[13]

- *Promotion.* Record companies use various techniques to persuade consumers to buy their products—placing advertisements in print media; distributing free music "samplers"; encouraging retailers to set up "listening stations" where consumers can hear new releases, and so on. By far the most effective and expensive of these strategies consists of radio promotion: the record companies persuade radio-station employees to add new recordings to their playlists; listeners then buy copies of albums containing those songs. (How exactly this "persuasion" is achieved and why it is so expensive will be considered in detail in Chapter 2.)[14]

- *Risk Spreading.* Most sound recordings, the record companies point out, "lose money." In other words, the revenue they generate is insufficient to cover the costs (just itemized) attributable to them. To offset these losses, the companies must collect from the few "hits" more money than is necessary to cover their associated costs. On the assumption that no one can accurately predict in advance which recordings will succeed and which will fail, this arrangement might be thought of as analogous to an insurance regime, in which an intermediary collects fees from all members of a group, then uses the revenue to cover the costs of injuries sustained by a subset of the group.

The new technology would likely make it possible to provide some of these services at lower costs—and perhaps to dispense with others entirely.

The most obvious opportunity for savings pertains to the production function. One of the major sources of the substantial cost of generating an album is the expense of purchasing or renting the necessary recording equipment. In 1980, those devices cost approximately $50,000; today, a laptop computer and less than $1000 worth of additional hardware and software provides comparable functionality. That extraordinary decline is enabling growing numbers of musicians to set up recording studios at home, a trend reinforced by the fact that the new equipment and software are substantially more user friendly than the old, enabling many musicians to dispense with the services of recording engineers. To be sure, home recordings are not altogether new. Since the 1980s, inexpensive tape recorders and mixing machines have allowed musicians to produce low-fidelity recordings. Sometimes this low-fi format has been used to advantage by established performers—as, for example, in Bruce Springsteen's album *Nebraska*. For the most part, however, the roughness of the sound has prevented mass circulation of home-made recordings. The quality of the recordings that can be produced on the new equipment is substantially better. In the past few years, "amateur" musicians have been able for the first time to produce "professional" albums.[15]

Less certain—but, in the long run, perhaps even more important—is an impending shift in the way that music is promoted. Radio stations are gradually losing their power as arbiters of popular taste. Increasingly, listeners are shifting to Webcasters for selections of streamed music. (An extraordinary compendium of the new channels can be found at the Website for Live 365, at live365.com.) The new services have at least two advantages: they offer many more "channels," corresponding to more finely sliced genres of music, and they typically contain many fewer advertisements than radio programs. For present purposes, their sheer numbers is the critical variable. The more there are, the harder it will become for the record companies—or the independent promoters they hire—to buy control over their programming.

The Internet is also making widely available other sources of information concerning recorded music. One of the best, until recently, was the now-defunct Website Gigabeat.com. It worked as follows. Suppose that, though I enjoy Joshua Redman's music, I'm becoming overly familiar with his CDs. I'd like to find some new music by other saxophone players of the same general sort. Instead of listening to my local jazz radio station, writing down the names of artists and albums that seem intriguing, I type "Joshua Redman" into the Gigabeat search engine, and it provides me two lists of saxophone players. Within each, the order of the players reflects how similar their styles are to Redman's. The first list consists of well-established musicians: John Coltrane, Sonny Rollins, and so on (no surprises yet). The second consists of less well-known artists: Roy Hargrove, James Carter, and so on. Next, I type a few of the latter set of names into the search engine of a peer-to-peer music distribution system. A few quick downloads, and I am able to listen, on my computer, to samples of Hargrove's and Carter's music. If I like them, I buy a few of their CDs. In any event, I discard my downloaded files. (Is this lawful behavior? We'll see.) The main lesson of this vignette is that an Internet-based intermediary, not a radio station and not affiliated with any of the record companies, has enabled me to expand my musical horizons. As such systems proliferate, the standard methods of promoting music will atrophy further.[16]

The two trends just discussed—the rapidly declining cost of making music and the slow weakening of the grip of the record companies on the marketing of music—are contributing to a third, even more fundamental shift: musicians are becoming less and less dependent upon record companies. For half a century, the only way recording artists could reach mass audiences was to sign on to "major labels," which then provided all of the services outlined above. Now they have other options. Already, as indicated, they are able to produce high-quality recorded music on their own—either by buying the necessary equipment or by renting it at modest cost. Their ability to conduct their own marketing campaigns is slowly increasing. And the new technologies enable them to distribute the music themselves. In response, a growing number of established artists are cutting their ties with the major record companies. If the technological and business trends described above continue, more and more new artists will be able to do the same.

Many nuances and uncertainties lurk in the analysis just completed. We will return to several in subsequent chapters. However, the central point for our present purposes is clear enough: Some of the services currently performed by record companies are becoming less expensive or, through full exploitation of the new technologies, could be dispensed with altogether. How much in the aggregate will society save? It's impossible to say with certainty, but a lot.

Let's take stock. The retail cost of a typical CD is about $18. By distributing recorded music in digital form through the Internet, we could save well over half of that amount—all of the $7.00 and $1.50 currently collected by the retail store and disc manufacturer, some of the $1.50 currently collected by the distributor, and a significant portion of the $8.00 currently collected by the record company. Those potential savings would then allow us either to increase the amount of money allocated to the composers and performers who create the music or to reduce substantially the prices paid by consumers for access to the music, or both.

Consumer Satisfaction

The second reason why we should try, if possible, to avail ourselves more fully of the new technologies is that we would be able to satisfy consumers' desires more fully, rapidly, and precisely. Through the Internet, consumers are able to obtain music instantaneously. They need not shop for CDs in stores, nor wait for Amazon to deliver them through the mail. Internet distribution also makes it easy to deliver to a consumer an individual song, not the entire collection of songs contained on a typical CD, which commonly contains "filler" tracks in which the consumer is uninterested.

A more subtle benefit of the same general sort is that the new technology improves the ability of each consumer to identify and then obtain music that corresponds to his or her tastes. The "sampling" technique outlined above —in which the consumer first ascertains some artists that might be within his or her zone of interest, then downloads and listens to a few recordings by each, and finally uses that information to decide what to buy—is likely to enhance his or her "listening pleasure" far more effectively than current customary purchasing systems. Similar gains in terms of customer satisfaction could be reaped through greater use of the "buy-it" buttons currently employed by many Webcasters. Suppose that you're listening to an ad-free "Indie Rock" Webcasting station. You very much like a new Indigo Girls song the station plays. While the song is playing (or within a limited period of time thereafter), you can, by clicking on the appropriate icon on the Webcaster's interface, add the song to your permanent musical collection. Simple, convenient, precise.[17]

But building better individual musical libraries is not the only way in which consumers stand to gain. Equally, perhaps more important, will be the emergence of what Paul Goldstein and Senator Orrin Hatch call the "celestial jukebox." As more and more consumers obtain broadband access to the Internet, as the "breadth" of those bands increases, as wireless Internet access becomes more common and reliable, and as improvements in compression systems reduce the size of streamed files, consumers will likely come to rely increasingly upon interactive streaming for musical entertainment, instead of replaying tracks permanently stored on CDs or in their computers. The potential terminus of this trend would indeed be divine: from your home, from your car, through your portable stereo, you would be able to gain access at any time to any musical recording ever made.

Similar systems are likely to take root in the video market. Instead of stopping on the way home from work at the local "video store," you will soon be able to "stream" on demand to your home entertainment center any movie ever made—and not have to worry about paying late fees.

Benefits to Artists

It is not just consumers who stand to gain from the new technologies. Vastly larger numbers of musicians would be able, in the new technological environment, to reach mass audiences. In part, this opportunity derives from two trends already discussed: the declining cost of high-quality recording equipment and the decreasing dependence of musicians on the major record companies, which for decades have acted as a bottleneck, limiting the set of performers who can reach the general public. An additional factor reinforces those effects. To illustrate, suppose that I write and perform music of a relatively exotic type—say, "trip hop" or "fried pop." A few people in Boston would like my stuff if they were aware of it, a few in Los Angeles, a few in Singapore, and so forth. Before the advent of the Internet, I would be unable to get my music into the hands of my potential fans. In combination, the difficulties I would face in locating my potential customers (and vice versa), the high costs of making a recording, and the costs of distributing CDs to them would be prohibitive. But the vastly reduced distribution costs and increased search capabilities associated with the Internet make it possible for me to overcome those barriers. (If this seems implausible, check out the "rare music and video index" of Radar Station, based in Brighton, England, available at www.beefheart.com.) The ability to exploit such niche markets plainly creates opportunities for a much larger and more diverse set of musicians to reach global audiences.

Cultural Diversity

An important by-product of the opportunities just summarized is greater variety in the entertainment opportunities available to consumers. To illustrate, see Figure 1.2, the main menu of Live 365, the compendium of musical Webcasters mentioned earlier.

If you click on any one of the displayed categories, you will find a generous list of stations, many of them specialized. For example, among the 860 folk Webcasters, you will find the Makossa Jukebox (offering "100 percent Cameroonian ethnic music: makossa, bikutsi, manganbeu, assiko and other freestyles"); Pagan Paradise Samhian (offering "a magical mix of neo-Pagan, XTC, Tull, McKennitt, Yes, Mediaeval Baebes, Genesis, Heart, Rush [and] traditional folk"); and Radio Free Boonie (offering a "one-hour show for the 0 to 4 crowd and their respective grownups"). The offerings under the jazz and rap headings are just as extensive.

Analogous diversity is already becoming evident in other sectors of the

All Genres
Alternative
  College
  Goth
  Indie Rock
  Punk
Americana
  Bluegrass
  Blues
  Country
  Folk
  Western
Blues
Classical
Comedy
Country
Dance
Electronica
  Ambient
  Breakbeat
  Downtempo/Leftfield
  Drum 'n' Bass
  Electro
  Experimental
  Hard House
  House
  Industrial
  Jungle
  Techno
  Trance
  UK Garage/2-Step
Easy Listening
  New Age
  Smooth Jazz
Folk
Funk
Jazz
  Smooth Jazz
  Swing

Oldies
  50s
  60s
  70s
  80s
  90s
Pop
R&B
Rap/Hip-Hop
Reggae
  Dub
Religious
  Christian
Rock
  Classic Rock
  Indie Rock
  Metal
  Punk
Talk
  Sports
International
  Asian
  Irish
  Latin
  World
Various
  College
  Community
  Holiday
  Government
  Music to ... to
  Reality
  Soundtracks
  Spoken Word
  Valentine
  Other

FIGURE **1.2.** *Live365.com, Complete Genre List.*
SOURCE: Live365.com.

entertainment industry—though, as yet, primarily in its "black" markets. For example, the range of sound recordings and movies that can be obtained from any of the currently popular peer-to-peer systems is extraordinary, dwarfing the holdings of the largest record and video stores. (The emergence of those systems will be examined in much more detail in Chapter 2.)

For two related reasons, diversity of this sort is socially beneficial. First, it reinforces the effect discussed previously—in which the new technology makes possible more precise satisfaction of consumer tastes. From the cornucopia, each consumer can pick out the entertainment products that give him or her the greatest pleasure and is not limited to products that have mass appeal. Second, the opportunity and responsibility to "pick," rather than just accept what Blockbuster or Kiss108 has to offer, has important secondary benefits. It makes consumers more active, more discerning, more alive.

The latter effect was noticed and celebrated long ago by John Stuart Mill, and his observations remain equally powerful today. Cultural diversity, Mill observed, has cumulative cultural effects: the more multifarious the lifestyles, ideas, and art forms on public display in a society, the more its members must decide for themselves what to think and how to act, thereby developing their own "mental and moral faculties" and rendering the culture as a whole even more "rich, diversified, and animating." The radical expansion of the range of readily available entertainment options that the new technology makes possible could move us closer to Mill's utopia.[18]

Semiotic Democracy

The final potential benefit of the new technology is the most revolutionary. Up to this point, we've been talking in familiar terms about "producers" and "consumers" of entertainment products. The new technology offers many opportunities to blur the boundary between those groups, enabling and encouraging the recipients of entertainment to reshape and redistribute it—to participate, in other words, in the process of creation. Some early, limited examples follow.

In the summer of 2001, Mike Nichols, a freelance film editor (no apparent relation to the famous director), prepared and circulated (anonymously) an edited version of *The Phantom Menace* (episode one of the *Star Wars* series of movies), deleting much of the footage involving the character Jar Jar Binks (whose depiction many viewers had considered racist) and altering several scenes involving Anakin Skywalker, making him appear stronger and less juvenile. Copies of the altered version, known as the "Phantom Edit," soon found their way onto eBay and then elsewhere on the Internet. Many viewers shared the creator's judgment that it is a "much stronger film." Soon other modified versions began to appear—"Episode 1.2," "Episode 1.14," "The Phantom Re-Edit NY"—each reflecting a different conception of how George Lucas's film could be improved. The following year, another film-maker—D. J. Hupp—did much the same thing to "Artificial Intelligence," a movie originally begun by Stanley Kubrick and finished, after his death, by Steven Spielberg. Annoyed by the sentimentality of Spielberg's product, Hupp sliced about thirty minutes out of it, reducing the roles of Professor Hobby, Gigolo Joe, and (above all) the cartoon character Dr. Know, and recapturing the "dark mood" of Kubrick's original vision.[19]

Moderately priced, user-friendly software is already available that would enable many people to engage in this kind of activity. Final Cut Pro, for example, enables the owners of ordinary Apple computers to make high-quality edits of digital copies of films. New users of the program can find instruction and support on the Website of the Los Angeles Final Cut Pro User Group.[20]

Gotuit Media Corporation hopes to enable even consumers with no software skills whatsoever to exercise some of this editorial power. Their prototype service, Gotuit TV, provides customers a combination of software, hardware, and "metadata" (information concerning where the "break points" lie in movies and television programs) that will allow the owners of personal video recorders to alter how they watch recorded programs. For example, viewers will be able to instruct their PVRs (by adjusting three virtual "knobs") as to how much violence, offensive language, and sexuality they would like to see in a given program; the machine will then automatically skip segments that exceed the specified levels. Future uses of the system could allow users to rearrange the order of scenes, delete material they consider redundant—and then save their settings and send them to their friends. The result: hundreds of sets of instructions, each of which would generate a different version of a movie, could circulate on the Internet.[21]

In the summer of 2001, the Internet Archive held a contest in which amateur filmmakers were asked to use excerpts of digitized films to create a "perspective" (a documentary, parody, or fictional depiction) concerning "an historical event associated with War." A wide variety of montages were submitted, including one from a fifth-grade class in a District of Columbia public school. The winner, titled the "ABC's of Happiness," combined World War Two footage with new animated characters to create a brief, sarcastic commentary on government propaganda and American complacency. (Because contestants were asked to limit themselves to digitized films that were no longer subject to copyright protection, the set of available materials was sharply limited. Access to digitized versions of material currently covered by copyright law of course would expand radically the opportunities for creativity of this sort.)[22]

The possibilities generated by the new technology for "consumer creativity" in the music industry are, if anything, even more dramatic. The sharp decline in the cost of recording equipment, mentioned earlier, has enabled thousands of amateur performers to record their music and make it available to the world. In some genres, one need not even be a trained musician to participate in the creative process. Hip-hop songs, for example, can be built electronically (from short slices of other sound recordings) by someone who cannot play a note on a traditional instrument. The newer compression formats, combined with hand-held devices like the recently released MadPlayer, will likely contribute to the ferment by making it far easier to disentangle, remix, and supplement the separate tracks that together make up a recording. Finally, Webcasting has created opportunities for thousands of nonprofessional "disk jockeys" to engage creatively with music in a different way—by selecting combinations of songs and streaming them to friends. Steve Albini is probably right in describing the intersection of these trends as "the triumph of the amateurs."[23]

These examples begin to suggest the range of opportunities for creativity that the new technology, unleashed, could make widely available. Is this a good thing? Are we sure we want to encourage this kind of behavior? From two perspectives, the answer seems clearly yes. (Other perspectives will be considered shortly.)

First, opportunities for creativity of this sort contribute to what has been called "semiotic democracy." Over the course of the twentieth century, the power to make cultural meanings in most Western countries has become ever more concentrated. The increasingly dense cloud of images, sounds, and symbols through which we move has been increasingly controlled by a shrinking group of record companies, movie and television studios, advertising houses, and political consultants. To be sure, as "cultural populists" have long insisted, ordinary citizens have not been altogether passive, uncritical recipients of the creations of the cultural industry; groups of resisters have striven to "recode" those creations, to invest them with meanings different from those intended by their designers. But their adulterated images have never had the wide circulation and cultural power of the originals. (Millions of television viewers saw President Bush (senior), when asked about his plans in Iraq, respond by hitching up his pants, in a powerful allusion to the gun-toting machismo of John Wayne; far fewer have seen the greeting cards, sold in gay bookstores, featuring a lipsticked John Wayne and the caption "It's such a bitch being butch.") Reversing the concentration of semiotic power would benefit us all. People would be more engaged, less alienated, if they had more voice in the construction of their cultural environment. And the environment itself—to return to a previous theme—would be more variegated and stimulating. The new technology makes that possible.[24]

The second perspective sees in the new technology opportunities for a different style of creativity—more collaborative and playful, less individualist or hierarchical. So far, the Internet-based culture of sharing has been limited for the most part to the exchange of completed cultural artifacts—as the habits of my daughter and her friends suggest. In the future, sharing could encompass more creativity. The circulation of artifacts would include their modification, improvement, or adaptation. To some degree, at least, such habits could help ameliorate the oft-lamented disease of modern culture: anomie, isolation, hyper-individualism. Collective creativity could help us become more collective beings.

Dangers

Large costs savings, faster and more precise satisfaction of consumers' desires, increased opportunities for creators, greater diversity in the publicly available menu of entertainment products, and dramatic gains in semiotic democracy—the potential benefits of the new technology seem extraordinary. Sadly, that's not the end of the story. Full exploitation of the technological opportunities could also have two serious social costs.

Erosion of Creators' Incomes

The more notorious of the two is that the flow of revenue that currently fuels creativity in the entertainment industry could be disrupted. Until recently, a combination of legal rules and practical impediments made it difficult for consumers to gain access to audio or video recordings without permission. To secure permission, they had to pay fees. Those fees came in various shapes and sizes—the purchase prices of CDs, the rental fees (and late charges) paid to video stores, the costs of admission to movie theatres, parts of the prices of products advertised on radio and television, and so on. To be sure, not all of that money ended up in the pockets of the original creators of those recordings, but some did, and that portion was essential to attract potential creators into the business and to support them in their endeavors. Consumers' willingness to pay those fees will drop if they can gain access to the same material without permission for little or no cost. The new technologies, by making it easy to create and distribute perfect, compressed,

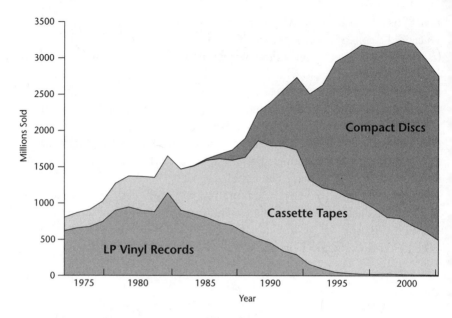

FIGURE **1.3.** *Global Sales of Record Albums by Format, 1973–2002.*

SOURCE: International Federation of the Phonographic Industry, *The Recording Industry in Numbers*, 10th ed., 2003, 210.

unencrypted copies of recordings, are steadily reducing the cost and inconvenience of such nonpermissive access. Already, this change has begun to produce symptoms in the record industry. After many years of growth (interspersed by occasional dips), unit sales of record albums (CDs, cassette tapes, and LP vinyl records) in the United States declined 3.7 percent in 2000, 9 percent in 2001, 9.9 percent in 2002, and 8.7 percent in 2003.[25]

Similar trends are apparent in other countries. Figure 1.3 shows total sales of record albums (broken down by format) throughout the world during the last thirty years.

Several aspects of the chart are striking: that, by 1994, sales of LP vinyl records had declined to insignificant levels; that sales of prerecorded cassette tapes have declined but remain vital; and that the compact disc is now the overwhelmingly dominant format. But, for present purposes, the most important feature is the sharp decline in total unit sales since 1999.

The movie industry is not yet symptomatic. Certainly gauging by box-office admissions and revenues, the industry looks healthy. After a mild dip in 1999 and 2000, the total number of admissions to American theatres rose sharply in 2001 and 2002 (by 4.7 percent and 10.2 percent, respectively). As one might expect, total box-office receipts have been rising even faster, reaching an all-time high of $9.52 billion in 2002. Meanwhile, sales and rentals of videotapes and DVDs—now an even larger source of revenue for the film industry—continued to rise at a healthy pace: $21.063 billion in 2000; $23.008 billion in 2001; $24.424 billion in 2002; and $27.503 billion in 2003. But spokesmen for the studios argue plausibly that, as compression technologies improve and the size of hard drives increases, consumers' willingness to pay for access to movies will similarly fall off.[26]

Some less obvious factors suggest that this doomsday scenario is not quite so inevitable or inexorable as is conventionally thought. As Stan Liebowitz has shown, the new technologies might stimulate consumers to buy *more* recordings. This might occur, for example, if the entertainment industry were characterized by strong "network effects"—if, in other words, the value to me of a particular Joshua Redman recording increased with the number of other people who owned it. Somewhat more plausibly, sales might rise if the proliferation of Internet-based promotion and distribution systems made consumers more aware of the breadth of attractive songs and movies available for purchase. Janis Ian provides some anecdotal support for the latter hypothesis, sometimes known as the "exposure effect":

My site (www.janisian.com) gets an average of 75,000 hits a year. Not bad for someone whose last hit record was in 1975. When Napster was running full-tilt, we received about 100 hits a month from people who'd downloaded *Society's Child* or *At Seventeen* for free, then decided they wanted more information. Of those 100 people (and these are only the ones who let us know how they'd found the site), 15 bought CDs. Not huge sales, right? No record company is interested in 180 extra sales a year. But . . . that translates into $2700, which is a lot of money in my book. And that doesn't include the ones who bought the CDs in stores, or who came to my shows.

Or take author Mercedes Lackey, who occupies entire shelves in stores and libraries. As she said herself: "For the past ten years, my three 'Arrows' books, which were published by DAW about 15 years ago, have been generating a nice, steady royalty check per pay-period each. A reasonable amount, for fifteen-year-old books. However . . . I just got the first half of my DAW royalties . . . And suddenly, out of nowhere, each Arrows book has paid me three times the normal amount! . . . And the *only* change during that pay-period was that I had Eric put the first of my books on the [the Internet-based Baen Free Library]. There's an increase in all of the books on that statement, actually, and what it looks like is what I'd expect to happen if a steady line of people who'd never read my stuff encountered it on the Free Library—a certain percentage of them liked it, and started to work through my backlist, beginning with the earliest books published. The really interesting thing is, of course, that these aren't Baen books, they're DAW—another publisher—so it's 'name loyalty' rather than 'brand loyalty.' I'll tell you what, I'm sold. Free works."

I've found that to be true myself; every time we make a few songs available on my website, sales of all the CDs go up. A lot.[27]

It is also conceivable, as Liebowitz points out, that the record and movie industries might offset the losses they sustain as a result of "piracy" by employing the technique of "indirect appropriation"—that is, by charging higher prices to the purchasers of legitimate CDs and DVDs, relying on those original purchasers to pass along a portion of their costs to the copyists.[28]

In the end, however, as Liebowitz acknowledges, none of these theoretically intriguing possibilities is likely to have much of an impact on the trajectory of the entertainment industry. Sooner or later, the "network" and "exposure" effects will be swamped by the corrosive effect of easy access to free recordings, and the feasibility of "indirect appropriation" in this particular context is sharply limited by the "asymmetric" pattern of the copying (in other words, the fact that the seller of two CDs cannot predict which will be used to make a thousand copies and which will not be used to make any).

Whether "promiscuous publication" has *already* begun to sap the strength of the entertainment industry is also somewhat harder to say than the industry's representatives assert. As many skeptics have pointed out, the declining revenues of the record companies in the past year could have been caused by the global economic crisis or by the paucity of "hit" records and movies, rather than by the proliferation of piracy. Again, however, doubts on this score are not likely to have much long-term significance. A recent study of the history of the music industry suggests that, over the past fifty years, sales of sound recordings and the overall state of the economy have not been positively correlated. Even if the most recent downturn could be traced to the fact that consumers have had less disposable income (or to consumers' disinterest in the major record companies' increasingly formulaic output), such modest effects would be dwarfed by the adverse impact on traditional sales caused by adoption of the Internet distribution systems sketched (and celebrated) in the preceding pages. In the end, therefore, I think we must face up to the fact that reaping the full economic and cultural benefits of the new technology would seriously threaten the ways in which for many years revenues have been collected and distributed in the entertainment industry.[29]

Should we be troubled by that effect? Some observers say no—on the ground that the people we really care about, the original creators, make so little money under the current system through sales of recordings that they will suffer no material injury. Again, Janis Ian:

[F]rom personal experience: in 37 years as a recording artist, I've created 25+ albums for major labels, and I've *never once* received a royalty check that didn't show I owed *them* money. So I make the bulk of my living from live touring, playing for 80–1500 people a night, doing my own show. I spend hours each week doing press, writing articles, making sure my website tour information is up to date. Why? Because all of that gives me exposure to an audience that might not come otherwise. So when someone writes and tells me they came to my show because they'd downloaded a song and gotten curious, I am thrilled! Who gets hurt by free downloads? Save a handful of super-successes like Celine Dion, none of us. We only get helped.[30]

If not musicians, who *does* get hurt by downloads? Only the record companies, Ian suggests. Should we care about them? Eben Moglen says no. After all, many of their traditional functions are becoming obsolete or are already being assumed by artists themselves. We should therefore be neither troubled nor surprised if, with a change in the technological climate, the dinosaurs die.

That response seems dangerously cavalier. At best, it seems to extend no further than the music industry; the established intermediaries in the film industry seem nowhere near so dispensable. It also seems a misdirected reaction to the plight of the average musician. If ordinary artists currently reap unfairly small shares of the revenues generated by sales of their recordings, an appropriate response would seem to be to restructure the pertinent business models or legal rules to increase that share, not to reduce it to zero. That seems especially true right now. For the reasons explained above, the new technology creates an opportunity to expand dramatically the revenues earned by artists—at the same time that the prices paid by consumers are reduced. If possible, we should strive to seize that opportunity, rather than forego it. In sum, the threat posed by the new systems to the current flows of revenues through the music industry is an effect we should take seriously —and should strive either to avoid or to offset in some other way.

The Hazards of Consumer Creativity

The second potential danger of the new technology is perhaps best seen by example. Suppose that "The Phantom Edit" were distributed not just among a few *Star Wars* aficionados in Hollywood but widely over the Internet—so widely, in fact, that consumers (having read negative reviews of the original) were more likely to download and watch it than they were to download and watch *The Phantom Menace*. Would this be troublesome?

Almost certainly, it would trouble George Lucas. When "The Phantom

Edit" was first released, he responded generously. Although he had not seen the modified film, he indicated that he was "delighted with the idea." "The Internet is a new medium, it's all about doing things like that," he reportedly told Zap2it.com. Most likely, however, he would be less generous if most consumers' experience of the first episode of the *Star Wars* series were derived from the modified version rather than his own creation. In the past, filmmakers have responded angrily to the production and performance of colorized versions of old black-and-white movies. More recently, the Directors Guild of America filed suit against CleanFlicks, a company that prepares and distributes expurgated versions of "R"- and "PG13"-rated films. The filmmakers' hostility to such activities does not derive from a desire to preserve their box-office or video-rental incomes. (Indeed, the availability of colorized or sanitized versions may under some circumstances increase their revenues.) Rather, they object to interference with the "artistic integrity" of the originals. As Steven Spielberg said, commenting on the CleanFlicks litigation, "No one is authorized to impose their truth on top of ours despite how strongly they may disagree with it."[31]

Scholars who write about the law and theory of intellectual property refer to the kind of injury at stake in such cases as interference with the "personality interest" of the creators. The underlying notion is that artists' identities are frequently bound up with their creations—sufficiently so that the destruction or modification of those creations threatens the artists' "personhood." In many European countries, this notion is deeply rooted and has found expression in laws that limit severely the freedom that the possessors of works of fine art otherwise would have to alter them. In the United States, it has been less widely accepted, but in the last two decades its popularity has been growing and art-preservation laws reflecting it have been gradually tightening.[32]

But it is not only filmmakers who stand to be hurt by the widespread distribution of modified films. Arguably, we should also be worried about viewers. As Justin Hughes has suggested, whenever a work of art is "recoded"—its meaning changed through the creation and distribution of an altered form—members of the general public may suffer three kinds of injury. First, their ability to use the work to help define themselves—"by identifying with it, by communicating with it, or by using it as a cultural reference"—may be impaired. So, in the hypothetical case, young boys would be less able to conceive of themselves as or in relation to the young Anakin Skywalker (a common phenomenon in 2001) if his character had been rendered indeterminate by the widespread circulation of inconsistent depictions of him. Second, the blurring of the meaning of the work ironically will make it less useful for future transformative or humorous recodings. It would be hard to construct a parody along the lines of the movie, "Space Balls," for example, if the targets of the mockery were unclear or moving. Finally and most broadly, the loss of a stable culture reference point may, if generalized, undermine the "constancy that gives the culture cohesion at any one time and the civilization cohesion over time." Thirty years from now, Americans would have a less clear sense of who we are if we had not shared the experiences of engagement with the special effects and innocent heroism of Episodes 4, 5, and 6, followed by disappointment with the increasingly fragmented and shallow Episodes 1 and 2.[33]

The relevance of these musings to the future of digital entertainment is apparent. Some (though not all) of the potential benefits of the new technology surveyed in this chapter entail empowering ordinary consumers to modify the cultural artifacts that come to them and then redistribute the altered forms. That capacity, I've suggested, should be embraced. A culture in which it was widely practiced would be freer, more energetic, and more egalitarian, than the one in which we currently live. But semiotic democracy, like all forms of democracy, carries with it risks and costs. In particular, it threatens the "personality" interests of creators and it threatens the interest of the general public in cultural stability and coherence. There are ways (which we will consider in due course) that these risks and costs could be substantially mitigated. But it is impossible to eliminate them altogether.

To sum up, the new technologies, applied to the field of popular entertainment, could provide us many wondrous benefits, but could also cause us some serious injuries. Plainly, we should strive to structure our business models and laws to maximize realization of the potential benefits while minimizing the associated harms. Have we done so? No. Could we? Yes. The next two chapters explain how and why we have failed to date. The balance of the book strives to show how we could do better.

2 The Baseline: Entertainment Law and Practice in 1990

In 1990, when the technological innovations examined in the previous chapter first began to affect the entertainment industry, the production and distribution of audio and video recordings were managed by a complex set of laws, government agencies, and private organizations. Between 1990 and the present, those rules and institutions were changed substantially through a series of efforts to meet the challenges presented by the new technologies. In Chapter 3, we will examine those changes in detail. To understand them, however, it is first necessary to understand the system they sought to remake. That's the task of the current chapter.

There are risks to choosing 1990 (or any single date, for that matter) for our baseline. Most important, it might leave the impression that the pertinent laws and institutions were stable until that moment. The reality, as one might expect, is that throughout the twentieth century the system was periodically modified in response to shifts in the technological and cultural climates. But the changes that have been made in the last fourteen years have been more rapid, dramatic, and interdependent than those that came before. Even more to the point, almost all of the recent changes have been responsive in some way to the combination of digital technology and the Internet. For our purposes here, therefore, it makes sense to take a snapshot of the system in 1990—and then examine how it has evolved since.

In this chapter, as in the rest of the book, we will concentrate on the law and associated business models in the United States. Both the relevant legal rules and the spirit in which they are interpreted differed significantly in other countries—too much so to make a comprehensive global analysis feasible, at least within a single volume.

Our analysis will begin with music, the branch of the entertainment industry in which the pertinent legal doctrines were the most complex. We'll then turn our attention to movies, where the law was simpler but the associated business models more intricate. (The present tense will be used throughout the presentation, but don't forget: all statements pertain to the state of the law in 1990.)

Music

Legal Rights in Compositions

Suppose I write a folk song. I select a rhythm (4/4), add a melody (a sequence of the twelve notes in the Western musical scale), harmony (a sequence of guitar chords), and some lyrics (a lament of the collapse of a love affair) to create a composition I find pleasing. What are my legal rights?

So long as the song is "original" (in the minimal sense that I did not copy it from another song) and so long as I "fix" it in some way (for example, by embodying it in sheet music or by playing it into a tape recorder), I own a copyright in the musical composition. That means that, subject to some important exceptions that we'll consider shortly, no one but me may do any of four things: reproduce the song; prepare a derivative work based upon it; distribute copies of it to the public; or perform it publicly. Each of these rights requires a bit more explanation.[1]

The exclusivity of my right of reproduction means, first, that no one without my permission may make a copy of a physical embodiment of the composition—for example, by photocopying the sheet music in which I notated it. Less obviously, it means that no one may make a "substantially similar" musical composition. So, for example, my friend Peggy may not, after listening to one of my performances, compose (and then write down or record) another song that closely tracks my melody or my lyrics. (How close is too close, and how would I prove that Peggy had copied my song rather than created hers independently? Both of these questions have generated much litigation and commentary, but neither is central to our enterprise here, so we won't pause to explore them.) Last but not least, my right of reproduction means that no one, without my permission, may make a "mechanical" copy of my song—for example, a tape recording of a performance of it.

A "derivative work" means a new work that alters or adapts an original work. Examples in other media include translations, dramatizations, and abridgments. Derivative works of a musical composition would include such things as a new arrangement or a combination of the original melody with new lyrics. So, for example, the popular Christmas carol "What Child Is This?," written by William Chatterton Dix in 1865, is a derivative work of the love song, "Greensleeves," believed by some historians to have been written by the ferocious, but talented, King Henry VIII of England. Had they both been working in the United States in the late twentieth century, Dix would have needed Henry's permission.

My exclusive right to distribute the song means that no one, without my authority, may sell, rent, or give away copies of it (including recordings of performances of it) to members of the general public. Nor may anyone without my authority import copies of the song into the United States. However, my rights in this regard are qualified by an important exception, which in turn is subject to yet another exception (a pattern sadly common in copyright law).

The exception: Once a person has lawfully acquired a copy of my song (including a phonorecord of a performance of it), he or she may resell or otherwise dispose of it to anyone he or she pleases, and I may not demand a share of the resale price. This rule, known as the "first-sale" doctrine, substantially limits my ability, when first selling copies of my song, to charge different consumers different prices. (The impact of this limitation on business models in the music industry is a theme to which we will return several times later in the book.)[2]

The exception to the exception: In 1984, the recording industry persuaded Congress that sales of record albums to the general public were being eroded by the proliferation of stores that purchased albums and then rented them to customers (for a few dollars for a few days), encouraging the customers to take them home and make cassette copies of them. (One such store advertised: "Never, ever buy another record.") In response, Congress forbade the owner of a phonorecord to rent it to the public for "commercial advantage" unless he or she had obtained the permission of the owner of the copyright in the recorded musical composition. (It is because of this rule that Blockbuster today does not rent CDs.) This is the first of many instances we will encounter in which Congress has altered a general doctrine of copyright law to protect a traditional system for distributing music.[3]

Finally, while the law permits private performances of musical compositions, it forbids unauthorized public performances. So Peggy, after hearing me play my song, could return home and play it for her family or friends. But she could not go to Harvard Square, stand on a street corner, and play it for the benefit of passersby. My rights under this heading extend, not merely to "performances" as that term is customarily used, but also to a variety of additional acts by which a rendition of my song might be transmitted or communicated to the public. To illustrate, all of the following would be covered: playing in public a CD containing a recording of my song, broadcasting a live or recorded performance of the song, and retransmitting such a broadcast over a cable system.[4]

This impressive catalogue of entitlements is, however, tempered by an even longer list of exceptions and qualifications. We've already seen one of them: the first-sale doctrine as a limitation on the right of distribution. Copyright law contains many others. Some are narrow, privileging specific activities that otherwise would run afoul of one of my four rights. For example, the law permits teachers and students to play my song in class without permission, members of religious congregations to perform it in the course of their services, and nonprofit "horticultural organizations" to play it at fairs. Some are broader, operating as limits on two or more of the four rights.[5]

Several of the exceptions take the form of what copyright lawyers call "compulsory licenses." In each of these contexts, an activity that ordinarily would violate one of my exclusive rights is nevertheless privileged if the actor pays me a fee determined by a government agency and abides by administrative regulations typically set by the same agency. In effect, the law gives me the right to prevent these activities, but then forces me to grant others permission to engage in them on specified terms—even if, given my druthers, I would charge more money or forbid the activities altogether. Hence the term *compulsory licenses*. Some examples follow:

- Public broadcasting organizations may play my song in noncommercial educational broadcasts without my permission, provided that the song has already been published and provided that they pay me fees either set through voluntary negotiation or (in the likely event that such negotiations break down) set by the Copyright Royalty Tribunal.[6]

- The operator of a jukebox (a "coin-operated phonorecord player" typically placed in a restaurant or similar establishment) may include a recording of my song in his or her machine so long as he or she abides by certain administrative requirements and pays license fees also determined by the Copyright Royalty Tribunal. The fees are not paid to me directly but instead are deposited with the Register of Copyrights. After the deduction of administrative expenses, the monies are periodically distributed to me and other copyright owners in accordance with estimates of the relative frequency with which our works have been played.[7]

- An extraordinarily complex set of rules governs the freedom of cable systems to receive over-the-air broadcasts containing my song and then retransmit those broadcasts to their customers. Under certain circumstances, such cable systems will not have to pay anything—for example, when the purpose of the retransmission is to facilitate primary transmissions made for specific educational purposes. In most instances, however, the retransmission will be permitted, but only upon the payment to the Copyright Office of administratively determined fees. Those monies are then redistributed to me and other similarly situated copyright owners.[8]

- An analogous system applies to satellite carriers who pick up broadcasts containing copyrighted programming from television stations (including so-called "superstations," like TBS in Atlanta) and retransmit those signals to home subscribers.[9]

What explains provisions of these sorts? Why not allow me and other songwriters to determine the amounts of money that other people must pay for the right to use our compositions in particular ways? They're our songs, after all. Shouldn't we be able to set the price of access to them—just as landowners ordinarily get to charge whatever they wish for access to their property? We'll address these questions in detail in Chapters 4 and 5. For the time being, here's a provisional set of responses. Three motivations, mixed in varying proportions, explain why Congress in many contexts has rejected the analogy between copyrights and rights to land—and instead has subjected songwriters like me to compulsory-licensing systems. First, lawmakers fear that it would be prohibitively time-consuming and costly for us to negotiate individual bargains with each PBS station, jukebox operator, satellite carrier, and so on that wants access to our material. Compulsory licenses are often intended at least in part to overcome those transaction costs and allow mutually advantageous uses of copyrighted works to occur. (Compulsory licenses are not the only devices that may be employed for this purpose. We'll consider others later.) Second, in some contexts, lawmakers fear that, left to our own devices, we would charge improperly high fees for access to our works—"improper" either because they are more than necessary to provide the necessary stimulus for creativity or because they reflect our efforts to drive competitors out of business. (The latter motivation will undoubtedly seem implausible so long as the copyright owners consist of individual songwriters like me. It will make more sense when, soon, more realistic descriptions of the organizations that actually hold the copyrights are introduced into the discussion.) Third and finally, compulsory licenses are occasionally employed to reduce the prices that organizations engaged in especially socially valuable activities (like public broadcasting) will be obliged to pay for access to copyrighted material.

Fair Use

The oldest, broadest, and most important of the many limitations on my rights as a copyright owner is known as the fair-use doctrine. In the middle of the nineteenth century, courts in the United States began occasionally to exempt from liability defendants who had violated some provision of the copyright statute but whose activities, in the courts' opinion, should nevertheless be deemed "reasonable" or "fair." During the next 150 years, as the set of rights enjoyed by authors and composers gradually expanded, so too did the set of circumstances in which courts would grant defendants free passes. Congress acquiesced in this practice, taking it for granted when it periodically modified the copyright statute. Finally, in 1976, as part of its general revision of the copyright system, Congress formally recognized what by then had come to be known as the fair-use doctrine. "Notwithstanding" the statutory provisions enumerating the rights of copyright owners, the new statute declared, "the fair use of a copyrighted work . . . is not an infringement." This declaration was not intended either to alter or to "freeze" the doctrine; it was designed, rather, to ratify the already well-established practice of the courts.

In that spirit, Congress went on to identify four factors that judges, when presented with invocations of the fair-use doctrine, had been considering and should continue to consider. First, the judge in such a case should determine "the purpose and character" of the defendant's use of the copyrighted material. For example, if the defendant's activity were "commercial" in nature, the judge should be less willing to deem his or her behavior "fair." By contrast, if the defendant were engaged in a "nonprofit educational" activity, the judge should be more willing to excuse his or her conduct. Second, the court should take into account the "nature of the copyrighted work" the defendant was accused of infringing. If, for example, the work were a news report, the judge should be more willing to apply the fair-use defense—in order to provide members of the public adequate room to discuss and use factual information. By contrast, if the work had not yet been published at the time that the defendant made use of it, the judge should be less willing to apply the defense—in order to protect the creator's economically valuable right of first public distribution and to avoid putting pressure on creators to release unfinished works prematurely. Third, the judge should consider how much of the copyrighted work the defendant used—specifically, "the amount and substantiality of the portion used in relation to the copyrighted work as a whole." Finally, the judge should consider the magnitude of the economic injury the copyright owner would sustain if the defendant and other similarly situated people were allowed to continue to engage in the activity in question. To escape liability, defendants need not show that all four of these factors incline in their favor; they need only show that, on balance, the factors point in their direction.

A congressional report accompanying the new statute provided an illustrative list of activities that, even though they appeared to violate copyrights, would nevertheless be permissible under this doctrine:

quotation of excerpts in a review or criticism for purposes of illustration or comment;

quotation of short passages in a scholarly or technical work, for illustration or clarification of the author's observations;

use in a parody of some of the content of the work parodied;

summary of an address or article, with brief quotations, in a news report;

reproduction by a library of a portion of a work to replace part of a damaged copy;

reproduction by a teacher or student of a small part of a work to illustrate a lesson;

reproduction of a work in legislative or judicial proceedings or reports;

incidental and fortuitous reproduction, in a newsreel or broadcast, of a work located in the scene of an event being reported.[10]

As this list suggests, the fair-use doctrine can be invoked in a wide variety of contexts. The case that best indicates how it applies in the specific context of the music industry is *Campbell v. Acuff-Rose Music.* (Though not decided until 1994, the case did not materially alter the doctrine and thus may legitimately be invoked to illustrate the state of the law as of our 1990 baseline.) The essential facts were as follows.[11]

In 1964, Roy Orbison and William Dees wrote the rock ballad "Oh, Pretty Woman" and assigned their copyright in the composition to Acuff-Rose Music, a publishing company. Orbison's subsequent recording of the song proved popular and later was incorporated (with permission) in the movie *Pretty Woman*, starring Julia Roberts. In 1989, Luther Campbell, one of the members of the popular rap group 2 Live Crew, wrote a parody of the song, also called "Pretty Woman." Campbell's lyrics differed from the original. For example, he replaced the first stanza:

Pretty Woman, walking down the street,
Pretty Woman, the kind I like to meet,
Pretty Woman, I don't believe you, you're not the truth,
No one could look as good as you,
Mercy.

with:

Pretty woman walkin' down the street,
Pretty woman, girl you look so sweet,
Pretty woman, you bring me down to that knee,
Pretty woman, you make me want to beg, please
Oh, pretty woman

The orchestration of Campbell's version was also different (as one might expect) from that of the original. However, the bass riffs used in their openings and refrains were identical, and their rhythms and melodies were similar. Campbell and 2 Live Crew offered to pay Acuff-Rose a royalty, but were refused. When they recorded and distributed the song anyway, Acuff-Rose brought a copyright infringement suit.

There was little doubt that Campbell and 2 Live Crew had abridged Acuff-Rose's exclusive right to reproduce the original song. The defendants did not suggest that they had developed their song without knowledge of the original, and the two versions were certainly "substantially similar." The defendants' only hope of avoiding liability thus rested on the fair-use doctrine. After protracted litigation, the defendants were exonerated. The decisive ruling by the United States Supreme Court acknowledged that several of the four statutory factors could be construed against the defendants: 2 Live Crew's activity was "commercial" in character; Orbison's song was "creative" rather than factual and thus deserved generous copyright protection; and the defendants had surely appropriated a substantial amount of the original. However, three other, closely related considerations inclined in the defendants' favor: they had "transformed" the original song, by mixing some of Orbison's and Dees's words and notes with new material; parodies are socially valuable and would be impossible if parodists were not free to mimic their targets; and copyright owners may legitimately complain of economic injuries only when copyists undermine demand for their products by offering the public substitutes for the originals, not when copyists undermine demand by making the originals look silly. Thus, in the absence of proof that 2 Live Crew's song impaired "the market for a non-parody, rap version of 'Oh, Pretty Woman'" (a matter the Supreme Court left to the lower courts to consider), the defendants were off the hook.[12]

Later in this book, we will consider many other invocations of the fair-use doctrine, but for now, the *Campbell* case should be sufficient to suggest its shape and power. What's the purpose of this doctrine, and what role does it play in the scheme of copyright law? Opinions vary on this topic, and the divergence of views partially explains the unfortunate ambiguity and unpredictability of the doctrine. An especially narrow view sees the doctrine exclusively as a device to facilitate uses of copyrighted material that otherwise would be blocked because of excessive transaction costs. (Note the parallelism with one of the justifications for compulsory licenses, discussed previously.) On this theory, as technology gradually reduces the impediments to arranging voluntary licenses of copyrighted works, the fair-use doctrine would atrophy. This view (and the associated prediction of the demise of the doctrine) are, however, rejected by most observers and courts, in part because fidelity to it would mean that defendants would always lose in cases like *Campbell*, in which the copyright owner was offered a license fee and simply refused. Rather, they see the doctrine as functioning in some way to prevent copyright law from curtailing socially valuable uses of ideas and information.[13]

But which socially valuable uses? For some observers, the primary goal is to prevent assertions of copyright from inhibiting future creativity. Others contend that its main function is to preserve opportunities for political or social commentary—supplementing, in this respect, the First Amendment's protection for freedom of speech. Other observers argue that the role of the doctrine is to leave members of the public free to "consume" copyrighted works in ways that do not undermine significantly the revenues that their authors need for sustenance and encouragement. For still others, the doctrine functions to protect activities whose aggregate economic benefits exceed their aggregate economic costs. In short, the fair-use doctrine can be understood as advancing a variety of loosely related social and economic objectives. Differences among judges concerning which is most important help to explain why, in practice, it's sometimes hard to predict how the doctrine will be applied to a particular set of facts.[14]

Composers' Rights in Action

The previous two sections mapped the various rights that copyright law affords me as a composer. Will I exercise those rights myself? For example, will I monitor the work of other folk artists to ensure that no one is performing my song in public or has composed a substantially similar song? Will I listen to the radio to ensure that commercial stations are not broadcasting my song without permission? Will I negotiate with record companies who wish to make recordings of it? Almost certainly not. I don't have the time or interest. Instead, I will assign my rights to a music publishing company, which will then assume responsibility for licensing access to my song and policing nonpermissive uses of it. In the United States, there are thousands of such publishers, so I will have no trouble finding one. Assume that, following Roy Orbison's lead, I sign up with Acuff-Rose Music, based in Nashville.

I could, if I wished, assign to Acuff-Rose only a subset of my entitlements. (A copyright is divisible in that way.) But it is customary—and most convenient for me—to assign to the company all of my rights in the song. What will I get in return? That will depend, of course, on the terms of the contract we negotiate. If I am naïve or poorly advised, I may end up with little. If I'm shrewd (or hire a shrewd lawyer), I'll do better—especially if I already have a track record as a songwriter. A very good contract might contain the following provisions:

- Acuff-Rose will enjoy all copyright interests in the song—throughout the United States and the rest of the world—for a period lasting forty years from the date of the contract or thirty-five years from the date on which the first commercial sound recording of the song is released, whichever comes first. After that, the copyright will revert to me or my heirs for the balance of the copyright term (which, in 1990, consists of my lifetime plus fifty years).

- Acuff-Rose must promote my song—most important, by securing a commercial recording of it. (For this purpose, Acuff-Rose will likely arrange to have a "demo" tape made of the song, which it will then use to pitch the song to performers and record companies. Acuff-Rose is permitted to deduct from my royalties 50 percent of the cost of making the tape.) If Acuff-Rose fails to obtain a commercial recording within a year, I may "recapture" the copyright.

- Acuff-Rose will pay me a portion of the royalties it receives in return for licensing any uses of my song. (The variety of licenses will be discussed in a minute.) In most instances, I will be entitled to 50 percent. Acuff-Rose will provide me semiannual accountings of my earnings. (Quarterly accountings are even better, but are very hard to get.)

- Acuff-Rose will pay me a modest advance—perhaps $500.

- Any disputes between us will be settled through arbitration.[15]

Once the deal has been struck, Acuff-Rose will set about using the song to make money—both for itself and for me. If the song is a good one (and especially if I am well known), it will be able to do so in many different ways.

Its first move, for the reasons just suggested, will likely be to arrange with a performer and a recording company to make a commercial recording. That performer might be me—in which case, the song would be called a "controlled composition," which would have various economic and legal implications. But suppose (to illustrate the full range of possible legal relationships) that another artist makes the recording. Chris Smither (an accomplished guitarist and singer) does a very nice rendition of my composition, and Adelphi Records would like to include it on Smither's next "album." (In a minute, we'll consider the various forms that "album" might take.) Acuff-Rose will make this possible by issuing to Adelphi a "mechanical license" for the song. (Remember that one aspect of my original right of reproduction was the exclusive right to make mechanical copies of my composition. It's that right, now held by Acuff-Rose, that's being licensed.) In theory, Acuff-Rose and Adelphi could arrange this deal on their own. But almost certainly they will rely instead upon an intermediary—specifically, the Harry Fox Agency, a wholly owned subsidiary of the National Music Publishers Association (NMPA), of which Acuff-Rose is a member.[16]

How much will Adelphi, assisted by Harry Fox, pay Acuff-Rose? Because this is the first recording of the song, they would be free as a matter of law to pick any price they wanted. In practice, however, the amount they select will be heavily influenced by a special provision of copyright law and a set of customs that have arisen in its shadow. Section 115 provides that, once a recording of a copyrighted musical composition has been distributed to the public, anyone else may make and distribute to the public another recording of the composition, provided that he or she does not alter the melody or character of the song and pays the copyright owner a prescribed fee. (It is because of this provision that you hear so many "covers"—recordings of one artist's song by someone else—being played on the radio.) In 1909, when this system was first instituted, the fee was 2 cents for each copy of the second recording. It has been adjusted several times since. In 1990 (our baseline), it is 5.7 cents for each copy (provided that the recording is less than five minutes long; more if it's longer).[17]

It is worth pausing to emphasize a few features of this system. First, it should be apparent that this is another example of a "compulsory license." The composer of a song enjoys, among other things, the exclusive right to make mechanical copies of it, but is "compelled" under certain circumstances to license that right to others for an amount of money that is likely to be less than what the composer would be inclined to charge. Why has Congress interfered in this fashion with the free market in mechanical licenses? The original motivation for the scheme was fear of monopoly. In

1908, the Supreme Court ruled that making a piano roll of a song did not infringe the copyright in the musical composition. The following year, Congress overturned that decision and for the first time gave songwriters control over "mechanical" embodiments of their songs. However, in making this important adjustment to copyright law, Congress confronted a problem: at the time, one piano roll manufacturer, the Aeolian Company, dominated the market. Congress feared that Aeolian would use its market power to acquire the exclusive rights to produce mechanical copies of all popular musical works, enabling it to drive its competitors out of business and then raise prices for piano rolls. The compulsory license, by enabling the competitors to use copyrighted compositions without permission, was designed to prevent that. The rule did what it was supposed to do; competition in the piano roll industry flourished and, to some extent, has continued in its successor, the record industry. Whether the rule has outlived its usefulness—or has had costs that exceed its benefits in terms of fostering competition—is a matter of some controversy, to which we will return in subsequent chapters.[18]

Back to our story. Because the Smither-Adelphi recording of my song is the first commercial recording of it, the cover license strictly speaking does not apply. However, according to long-standing custom in the music industry, first recordings are licensed on the same terms as subsequent recordings, which are of course governed by the cover license. So, under the deal arranged by the Harry Fox Agency, Adelphi will pay 5.7 cents for each copy it sells of Smither's album. Suppose that Smither's album is moderately successful. In the first year, Adelphi sells one hundred thousand copies. Adelphi would thus be obliged to pay Acuff-Rose $5,700. The Harry Fox Agency would likely keep 4.5 percent of that amount ($256.50) as a commission, leaving Acuff-Rose with $5,443.50. Acuff-Rose would, in due course, give me half of that amount: $2,721.75.

So that's the first and most important of the licensing strategies available to Acuff-Rose. It's not terribly lucrative, as we can see. But getting a recording of the song out into the world is critical to the other licensing possibilities. Those include the following.

Once Smither's album begins to circulate among folk-music fans, some amateur guitarists and singers may wish to purchase copies of the sheet music containing my composition. To satisfy that demand, Acuff-Rose could print sheet music itself. More likely, however, it will license the right to do so to one of the four major American sheet-music publishing firms, paying me, in turn, five or six cents per copy.[19]

A motion-picture producer who wishes to use my song in a movie will have to obtain from Acuff-Rose a "synchronization" license. If the studio is small, it is likely to arrange the deal through the Harry Fox Agency, in which case Harry Fox will likely retain 10 percent of the revenue, and I will likely be paid 50 percent of the remainder. If the studio is large, it will probably negotiate directly with Acuff-Rose, and the amount I earn will be determined by the bargain they strike.

The most lucrative licensing opportunity available to Acuff-Rose involves the right to perform my composition publicly. Recall that copyright law defines "public performance" expansively, including all means of communicating recordings of the song to the public. That means, among other things, that radio stations must obtain copyright owners' permission before playing their songs over the air. Music publishers are in a somewhat better position than individual composers to negotiate such licenses. But still, it would be difficult and costly for each music publisher to negotiate contracts with each radio station that wishes to broadcast songs in the publisher's repertoire. To facilitate such transactions, there have arisen in the United States three private "performing rights organizations" (PROs): the American Society of Composers, Authors, and Publishers (ASCAP); Broadcast Music, Inc. (BMI); and SESAC. ASCAP is the oldest. As of 1990, its members included approximately twenty-nine thousand songwriters and twelve thousand publishers. BMI is its principal competitor, with a membership of approximately fifty-three thousand writers and thirty-two thousand publishers. SESAC is much smaller. As of 1990, it represented approximately two thousand writers and one thousand publishers. Both ASCAP and BMI are not-for-profit organizations, while SESAC is a private, for-profit corporation, but that formal difference does not matter hugely in practice.[20]

The business models of the three PROs differ somewhat, but the primary and most lucrative function of all three is to issue "blanket" performance licenses for all of the songs in their catalogues to radio and television stations. (They also offer licenses for individual songs, but they are significantly more expensive [per song] and so are rarely used.) To obtain a blanket license, a station pays the relevant organization a single fee. Typically, the fees paid by radio stations are flat percentages (roughly two percent in the cases of ASCAP and BMI; less in the case of SESAC) of their gross revenues minus certain deductions. The formulae used by the PROs to determine the fees paid by television stations and networks are more idiosyncratic and complex. Almost all radio and television stations obtain licenses from all three organizations. (Similar, although much less expensive, licenses are commonly obtained by other institutions interested in performing large numbers of compositions publicly—such as restaurants that provide their patrons background music.)[21]

In 1990, the total amount of money generated in this fashion is approximately $700 million. Where does the money go? ASCAP and BMI each keeps somewhere between 15 percent and 20 percent of its gross revenues to cover its overhead and divides the rest between its members. SESAC pays its members negotiated fees, keeping the balance as profits. Do all writers and publishers of all songs share equally? In the early history of ASCAP, the answer was yes. No longer. Now all three organizations use a combination of self-reporting by licensees and sophisticated sampling techniques to estimate the frequency with which each composition within their repertoires is being performed. The fees paid to the member writers and publishers are then adjusted accordingly.[22]

This system has been remarkably successful. Total overhead charges are relatively low. The techniques employed by the PROs to estimate consumption and then to distribute revenue have gradually become increasingly precise. To be sure, the concentration of licensing power in a few organizations creates a danger of oligopolistic behavior and pricing. Partly as a result, ASCAP and BMI, the two largest PROs, are now subject to antitrust consent decrees which, among other things, prevent them from demanding from members exclusive rights to license their compositions and enable potential licensees unhappy with the rates they are offered to appeal to a "rate court" administered by a federal court. But invocations of the rate court have been rare, and most members of the organizations seem satisfied with the ways in which they are treated and compensated. (In Chapters 4 through 6, the success of this system will be an important point of reference when considering how copyright law as a whole might be sensibly reformed.)[23]

The last of the licensing opportunities available to Acuff-Rose concerns the reproduction, distribution, and public performance of my song in other countries. Unless Acuff-Rose has branch offices abroad, it is likely to enter into contracts with foreign music publishers, conventionally known as "subpublishers." In return for the right to exploit the various entitlements I enjoy under the copyright laws of their respective jurisdictions, the subpublishers will pay Acuff-Rose fees that vary, depending on the rights at issue, from 10 to 50 percent of the money they collect. Acuff-Rose, in turn, will pay a portion of those fees to me.[24]

Figure 2.1 summarizes these various transactions.

To review, the composer of a song typically assigns all of his copyright interests in his creation to a music publisher. With the aid of intermediaries (in rounded rectangles), the publisher then issues licenses to a wide variety of organizations (in ellipses), empowering them to use the composition in specified ways. Money flows through the channels cut by the transfers of legal

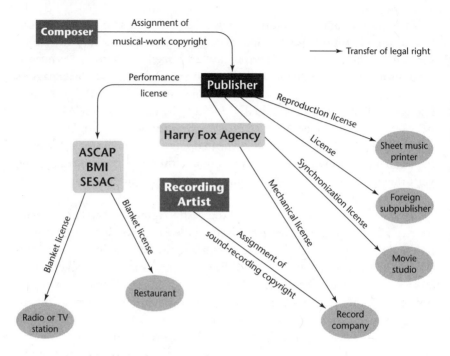

FIGURE 2.1. *Legal Rights in the Music Industry (1990).*

rights—but in the opposite direction. Each licensee uses the musical composition to fuel a profit-making business model—selling sheet music, selling sound recordings, selling radio and television advertisements, and so on. Each licensee then pays a portion of its income to the music publisher. The publisher pays a modest commission to the pertinent intermediary, and then turns over to the original composer a share determined by contract. (In a slight variation on this pattern, the PROs pay the composer's share to him or her directly, rather than through the publisher.)

Legal Rights in Sound Recordings

We have thus far paid scant attention to one crucial player in this drama: the recording artist. What rights does he have? Chris Smither, remember, developed and recorded an especially attractive rendition of my song, the distribution of which was critical to all of my other sources of revenue. Doesn't he receive intellectual-property rights? For decades, the answer was no; federal copyright law did not accord recording artists any entitlements (although some states did). Thus artists' principal rights were those they acquired through their contracts with the record companies. In 1972, however, Congress strengthened their position. The net result is that, now (that is, in 1990), Smither, like a composer, gets a copyright. Specifically, as soon as he "fixes" his rendition of my song in a tangible medium of expression, he acquires a copyright in the resultant sound recording, which parallels Acuff-Rose's copyright in the underlying musical composition.[25]

In three respects, however, Smither's copyright is more limited than Acuff-Rose's. First, Smither's right of reproduction is defined more narrowly. Recall that Acuff-Rose's rights would be violated if someone, after hearing a rendition of the song, composed and then recorded a "substantially similar" song. Not so with Smither. His rights would be violated only if the copyist "directly or indirectly recapture[d] the actual sounds fixed in [his] recording." In other words, mimicking a sound recording does not abridge the performer's rights; only dubbing does so.[26]

The most important practical implication of this limitation is that it prevents the first person to record a song from controlling subsequent recordings. Suppose, for example, that Paul Simon hears Smither's recording of my composition on the radio and decides to make a commercial recording of it himself. He will have to pay Acuff-Rose the amount specified by the compulsory license for "covers," discussed earlier. But he will not have to pay Smither anything.

Smither's exclusive right to prepare derivative works based upon his sound recording is limited in the same fashion. Only adaptations "in which the actual sounds fixed in the [original] sound recording are rearranged, remixed, or otherwise altered in sequence or quality" will violate Smither's right. That means that if Simon substantially altered the orchestration or rhythm of Smither's rendition of my song (for example, by resetting it to an African beat and interweaving it with a performance by the Zulu a capella group Ladysmith Black Mambazo), he would still have to pay Acuff-Rose (indeed, would have to pay the publisher whatever fee it demanded, not limited by the compulsory license), but again would not have to pay Smither.

The third and most important limitation (as of 1990) on Smither's copyright is that, unlike me, he does not enjoy an exclusive right of public performance. That means that Peggy can play his album on her boombox in Harvard Square without his permission. More important, it means that, when a radio or TV station broadcasts his recording of my song, it has to pay Acuff-Rose and me (through the system of blanket licenses described previously) for the right to use my composition, but, unless it makes a copy of his recording while preparing the show, does not have to pay Smither.

Why not? Doesn't Smither deserve a share of the revenue reaped (indirectly) by the station because of its ability to offer listeners access to his creation? There are two explanations for this apparent gap in the system of legal rights—one political, the other principled. The political explanation is that radio and television stations and their respective trade associations have considerable legislative clout. In 1972, when copyrights in sound recordings were first created, the stations lobbied successfully against the inclusion of a public-performance right, and they have held that line ever since.

The principled explanation is that the owners of sound-recording copyrights benefit whenever their recordings are broadcast, because listeners become aware of the recordings and are stimulated to buy albums containing them, and a portion of the purchase prices of those albums ends up in the pockets of the performers. If anything, the owners of the copyrights in the sound recordings should be paying the radio and TV stations for advertising their wares, not vice versa. (More on that shortly.) A possible retort: But doesn't this argument suggest that music publishers shouldn't be compensated either when records containing their compositions are broadcast? After all, their incomes also rise, because the "mechanical fees" that the record companies must pay them vary with the number of albums sold. The response: yes, but remember that those mechanical fees are capped by the compulsory license. The result is that the holders of musical-works copyrights benefit less from increased album sales than the holders of sound-recording copyrights, whose incomes are not similarly limited. Thus it's appropriate for the former and not the latter to receive public-performance license fees from the stations.

Which is the "real" explanation? It's hard to tell, in part because the stations, when lobbying, rely not surprisingly on the principled argument just sketched. So the extent to which the members of Congress, when repeatedly rejecting requests to create public-performance rights for sound recordings, have been responding to political pressure or have been persuaded by the lobbyists' arguments remains unclear.

Performers' Rights in Action

Back to our narrative. Will Smither exercise his sound-recording copyright himself? Almost certainly not. Instead, he will follow the widespread industry custom and assign his rights (not just to his recording of my song, but for all his recordings) to Adelphi, the recording company. Several circumstances will push him in this direction. First, Smither probably lacks the equipment and resources necessary to make the recording without Adelphi's assistance. In 1990, it costs approximately $150,000 to produce a high-quality master for a ten-track album; to produce an individual track would of course cost at least 10 percent of that. Even if he could obtain the necessary funds, Smither lacks the expertise and contacts necessary to promote the recording effectively and the distribution system necessary to deliver it to retailers. As of 1990, only a record company is in a position to supply those services. In return for supplying them, the company—in this case, Adelphi—will demand that Smither assign to it the copyright in the recording.[27]

What is Smither likely to get in return for his assignment? Here we return to the subject broached in Chapter 1. If he is naïve or poorly advised, he is likely to end up with very little. An experienced and moderately well-known artist, like Smither, is likely to do somewhat better—but not so well as one might expect. If it's typical, the contract he signs with Adelphi will include the following terms:[28]

- Smither agrees to provide Adelphi his "exclusive personal services as a recording artist" for the term of the contract.
- Within twelve months, Smither agrees to deliver to Adelphi a sufficient number of recordings to constitute one "album."[29]
- The term of the contract shall consist of the period necessary to produce one album plus nine months. However, Adelphi shall have the option to extend the contract for additional periods thereafter.[30]
- Adelphi has the right to select the compositions to be recorded.
- Smither shall receive 15 percent of the "suggested retail list price" (SRLP) of all copies sold of his recordings. (As one might expect, this percentage varies with artists' stature. A new artist is likely to get only 9 or 10 percent. A "superstar" may get as much as 20 percent.) However, his royalties shall be reduced by the following deductions:[31]
  - A 3 percent share for the producer of the recordings (reducing Smither's share from 15 percent to 12 percent).[32]
  - A reduction corresponding loosely to the cost of "packaging" the recordings into containers, the amount of which will vary by format. As of 1990, typical numbers were 10 percent for vinyl albums, 20 percent for cassettes, and 25 percent for CDs. (It doesn't actually cost that much to make the containers; the inflated percentages are just a way of semi-covertly reducing Smither's share of the pot.)[33]
  - A 15 percent reduction for "free goods"—copies of the recordings ostensibly distributed for "promotional purposes," even though most are sold to consumers.[34]

- A 25 percent reduction in the standard royalty rate for containers in formats relying on "new technologies," the most important of which, as of 1990, is the compact disc.[35]
- Perhaps a 10 percent reduction for "breakage"—a leftover from the days when sound recordings were distributed primarily in the form of shellac "78"s, many of which did indeed break in transit. (As of 1990, this ploy was still used by two and perhaps three record companies.)[36]
- A 35 percent reduction for "reserves"—a (generous) estimate of the percentage of recordings delivered to retailers that will not be sold and thus will eventually be returned. (Unlike all the preceding deductions, this one is temporary; typically within two years of the date of shipment, Adelphi would be obliged to "liquidate"—that is, pay Smither—the amount held in reserve for recordings that had not, in fact, been returned.)[37]

- Adelphi agrees to pay all recording costs (including studio and equipment rental charges, mixing and editing costs, and fees for backup musicians), but all such payments will be deducted from Smither's royalties. (If, as is conventional, Smither is paid an advance on the record, both these expenses and the advance will be "recouped" from the royalties owed to Smither before he is paid anything more.)[38]
- Adelphi will pay the fees charged by "independent promoters" (more on these shortly) and the costs of producing a promotional music video, but (at least) half of those costs will then be deducted (in the same fashion) from Smither's royalties.[39]

The contract is likely to contain an additional, potentially explosive provision: it will purport to characterize Smither's contribution to the sound recording as a "work for hire." We will consider the legal significance of that phrase in some detail in the next section of this chapter, when we turn our attention to the film industry. For the time being, it's sufficient to say that, at least until the year 2013, that provision, even if valid, will not materially affect the relative rights of Smither and Adelphi.[40]

Looking over the enforceable terms of this representative contract, it becomes easier to understand why, as we discussed in the previous chapter, recording artists so often end up with so little. Ostensibly, Smither is entitled to 15 percent of the retail sales of his records. But once the various customary deductions are applied, his share turns out to be much smaller. How

Cassettes

$9.00	SRLP
x .80	20% deduction for packaging
$7.20	Royalty base
x .12	Royalty rate (Smither's 15% "all-in" rate, minus 3% for the producer)
$.864	Gross royalty
x 60,000	Number of cassettes sold
$51,840	
x .85	15% reduction for "free goods"
$44,064	Subtotal

CDs

$16.00	SRLP
x .75	25% deduction for packaging
$12.00	Royalty base
x .75	25% reduction for "new technologies"
$9.00	
x .12	Royalty rate (Smither's 15% "all-in" rate, minus 3% for the producer)
$1.08	Gross royalty
x 40,000	Number of CDs sold
$43,200	
x .85	15% reduction for "free goods"
$36,720	Subtotal
$80,784	TOTAL

TABLE **2.1.** *Calculation of Smither's Royalties.*

much, exactly? We've been assuming that Adelphi sells 100,000 copies of the album in the first year. (Most likely, sales after the first year would be modest.) Suppose that 60 percent of those sales were in the form of cassette tapes, which carried a suggested retail list price (SRLP) of $9, and 40 percent were in the form of CDs, which carried a SRLP of $16. On these assumptions, the conventional way of combining all of the contractual terms reviewed previously would be as indicated in Table 2.1.[41]

$80,784 is nothing to sneeze at. However, the charges for which Smither is responsible—the various recording costs and half of the promotional costs of the CD—will almost certainly exceed that number. The net result is that Adelphi, in the end, will not pay Smither anything.[42]

Will Adelphi seek to collect from Smither the amount by which his obligations under the contract exceed the royalties due him? Or if (as is customary) Adelphi has paid Smither an advance, will it seek to recover that amount? No. However, Adelphi will keep track of how much Smither "owes"—that is, how much of the expenses for which he is responsible are "unrecouped." If Adelphi later exercises its right to extend Smither's contract and induce him to make another album in the future, it will deduct from any net royalties Smither earns from the new album the amount by which he was in the hole on the original album. (This is known as "cross-collateralization.")

Not all performers in 1990 fared as badly as Smither in our imagined example. Suppose, to return to an earlier example, that Paul Simon recorded my song (along with various other compositions) on a Warner Bros. album. His position is likely to be better than Smither's in two respects. First, his fame will probably enable him to cut a somewhat better deal with Warner Bros. than Smither was able to secure with Adelphi. Second, and more important, his fame, talent, and seemingly ageless optimistic voice will enable Warner Bros. to sell many more albums. Assume, for example, that, like his 1986 classic *Graceland*, Simon's new album "goes multi-platinum"—meaning that it sells more than two million copies. Even if the terms of his contract with Warner Bros. were identical to Smither's with Adelphi, Simon would earn in royalties at least $1,615,680. An "escalation" clause in his contract (increasing the size of his "all-in" royalty if the album sells more than a designated number of copies) and other contractual concessions would likely push the number substantially higher. After deducting recording and promotional costs, he would still likely earn somewhere in the vicinity of a million dollars. A very different picture indeed.

There remains to be discussed one final, important piece of the puzzle. As noted previously, because of the absence of a public-performance right for sound recordings, there is no legal relationship in our hypothetical story between the radio stations that broadcast Smither's recording of my song and Adelphi, the holder of the copyright in the song. Most likely, however, there is a significant economic bond between them, commonly known as "payola" (a term originally derived from a combination of the words *pay* and *Victrola*). Early in the development of the music industry, record companies began semi-secretly paying key radio-station employees—either disk jockeys or program managers—to air particular tracks, in hopes that listeners would then purchase copies of those recordings. The type of compensation varied. Cash was of course the simplest, but "gifts" in the form of drugs, access to prostituted women, and free concert tickets were also common. After a series of scandals in the late 1950s, Congress amended the Federal Communications Act to forbid undisclosed payments of these sorts, but criminal prosecutions under the revised statute were rare, and the potential fines were modest. Significant reform came only in the late 1970s, when federal prosecutors' increased use of the Racketeer Influenced and Corrupt Organizations (RICO) Act for the first time threatened record companies with substantial penalties for bribing station employees.

Payola did not disappear, however. The importance of air play to sales of records was too great for the companies to abandon the practice altogether. Instead, taking advantage of the clumsy way in which the pertinent laws were written, the record companies simply changed the form in which they made payments to the stations. The new system was known as "independent promotion." Under this regime (which survives largely unchanged today), the companies pay separate firms or individuals—commonly known as "indies"—to persuade stations to add particular songs to their playlists. The most effective of the various techniques employed by the indies is, as one might imagine, cash payments—typically in the vicinity of $1,000 per song for a major metropolitan station. (Ordinarily, the money is ostensibly for "promotional support." The station is supposed to use it to purchase T-shirts, billboard ads, and so forth. In reality, the station can use the funds however it pleases.) So long as the station does not promise to give the song in question a minimum number of "spins," such an arrangement is lawful. In any event, the record companies, deliberately ignorant of the techniques employed by the indies, cannot be held responsible if they occasionally stray across the line of legality. This new system quickly became expensive—more expensive, in fact, than old-style payola. By the late 1980s, the record companies collectively were paying independent promoters between $60 and $80 million a year.[43]

Figure 2.2 adds this final, critical revenue stream to the pattern of entitlements and payments we have already mapped.

Film

The Creation of a Motion Picture

The film industry is just as complicated as the music industry, but the legal doctrines that help structure it fortunately are simpler. Most of the relevant rules can be understood as variations on the rules we've already discussed.

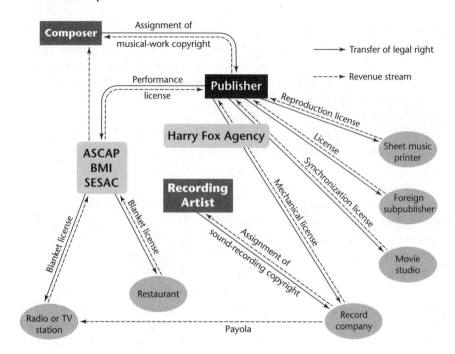

FIGURE **2.2.** *Revenue Streams in the Music Industry (1990).*

With respect to each piece of recorded music, you will recall, there are two copyrights: the copyright in the musical composition, which vests initially in the original composer but typically is later assigned to a music publishing company; and the copyright in the sound recording, which vests initially in the recording artist but typically is later assigned to a record company. With respect to a film, there is only one: the copyright in the "motion picture."[44]

Typically, this copyright is first acquired by a "production entity." On rare occasions, that entity is an individual person, acting on his or her own. Somewhat more often, it is an independent production company. Most commonly (as of our baseline), it consists of a person or a group of people hired by one of the major film studios—who then work in conjunction with an in-house "creative executive." (During the remainder of this discussion, we will assume that the production entity is separate from the studio, but keep in mind that they may be closely affiliated or even identical.)[45]

But what about the many other people who make creative contributions to the venture—screenwriters, directors, cinematographers, actors, soundtrack composers, costume designers, and so on. Don't they get shares of the copyright? In many countries, the answer is yes, and a complex set of contracts is then necessary to collect their various interests in one place. In the United States, however, the answer (with a few qualifications) is no; the production entity holds all of the rights.

The legal rule that makes this result possible is known as the "work-for-hire" doctrine. In most countries, a copyright always vests in the individual person who makes a creative work. American copyright law generally adheres to the same principle, but recognizes two exceptions to it. The first arises when a work is "prepared by an employee within the scope of his or her employment." The second arises when all of the following requirements are met: (a) a creative work is "specially ordered or commissioned," (b) the parties agree in writing that the copyright in the work shall vest in the party who places the order, and (c) the work falls into one of nine carefully limited categories. (A motion picture is one of the nine categories. A sound recording is not—which is why, as mentioned in the previous section, it is far from clear that the boilerplate provision in most sound recording contracts indicating the recording shall constitute a "work for hire" has any effect whatsoever.) In both of these cases, the work in question will be deemed a "work for hire." That designation has many implications, but the most important, for our purposes, is that the copyright belongs to the person or institution for whom the work is made, rather than the person who actually makes it.[46]

During the early history of the film industry, studios customarily employed actors and directors for long periods of time (often on onerous terms). As a result, any copyrights that might have arisen from the actors' and directors' contributions to the films belonged to the studios under the first of the two legal theories just mentioned. Today (meaning, as of our baseline of 1990), such long-term employment contracts are much rarer. Instead, production entities (often with the aid of talent agencies and casting consultants) generally hire actors and directors (either directly or through paper intermediaries known as "loan-out companies") to work on individual films. The contributors thus might plausibly claim the status of "independent contractors." However, the agreements that they sign when they are hired routinely include clauses specifying that their contributions to the projects shall be deemed works for hire—thus triggering the second of the two legal theories. The net result is the same: the production entity, and not the individual contributors, acquires a copyright interest in the final product.

But what if material that the production entity wants to include in the film is already in existence when the project gets under way? For example, suppose that the entity wants to make a motion-picture adaptation of a novel, or wants to use a screenplay "pitched" by a screenwriter, or wants to include a recording of a currently popular song in the soundtrack for the film. The copyrights in those materials will already have vested in the people who created them; the work-for-hire doctrine is thus inapplicable. In such cases, the production entity will instead obtain either an assignment of the copyright from the copyright owner or, more typically, a license to use the material in a specified way. For example, it will obtain from the novelist a license to prepare a "derivative work" based on the novel. (In practice, such agreements often are struck in two stages. First, the production entity acquires an option to make use of the novel. If it is then successful in obtaining the necessary actors, financing, and so on, it exercises the option.) Similarly, it will obtain "synchronization" and performance licenses from the music publisher that owns the copyright in an existing musical work and a "master use" license from the record company that owns the copyright in the associated sound recording. The fact that, under these arrangements, the copyrights in the materials are still held by their creators sometimes complicates the process of distributing the film outside the United States, but those intricacies need not detain us.[47]

What will the individual contributors receive in return for participating in the venture and surrendering their possible copyright interests? Money, of course. For the majority of the contributors, this will consist of a fixed amount, agreed upon at the time of the contract. Many will belong to organizations—for example, the Writers Guild, the Directors Guild, and the Screen Actors Guild—which ensure that their members are provided various other contractual benefits (minimum salaries, health insurance, and the like). Finally, a few of the crucial players—the lead actors and perhaps the lead screenwriter—may also obtain "back-end participation" agreements, which entitle them to a share of the net profits of the film. (Determination of what counts as net profits is often, as one might imagine, a complex and hotly contested aspect of the contract negotiation.) The key participants are also likely to insist upon some noneconomic rights. Writers and actors typically are especially interested in the details of the screen credit they are given. Directors may demand the right to make the final cut of the film—the decisive edit.[48]

The production entity will, of course, seek from the contributors the broadest possible grant of rights. For example, from the screenwriter, it will seek and usually obtain, not merely the right to produce the script, but also the rights to modify it freely, to make sequels and remakes, and to exploit all other derivative rights in all present and future formats.

Finally, the production entity will sometimes obtain permissions (for free or for a fee) from any real people who will be depicted in the film and from the owners of the properties that will be seen in the background. It is far from clear that such permissions are legally necessary. In their absence, depicted people might argue that their privacy has been invaded, that they have been defamed, or that (if they are celebrities) their "rights of publicity" have been abridged. But many studios plausibly take the position that the First Amendment protects their freedom to create truthful depictions of real people. The legal rights that might be asserted by the owners of the physical locations that will be seen in a film are even less clear. Nevertheless, the risk-averse companies that provide production entities so-called "errors and omissions" insurance sometimes insist that such releases be obtained anyway.[49]

At least as important as the licenses and "talent" necessary to make a film is the financing for the venture. For the typical "wide-release" picture, this is a sizeable sum. As of 1990, it costs on average $26.8 million to produce a major studio film in the United States. Where does this money come from? In a small percentage of the cases, the production entity raises the necessary funds from banks and individual investors. More typically, however, the money comes from one of the "major" American film studios—which in turn raises the money from a variety of internal and external sources. As of 1990, there are seven dominant studios: Disney; MGM/UA; Paramount Pictures (a subsidiary of Viacom); Sony Pictures (formerly Columbia); Twentieth-Century Fox; Universal Pictures; and Warner Bros. (a division of Time Warner). The majors control only about half of the films released in the United States, but that half accounts for 95 percent of theatrical admissions and revenues.[50]

If the production entity and the studio are separate, the financial arrangements between them commonly proceed in stages. In the initial development period, the studio pays the production entity a modest amount of money to supervise the clarification and refinement of the project. After the venture is "green lighted" (by no means a certainty), the studio puts up increasing amounts of money to fund each of the phases in the creation of the movie: the pre-production phase, in which the script is developed, the cast is assembled, the location is selected, the sets are constructed, the costumes are made, the scenes are rehearsed, and the budget is drafted; the production phase, when most of the shooting occurs; the post-production phase, when the scenes are edited (and sometimes reshot), sound and special effects are added, and so on; and the prints and advertising phase, when positive prints of the final negative are made and the finished product is marketed. (The marketing of a movie typically begins long before the process of producing the film is complete, but is conventionally considered financially separate. In 1990, it cost the studio, on average, an additional $12 million.) A film produced "in house" typically goes through the same phases, but the associated financial arrangements are simpler because they are handled internally.[51]

If the production entity and the studio are separate, the latter ordinarily acquires two things in return for putting up the necessary funds: creative control, and very extensive rights to distribute the film. In the 1950s and 1960s, such distribution agreements often attempted to specify in some detail the rights of the studio. This practice, in turn, gave rise to much controversy and litigation when new marketing possibilities unforeseeable at the time a picture was made arose. Nowadays, it is more common for the studio to acquire "comprehensive and perpetual worldwide rights" to distribute the film in all ways in all present and future media.

That, in brief, is how legal interests in a film are created, collected, and transferred. We now turn to the question of what entitlements are included in this bundle of rights.

The Copyright in a Film

Like the composer of a song, the holder of the copyright in a motion picture enjoys four exclusive rights. However, each of those rights takes a slightly different form in this new context.

The exclusive right of reproduction means that no one, without the permission of the copyright owner, may make either a verbatim copy of the film or a "substantially similar" film. Thus, for example, in 1983 a federal court ruled that the plots of *Star Wars* and *Battlestar Galactica* were sufficiently close that Twentieth-Century Fox (the owner of the copyright in the former) could try to persuade a jury that the latter constituted copyright infringement. The owner's right of reproduction also extends to well-delineated characters who appear in the film. Thus, for example, in 1995 (a bit after our baseline), a court required the Honda Motor Company to stop airing an advertisement for its "Honda del Sol" convertible, in part because the "suave, . . . young, tuxedo-clad, British-looking" spy depicted in the ad too closely resembled James Bond, the central figure in a series of movies whose copyright was owned by MGM.[52]

The copyright owner's exclusive right to prepare derivative works based on the movie enables him or her to control all adaptations of it (including translations and versions edited for television), all "remakes," and all sequels (an increasingly valuable entitlement). In addition, it enables the owner to control the increasingly lucrative market in movie-related merchandise: toys, dolls, clothing, posters, and so on derived from or based upon the film.[53]

The owner's exclusive right to "distribute" the film means that no one, without permission, may sell, rent, or give away copies of it to the general public. As was true of musical compositions, the owner's rights in this regard are tempered by the "first-sale" doctrine. In contrast to the situation in the music industry, however, that doctrine is not limited by a prohibition upon commercial rentals. Thus, once Blockbuster has purchased a copy of the film, it is free to rent it to customers without the permission of the copyright owner.

Finally, the owners' exclusive right to "perform" the film publicly prevents anyone, without permission, from presenting it to a general audience or from transmitting it to remote viewers (for example, over a cable or satellite system). Exactly how "public" does a performance of a film have to be in order to trigger this right? Generations of law students have cut their teeth on a series of cases addressing that question in borderline situations. Among the contested scenarios are the following:

1. Using a VCR located at the front of a store to transmit a film selected by a customer to a small, private room at the back of the store;
2. Renting videocassettes of a film to customers, who then play them on VCRs in private booths located in the store;
3. Renting videodiscs to hotel guests, who then play them on videodisc players in their rooms.

Situations 1 and 2 were held to be "public performances"; 3 was not. Such troublesome cases will likely continue to arise, and law students will continue to struggle to differentiate them, but the general principle is not in doubt: the copyright owner controls all economically significant performances of the movie.[54]

As we've seen, by the time the typical American film is complete, one of the seven major studios will hold this constellation of rights. The studio is quite unlikely to exercise any of these rights itself. Instead, it will seek to recover the cost of producing the film by licensing other parties to engage in the specified activities. Figure 2.3 identifies the most important of these licensing opportunities.

The first and foremost distribution channel involves performances of the film in theatres. During our baseline year, this was a large and growing market. (In 1989, the typical "major" film was shown on a total of 1,177 movie screens in the United States, up from 850 screens only three years earlier.) Ordinarily, the studio rents to each theatre a copy of the film and grants it a license to show the film to public audiences. The commitments that the

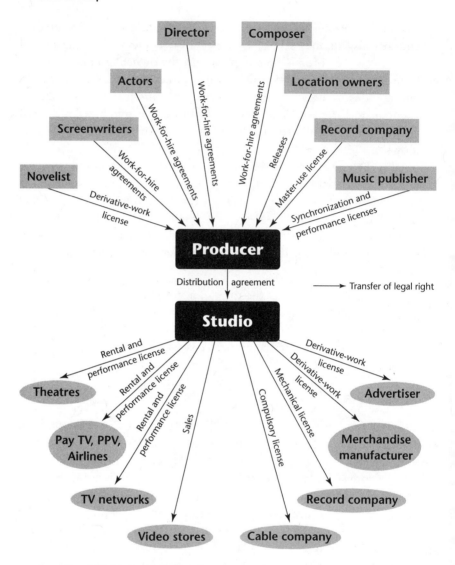

FIGURE 2.3. *Legal Rights in the Film Industry (1990).*

theatre makes in return are heavily shaped by industry custom. The standard contract allows the theatre to keep a portion of its box-office receipts (known as the "house nut") to cover its operating costs. Ten percent of the receipts in excess of that amount are kept by the theatre; the remaining 90 percent go to the studio. This division of the spoils is overridden, however, by a guarantee to the studio of a minimum percentage of the total receipts (including the "house nut"), the amount of which declines over time—for example, 70 percent during the first two weeks, 60 percent during the next two weeks, 50 percent during the next two weeks, and so on. When all is said and done, the studio commonly ends up with somewhere between 40 percent and 50 percent of the money that theatre patrons have paid to see the film.[55]

It's a bit surprising that the studios don't get a larger share of this pie. After all, there are only a few major studios, and they control a commodity that the theatres cannot live without. Why don't they use their bargaining power to squeeze the theatres harder? The explanation lies in a combination of three circumstances. First, the bargaining position of the theatres has been improved through consolidation into "chains." (In 1990, nine chains controlled 35 percent of theatre screens in the United States. Because those screens tended to be located in optimal urban or suburban spots, they accounted for 80 percent of total exhibition revenues.) Second, a series of state statutes and judicial antitrust rulings over the course of the twentieth century have shielded the theatres from the most heavy-handed of the bargaining tactics once employed by the studios. Third, the studios have an obvious financial interest in keeping the theatres alive. In 1990 (like today), many theatres teetered on the brink of bankruptcy. Demanding more of their revenues might well have pushed them over the edge.[56]

Despite these limitations, the studio is likely to make a good deal of money from its theatre contracts. But this is by no means the end of the story. A few months after its first theatrical release in the United States, the studio will license the film for theatrical performances in other countries. Soon thereafter, the studio will begin to authorize a series of other institutions—pay-per-view companies, "premium" cable channels, airlines, and so on—to show the film to their customers. Next, the studio (or its subsidiary) will begin to sell videocassette copies of the film to video rental stores. (During the 1980s, this source of revenue grew very rapidly. By the middle of the decade, Disney's animated features were generating more money from video sales and rentals than from box-office admissions. As of 1990, this is true of most films.) When the revenues that can be earned in those "windows" begin to fall off (approximately two years after its initial theatrical release), the studio typically licenses the film to television networks (both domestic and foreign), which, in turn, broadcast it over the airwaves leavened with advertisements. (We'll return to this business model shortly, when we discuss the *Sony* case.) Finally, roughly five years after its initial release, the studio licenses the film to local television syndicators. Usually, the revenues generated by this last set of deals are significantly smaller than those generated by

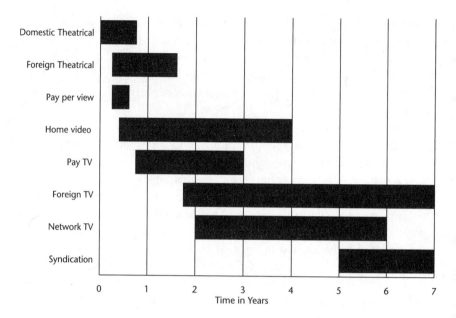

FIGURE 2.4. *Market Windows for Major Films from Release Date, circa 1990.*

theatre performances, but there are exceptions. Hitchcock's *The Birds* was a dud at the box office, but a lucrative hit on television.

Figure 2.4, derived from the 1990 edition of Harold Vogel's thorough guide to the economics of the entertainment industry, shows the relationships among these various outlets.[57]

To some extent, the studios' custom of releasing their films in different markets at different times represents a form of what economists call "price discrimination," which they define as charging different consumers different prices for access to the same good or service—or, more subtly, as charging different prices for different versions of a particular good or service when the variation cannot be explained by cost differences. A stylized explanation of the way this technique is employed in the movie industry goes as follows. The studios recognize that people vary in their willingness and ability to pay for access to films. Type-1 customers are eager to see films and will pay the substantial cost of admission to first-run theatres. Type-2 customers are less eager or less wealthy; they won't or can't pay the theatre ticket prices, but will pay the lower cost of renting videocassettes from Blockbuster (plus the customary late fees). Type-3 customers are unwilling or unable to pay the rental charges, but are willing to "pay" (by enduring the embedded advertisements) to watch films when broadcast over television networks. If films were released in all three markets simultaneously, the low-margin markets would erode the high-margin markets. For example, some of the type-1 customers would not go to the theatres, but would rent videocassettes instead. To avoid this outcome, the studios don't release films in a given market until all higher-margin markets have been substantially exhausted. In effect, what the studios are doing is dividing the universe of movie consumers into segments, defined by differences in their willingness and ability to pay for access to the product, and then charging the members of each group prices that will maximize the studios' profits.[58]

But can't the studios' conduct be explained in more benign terms? After all, some people (such as parents of young children who have trouble finding baby-sitters, or the owners of large home-entertainment systems) would prefer to watch films in the comfort of their living rooms than in theatres. One might thus argue that, what the studios are really doing, by making films available in a variety of formats, is enabling consumers to choose the viewing modes that best suit their tastes and schedules. In part, that's certainly true. But the best indication that it's not a full explanation of the studios' marketing strategy—that at least one of the purposes of this system is price discrimination—is the fact that the studios do not make all the formats available simultaneously. (Another indication is the fact that the studios typically make less money per "viewing" in each successive window.)[59]

Unfortunately, the term *price discrimination* has unpleasant connotations—suggesting both price gouging and injustice. (It's for that reason that the studios prefer the second explanation.) In fact, a serious argument can be made that price discrimination is socially desirable—and thus that we should commend the studios' conduct in this respect, not condemn it. But examination of that claim would take us far afield of our current topic. We'll take it up in Chapter 4, when we discuss some far more elaborate and precise price-discrimination systems that could be facilitated by a combination of technological innovation and legal reform.

Back to the subject. At the same time that the studio is making the film available to successive categories of viewers, it typically will be exploiting ancillary markets. For example, it may enter into licensing agreements with merchandise manufacturers (sometimes in combination with fast-food chains) to produce toys, Styrofoam cups, and so on based on characters in the film. It may license advertisers to use those same characters to sell products. It may license the creation of a videogame based on the film. It may license a record company to produce and distribute albums containing an edited version of the soundtrack of the movie (typically for a royalty of between 10 percent and 19 percent of the retail prices of the albums, half of which the studio will then distribute to the soundtrack composer). Once trivial, these ancillary sources of revenue can now be quite lucrative.

Finally, the studio will receive some additional income through the compulsory licensing systems we discussed earlier in this chapter. When a cable system picks up an over-the-air television broadcast and retransmits it to its customers, the system must pay an administratively determined fee to the Copyright Office. If the broadcast contains a film, a portion of that money will eventually end up in the coffers of the studio that owns the copyright in the film. The same system, as we've seen, applies to satellite carriers who retransmit television broadcasts.

Fair Use Revisited

Like copyrights in musical compositions and sound recordings, copyrights in motion pictures are subject to a list of exceptions and limitations. The list applicable to the film industry is shorter than the list applicable to the music industry, but it is still important. Some of the exceptions we have already seen: the "first-sale" doctrine, which tempers the studio's right of distribution, and the compulsory licenses that temper its public-performance right. But more important than any of these is the fair-use doctrine.

That doctrine, you will remember, permits a defendant who has violated one or more of a copyright owner's exclusive rights to avoid liability if the defendant's activity is deemed, on balance, "fair." The case that best illustrates how this doctrine affects the music industry is the *Campbell* decision (reviewed earlier), which permitted 2 Live Crew to make and distribute a parody of "Oh, Pretty Woman." The case that best illustrates how the doctrine affects the film industry is the *Sony* decision, decided by the United States Supreme Court in 1984. As we will see in the next chapter, after 1990, the ruling in *Sony* would powerfully shape the ways in which American courts reacted to the emergence of new distribution technologies. Accordingly, we will review the decision in some detail.

The essential facts were as follows. In the mid-1970s, the Sony Corporation began manufacturing and distributing videocassette recorders (VCRs), which among other things enabled users to record films and other copyrighted programs broadcast by television stations. In 1976, two of the major studios—Walt Disney Productions and Universal City Studios—sued Sony, arguing (A) that the use of VCRs to copy the studios' films violated their exclusive right of "reproduction" and (B) that Sony, by putting the machines into the hands of consumers, was guilty of "contributory copyright infringement." The studios ostensibly sought both damages and an injunction against the further distribution of VCRs. What they really wanted was a ruling that would enable them to cut a deal with Sony and other VCR manufacturers—a deal that most likely would have obliged the manufacturers in the future to pay the studios a fee whenever a VCR was sold to a consumer.

Argument B requires a bit of explanation. Copyright law contains a pair of doctrines that enable copyright owners to go after people who help others to engage in infringement. The doctrine of "contributory infringement" imposes liability on a person "who, with knowledge of [an] infringing activity, induces, causes or materially contributes to" the activity in question. The doctrine of "vicarious infringement" imposes liability on a person who has both "an obvious and direct financial interest" in an infringing activity and the "right and ability to supervise" that activity, but fails to forbid it. Paul Goldstein uses the following hypothetical example to illustrate the relationship between the two rules:

> When a musical group performs a copyrighted work in public, each member of the group will directly infringe the performance right unless the group has obtained permission from the copyright owner or unless one of the statutory exemptions or defenses applies. The group's manager, who selects the musical compositions to be performed, will be liable as a contributory infringer because she effectively induces the infringing performance. The owner of the theatre in which the performance occurs, and who is compensated from ticket sales for the performance, will be vicariously liable if he has the ability to control the content of the performance.[60]

In the studios' view, the people who used VCRs to make verbatim, full-length copies of copyrighted movies were clearly engaged in direct infringement. But even if it were feasible for the studios to identify and sue the individual consumers who were using their machines for this purpose, such a litigation strategy would have made the studios very unpopular. So instead, the studios pursued the manufacturer who, in their view, was making this rampant piracy possible. Because Sony did not itself use its products to copy programs, the studios could not charge Sony with direct infringement. But, relying on the first of the two doctrines just mentioned, they accused Sony of "contributing" to the illegal conduct of its customers. (As we will see in the next chapter, the *Napster* case took a very similar form.)

Why, exactly, were the studios so exercised? In their view, the VCR threatened one of the most important of the various business models upon which their income depended. Figure 2.5 shows what they were worried about.

During the 1960s and 1970s, the studios would commonly grant licenses to television networks to broadcast their films (after the revenue streams from theatre performances and subscription broadcasts had petered out).

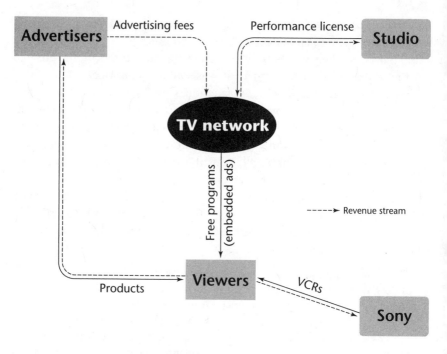

FIGURE 2.5. *Compensation System for Network Broadcasts of Films.*

The networks would remove scenes inappropriate for general audiences, divide the remaining material into roughly ten-minute segments, intersperse them with commercial advertisements, and then, through their local affiliates, broadcast the modified films to the viewing public for free. Viewers, after seeing the ads, would buy more of the products featured in the ads (or at least so the advertisers believed). Anticipating this effect, the advertisers would pay the networks for the right to place their ads in the films. The networks would use a portion of those advertising fees to pay license fees to the studios—thus completing the circle of rights and revenue.

The advent of VCRs threatened to disrupt this long-standing arrangement. In two ways, the machines reduced the number of ads that viewers watched. First, some viewers would record broadcasts without watching them and then, when replaying the tapes, "fast forward" through the ads. Second, in other households, one family member would record a program, stopping the tape whenever an ad appeared. The rest of the family could then later watch the program ad-free. These scenarios seemed sufficiently common or likely to the advertisers that they threatened to reduce the fees they would pay the networks for advertising slots. The networks, in turn, threatened to reduce the fees paid to the studios. The studios wanted to recoup this endangered revenue—and to reap a share of the net benefits of the new technology—by demanding a fee from Sony, the original source of the threat.

The case was closely and furiously fought. Jack Valenti, president of the Motion Picture Association of America, argued that it was a life-and-death battle for the film industry. "The VCR is to the motion picture industry and the American public," he claimed, "what the Boston strangler is to the woman alone." In the end, the Supreme Court, by a vote of five justices to four, found in Sony's favor.[61]

The Court's judgment was founded on two interlocking rulings. First, the Court held that the manufacturer of a device that is sometimes, even often, used to reproduce copyrighted material in violation of the copyright laws is not necessarily liable for contributory copyright infringement. So long as the device is "capable of substantial noninfringing uses," the manufacturer cannot be held responsible. The Court's stated objective, in drawing this line, was to "strike a balance between a copyright holder's legitimate demand for effective—not merely symbolic—protection of the statutory monopoly, and the rights of others freely to engage in substantially unrelated areas of commerce." But in fact, the way the Court phrased its judgment strongly favored the latter interest. To repeat: to avoid liability, a defendant who provides to the public a technology that can be used to violate copyrights merely needs to show that it is also capable of substantial legal uses.

Second, the Court ruled that using a VCR to "time-shift" a copyrighted program does not violate the copyright laws. "Time-shifting" (a phrase that was invented in this litigation) consists of "the practice of recording a program to view it once at a later time, and thereafter erasing it." The Court acknowledged that such behavior violates the copyright owner's exclusive right to reproduce the program. However, that apparent violation is overridden by the fair-use doctrine. To reach the latter conclusion, the Court reviewed and applied the four factors that the copyright statute identifies as relevant to a fair-use analysis. Factor one—"the purpose and character" of the behavior in question—tilted in favor of a finding of fair use, because "time-shifting for private home use must be characterized as a noncommercial, nonprofit activity," which is unlikely to threaten significantly the revenues of the copyright owner. Factor two—"the nature of the copyrighted work"—is not mentioned in the Court's opinion, but would seem to tilt against a finding of fair use, insofar as a film is a highly creative work, which (unlike a news report, for example) is generally thought to deserve strong copyright protection. Factor three—"the amount and substantiality of the portion used"—would also seem to tilt against fair use, insofar as time-shifters typically copy entire copyrighted works, but the Court discounted this factor in light of the fact that "timeshifting merely enables a viewer to see such a work which he had been invited to witness in its entirety free of charge." Last but not least, factor four—"the effect of the use upon the potential market for or value of the copyrighted work"—titled toward a finding of fair use, because the studios had failed to prove that there was a "meaningful likelihood" that, in the future, time-shifting would harm the "potential market" for the studios' films. In sum, the majority of the relevant considerations suggested that time-shifting should be deemed fair. Because time-shifting was a major (indeed, the predominant) use of VCRs, it was evident that the machines were "capable of substantial noninfringing uses." Consequently, Sony could not be held liable for contributory infringement—even if, some of the time, its products were used for other, illegal purposes.

The last step in the Court's analysis—its interpretation and application of the fourth factor—merits close attention, because it has colored the way in which courts ever since have considered fair-use cases. How could the Court have concluded that the use of VCRs posed no threat to the studios' revenues? The answer hinges in part on a procedural nicety: the factual record in the case had been developed in 1978, when the studios first brought suit against Sony. At the time, evidence was scant that viewers were regularly using their "fast-forward" buttons to avoid ads, and it was not yet clear that advertisers would refuse to pay for time-shifting audiences. In 1983 and 1984, when the case was being considered by the Supreme Court, much more evidence of both sorts was available—and was pressed upon the Court by *amici curiae* (other parties offering their views as "friends of the Court"). But the Supreme Court, appropriately, ignored that evidence, limiting itself to the facts as they appeared to the trial court back in 1979.

More important than this procedural nuance, however, was the way in which the Court interpreted the phrase "potential market." Justice Blackmun, in his dissenting opinion, argued that the phrase should be construed to encompass "any group of people who . . . would be willing to pay to see or hear the copyrighted work"—and specifically should include sets of potential customers that the defendant had helped to make available. Thus, for example, Spanish readers would constitute a potential market for a novel originally written in English. A person who, without permission, translated the novel into Spanish and then began selling copies of the translation surely should not be able to invoke the fair-use doctrine by claiming that such behavior did not undermine any *existing* market for the English version and thus did not impair the novelist's *existing* royalty stream. Rather, the novelist has the right, by licensing a translation of his or her work, to exploit the "potential market" of Spanish readers. Analogously, Blackmun suggested, the set of people who wished to watch movies at times different from the times they were originally broadcast constituted a "potential market" for the studios' films. Surely that market had been impaired by the practice of free, unauthorized time-shifting.

The majority of the Court implicitly rejected this view of the case. Regrettably, the majority did not explain why. By focusing on the impact of time-shifting on business models that had existed prior to the advent of VCRs, the majority tacitly took the position that only ordinary, normal, or foreseeable markets—and not markets unexpectedly created by the emergence of new technologies—should be taken into account when, in the course of applying the fair-use analysis, a court assesses the harm caused by a challenged activity to copyright owners. But, as we will see in the next chapter, the Court's failure to make this point explicit—or to justify it—would cause trouble when, during the 1990s, many more fair-use cases began to appear in the lower courts.

Taking Stock

This concludes our review of the combination of legal rules, customs, and business models that gave shape to the music and film industries as of our baseline date of 1990. How well did these systems work?

By some measures, very well indeed. Certainly, they succeeded in generating and distributing lots of music and movies. In 1990, approximately 856 million audio CDs, cassette tapes, "albums," and "singles" were sold in the United States, generating revenues at the retail level of approximately $7.369 billion. Roughly 90 percent of those sales consisted of recordings produced and distributed by American record companies. Retail sales of American recordings abroad generated an additional $5.4 billion at the retail level. All of these figures were increasing.[62]

The output of the film industry was similarly impressive. In 1990, 169 films were released in the United States by the major American studios. An additional 241 were released by smaller film companies. Consumers were admitted to American movie theatres a total of approximately 1.189 billion times, generating $5 billion in box-office revenues. Roughly $2.1 billion of those revenues were collected by the major studios. In addition, the studios earned roughly $1.2 billion from foreign theatrical licenses; $5.1 billion from sales and rentals of home videos; $1.1 billion from cable TV licenses; $0.1 billion from network TV licenses; $0.6 billion from syndication; and

$1 billion from foreign TV licenses—for a total of $11.2 billion. Most of these numbers had been rising steadily for many years.[63]

To some extent, these impressive statistics must be attributed to the efficiency of the rules and customs that regulate the interaction of the myriad participants in the two industries. To induce tens of thousands of composers, publishers, performers, producers, distributors, and broadcasters to work cooperatively to make sound recordings available to the public might seem an impossible—or at least very expensive—task. But through a combination of standardization (of contracts and business models) and intermediaries (above all, the PROs and the Harry Fox Agency), the job got done without undue expense. Similarly, aggregating the creative contributions of tens of thousands of actors, directors, screenwriters, and costume and set designers—and then exploiting their joint products in a wide variety of changing markets—would seem hugely difficult and costly. But again, the combination of (1) reasonably clear copyright rules (including the "work-for-hire" doctrine); (2) stable industry-wide customs—reinforced in some instances by union standards—concerning the contractual relationships among the various players; and (3) the studios' capacity to serve as intermediaries between the worlds of creators and consumers facilitated the production and distribution of films.

The systems were by no means perfect, however. Unnecessary transaction costs were incurred by several of their features. An especially notorious example was the system by which record companies obtained radio airtime for their products. It is possible that, as some economists have argued, old-style payola, though sordid, was economically efficient—a sensible way of allocating scarce advertising opportunities. However, even those economists acknowledge that the modern system of "independent promotion"—sustained, as we've seen, by clumsily phrased legal prohibitions and the record companies' understandable desire to avoid liability if their agents ran afoul of those laws—was (and is) wasteful, unnecessarily siphoning millions of dollars annually out of the music industry. The existence of three performing rights organizations was similarly inefficient. Virtually all radio stations obtained blanket licenses from all three. Total administrative costs would have been lower if the United States, like most other countries, had had just one such institution.[64]

More serious than such instances of avoidable waste was the inequality in the way the fruits of the two industries were distributed. This inequality was especially glaring in the music business. The record companies, as we have seen, got generous shares of the pie. By contrast, most members of the groups of true creators—the composers and the performers—did not. To be sure, a few stars (exemplified in our hypothetical story by Paul Simon) enjoyed very large incomes. But the typical performer (exemplified by Chris Smither) and the typical composer (exemplified by me, unless my song is picked up by Simon) struggled to make ends meet.

It had not always been so. As Robert Frank and Philip Cook point out, in the early twentieth century, the gap between the incomes of an average professional musician and a "top" professional musician had not been terribly great. Since then, however, the industry had increasingly resembled a contest in which "the winner takes all." A recent study by F. M. Scherer of sales of popular-music CDs in 1997 provides empirical support for Frank and Cook's generalization. Using sales figures supplied by *Billboard* magazine, Scherer found that the data conform closely to what statisticians refer to as a "skew log normal distribution." Roughly speaking, that means that the large majority of CDs sold relatively few copies, while, at the other extreme, a very few CDs sold huge numbers of copies. As we've seen, the incomes of recording artists track sales figures closely. It is thus not surprising that a few soloists and groups earned a great deal of money, while most earned little.[65]

It was not merely popular music that fits this pattern. A similar distribution of sales (and incomes) could be observed in the field of classical music. In 1981, Sherwin Rossen reported the following:

> The market for classical music has never been larger than it is now, yet the number of full-time soloists on any given instrument is on the order of only a few hundred (and much smaller for instruments other than voice, violin, and piano). Performers of the first rank comprise a limited handful out of these small totals and have very large incomes. There are also known to be substantial differences in income between them and those in the second rank, even though most consumers would have difficulty detecting more than minor differences in a "blind" hearing.[66]

What causes this pattern? Two forces appear to be at work. First, technology has magnified the competitive advantage of the best musicians. Suppose that soprano X is slightly better than soprano Y. If (as was true in 1900), the only way in which they can reach audiences is to perform in person, their earning power will not be dramatically different. X can sing in only a limited number of cities per year. Many people in other cities—or in the same cities at different times—will thus still be eager to hear Y sing. But if (as is true today), they can reach audiences by making high-quality recordings of their performances and then reproducing them at modest cost, X's competitive advantage will be much greater. If a consumer can buy a recording of *La Traviata* in which X sings the lead, why would he or she buy a recording of the same opera in which Y sings the lead? One would expect, therefore, sales of the former vastly to exceed sales of the latter, and the incomes of the two performers to diverge accordingly.

The structure of the modern music industry reinforces this bias. In 1990, six record companies—CBS, Warner, RCA, Capitol-EMI, Polygram, and MCA—either produced or distributed the large majority of the recorded music sold in the United States. Those companies had discovered (or decided) that it is more profitable to select a few individual performers and musical groups, promote them heavily, and market their recordings aggressively than it is to spread resources more thinly over a larger set of musicians. Consequently, only a few musicians received the exposure and support necessary to become stars and to earn correspondingly generous royalties.[67]

The radical distributive inequality that characterizes the music industry is not quite so pronounced in the movie industry. Both of the forces just described are equally relevant in the film context. Unlike stage actors, film actors can "perform" for unlimited numbers of people simultaneously. Thus, a slight difference in the abilities of two otherwise similar actors gives the better of the two a huge advantage. (Why would any customer pay to see James Coburn play the Sundance Kid, when he can see Robert Redford in the role?) And the structure of the industry reinforces the tendency for money and talent to be concentrated on a small number of high-cost productions; the seven studios that dominate the business have found that they make larger profits by cultivating a few celebrity actors and placing them in a few high-cost, heavily promoted "blockbusters" than they can by spreading their resources more evenly. (Twenty-five of the 380 films released in the United States during 1989 accounted for almost half of the box-office revenues.)[68]

However, these pressures are partially offset by two related circumstances. First, it takes many more people to make a film than it takes to produce a CD. Thus, a much larger set of "creators" must be enlisted (and paid) to generate the relatively few major movies. Second, powerful unions (the Screen Actors Guild, the Writers Guild, the Directors Guild, and the Producers Guild) protect the salaries (and other benefits) of the second-tier participants.[69]

The net result: in the film industry, like the music industry, a few people make an enormous amount of money. Stars such as Warren Beatty, Mel Gibson, Dustin Hoffman, Eddie Murphy, Robert Redford, Sylvester Stallone, Arnold Schwarzenegger, and Meryl Streep can demand (as of 1990) up to $20 million to play the lead in a film. A small number of directors (for example, James Cameron) and screenwriters (such as Joe Eszterhas) can extract compensation packages approaching those numbers. Also as in the music industry, large numbers of aspiring actors, directors, and writers hover on the margins, occasionally participating in projects and earning meager incomes. Unlike in the music industry, however, there exists a sizeable intermediate group—supporting actors, low-profile directors, film editors, and so on—earning quite generous salaries, despite the fact that hundreds, even thousands, of equally talented people would be willing to do their jobs for far less.[70]

Many observers regard the inequality in the incomes of the members of each set of creators—severe in the context of music, somewhat less so in the context of films—as unfortunate. Why? In part, because it seems unjust. The stars may well be talented and may well work hard—but not enough to justify the extraordinary incomes they enjoy. By contrast, the typical professional in the music business, who often works even harder than the stars, deserves more than he or she receives under the current regime.

The sense that the degree of inequality in both industries is excessive also reflects in part the suspicion that society as a whole would be better off if the distribution of incomes among creators were less skewed. The average creator would likely be more skilled, creative, and productive—and thus would contribute more to the welfare of consumers—if he or she did not have to wait tables to keep body and soul together. And some economists believe that the enormous incomes (and other benefits) currently enjoyed by the few highly visible stars have a pernicious impact on society at large—by attracting, like moths to a flame, an inefficiently large number of aspirants into the music and film industries.

The last point merits elaboration. Why, exactly, would an excessively large number of contestants be attracted by the spectacle of a few very well-paid stars? Professors Frank and Cook offer two reasons. First, people (especially young people) consistently overestimate their chances of winning gambles, and their tendency to do so is magnified when the prizes are highly visible and memorable. As a result, a teenage guitarist is almost certain to exaggerate his chances of becoming the next Paul Simon, and a teenage actor will overstate his chances of achieving the status of Robert Redford. Second, even if potential creators accurately assessed their chances of great success, too many (from the standpoint of society at large) would enter the business, because each one, when selecting his or her career, will pay attention only to the probability that he or she will succeed, and will ignore the extent to which his or her entry into the profession will diminish the chances of all other contestants. The net result, argue Frank and Cook, is that the music and film industries—like all other "winner-take-all" industries—are currently overpopulated.[71]

Not everyone agrees. For example, Professor Scherer (focusing on the music industry) points to one way in which the current distribution pattern might be socially beneficial. His argument hinges on the speculation that some gifted musicians may be "skewness-lovers." Like gamblers at horsetracks (or in convenience stores) who select bets that have a low probability of producing very high returns, they may know that the chances of making a hit record and becoming truly wealthy are slim, but are willing to take the gamble anyway. Why would people *rationally* behave this way? In other words, why would they make such wagers with full knowledge of their long odds? The technical answer is that their utility functions are "ogee" shaped —meaning that, at the upper reaches of their potential wealth, each additional dollar (contrary to conventional wisdom) would give them more pleasure than the previous dollar. A more prosaic answer is that such persons recognize that winning the long-shot bet would enable them to make a quantum jump in "material and social status"—to enter an entirely new class, whose perquisites would fulfill their "optimistic, or perhaps wildly optimistic, dreams." If persons with great musical talent think and feel this way, we should be reluctant to diminish the size of the monetary prizes to which they can aspire, for fear that they would decide to become investment bankers instead.[72]

Scherer's argument is intriguing as a possible explanation of the behavior of high-technology entrepreneurs or the distressing tendency of poor Americans to dissipate their meager incomes on lotteries, but is less plausible as a map of the motivations of musicians. To be sure, as he points out, some great composers, like Beethoven, have been "notoriously avaricious." Perhaps some of these have indeed been "skewness lovers." But most of our greatest musicians—from Mozart to Coltrane to Clapton—seem to have been motivated more by love of the art, devotion to the music culture, or hunger for recognition than by dreams of great wealth. In sum, a more egalitarian distribution of musicians' incomes, which would provide a much larger group the financial security necessary to free them to explore and apply their talents, would seem preferable, from the standpoint of aggregate social welfare, to an arrangement in which the majority scrape by while a few live in luxury.

A final disadvantage of the structure of the two industries, as of 1990, grew out of the same configuration of forces. The principal companies in both fields apparently had come to the conclusions that they could only make money on high-cost, high-volume products, and that the only movies and songs likely to generate very large sales were those that appeal to middle-of-the-road popular tastes. Pursuit of this strategy was self-sustaining: by filling the theatres and the airwaves with repetitive varieties of action films, romantic comedies, and popular music, the companies helped to *keep* most consumers' tastes in the middle of the road. The net result was that the menu of entertainment products available to the public was distressingly homogenous.

This judgment, largely aesthetic in character, is difficult to document statistically. But the following figures are suggestive. In 1980, the American record industry produced approximately four thousand albums; by 1990, that number had shrunk to approximately two thousand. In 1980, the major American film studios released 161 films; in 1990 (as indicated previously), they released almost the same number, 169—despite the facts that, in the interim, per-capita theatre admissions, average ticket prices, the total number of movie screens, and total theatre admissions had all risen substantially; domestic box-office revenues had roughly doubled; and major new sources of licensing revenue had become available. (Where, you might ask, did all the new-found money go? Instead of making more movies, the studios spent more on each film. In 1980, the average production cost of a major release was $9.4 million, and the average marketing cost was $4.3 million. By 1990, as indicated previously, those numbers had risen to $26.8 million and $11.97 million respectively.)[73]

In sum, measured by their capacity efficiently to generate large numbers of products highly valued by consumers, the complex sets of rules, customs, and institutions that gave shape to the music and film industries in 1990 were remarkably effective. However, the persistence of unnecessary transaction costs, radical inequality in the pattern of incomes they produced, and the limited range of material they generated and disseminated were causes for concern. Would these imperfections have triggered significant reforms in the two industries? Almost certainly not. Change, rather, was spurred by technological innovations that undermined the business models upon which both industries depended. What those innovations were—and how the principal players in the two industries sought to meet them—are considered in the next chapter.

3 What Went Awry

Beginning in approximately 1990, a series of technological innovations destabilized the business models described in Chapter 2. Each of these innovations made it more convenient or less expensive to obtain, store, or enjoy audio or video recordings. But each one also undermined the existing systems by which copyright owners made money. Not surprisingly, the copyright owners resisted the deployment of these technologies. Sometimes their resistance took the form of litigation, relying on existing copyright law. Sometimes they sought to change the law. And sometimes they relied upon technological self-help measures. Each time, through one or another of these strategies, they were able to block or tame the threatening innovation. The war is not yet over. The outcomes of the most recent battles are still in some doubt. But so far, the copyright owners have been consistently winning.

The net result has been unfortunate. Widespread adoption of the technological innovations would have enabled us to realize many of the economic and cultural opportunities sketched in Chapter 1. The cost of protecting the traditional business models has been forfeiture of those potential gains.

The copyright owners are not to be blamed for initiating and, at least until now, winning this fight. Most of them, as we saw in the last chapter, are private corporations, whose managers have a legal responsibility to protect the financial interests of their shareholders. If they are to be faulted, it is only for short-sightedness—for failing to imagine combinations of legal reforms and new business models that would enable them to flourish in a more technologically open environment. In the last three chapters of this book, we will explore some of those alternative visions. The task of this chapter is to describe how the war has proceeded to date.

Digital Audiotape Recorders

The convergence of two lines of technological innovation provoked the first of the battles. As Chapter 1 showed, the introduction during the early 1980s of compact discs transformed the manner in which recorded music was distributed. The quality of the sound generated by CDs was close to the quality that could be obtained by playing LP albums on the best turntables, and CDs were substantially more convenient and durable. In the mid-1980s, consumers shifted to the new format remarkably quickly. By 1990, 28 percent of American households owned CD players, and annual sales of the discs had reached 288 million.[1]

The other technological initiative was the development of several devices that enabled consumers to make digital copies of CDs. The quickest out of the box were digital audiotape (DAT) recorders, introduced in 1986 by Sony and Philips. The tapes used in these machines were about half the size of analog cassette tapes, could record music at better-than-CD quality, and could play for up to 180 minutes. Soon afterward, Philips developed digital compact cassettes (DCCs), which operated similarly, and Sony developed minidiscs (MDs), which used a compression system to record music (or other audio material) on small discs encased in durable plastic housings. These formats had different advantages and disadvantages, but shared two features: the quality of the sound they were capable of generating was excellent, and they enabled consumers to make, serially, an unlimited number of identical copies of a single CD. In combination, these features terrified the recording industry.[2]

To be sure, consumers had been making copies of CDs for years. During the mid-1980s, it was customary, especially for young people, to use analog cassette recorders to reproduce commercial CDs—both for their own use and to share with others. (My daughters were far from unique in making many "mixes" of their favorite songs for their friends.) The legal status of this practice was uncertain. At least one court suggested that the 1972 statute that first granted copyright protection for sound recordings tacitly recognized an exemption for home taping of those recordings, and other observers thought that the decision of the Supreme Court in the *Sony* case (reviewed in Chapter 2) lent support to the proposition that home taping of audio recordings, like the use of VCRs to "time-shift" broadcasts of video recordings, qualified as a fair use. Other scholars rejected both of these arguments, concluding that each time a consumer used a cassette deck to record a song, he or she violated both the copyright in the musical composition and the copyright in the recording. The record companies, not surprisingly, took the latter position but nevertheless made no effort to halt the practice. Why not? Partly because they feared alienating their customers, many of whom believed they

were entitled to engage in this behavior. And partly because of the technological limitations of the analog recording systems. Analog tapes (even those
produced using Dolby noise-reduction systems) "hiss" audibly. And each
time a tape is made from another tape, the quality of the sound diminishes.
To be sure, analog tapes were good enough to cut significantly into the record companies' profits. In 1984, the RIAA estimated that it lost $1.5 billion
in retail revenues because of home taping, and a 1990 study commissioned
by the recording industry estimated that home taping diminished commercial
sales by over 322 million units per year. But the companies apparently concluded that this amount of "leakage" was tolerable.[3]

The copyright owners drew the line, however, at digital recording. The
new recording devices did not suffer from either of the features that limited
the attractiveness of analog tapes. The copyright owners consequently feared
that they would be used in two pernicious ways. First, commercial "pirates"
would employ them to make large numbers of perfect copies of commercial
recordings, which would then be sold on black markets. Second, ordinary
consumers would use them to make myriad copies of CDs—and of digital
tapes originally made from CDs—which they would then distribute free to
their friends, their neighbors, and members of their "swap clubs"; the high
quality of the resultant recordings would sharply undermine demand for
the originals. The copyright owners therefore set out to block the distribution in the United States of the machines that would unleash this apparent
nightmare.[4]

How? Their first move was to threaten to sue the manufacturers of the
devices for contributory and vicarious copyright infringement—the same legal theory that the studios had used (unsuccessfully) in the *Sony* case. The
manufacturers found the threat credible. Accordingly, they held off introducing the devices into the American market, and, in 1989, attended a meeting
in Athens, Greece, with representatives of the international recording industry in hopes of securing a mutually acceptable solution to the situation. The
fruit of that meeting was an agreement, known as the Athens Compromise,
that contained two main provisions. First, the manufacturers promised to incorporate into their machines a "serial copy management system" (SCMS),
which would prevent the machines from making third-generation copies of
copyrighted material. In other words, the machines so equipped could make
copies of CDs, but not copies of copies of CDs. Second, the record companies would seek new legislation that would enable them to earn royalties
when the machines—or the tapes and discs they processed—were distributed
to consumers.[5]

The deal unraveled, however, primarily because it did not adequately address the interests of the holders of copyrights in musical compositions. In 1990, Senator Dennis DeConcini introduced the Digital Audio Tape Recorder Act, which would have required the inclusion of an SCMS in every digital recorder. However, because the bill lacked any provision for the payment of royalties, representatives of the songwriters and music publishers opposed it, and it died in committee. When Sony, in this legislative vacuum, decided to begin importing into the United States DAT recorders unencumbered by SCMS systems, the holders of copyrights in musical compositions took the initiative. Lyricist Sammy Cahn and three music publishers filed a class-action suit on behalf of all music copyright owners against Sony, once again relying on the theories of contributory and vicarious infringement. Another flurry of negotiations enabled the parties to settle the suit. Both sides agreed to support legislation that would include a provision for royalties.[6]

The final outcome of all this maneuvering was the Audio Home Recording Act. Introduced into both the House and the Senate less than a month after the settlement of the *Cahn* lawsuit, it essentially codified the deal struck by the various combatants. In its final form, the statute contained three main provisions. First, like the aborted Digital Audio Tape Recorder Act, it required the installation of an SCMS in any "digital audio recording device or digital audio interface device" imported, manufactured, or distributed in the United States. Second, it required payment of two percent of the "transfer price" (as a practical matter, this means the wholesale price) of any digital audio recording device and three percent of the transfer price of digital media (DAT tapes, minidiscs, and so on). The money collected in this fashion was to be deposited into two U.S. Treasury funds. Two thirds of the money would go to the Sound Recordings Fund (for payment to record companies as well as featured and nonfeatured artists); the other third would go to the Musical Works Fund (for payment to songwriters and publishers), based on the frequency with which their creations were distributed to the public via recordings or "disseminated to the public in transmission". Finally, the statute barred any copyright infringement suit brought for the manufacture, distribution, or importation of digital or analog recording devices or media, or the "noncommercial use by a consumer of such a device or medium for making digital . . . or analog musical recordings."[7]

As compromises go, the Audio Home Recording Act (now known as the AHRA) was not bad. It at least aspired to accommodate both the interests of consumers in gaining access to the new technologies and the interests of copyright owners in getting paid. And the tax-and-royalty scheme it pioneered has much to recommend it. (In Chapter 6, we will consider a much expanded version of the same basic idea.)

Unfortunately, the statute had three flaws, which have become increasingly glaring over time. First, it came too late. It was adopted in 1992, six years after the technology in question was first developed. In the interim, actual or threatened litigation kept the new digital recorders out of the hands of American consumers. That delay contributed to the eventual commercial failure of DAT technology. To be sure, other factors were also at work. The machines were (and are) expensive, and many consumers, confronted with several competing digital-recording formats, decided to wait until one defeated its rivals before investing in new machines. But the six-year limbo period at least helps to explain why very few American consumers currently own digital audio recording devices.[8]

Second, the statute was very technology-specific. It defined a "digital audio recording device" as "any machine or device of a type commonly distributed to individuals for use by individuals, whether or not included with or as part of some other machine or device, the digital recording function of which is designed or marketed for the primary purpose of, and that is capable of, making a digital audio copied recording for private use"—with some exceptions not relevant here. A "digital audio copied recording," in turn, was defined as "a reproduction in a digital recording format of a digital musical recording, whether that reproduction is made directly from another digital musical recording or indirectly from a transmission." Finally, "a digital musical recording" was defined as "a material object—(i) in which are fixed, in a digital recording format, only sounds, and material, statements, or instructions incidental to those fixed sounds, if any, and (ii) from which the sounds and material can be perceived, reproduced, or otherwise communicated, either directly or with the aid of a machine or device." The restrictions built into these definitions rapidly consigned the statute to a marginal role in the development of the music and consumer-electronics industries. In 1999, the Court of Appeals for the Ninth Circuit ruled that it did not apply to the Rio, one of the first popular portable players of MP3 recordings, because the recordings housed on that device were typically downloaded from a computer hard drive (which, since its primary uses are unrelated to musical recordings, did not qualify under the AHRA as a "digital musical recording") and therefore did not fit within the narrow definition of "digital audio copied recording." As computers rapidly became increasingly important in the creation and distribution of digital recordings, the AHRA equally rapidly declined in significance.[9]

Today, only three commercially significant types of equipment fall within the purview of the statute: DAT recorders (of which very few are sold), minidisc recorders (still being produced in modest numbers by Sony); and the CD

burners designed as components of stereo systems (not the much more popular burners housed in personal computers). As indicated above, the tax created by the statute applies not only to the machines themselves, but also to
the storage media they use: DAT tapes, minidiscs, and blank "audio" CDs
(not the general-purpose blank CDs that the overwhelming majority of consumers use to reproduce commercial CDs). This modest tax base helps to explain the small amounts of money collected and redistributed under the
statute. The total amount of royalties peaked at $5.5 million in 2000, and
since then has been hovering around $3.5 million per year—roughly .03 per-
cent of the total amount of revenue that American consumers pay each year
for musical recordings.[10]

The third of the limitations of the AHRA is related. When it was adopted,
many supporters thought that it had established, finally, that home "taping"
of music was lawful. For two reasons, that proved to be wrong. First, the
narrowness of the definition, just discussed, of a "digital audio recording device" means that the most common ways in which consumers copy music at
home (such as CD burning using personal computers) are not reached by the
statute. Second, the relevant provision of the statute, closely read, merely de-
clares that a consumer may not be sued for copyright infringement for using
a recording device for noncommercial purposes, not that that activity is lawful. What difference does that subtlety make? When we get to the *Napster*
case and its aftermath, you'll see.[11]

In sum, the first of the battles in this war resulted in a truce, the terms of
which at first seemed promising, but which proved to have minimal impact
on the widening conflict.

Encryption Circumvention

In the early 1990s, as the power of the new technologies to facilitate unauthorized copying became increasingly apparent, entertainment companies
began exploring systems for encrypting their products. It was far from obvious that effective encryption systems were feasible. Encrypting material
sent over the Internet is relatively easy when both the sender and the receiver
of the material are committed to keeping it confidential. It is much more difficult to package a digital recording in a way that prevents a recipient who
wants to copy or redistribute it from doing so. Why? Because, in order to
produce music or to display a motion picture, a recording must at some
point generate an unencrypted stream of data that can be interpreted by a
sound system or screen. It is hard to prevent the possessor of the recording
from capturing that stream in a new, unencrypted recording. To be sure,

only a small percentage of the millions of Internet users have the skill and inclination to evade copy-protection technology. But, the entertainment companies worried, it would only take a few "hackers" to wreck their business models—because those few would then use the Internet to make available to the rest of the world unencrypted copies of their products. Thus, establishing and defending robust encryption methods came to seem to the companies ever more important.[12]

The first major initiative inspired by this concern was the effort to prevent unauthorized reproduction of digital versatile discs (DVDs). In the early 1990s, two teams of engineers—one from Sony and Philips, the other from Toshiba—independently developed systems for storing motion pictures on high-capacity videodiscs the size of CDs. However, two problems prevented the use of these systems to distribute films commercially. First, the two technologies were incompatible. Second, the movie studios feared that, once released to the public, the discs would be copied promiscuously, undermining both theatre attendance and future disc sales.

The first problem was solved quickly; by the end of 1995, the competing teams had settled on a common DVD standard. The second was more formidable. Initially, the Motion Picture Association of America (MPAA), through negotiations with the Home Recording Rights Coalition, sought to address the problem by securing federal legislation requiring the installation in all DVD players of a copy generation management system (CGMS)—a serial-copying-prevention technology similar to the SCMS system mandated under the AHRA. A bill embodying that plan was drafted but never introduced in Congress, largely because of strong resistance from the computer and personal-electronics industries. Thwarted, the studios tried a different tack. Instead of relying on Congress for aid, they facilitated the formation of a trade association, the DVD Forum, which brought together more than 230 companies that either owned copyrights in motion pictures, manufactured consumer electronic devices, or created DVD-related software. In 1996, the DVD Forum developed the Content Scramble System (CSS), which used a set of "keys" and an accompanying algorithm to rearrange the data in a digital video recording. A file that had been "scrambled" using this system could only be played, intelligibly, by a machine that included the same keys and algorithm. The Forum then licensed this technology both to firms wishing to encrypt motion pictures and to electronics manufacturers wishing to sell DVD players. In return for such a license, a manufacturer was obliged to pay a fee, agree to keep the keys and algorithm secret, and (most important) design its player so that it was incapable of reproducing the decrypted content. In 1997, licensed DVD players incorporating this technology became available to consumers, and the studios, assured that their markets were now safe, began producing and distributing large quantities of "scrambled" discs.[13]

The analogous effort within the music industry to promulgate common encryption standards was known as the Secure Digital Music Initiative (SDMI). In 1998, over 120 "companies and organizations representing information technology, consumer electronics, security technology, the worldwide recording industry, and Internet service providers" formed a consortium for the purpose of developing a "voluntary, open framework for playing, storing and distributing digital music to enable a new market to emerge." The members hoped to develop such a framework in two phases. In the first, they would develop a set of technical specifications and agree upon the common platform for the operation of all portable MP3 players. The second phase would then develop a screening technology suitable for incorporation in the next generation of electronic equipment. The precondition for the deployment of that technology was the creation of inaudible, durable digital "watermarks," which recording artists and record companies could, if they chose, insert into legitimate copies of their products. The watermarks would contain "usage rules," indicating, for example, how the recordings in which they were embedded could be played and how many times (if any) they could be legitimately copied. Devices incorporating the proposed screening technology would recognize those watermarks and obey the instructions contained therein. The ultimate goal, in Cary Sherman's words, was to "secure music in *all* forms, across *all* delivery channels." The first phase of the project was completed in short order; by July of 1999, the organization had released Portable Device Specification 1.0. The second phase, as we will see, encountered obstacles.[14]

A final example of an encryption initiative involved streaming. During the 1990s, many entertainment companies were willing, even eager, to allow consumers to listen to their audio recordings or watch their video recordings over the Internet, so long as they could not make permanent copies of those recordings. RealNetworks, Inc., developed an interlocking set of proprietary programs that enabled them to stream material to consumers in this restrictive fashion. A content provider would use the RealProducer program to encode a recording in either RealAudio or RealVideo format. When doing so, the provider could either enable or disable a "copy" switch. The provider would then make the encoded material available to the public at large on a specially configured Web server, known as a RealServer. To gain access to the material, a consumer would use RealPlayer, a (free) piece of software that resided on the consumer's own computer, which was designed to recognize and respect the provider's choice concerning the permissibility of copying. The system worked so well that, by the end of the decade, "a large majority of all Internet Web pages that deliver[ed] streaming music or video use[d] the RealNetworks' format."[15]

From the beginning, the developers of encryption systems of these sorts worried that they would be circumvented. Of course, they tried to design the technological shields to be as resistant as possible to evasion. But they feared, even expected, that sooner or later determined hackers would break them. If that occurred, they hoped that the law would come to their aid, penalizing the hackers and preventing the distribution of circumvention technologies.

The legal system, however, was not well configured to provide them this support. Scattered through federal statutory law were a few provisions that forbade the circumvention of specific sorts of encryption systems. For example, it was illegal to manufacture or distribute devices designed to "descramble" the signals provided by cable television systems or digital satellite systems. Similarly, the recently enacted Audio Home Recording Act (discussed in the previous section) prohibited the production and distribution of devices that circumvented an SCMS. But there was no provision forbidding encryption circumvention in general.[16]

Nor had the federal courts in the past been especially receptive to lawsuits against hackers. In *Vault Corporation v. Quaid Software*, for example, the Fifth Circuit Court of Appeals had ruled that the creation and sale of a software program designed to circumvent the copy controls on a diskette did not make its creator liable for contributory copyright infringement, because the program had a substantial noninfringing use—namely, enabling the making of archival copies. In *Sega Enterprises v. Accolade*, the Ninth Circuit had refused to find a company liable after it circumvented the lock-out mechanism preventing unlicensed game developers from building games compatible with Sega's Genesis console, ruling that the temporary copying of the lock-out program for the purpose of achieving interoperability was excusable as a "fair use." Finally, in *Lasercomb v. Reynolds*, the Fourth Circuit sided with a defendant who had circumvented a technological protection system placed on purchased software and then had marketed an infringing version of the software. In the court's view, the plaintiff's deployment of the protection system constituted copyright misuse, because it would have lasted for ninety-nine years and thus impeded competition for a period longer than that contemplated by the copyright statute.[17]

Worried, the entertainment industries set out to change the law so as to provide their new encryption methods greater legal protection. The road to that reform was long and circuitous. But in the end, they were successful.

The first step was to make their case to the Information Infrastructure Task Force (IITF), which had been appointed by President Clinton "to articulate and implement the Administration's vision for the National Information Infrastructure." The crucial subcommittee within the IITF was the Working Group on Intellectual Property Rights, chaired by Bruce Lehman, a former copyright industry lobbyist who had recently been appointed the Commissioner of Patents and Trademarks. The Working Group proved receptive to the entertainment industry's pleas. In its preliminary report (known as the Green Paper), it found that "legal protection alone may not be adequate to provide incentives to authors to create and to disseminate works to the public, unless the law also provides some protection for the technological processes and systems used to prevent unauthorized uses of copyrighted works. . . . The Working Group [also found] that prohibition of devices, products, components and services that defeat technological methods of preventing unauthorized use is in the public interest." In a second round of public hearings, some critics of this recommendation argued that it threatened to curtail fair uses of copyrighted materials and would constrict the public domain. The Working Group was unpersuaded. The IITF's final report, known as the "White Paper," hewed to the original recommendation, arguing that a general ban on circumvention-enabling products and services would be in the "public interest" because "[c]onsumers of copyrighted works pay for the acts of infringers." In addition, "[t]he public will also have access to more copyrighted works via the NII if they are not vulnerable to the defeat of protection systems."[18]

Somewhat surprisingly, however, the initial effort of the Clinton Administration to persuade Congress to embody the IITF's proposals in a federal statute—reinforced by intense lobbying on the part of the entertainment companies—came to naught. In combination, the timing of the effort (in the shadow of a presidential election); opposition from a miscellaneous collection of librarians, law professors, and consumer advocates; and (perhaps most important) the absence of any pressing circumvention controversy were enough to kill the bill.[19]

Undiscouraged, Lehman selected an alternative strategy. Instead of continuing to make his case to an unreceptive Congress, he turned to the international arena. In 1996, in his capacity as the United States delegate to the World Intellectual Property Organization (WIPO), he pressed for adoption of a new copyright treaty that would embody the critical provisions of the White Paper. If successful, he could then return to Congress, seeking domestic legislation implementing the treaty. In the treaty that finally emerged from this process, Lehman did not get all that he wanted. Continued noisemaking by American opponents of the plan, plus resistance from some of the other delegates to the WIPO conference, forced him to abandon some of his more ambitious proposals. But the final treaty did contain at least a moderate anti-circumvention provision:

> Contracting Parties shall provide adequate legal protection and effective legal remedies against the circumvention of effective technological measures that are used by authors in connection with the exercise of their rights under this Treaty or the Berne Convention and that restrict acts, in respect of their works, which are not authorized by the authors concerned or permitted by law.[20]

Back in the United States, the opponents of anti-circumvention legislation argued that the existing doctrines of contributory and vicarious copyright infringement were sufficient to provide the "effective legal remedies" mandated by the new treaty. But the proponents of legislative reform now had the upper hand. Relying on a combination of the new treaty provision, the rapidly growing use of encryption systems, and the increasing amounts of money at stake, they were able this time to persuade Congress to act.[21]

This is not to suggest that the legislation slid through easily. Several competing bills were introduced, and many groups sought to influence their shape. In the end, the two most influential clusters of lobbyists were the entertainment companies and the electronics industry. Professor Pam Samuelson explains the character and outcome of their struggle:

> It would oversimplify the facts—although not by much—to say that the battle in Congress over [anti-circumvention legislation] was a battle between Hollywood and Silicon Valley. Hollywood and its allies sought the strongest possible ban both on the act of circumventing a technical protection system used by copyright owners to protect their works and on technologies having circumvention-enabling uses. Silicon Valley firms and their allies opposed this broad legislation because of deleterious effects it would have on the ability to engage in lawful reverse engineering, computer security testing, and encryption research. They supported legislation to outlaw acts of circumvention engaged in for the purpose of infringing copyrights and would have supported narrowly drawn device legislation had the Congressional subcommittees principally responsible for formulating WIPO treaty implementation legislation been receptive to a narrower bill. Silicon Valley and its allies warned of dire consequences if the overbroad anti-circumvention provisions Hollywood supported were adopted. Yet, by colorful use of high rhetoric and forceful lobbying, Hollywood and its allies were successful in persuading Congress to adopt the broad anti-circumvention legislation they favored, even if it is now subject to some specific exceptions that respond to some concerns raised by Silicon Valley firms and their allies in the legislative process.[22]

In the course of the struggle, many other groups came forward, seeking protective legislation of their own—Internet Service Providers, companies that repair or maintain computer software, the manufacturers of recreational boats, and so on. Congress sought to satisfy almost all of them in a single piece of legislation, to which it affixed the ponderous label, Digital Millennium Copyright Act (DMCA). An enormous, gangling, and poorly edited piece of legislation, it more than doubled the length of the federal copyright statute. We will have occasion to consider various of its collateral provisions later in this chapter. But the crucial portion of the statute was Title I, formally known as the "WIPO Copyright and Performance and Phonograms Treaties Implementation Act of 1998," which pertains to encryption and the circumvention thereof.

That section of the statute contains three main provisions. Section 1201(a)(1)(A) provides that "[n]o person shall circumvent a technological measure that effectively controls access" to a copyrighted work. A supplementary provision, section 1201(a)(2), provides that "[n]o person shall manufacture, import, offer to the public, provide, or otherwise traffic in any technology, product, service, device, component, or part thereof, that . . . is primarily designed or produced for the purpose of" such circumvention. Finally, section 1201(b) contains a similar ban on the production or distribution of technology primarily designed to circumvent technologies that effectively protect the exclusive rights of a copyright owner—the exclusive rights to reproduce the work, adapt it, perform it publicly, and so on. Parties injured by violations of these rules can bring civil lawsuits to halt the practices and collect damages. In addition, willful violation of the rules (for commercial advantage or personal gain) subjects the offender to substantial criminal penalties.[23]

Myriad ambiguities lurk in these provisions. For example, what does it mean "effectively" to control access to a copyrighted work? What activities, other than manufacturing and distributing, are encompassed by the ban on "trafficking" in circumvention technologies? Some of these ambiguities are addressed—though not with great clarity—by other statutory provisions.[24]

The resultant complexity is enhanced by a long list of exceptions and reservations to the statute's prohibitions, many of them equally vague. For example, technologies that are not "primarily designed" for circumvention, have more than a "limited" commercially significant purpose other than circumvention, and are not "marketed" for circumvention are exempt. Nonprofit libraries, archives, and educational institutions are sometimes permitted to engage in circumvention in order to decide whether to acquire a copyrighted work. Circumvention activities for the purpose of (1) reverse engineering to achieve interoperability among computer programs, (2) security testing, (3) encryption research, and (4) controlling minors' access to pornography are all privileged. Every three years, the Librarian of Congress is required to promulgate regulations exempting from the anti-circumvention provision persons who would otherwise be "adversely affected" in "their ability to make noninfringing uses." Last but not least, the statute provides that it should not be interpreted to "affect . . . defenses to copyright infringement, including fair use," or to "enlarge or diminish any rights of free speech or the press for activities using consumer electronics, telecommunications, or computing products."[25]

Most of the provisions of the statute became effective in 1998. In the view of the entertainment companies, this was just in time, because many of their new encryption systems were succumbing to the assaults of hackers. In a series of cases initiated during the next four years, the entertainment companies invoked the new law (either directly or with the aid of sympathetic federal prosecutors) to defend their technological protections. The outcomes of these cases varied, but in the end, all of the principal ambiguities in the statute were resolved by the federal courts in ways favorable to the entertainment industry.

The first two major cases set the trend. In 1999, a company called Streambox began to distribute a piece of software that imitated RealNetworks' RealPlayer. The key to the program was a replica of the "secret handshake" that each RealPlayer uses to authenticate itself to a RealServer. The replica enabled Streambox's program to induce a RealServer to stream information to it. Unlike a RealPlayer, the new program would then ignore instructions by the content provider not to permit reproduction of the streamed material. The program was appropriately called the "VCR," because it enabled users without permission to make permanent copies of streamed audio and video files. At RealNetworks' behest, a federal court in the state of Washington ordered Streambox to cease manufacturing or distributing the VCR, ruling that it violated both the access-control and the copy-control provisions of the DMCA. Crucial to this ruling was the Court's judgment that the fair-use doctrine—and, specifically, the safe harbor recognized by the *Sony* court for technologies with "substantial noninfringing uses"—could not be invoked to justify a violation of the new statute.[26]

The second case had less practical effect but was even more important in clarifying the reach of the law. In September of 1999, Jon Johansen, a fifteen-year-old Norwegian, assisted by two other people he met through the Internet, reverse-engineered a licensed DVD player and used the information he obtained to write a short program designed to "descramble" a signal that had been scrambled by the CSS security system. The program, which he called "DeCSS," was relatively simple. The original version consisted of sixty lines of computer code; it has since been reduced to seven. Although Johansen's original purpose apparently was the relatively benign goal of developing a DVD player that could operate on the Linux operating system, his creation enabled many other, less innocent uses of the video recordings distributed on DVDs. Once descrambled, they could be stored, compressed, reproduced, and redistributed. Copies of DeCSS spread quickly over the Internet; within a month, many Websites offered user-friendly, downloadable versions of the program in both source code and object code. The major film studios, seeking to stop or at least slow the spread of the infection, invoked the DMCA to demand that the operators of those Websites remove the program from their servers. Some of the operators—including Eric Corley, the editor of a print magazine brazenly named *2600: The Hacker Quarterly* and an accompanying Website—refused to comply. In response, the studios brought suit, accusing Corley and others of "trafficking" in circumvention technology.

The case slowly wound its way through the federal court system, gaining notoriety as it rose. At the trial-court level, Judge Lewis Kaplan found that the defendants had indeed violated the DMCA's ban on "trafficking" in technology designed to circumvent restrictions on access to copyrighted works. Kaplan agreed with the judge who decided the *Streambox* case that the fair-use doctrine offered no aid to violators of that provision. He also ruled that the "reverse-engineering" exception, even if it could be applied to justify Johansen's behavior, did not excuse Corley's subsequent public distribution of the code-breaking program. Nor, in his judgment, were any of the other statutory exemptions applicable. Kaplan then rejected the defendants' argument that the statute, so construed, would violate the federal Constitution. In his final ruling, Kaplan ordered the defendants to remove the program from their servers and (more controversially) to disable all hyperlinks to other Websites where copies of the program could be found.[27]

Widespread unease concerning the scope of the latter portion of Kaplan's ruling helped fuel public interest in the appeal of the case. A variety of public-interest groups and academics urged the Second Circuit Court of Appeals either to interpret the statute narrowly or to declare it unconstitutional. An equally vocal group, including the Justice Department, urged affirmance of Kaplan's ruling. In the end, the Court of Appeals sided with the latter. None of the limitations and exceptions built into the statute, the court ruled, prevented it from applying to Corley's behavior. Nor did the statute, even when broadly construed, violate the First Amendment. The court conceded that the anti-trafficking provisions (in general, and as applied in this case) did restrict speech. But that restriction, it ruled, is "content neutral," advances a "substantial governmental purpose" unrelated to the suppression of free expression (namely, assisting copyright owners in preventing unwanted access to their "property"), and burdens freedom of speech no more than necessary to achieve that end—and is therefore constitutional. A separate constitutional objection—that the statute exceeds Congress's authority to create intellectual-property rights that last "for limited times"—the court rejected on procedural grounds.[28]

The rulings in the *Corley* case did little to impede distribution of the offending program. While the case was ongoing, hackers and Corley sympathizers continued to distribute DeCSS in a wide variety of formats: on T-shirts; in the form of a Haiku, set to music, and so on. (Dr. David S. Touretzky of Carnegie-Mellon University created a Website cataloguing the many variants—and received for his pains a cease-and-desist letter from the MPAA, with which he refused to comply.) But the precedent set by the case was powerful. The Court of Appeals had upheld the statute against a serious constitutional challenge, despite simultaneously ruling that it trumps the fair-use doctrine, an exception to copyright entitlements that had long been thought to be necessary to accommodate the public interest and freedom of speech. The DMCA had withstood its first major test.[29]

Most of the other cases brought by the entertainment industry under the new statute met with equal success. Not all, however. One embarrassing and short-lived attempt to bring the law to bear on hackers occurred during the late stages of the ill-fated SDMI project, described earlier. The effort to develop a common format for music encryption was plagued from the beginning by technical difficulties and increasing dissension among the companies participating in the venture. In September of 2000, after several delays, the leaders of the consortium finally announced to the world that they had developed prototypes of four watermarking systems. They were sufficiently confident of the durability of the new technologies that they used them to encode some digital recordings, made them available on the Internet, and dared anyone to break the codes—specifically, to strip the watermarks out of the recordings without degrading the quality of the music. To their dismay, a group of computer scientists led by Professor Ed Felten of Princeton succeeded within three weeks. Adding insult to injury, Felten renounced the $10,000 reward offered by the consortium (acceptance of which would have required him to tell the consortium in confidence how he broke the codes) and instead made preparations to publish the fruits of his research. The Recording Industry Association of America, which had been following these events closely, then sent Felten a letter, suggesting that such publication "could subject you and your research team to actions under the DMCA." Felten responded by filing a declaratory judgment suit (essentially, a pre-emptive lawsuit to clarify his legal rights) against the RIAA, the SDMI, and the United States, seeking a judicial ruling that the application of the DMCA threatened by the RIAA would violate the First Amendment. The RIAA, recognizing the force of Felten's contention, beat a hasty retreat, insisting that they had no intention of invoking the statute against Felten and would have no objection to the publication. The New Jersey federal court then dismissed Felten's lawsuit on the ground that there was no longer any live "case or controversy."[30]

The other failed litigation effort took longer to unfold. Adobe's eBook Reader, the software system most widely used to distribute electronic books, contains a copy-protection system. In 2001, the Russian software company ElcomSoft made a program called the Advanced eBook Processor, created by employee Dmitry Sklyarov, available for purchase over the Internet. The program enabled users to convert files from Adobe's proprietary eBook format to a normal PDF file—in effect, defeating the copy-protection system and making it possible to distribute free copies of eBooks online. In July of 2001, Sklyarov came to the United States to present parts of his dissertation discussing eBook's security flaws at the annual "Defcon" Conference held in Las Vegas. Nudged by Adobe, federal officials arrested him. He was subsequently indicted on four counts of criminal violations of the DMCA. This dramatic, well-publicized case ultimately ended in a whimper. Charges against Sklyarov were dropped in return for his pledge to testify against his former employer. Despite that testimony, ElcomSoft was finally acquitted, apparently because the jury was unconvinced that its executives had the requisite criminal intent.[31]

In short, the entertainment industry occasionally lost skirmishes. But they won all the critical battles. The crucial provisions of the DMCA have been broadly construed by the courts and have been upheld against constitutional challenges. Today, they constitute powerful weapons that can be deployed both against persons who engage in circumvention of encryption technologies and against companies that develop technologies that facilitate such behavior.[32]

Meanwhile, the statute has begun to be applied in troubling ways well outside the zone of the entertainment industry, which it was originally designed to protect. In one recent case, for example, Lexmark argued that the unauthorized manufacturer of replacement toner cartridges compatible with Lexmark's printers had circumvented the printers' "authentication sequence" and thus violated the DMCA. A federal district court in Kentucky agreed, ruling that the defendant was unlikely to escape liability on the basis of the "reverse-engineering-for-interoperability" exception. Legitimate cryptographers are also finding the threat of criminal sanctions chilling. For example, Niels Ferguson, a Dutch cryptography expert whose research has discovered a serious flaw in Intel's encryption scheme for firewall connections (the High-Bandwidth Digital Content Protection System) has refused to publish his results for fear of being sued by Intel under the DMCA. Other cryptography experts have also withdrawn work from publication, citing similar concerns.[33]

Was it really necessary to give the entertainment industry such a large, blunt club? The second half of this book will consider that question, among others. Before then, however, we must finish setting the stage.

Music Lockers

For decades, consumers have listened to music in two main ways: either they have bought sound recordings in semi-durable containers (LP albums, cassette tapes, or CDs) and then replayed those recordings using their own equipment (turntables, cassette decks, or CD players) or they have used radios to listen to recordings broadcast by radio stations. Each method has advantages and disadvantages. The first gives listeners greater control over what they hear but is expensive and often inconvenient. The second gives listeners less control, poorer fidelity, and the annoyance of advertisements, but allows them to listen to music almost anywhere on inexpensive devices and avoids the risks of damage and deterioration to which all of the containers are vulnerable.

In combination, the popularization of the MP3 compression technology and the spread of broadband Internet access made possible a third, hybrid method that combined some of the advantages of each of the traditional models. A consumer could buy a CD, use widely available "ripping" software to convert the music on it to MP3 format, upload copies of those files to a remote server, and then "stream" them at any time to any device connected to the Internet. The quality of the resultant music was good—typically, better than a radio broadcast, though not as good as the sound produced by a decent home stereo. The MP3 files stored remotely in this fashion were not vulnerable to the many hazards (toddlers, fires, careless handling, and so on) that endanger personal music collections. And this system significantly increased the locations from which one could gain access to ad-free music of one's choice.[34]

In 1998 and 1999, a rapidly growing group of companies began to offer consumers the Internet storage facilities—dubbed "music lockers"—essential to this new listening system. Among the more popular were I-drive, RioPort, MyPlay, myMP3storage.com, x:drive, Driveway, Epitonic, and @Backup. Their services varied slightly. Some were designed specifically for storage of MP3 files, while others hosted generic data lockers or partnered with dedicated media sites. A few charged nominal fees, but most were free.[35]

Consumers' use of these services increased quickly, but one factor still limited signups: many people lacked the patience or skill to "rip" and then upload their entire CD collections. Michael Robertson, the creator of the pioneering Website, MP3.com, saw a way to eliminate this impediment. Instead of merely offering consumers storage facilities where they could keep MP3 recordings they had created for themselves, he would stock their music lockers for them. To do so, he purchased over forty thousand CDs, made copies of them in MP3 format, and then loaded the copies onto his Website's servers. Those files were not available to the world at large. Rather, to gain access to them, a consumer had to "prove," in one of two ways, that she already owned a CD containing the songs in question. Either she would place a copy of the pertinent CD in the CD-ROM drive of her home computer, which would then communicate with the MP3.com Website, or she would order a copy of the CD from an affiliated online retailer. After receiving verification in one of these two ways, Robertson would place copies of the relevant songs in the consumers' password-protected "virtual locker," enabling her to stream the songs to any Internet-connected device. Users of the service were required to sign an agreement pledging not to allow others to use their accounts, and, since the technology did not permit them to "save" the streamed songs, they could not email their MP3 files to others.[36]

Several of Robertson's employees were worried about the legality of this system—and with good reason. The legal status even of the traditional music-locker services was doubtful. When customers of those services made MP3 copies of their own CDs, they were violating section 106 of the Copyright Act. Because the personal computers they used to make those copies did not fit within the definition of an "audio home recording device," the safe harbor for home copying created by the Audio Home Recording Act was inapplicable to their behavior. Had they been sued, the customers who engaged in this activity would likely have invoked the fair-use doctrine, but the permanence of the MP3 recordings they made and the scale of their behavior made it far from clear that they could escape liability. If their customers were engaged in copyright infringement, then arguably the services themselves, by facilitating and encouraging their behavior, were engaged in contributory copyright infringement. (A few, sensing this hazard, had negotiated agreements with the record companies, but most had not.) The record companies had not pursued the first generation of music-locker services, despite the questionable legal status of their behavior, apparently because most were not terribly popular and because the record companies had bigger fish to fry. Robertson's innovation, however, raised the stakes sharply. The primary relevant difference between his system and those of his predecessors is that MP3.com, not individual consumers, was making the MP3 files. Thus Robertson, unlike his predecessors, risked a suit for direct copyright infringement, not just contributory infringement.[37]

In January of 2000, despite his advisers' misgivings, Robertson launched his new service, which he called My.MP3.com (or, privately, "Da Bomb"). It was popular almost instantly. Within three weeks, over 4.4 million songs had been added to his customers' accounts. Almost as quickly, the record companies brought suit. Robertson tried to persuade them that they should be pleased, not angered, by his new service; it helped them, as well as all other participants in the music world:

> On behalf of consumers, we are disappointed that the positive benefits and security features of our newly upgraded My.MP3.com service are misunderstood by the RIAA and its member companies. My.MP3.com provides more choices for consumers to do what they want with the music they already own. Our technology also empowers artists to communicate directly with their fan base. We believe My.MP3.com will stimulate CD sales and expand the music industry overall.[38]

The companies were unmoved.

On April 28, Judge Rakoff sided with the companies. The case was straightforward, he argued. MP3.com had engaged in massive unauthorized copying of copyrighted sound recordings. Its only colorable defense was the fair-use doctrine. An examination of the four fair-use factors, however, persuaded Rakoff that even that line of defense was untenable: (1) unlike a home copyist, Robertson was making copies for "commercial" purposes, and, unlike a parodist, he did not "transform" the underlying sound recordings in any significant sense; (2) the songs he copied were "creative" in nature (unlike news programs) and thus deserved strong copyright protection; (3) he reproduced sound recordings in their entirety, not merely parts of them; and (4) although it might be true that the availability of Robertson's service increased CD sales, his conduct nevertheless undermined an important "potential market" for the record companies—namely, their ability "to license their copyrighted sound recordings to others for reproduction."[39]

The fourth of Judge Rakoff's findings was the most important. You may recall, from Chapter 2, that the rulings of the United States Supreme Court interpreting the fair-use doctrine failed to resolve a crucial ambiguity in the statutory provision that codifies that doctrine: When determining whether a defendant's conduct (if it became widespread) would impair a "potential market" for the plaintiff's copyrighted work, should a judge focus solely on the markets that the plaintiff has already begun to exploit and would naturally exploit in the future, or should the judge also consider possible impairments of all conceivable markets for the work, including markets that the defendant himself may have created? In the *Sony* decision, the Supreme Court adopted the first (narrower) approach, but in subsequent cases, the Court has wavered. Judge Rakoff implicitly adopted the second, broader approach—thus favoring the record companies and constricting the zone of privileged unauthorized uses of their products. As we will see shortly, the courts in the *Napster* litigation would take a similar tack.

The bottom line: Robertson lost, and lost big. For a while, it looked like he might snatch a truce from the jaws of defeat. Between May and August of 2000, he negotiated settlements with four of the five major record companies. Those deals were expensive, obliging him to pay each plaintiff a lump sum of approximately $20 million plus roughly half that amount per year in future license fees. But at least they would have enabled him to reopen his music-locker service. He was unable, however, to come to terms with Universal, the fifth of the plaintiffs. Pressing its litigation advantage, Universal contended that Robertson's copyright infringement had been "willful," and thus that Universal was entitled to heavy "statutory damages." Judge Rakoff agreed, ordering MP3.com to pay approximately $188 million in damages—an amount he selected in large part to deter future innovators in "the rapidly expanding world of the Internet" from breaking the law. Rakoff's order enabled Universal to extract from MP3.com a settlement more lucrative that those it had reached with the other plaintiffs: $53 million in cash plus warrants allowing Universal to purchase up to three million shares of MP3.com common stock.[40]

As these legal and financial obligations multiplied, Robertson sought relief from Congress. In September of 2000, four sympathetic congressmen— Rick Boucher of Virginia, Richard Burr of North Carolina, Fred Upton of Michigan, and Ray LaHood of Illinois—proposed the Music Owner's Licensing Rights Act (MOLRA), which would have amended the Copyright Act to legalize services like My.MP3.com. When introducing the bill, Rep. Boucher pointed out that 79 percent of frequent Internet users believed that "copyright laws should not infringe on an individual's access to music that they have legally purchased." The bill was supported by the Digital Future

Coalition, the Electronic Frontier Foundation, and a host of individual Internet users, whom Robertson had organized under the aegis of a "Million Email March." It was opposed, as one might expect, by the RIAA, the National Music Publishers Association (NMPA), the Songwriters Guild of America, ASCAP, BMI, and the Motion Picture Association of America. The bill died in committee.[41]

Facing enormous settlement costs (more than $160 million) and the prospect of future suits by still other parties, MP3.com briefly tried to restart its service on a subscription basis, charging customers $50 per year for the right to store up to five hundred CDs online. But the company could not bear the weight of its mounting debts. In May of 2001, Universal (the most aggressive of the plaintiffs) bought the company for a total of $350 million. For a while, Universal kept the site alive, but in a much reduced form. The locker service that had provoked the litigation was eliminated. Finally, in November of 2003, Universal's parent company sold MP3.com's remaining assets to CNET Networks, which planned to use them to create a new site that would provide consumers "a source for information for digital music."[42]

The defeat of Robertson's innovation was the death knell for music lockers in general. One after another, the companies that had pioneered such services either closed down or shifted their attention from free MP3 storage for individual Internet users to subscription data-backup services for other companies. Today, consumers' use of the few survivors is minimal.[43]

During the heat of this battle, Michael Robertson argued that the music companies were being foolish. In their determination to maximize their short-term profits, they were attacking a service that benefited not only consumers but also the record companies themselves. Not only would destroying My.MP3.com be selfish, it would also fuel consumer interest in less benign music-distribution systems. He warned, presciently:

> The labels made the decision to challenge a technology that will protect their intellectual property interests and grow their business. They will be left with copyright chaos, as we're witnessing today.[44]

Webcasting

You will recall from Chapter 2 that, since the early 1970s, the legal rights of composers and recording artists have differed. In brief, composers have enjoyed the full set of entitlements enjoyed by the creators of most other kinds of copyrighted materials (novels, movies, and so forth): the exclusive rights to make copies of their works, to make "derivative works" incorporating them, to distribute them to the public, and to perform them publicly. The creators of sound recordings have enjoyed somewhat narrower versions of the first three of those entitlements, but have lacked the right to control public performances of their recordings. The main effect of that difference has been that radio stations and other broadcasters have been obliged to pay royalties (typically through blanket license agreements) to the music publishers (the assignees of the composers' copyrights) whenever they broadcast music, but have not been obliged to pay anything to the record companies (the assignees of the performers' copyrights in the accompanying sound recordings).

The record companies have repeatedly sought legislation correcting this imbalance. Until recently, Congress consistently refused—partly because of effective lobbying by the broadcasters (who did not want to pay increased royalties) and partly because Congress was persuaded that (for the reasons explored in Chapter 2) radio broadcasts of music *helped* the record companies by stimulating consumers' tastes for new music and thus promoting retail sales of records—and helped them more than it helped the music publishers, whose incomes from record sales were capped by the compulsory license for "mechanical" copies of their compositions.[45]

In the mid-1990s, the advent of Webcasting destabilized this equilibrium. When they approached Congress this time, the record companies argued, plausibly, that the streaming of music over the Internet posed substantially greater danger to their traditional sources of revenue than did radio broadcasts. The fidelity of streamed music was better than that available through over-the-air radio signals, the variety of streamed music was much greater, some of the streamers leavened their broadcasts with fewer (or no) advertisements, and some offered to stream to individual listeners specific songs on request. All of these characteristics increased the likelihood that streaming, instead of stimulating record sales, would diminish them by providing consumers a plausible substitute for playing recorded music on their home stereos.

Congress was persuaded that, to meet this threat, the copyright statute should be amended. The record companies, of course, argued that this was the appropriate occasion to give them the full, unqualified public-performance right they had long sought. Congress once again refused. However, Congress did give the record companies a new set of limited public-performance rights focused specifically on the emergent distribution technologies. The necessary adjustments to the law came in two stages—an initial set of changes effected by the Digital Performance Right in Sound Recordings Act of 1995 (DPRA) and a second set of adjustments three years later in Title IV of the omnibus Digital Millennium Copyright Act.[46]

The new rights were very complex and, as we will see, contained some unfortunate ambiguities, but the overall thrust of the reform was clear enough.

On one hand, Congress recognized that Webcasting was socially valuable and should be encouraged. "These new digital transmission technologies may permit consumers to enjoy performances of a broader range of higher-quality recordings than has ever before been possible. . . . Such systems could increase the selection of recordings available to consumers, and make it more convenient for consumers to acquire authorized phonorecords." It was consequently important to nurture, not stunt, the infant Webcasting industry. On the other hand, Congress recognized that it was equally important to ensure that the creators of music not be harmed by the new technology—in other words, that any disruption of the traditional systems by which they earned money would be repaired by new sources of revenue.[47]

In hopes of reconciling these goals, Congress granted to the owners of copyrights in sound recordings a new entitlement—the exclusive right to control public performances of their works in the form of "digital audio transmissions"—but qualified it with various exceptions and limitations designed to prevent the record companies from reaping a windfall. For example, over-the-air broadcasts by FCC-licensed radio stations were exempted from the coverage of the new right (even if those broadcasts were made using new, digital technology) for essentially the same reasons that radio stations had long been allowed to broadcast music without compensating the record companies. Similarly, digital transmissions for the purpose of "store-casting" were exempt, on the theory that the availability of better-quality background music in Walmart and Stop & Shop would not cause consumers to buy fewer CDs.

The primary activities that did come within the ambit of the new right were interactive streaming and noninteractive streaming. You will recall, from Chapter 1, that the difference between these two forms of Webcasting is that, in the first, the recipient selects the songs sent to him or her, while in the second, the sender selects the songs. The first thus resembles pay-per-view movie broadcasts; the second resembles traditional radio. This difference was crucial, Congress concluded, when assessing the danger that the two activities posed to the revenues of the record companies. The first posed a substantial danger of injury through "substitution." If I can have a decent-quality stream of whatever music I want sent to me at any time, my eagerness to buy cumbersome CDs could well diminish. The second posed a less serious risk of that sort. If I can control only the genre of music I listen to (by selecting a particular noninteractive "station"), my desire to buy music for my own collection is not likely to decline dramatically. Moreover, noninteractive streaming, like traditional radio broadcasts and unlike interactive streaming, would expose consumers to music they had not selected and did not know about—and thus would have a promotional effect on record sales. Indeed, that promotional effect would likely be even greater than the one associated with radio broadcasts, because most Webcasters included on their sites "buy-it" buttons that enabled listeners easily to order, online, CDs containing songs they enjoyed.[48]

Awareness of these differences prompted Congress to treat the two types of Webcasting differently when crafting the modifications of copyright law. With respect to interactive streaming, the new right of a sound-recording copyright owner to control digital public performances of his work was unqualified. The DPRA and then the DMCA compelled a Webcaster that wished to stream music on demand to consumers (or to provide functionally similar "interactive" services) first to obtain from the owners of the copyrights in the relevant sound recordings freely negotiated licenses. With respect to noninteractive streaming, Congress adopted a different strategy. So long as a noninteractive Webcaster conformed to some detailed rules intended to reduce the ability of listeners to make copies of their broadcasts, and so long as it paid a compulsory royalty to be determined by the government, it, like a radio station, could perform copyrighted recordings without permission. The compulsory royalties paid by the Webcasters would then be allocated (half to the record companies, half to the recording artists) in proportion to the frequency with which each song was broadcast.[49]

The general structure of Congress's response to the advent of Webcasting was sensible. Certainly, its aspiration both to facilitate the development of this new technology and to ensure that copyright owners were not injured thereby was commendable. The distinction Congress drew between interactive and noninteractive Webcasting also seems wise. And the requirement that half of the compulsory royalties be paid to the artists themselves was laudable, providing them a much larger piece of the revenue pie than (as we saw in Chapter 2) they earned from sales of their records. The only flaw in the statutory regime it created was the absence of any limitations whatsoever on the rights of the record companies vis-à-vis interactive services—empowering the companies, if they saw fit, to refuse to grant any licenses and thus block the development of the technology altogether. Congress's confidence that the companies would recognize that it was in their long-term best interest not to do so may have been unduly sanguine. While some interactive services have been able to negotiate licensing agreements with the record companies, they are still fairly limited in their reach. But with that exception, the overall strategy was sensible enough.[50]

The devil, as usual, was in the details. Several features of the scheme were troublesome. First, Congress delegated the task of setting the compulsory licensing fees applicable to different subcategories of Webcasters not to the courts or even to the Copyright Office but instead to groups of arbitrators (known as Copyright Arbitration Royalty Panels) without any special expertise either in copyright law or in the music business. (A panel's ruling could be appealed to the Librarian of Congress and ultimately to the Court of Appeals for the D.C. Circuit, but could be overturned only if "contrary to law".) Next, the statutory provision applicable to the most important subcategory (all nonsubscription noninteractive Webcasters and certain subscription noninteractive Webcasters) was far from crystalline, instructing the arbitrators to establish rates "that most clearly represent the rates and terms that would have been negotiated in the marketplace between a willing buyer and a willing seller," while also encouraging them to take into account such varied factors as "whether use of the service may substitute for or may promote the sales of phonorecords or otherwise may interfere with or may enhance the sound recording copyright owner's other streams of revenue from its sound recordings" and the relative contributions of the record companies and the Webcasters in making streamed music available to the public. (Every two years, a new panel would be asked to reset the rates to respond to changing economic conditions.) Finally, although (as previously indicated) radio stations continued to be exempt from the new fee system so long as they broadcast their programming through the airwaves, the statute could be construed to require them to pay fees if they "simulcast" exactly the same programming over the Internet.[51]

This system, awkward enough on paper, proved even worse in practice. In the primary arbitration proceeding under the statute, both the record companies and the Webcasters hired large teams of lawyers and expert witnesses. (I was one of the experts to testify for the Webcasters. My participation in the proceeding—and the fact that the arbitrators in their final ruling did not pay much attention to my testimony—may color the comments offered in the following.) The record companies, emphasizing the reference in the statutory standard to the amount that would be negotiated "between a willing buyer and a willing seller" (a phrase they themselves had inserted during the late stages of the DMCA lobbying), argued that the arbitrators should strive to mimic in their ruling an unregulated market. On that basis, the companies asked that Webcasters be required to pay them royalties between five and twenty times greater than the amount that they were already paying to the owners of copyrights in musical compositions. They argued that this proposed rate was consistent with the terms of the voluntary licensing agreements that a few Webcasters had already agreed to. The Webcasters, emphasizing the infancy of their industry, Congress's stated goal of fostering it, and the references in the statute to factors other than market prices, sought a much lower compulsory rate. In response to the record industry's contentions regarding previously negotiated rates, Webcasters argued that those contracts should not be treated as representative, because the record companies had been "cherry-picking" and had used various kinds of economic pressure to extract misleadingly lucrative concessions. The proceedings in which these various arguments were deployed and documented lasted for six months (not counting the preliminary negotiations) and cost the parties a total of approximately $25 million.[52]

In the end, the arbitrators sided, for the most part, with the record companies. The crucial figure in their final order was 0.14¢—the amount of money that eligible nonsubscription Webcasters would have to pay for each performance of a sound recording. This seems like a very small number, until one recognizes that each transmission of each song *to each listener* is counted as a "performance." Application of this rate would mean, for example, that a small hip-hop Webcaster, streaming an average of fifteen songs per hour to an average of one thousand listeners, would pay royalties to the record companies of approximately $200,000 per year.[53]

Announcement of the arbitrators' decision provoked furious protests by Webcasters. A common complaint was that the panel's ruling would enable only the largest Webcasters—typically those affiliated with other companies—to survive. For example, Vice President Bill Rose of Arbitron predicted, "If the proposed fees are enacted, we foresee that very few companies if any would be able to pay the cost. The proposed fees are likely to create a business/regulatory environment that will limit competition, stifle innovation, reduce consumer choices and diminish diversity by concentrating the distribution of music to a handful of sources." Not surprisingly, small stations were especially dismayed by the panel's ruling. One reported that the royalty payments mandated by the panel would be twice the size of its total current revenues. On May 1, 2002, a consortium of Webcasters, in hopes of stimulating public awareness of their plight, voluntarily either shut down their operations for a day or replaced their usual programming with a twelve-hour broadcast called, "The Emergency Webcasting System." For their part, the record companies insisted that the new rates were, if anything, too low.[54]

The Copyright Office seems to have had its ear to the ground. In May, the Librarian of Congress, on the advice of the Copyright Office, rejected the panel's ruling as "arbitrary and contrary to law." The Librarian did not, however, reject the overall approach adopted by the arbitrators. The Librarian's final ruling, issued in June, cut the panel's rate in half—from .14 cents to .07 cents per performance—a significant reduction but not enough to assuage the concerns of the Webcasters. A growing number, concluding that they could not pay the new fees, shut down their operations. By September of 2002, the total number of Webcasters was more than 31 percent smaller than it had been in 2001. The attrition rate was especially high among small Webcasters serving niche markets and among college radio stations that had been "simulcasting" over the Internet. Other Webcasters considered going "underground"—using recently developed software to conceal their operations from the RIAA and its fee-collection affiliate, SoundExchange. Both sides, unhappy with the Librarian's decision, appealed to the United States Court of Appeals for the D.C. Circuit, but few observers expected the court to overturn the ruling.[55]

Various bills were introduced in Congress seeking in different ways to reduce the pressure that the new rates exerted, especially upon small stations. A flurry of negotiations led to a compromise—the Small Webcaster Settlement Act—that empowered (and tacitly encouraged) the RIAA to reach a new, less onerous agreement with small and noncommercial Webcasters, including college radio stations. A month later, a short-term deal of that sort was struck. Small operators would be allowed to pay, through 2004, relatively modest percentages of their revenues or expenses rather than the harsh per-performance fees mandated by the arbitrators and the Librarian. Most Webcasters thought that, for the time being, such an arrangement was acceptable, but a group of the smallest operators, known as the Webcaster Alliance, continued to denounce the rates.[56]

Where do things stand at present? Unlike commercial radio stations broadcasting over the airwaves, commercial noninteractive Webcasters are now obliged to pay substantial fees to the record companies. Several have recently altered their business models in an effort to raise the necessary funds. The prospect of paying similar fees prompted many smaller Webcasters to close down, but those that survived were eventually given at least a brief reprieve. How they will fare in the next round of arbitration remains to be seen.

The establishment of these new rights and obligations requires us to modify once more the diagram we developed in Chapter 2 of the complex patent of legal rights in the music industry (Figure 3.1).

In retrospect, the process of setting the compulsory rates governing noninteractive Webcasting was wasteful and nearly disastrous. Four aspects of the process turned out to be especially problematic. First, it makes little sense to confer the crucial responsibility for setting the rates upon a group of arbitrators with no special expertise in this area. A judge, preferably one with some background in copyright law, charged with first setting and then

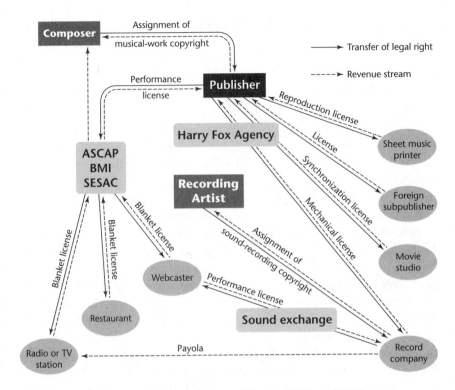

FIGURE 3.1. *Legal Rights in the Music Industry After the DPRA and DMCA.*

periodically adjusting the compulsory rates applicable to the various sub-categories of Webcasters, would almost surely do a better job.[57]

Second, partly because the parties (rather than the government) pay the salaries of the arbitrators, the attorneys, and the expert witnesses, and partly because of the extraordinary complexity of the pertinent statutory provisions, the process was extremely expensive. Participating Webcasters ultimately paid, on average, approximately $300,000 apiece. The result, of course, is that most smaller Webcasters could not afford to get involved. It is not terribly surprising that their interests were poorly reflected in the Librarian's final ruling.[58]

Third, the aspect of the relevant statutory standard that was emphasized by both the arbitrators and the Librarian—which tries to estimate the licensing fees that would have been agreed upon, in an unregulated market, by "willing" record companies and "willing" Webcasters—is misguided. Such a guideline fails to take into account the many reasons, reviewed earlier, why noninteractive Webcasters should pay less for the right to broadcast copyrighted sound recordings than should interactive Webcasters. It also ignores the danger (emphasized by the Justice Department as the statute was being drafted) that the record companies, authorized to negotiate rates in concert, would act like a cartel, extracting supracompetitive licensing fees from the dispersed Webcasters. A standard that gave the decision-maker more discretion to set "fair" rates (as the original DPRA did) would be more sensible.[59]

Finally and most fundamental, the process enables, even encourages, the record companies to act in a shortsighted fashion. The long-run best interests of society at large would have been served by initially charging the infant Webcasters very low compulsory rates, allowing the industry to flourish, and then, once it had matured, increasing those rates to levels sufficient to compensate musicians fairly. But two circumstances prompted the record companies to seek to extract the maximum possible fees from the beginning. First, they feared that, if the rates were set low at the outset, they would be hard to raise later. (The manner in which the compulsory "cover license" rates have been adjusted over time makes that anxiety reasonable.) Second, the record companies had a financial interest in thinning the field of the Webcasters. As one of their expert witnesses testified, a profit-maximizing strategy for the companies would be to set rates that would, in reasonably short order, drive two-thirds of the enterprises into bankruptcy and enable the record companies to buy the remainder, thus maintaining their control over the channels through which music was distributed. Such a strategy would indeed protect the companies' existing business models and perhaps maximize their near-term profits, but for obvious reasons would be highly regrettable from the standpoint of the public interest.[60]

Centralized File Sharing

Consumers have been sharing audio recordings for decades; teenagers making "mixes" for their friends is perhaps the clearest example. But the limitations of analog copying technology and the absence of a convenient system for mass distribution of those copies limited the scale of the practice. The same three innovations with which we have been concerned throughout this book—the shift from analog to digital recordings; the development of convenient compression-decompression software; and the popularization of the Internet—created the potential for massive expansion of this custom.

The first person to exploit that potential was Shawn Fanning. In 1998, while a freshman at Northeastern University, Fanning (with the help of friends) began work on a program that would make it substantially easier for consumers to trade MP3 files. That winter, he left school to develop the system. With his uncle's help, Fanning incorporated Napster in May of 1999 ("Napster" was Fanning's nickname). A beta version of the software was released to the public in the summer.[61]

The system worked as follows. From the Napster Website (www.napster.com), a prospective subscriber would download a free copy of the "Music-Share" software, selecting at the same time a unique "user name" and password. He would then create on his computer a "user library," into which he would copy any MP3 files he wished to share with other subscribers, labeling them with self-designated filenames. To trade files, he would log onto the Napster system. So long as he remained connected, a list of the files contained in his own library would appear in the central "collective directory" of the Napster Website. (The files themselves would not be copied onto the servers of the Napster site, just their names.) Suppose, then, that he wanted to enhance his Bruce Springsteen collection. He would enter "Springsteen" into the Napster search engine and would be provided, in return, with a list of all the Springsteen songs located in the "user libraries" of all of the other Napster subscribers connected to the system at that time. To obtain a copy of a song, he would merely "click" on the appropriate filename, whereupon the Napster server would supply his computer with the IP (Internet Protocol) address of the "host" computer where the file was located. That information would enable his computer to download a copy of the file directly from the host (hence the name, "peer-to-peer" copying). He could then either play the file directly from his computer or, if he had a CD burner and the appropriate software, convert the MP3 file to a WAV file and copy it onto a CD, which could be played on any CD player.

No money changed hands in this sequence. Napster offered both its software and its indexing service for free, and subscribers exchanged files for free. The company hoped at some point to make money—through advertising, through direct marketing of other products, or through the creation of a fee-based "premium" service. But, during its brief life, the company did not adopt any of those business models, surviving instead on loans and injections of venture capital.

Partly because it was free, partly because it was highly convenient, the system was enormously popular. By October of 2000 (roughly a year after its launch), it claimed thirty-two million subscribers. Four months later, the number had risen to eighty million. In its last month of operation, its members exchanged 2.79 billion files. Approximately 40 percent of its subscribers were American high-school or university students. But it also attracted many older music consumers. And, as the anecdote offered in the Introduction suggests, it drew large followings in other countries. Indeed, the percentage of Napster users among people with Internet access was higher in Canada, Argentina, Spain, and Brazil than in the United States.[62]

Close on the heels of Napster was Scour.net. "Scour," as its name suggests, was originally created in 1997 by a group of UCLA students as a multimedia search engine. Two years later, the company received a boost when Michael Ovitz, a wealthy and savvy former Disney executive, invested a substantial amount of money. In April of 2000, the organizers of the firm decided to add to their Website a file-trading system, which they dubbed the "Scour Exchange" or "SX." Like Napster, SX was centralized. (Indeed, because it relied upon a "server farm connected in a hierarchical fashion," it was even more centralized than Napster, which, as it grew, relied upon many unconnected servers to coordinate trades among subsets of its subscribers.) Also like Napster, it was free. However, SX differed from Napster by allowing subscribers to exchange, not just MP3 files, but also movies, music, and other media in a variety of formats. It too attracted large numbers of users. By August, 2.5 million people had downloaded its free software. At any given time, up to seventy thousand people were signed on, sharing nearly five million files.[63]

The third such system out of the blocks was "Aimster"—so named because it piggybacked on AOL's Instant Message System (AIM). (The name was later changed to "Madster" after AOL persuaded an arbitration panel that the original name encroached upon its trademarks.) Aimster differed from Napster and Scour in three main ways. First, because of its design, it was only available to users of instant messaging services. Second, files exchanged through the system were encrypted. Thus, even the operators of the system did not know and could not learn what those files contained. Third, Aimster did not maintain a central directory of files available for downloading at any given time. Instead, each time a subscriber submitted a search request, the Aimster servers would conduct an ad-hoc search of the computers of connected users to locate a copy of the file in question—and would then instruct the computer on which the file was found to transmit it, via the Internet, to the requester. Nevertheless, like Napster and Scour, Aimster was "centralized" in the sense that the company's own servers managed all search requests, and thus closing down those servers would destroy the network. Like its ancestors, Aimster attracted subscribers with extraordinary speed. It was launched on August 8, 2000. Within three days, twenty thousand people had signed up. By early 2001, it had 2.5 million registered users. By the end of April, the number had grown to 4.2 million.[64]

The music and film companies watched the rapid growth of these systems with alarm. The large majority of the files exchanged through all three consisted of copyrighted recordings, the owners of which had not given permission for them to be reproduced or distributed over the Internet. Because none of the services copied any recordings onto their own servers, they were largely immune to suit for direct copyright infringement. However, the media companies believed, all three were plainly designed to facilitate "piracy" by their subscribers—and thus were guilty of contributory and vicarious copyright infringement. They quickly sought confirmation of that belief from the courts.

The primary lawsuit against Napster was filed by the major record companies on December 6, 1999, in the U.S. District Court for the Northern District of California. (Separate suits by the band Metallica and the major music publishers unfolded in its shadow.) The case proceeded through the federal courts with highly uncharacteristic speed. On May 5, 2000, Judge Marilyn Patel rejected Napster's effort to seek protection in the "safe-harbor" provisions of the DMCA, ruling (1) that 17 U.S.C.S §512(a) was inapplicable because Napster did not "transmit, route, or provide connections for allegedly infringing material through its system" and (2) that Napster may have failed to comply with the statutory obligation of all Internet service providers to implement a copyright compliance policy and thus might not be able to invoke any of the DMCA safe harbors. On July 26, Judge Patel ruled that the record companies would likely prevail on their primary claims of contributory and vicarious copyright infringement and consequently granted the companies a preliminary injunction, ordering Napster to cease "facilitating others in copying, downloading, uploading, transmitting, or distributing plaintiffs' copyrighted musical compositions and sound recordings" within two days. On July 28, the Court of Appeals for the Ninth Circuit stayed that ruling, allowing Napster to continue operating while the appellate court considered the "substantial questions of first impression going to both the merits and the form of the injunction." The Ninth Circuit issued its own opinion on February 12, 2001, upholding many aspects of Judge Patel's shut-down order, but requiring that the plaintiffs first provide Napster with notice of those specific copyrighted sound recordings that were being exchanged unlawfully through its service. On March 5, Judge Patel issued an appropriately modified injunction, and four days later the record companies provided Napster a list of 135,000 copyrighted songs that Napster would be obliged to block. Napster then struggled for a few months to comply with the order without shutting down its system altogether. Judge Patel took a hard line concerning these efforts, ordering Napster to remain offline until and unless it was capable of filtering out infringing material with 100 percent effectiveness. The Court of Appeals again temporarily stayed Patel's order, but ultimately, on March 25, 2002, upheld it. On June 3, Napster filed for bankruptcy.[65]

The analogous suit against Scour resulted in an even more rapid shutdown, mainly because Scour lacked the financial resources to fight it. On July 20, 2000, a group of thirty record companies, music publishers, and movie studios filed a complaint, asserting claims very similar to those that had been deployed against Napster. In several respects, Scour's legal position was stronger than Napster's: it had been more careful in complying with the DMCA; a larger percentage of the traffic on its system was noninfringing (thus increasing the chance that it could invoke the *Sony* defense successfully); and it was not saddled with self-incriminating emails from its founders proclaiming their desire to break the backs of the record companies. Nevertheless, potential investors, fearing entrapment in a maelstrom like that engulfing Napster, backed away from the company. As a result, Scour quickly collapsed. In early September, it laid off most of its employees; on October 12, it filed for Chapter 11 bankruptcy protection; on November 16, it shut down the SX service; and on December 12, its remaining assets were sold in a court-supervised bankruptcy auction.[66]

Victory against Aimster was achieved almost as fast. Beginning in May of 2001, the music publishers and more than forty media companies of various sorts filed a series of lawsuits against Johnny Deep, the creator of Aimster, and the corporate entities he controlled. By November, the separate suits had been consolidated in the Northern District of Illinois. On September 4, 2002, Judge Marvin Aspen issued a preliminary injunction against the company; three months later, he ordered Aimster to shut down immediately. The following June, the Court of Appeals for the Seventh Circuit, in an opinion by Judge Posner, upheld Aspen's order, emphasizing Aimster's failure to show (1) that the system was actually being used for any lawful purposes or (2) that it would have been "disproportionately costly" to design the system so as to reduce its susceptibility to illegal uses. In the meantime, both Deep and his companies had filed for bankruptcy. He has vowed to carry the fight to the United States Supreme Court, but the chances that the Court will take his case are slim.[67]

The media companies expressed satisfaction concerning the outcomes of the lawsuits. Their view that such services facilitated "piracy" on a massive scale and thus were clearly illegal had been upheld by the courts, and all three enterprises had been rapidly driven out of business. The response of the community of artists—the musicians and filmmakers on whose behalf the media companies consistently claimed to be acting—was more mixed. Some denounced Napster, Scour, and Aimster while they were in operation, and cheered when they were shut down. Other artists, however, thought that file-sharing services helped rather than hurt them—either because they stimulated rather than eroded sales of recordings or because they increased public awareness of the artists' work and thus enhanced ticket sales for live performances. The big losers were entertainment consumers. Millions had discovered that these services were fast, convenient, and reasonably reliable —vastly more efficient mechanisms for distributing entertainment than those afforded by the media companies' existing business models. Many lamented their demise—and, as we will see, immediately began to look elsewhere for substitutes.[68]

The story could have had a happier ending. At least two of the many choices that led to this particular conclusion easily could have been made differently. First, the media companies could have cut deals with the file-sharing services. At least with respect to Napster and Scour, they had many opportunities to do so. The Napster executives repeatedly approached the record companies, proposing to introduce a new fee-based "premium" service and to pay the companies 80 percent of the revenues reaped through it. Some of the record-company executives were tempted. The most enthusiastic was Bertelsmann, Inc., the German parent company of UMG, one of the big-five record companies. In October 2000, Bertelsmann announced that it had extended a $50 million loan to Napster, hoping to catalyze its conversion to an authorized subscription service. (The amount was later increased substantially.) Many other industry leaders, though privately uneasy with the leading role that Bertelsmann was taking, nonetheless publicly expressed support for the initiative. As late as February 20, 2001, Napster offered the companies $1 billion to settle their suit. But, in the end, the majority of the companies refused to play ball unless and until Napster had completely shut down its existing system.[69]

The executives of Scour were even more assiduous in seeking copyright owners' permission to have protected materials exchanged through their service. Founder and President David Rodrigues insisted

> We came with a fundamentally different philosophy to these guys [than had Napster] and we said we really want to work out a business solution because there's this huge consumer demand here that it only makes sense to harness. . . . What we've talked to the record labels about is a model where we could operate in a licensing environment, providing users premium offerings that aren't available now. We could then get users to pay for that type of service. So while I can't go into the specifics, we have identified a model that allows us to monetize Scour's activity, and allows us to take the Scour Exchange—which is a raw search engine technology now—and transition it to being a distribution

platform for content that would let us identify what's being traded, provide some means of security and ultimately pay royalties to content owners for the use of their work. We think it's a great business model that can be profitable and that can work.[70]

Rodrigues persuaded Miramax and Hollywood Records to grant him permission to distribute at least some of their copyrighted recordings. He was actively engaged in discussions with several other media companies when, to his surprise, they filed suit. He continued for some time to hope that litigation was just "part of the negotiation process." He was wrong.[71]

In both instances, an important opportunity was lost. Fee-based subscription versions of the two services would have continued to provide consumers a highly efficient distribution mechanism while simultaneously fairly compensating the creators of the exchanged recordings. It is at least possible that such win-win solutions could have been engineered. Certainly, the Napster and Scour executives were willing. And polls conducted at the time suggested that most users of the systems would have been willing to pay modest subscription fees. Were their protestations sincere? If actually asked to pay for access to Napster or Scour, would they instead have defected to one of the infant decentralized peer-to-peer systems (whose structures and trajectories we will consider shortly)? One can't be sure. But it might have worked. That the media companies balked is regrettable.

The second chance to fashion an alternative ending to the story came during the Napster litigation. The courts, had they wished, easily could have ruled in favor of Napster on one critical issue, thus allowing the system to survive. With respect to most of the issues in the case, the media companies had solid arguments, and the courts were right to rule in their favor. For example, the media companies (and the Justice Department, which filed a "friend of the court" brief) persuasively argued that the conduct of Napster's subscribers could not plausibly be shoehorned into the safe harbor created by section 1008 of the Audio Home Recording Act for the "noncommercial use" of a "digital audio recording device." Similarly, the media companies were probably correct that Napster could not fairly avail itself of the qualified immunity created by the DMCA for Internet service providers.[72]

But there was one crucial issue for which Napster had the better argument. Remember that, in the *Sony* case, the United States Supreme Court had ruled that the distributor of technology that is often used for infringing purposes is nevertheless not liable for contributory copyright infringement if the technology is "capable of substantial noninfringing uses." In that case, the Court concluded that the use of a VCR to "time-shift" a copyrighted program, although presumptively a violation of the copyright owner's exclusive right to reproduce the program, nevertheless qualified as a fair use and was therefore lawful. Because time-shifting was a common use of VCRs, the machines themselves plainly were capable of at least one substantial noninfringing use—and thus Sony escaped liability.[73]

Napster argued, plausibly, that it should prevail for very similar reasons. Specifically, Napster argued that at least three uses of its system were non-infringing: "sampling, where users make temporary copies of a work before purchasing; space-shifting, where users access a sound recording through the Napster system that they already own in audio CD format; and permissive distribution of recordings by both new and established artists." Each of these activities, Napster claimed, either was authorized by the relevant copyright owners or, like time-shifting, constituted a fair use and was therefore lawful. Thus even if most of Napster's subscribers were engaged in illegal behavior, the fact that a significant subset were engaged in lawful conduct should have excused Napster from liability for contributory or vicarious infringement.[74]

The grounds on which the courts rejected this contention were shaky at best. Their weakness is most evident with respect to "sampling," so we will concentrate on that activity. Napster argued, accurately, that some of its subscribers used its system only to determine what CDs to buy. In other words, they would download songs from albums they were considering purchasing and then listen to them through the speakers on their computers. If they liked particular songs, they would buy the corresponding CDs. If they didn't, they wouldn't. In either event, they would delete the MP3 files after listening to them once or twice. (Why wouldn't they simply keep the songs they downloaded and avoid the cost and inconvenience of buying CDs? Some did not want to deprive the recording artists and composers of the revenue they would have reaped from CD sales. Others had poor-quality sound systems on their computers and lacked the skill or equipment to convert downloaded MP3 files to CDs that they could play in their home stereos. Still others valued the slightly better sound that could be obtained through uncompressed files.) If time-shifting movies constitutes a fair use, then surely "sampling" in this sense constitutes a fair use. Both activities involve temporarily making full-length copies of highly creative materials—circumstances that would ordinarily suggest they could not qualify as "fair." However, both activities are "noncommercial" at least in the sense that (unlike, for instance, the behavior of MP3.com) they are not associated with profit making. And neither undermines the normal markets for the copyrighted works in question. (Indeed, sampling MP3 recordings, unlike time-shifting movies, *enhances* the normal market for sound recordings by stimulating CD sales.) Thus, if time-shifting movies is legitimate, then sampling songs ought to be also.

How did the courts—and, specifically, the Court of Appeals for the Ninth Circuit in its decisive ruling in the case—avoid this conclusion? First, the appellate court rejected the characterization of sampling as "noncommercial" in nature, reasoning that, if they were unable to sample songs through Napster, its users would visit ad-supported Websites where (free) authorized "promotional downloads" (either excerpts of songs or full-length versions which self-destructed after a brief period) were available, and record companies are paid fees by those Websites. In other words, the court claimed, the samplers' behavior is "commercial" because, if they were prevented from engaging in it, the copyright owners could make more money. But this is surely not the definition of "commercial" that underlay the Supreme Court's ruling in the *Sony* case. On this definition, time-shifting would be "commercial" too, because, if forbidden to engage in it, VCR users would pay for access to films and TV shows broadcast at times they were not home. Nor does the Court of Appeals' definition make much sense. Viewed through this lens, virtually every unauthorized use of a copyrighted work would be "commercial" in character.[75]

Next, the Court of Appeals upheld a factual finding by the trial court that "the more music that sampling users download, the less likely they are to eventually purchase the recordings." This ruling either misunderstands the nature of sampling (by assuming that samplers keep the recordings they download) or presupposes, implausibly, that samplers buy less music because they conclude they don't like any of the songs they temporarily download.[76]

Finally, the Court of Appeals ruled that, even if the activity of sampling increased CD sales, it still deprived the record companies of a "potential market"—namely their right to charge money for licenses to engage in sampling. Remember that Justice Blackmun made a precisely analogous argument in his dissenting opinion in the *Sony* case. The majority of the Supreme Court rejected the argument, implicitly adopting a narrower conception of what counts as a "potential market" when assessing alleged injuries claimed by copyright owners. To be sure, as noted in the previous chapter, both the Supreme Court and the lower federal courts have since vacillated on this topic, and thus the Ninth Circuit's analysis is not wholly unprecedented. But it is inconsistent with the approach taken by the majority of the Supreme Court in *Sony*, the case whose facts most closely resemble those of *Napster*.[77]

(Judge Posner, in the *Aimster* case, had an easier time dealing with this issue, because he could stress Aimster's failure to offer any evidence that any of its subscribers were engaged in benign activities. But even Posner, in order to rule for the entertainment companies, had to contort the *Sony* decision a bit. The Supreme Court, you will recall, had indicated that a company could escape liability for contributory infringement if it showed that its technology was "capable of substantial noninfringing uses." For Posner, merely being "capable" of legal uses was not enough. The company would have to "demonstrate that its service *has* substantial noninfringing uses.")[78]

The bottom line: the courts had to strain to find against Napster on this score. On balance, Napster had the better argument. To rule in favor of the record companies, the courts were obliged to misconstrue the Supreme Court's judgment in *Sony* and reconfigure the fair-use doctrine. That they saw fit to chart their own course should not necessarily be considered an outrage. When interpreting copyright law, lower federal courts frequently deviate from the lines drawn by the Supreme Court, and this habit probably helps the law adapt to new technological and economic conditions. But, in this particular instance, their doctrinal creativity had at least one and perhaps two unfortunate consequences.

First, the Ninth Circuit's *Napster* ruling has precedential power that will affect the legal status of many activities in addition to file sharing. Taken literally, its expansive definitions of "commercial" activity and "potential market" would radically constrict the zone of unauthorized uses of copyrighted materials that would qualify as "fair," upsetting in many contexts the balance that the fair-use doctrine seeks to strike between the rights of creators and the interests of the public. Other courts will have to work to restore the proper balance in future cases. Some will likely fail.

Second, a ruling in favor of Napster *might* have been better from the standpoint of the public at large. Merely letting Napster off the hook and permitting file sharing to flourish unchecked would not have been a wonderful outcome. But, most likely, the tale would not have ended there. Instead, the record companies would have sought relief from Congress. Congress, in turn, might have responded to their entreaties by merely overturning the courts' decision—in which case nothing would have been gained. But the record companies' demand for aid probably would have triggered a general public discussion of alternative ways in which copyright law might be restructured so as both to preserve the abilities of creators to make money and to exploit the enormous potential benefits of the new technologies—a discussion that, in turn, could have led to a more sophisticated legislative response. This is all highly speculative, of course. Many other scenarios are imaginable. But a judicial decision that, in effect, compelled the legislature to get involved—what Judge Robert Bork once referred to as a "remand to Congress"—could, in the end, have left us all better off.

There's still a possibility that centralized file sharing will someday re-emerge in a form that benefits everyone. Indeed, there's a chance that a transformed, fee-based version of Napster itself will once again sweep the field. But we will wait to consider that possibility until Chapter 4, when we will discuss a variety of preliminary efforts by the record industry to create, at long last, an online market in sound recordings.

Decentralized File Sharing

The file-sharing systems created by Napster, Scour, and Aimster were vulnerable to litigation because, in each, a single set of servers controlled the process by which one subscriber located a file on another subscriber's computer and then copied it. Force the company to take its servers offline, and you stop the illicit traffic. The members of the next generation of file-sharing systems were designed to eliminate or at least reduce this source of weakness.

The pioneer was Gnutella. Its creator was Justin Frankel, a brilliant programmer employed by Nullsoft, a subsidiary of AOL. In the spring of 2000, Frankel created a beta version of a new file-sharing program and posted it on the AOL Website. Within hours, his employers removed the program and disavowed it as an "unauthorized freelance project." They were too late. Thousands of copies had already been downloaded and were now being exchanged on the Internet. A few of the recipients reverse engineered the object code that Frankel had made available and began to redistribute and improve upon the source code as a collaborative open-source project.[79]

The system worked as follows:

> Unlike a centralized server network, the Gnutella network does not use a central server to keep track of all user files. To share files using the Gnutella model, a user starts with a networked computer, which we'll call "A," equipped with a Gnutella "servent" (so called because the program acts as a combination of a "server" and a "client"). Computer "A" will connect to another Gnutella-networked computer, "B." A will then announce that it is "alive" to B, which will in turn announce to all the computers that it is connected to, "C," "D," "E," and "F," that A is alive. The computers C, D, E, and F will then announce to all computers to which they are connected that A is alive; those computers will continue the pattern and announce to the computers they are connected to that computer A is alive. Although the reach of this network is potentially infinite, in reality it is limited by "time-to-live" ("TTL") constraints; that is, the number of layers of computers that the request will reach. Most Gnutella servents will reject any network messages which have TTL's that are excessively high.
>
> Once "A" has announced that it is "alive" to the various members of the peer network, it can then search the contents of the shared directories of the peer network members. The search request will send the request to all members of the network, starting with B, then to C, D, E, F, who will in turn send the

request to the computers to which they are connected, and so forth. If one of the computers in the peer network, say for example, computer D, has a file that matches the request, it transmits the file information (name, size, etc.) back through all the computers in the pathway towards A, where a list of files matching the search request will then appear on computer A's Gnutella servent display. A will then be able to open a direct connection with computer D and will be able to download that file directly from computer D. The Gnutella model enables file sharing without using servers that do not actually directly serve content themselves.[80]

Gnutella was a breakthrough in network design. However, four characteristics of the initial version of the system limited its utility and popularity. First, it did not "scale" well—meaning that the set of users could not be increased indefinitely without reducing its performance. Unlike Napster, which enabled each subscriber to share files with hundreds of thousands of comrades simultaneously connected to a given server, Gnutella limited each subscriber's reach to approximately four thousand other users. Second, because the system did not differentiate users with broadband connections from users with dial-up modem connections, search times were limited by the speed of the slowest link in each search chain. Third, it was vulnerable to "denial of service attacks"—efforts (by the recording industry or others) to overwhelm the system with false search requests. Finally, it encouraged "free riding"—meaning that, typically, a few users offered a large number of files for downloading, while the majority of users did not offer any. This circumstance not only threatened the culture of openness and sharing that helped to sustain the system, but also made the relatively few generous hosts more vulnerable to attack or lawsuit.[81]

In late 2000, two companies—Lime Wire LLC and Free Peers, Inc.—set out to correct the most serious of these defects. Their new versions of Frankel's program, dubbed Limewire and Bearshare, incorporated "connection-preferencing rules" that had the effect of "driv[ing] slower hosts to have fewer connections and sit at the edge of the network, a bit like a poor conversationalist might find himself marginalized at a party." Users flocked to the improved versions. By March 2002, as many as 320,000 people were connected at a given time.[82]

In late 2000, the Dutch programmers Niklas Zennstrom and Janus Friis developed an even better protocol for file sharing. Dubbed FastTrack, it differed from even the enhanced versions of Gnutella in three main ways. First, it was proprietary, rather than open source. Zennstrom and Friis founded a company, KaZaA, that offered subscribers (free) access to the network, and subsequently charged two other companies, Morpheus (a.k.a. MusicCity and StreamCast Networks) and Grokster, for permission to gain access to it. Second, FastTrack relied upon a subset of the computers employing the system to function as "supernodes," coordinating the searches of ordinary users. Third, the companies providing access to the system played at least modest roles in its operation—maintaining user registrations, logging their subscribers into the system, and helping them to locate supernodes.[83]

These features made the FastTrack services very popular very fast. Within a year, between two and four million people were connected to the network at any given time. They also, however, offered the copyright owners attractive litigation targets. Each of the three companies employing the system soon found itself accused of contributory and vicarious copyright infringement.[84]

In pursuing these lawsuits, however, the copyright owners encountered difficulties. Two of the target companies, KaZaA and Grokster, were incorporated in countries other than the United States (KaZaA first in the Netherlands and then in Vanuatu, a cluster of South Pacific Islands; Grokster in Nevis). As one might expect, the copyright laws of those countries are less favorable to the interests of the record and film industries than the laws of the United States, and suing the companies in the United States was jurisdictionally complicated. In addition, all three companies could argue, plausibly, that their subscribers could use the network for various lawful purposes in addition to the unauthorized exchange of audio and video recordings. (Professor Larry Lessig, for example, at one time used KaZaA to facilitate the distribution over the Internet of some of his essays—to the consternation of the administrators of the Stanford University network.)

Partly (but only partly) for these reasons, the FastTrack litigation campaign did not proceed as smoothly as the campaign against the centralized file-sharing services. It started out well enough. In November of 2001, a Dutch trial court ruled in favor of Buma/Stemra (the Dutch copyright organization) in its suit against KaZaA, ordering the company to prevent its product from facilitating copyright infringement or face fines of approximately $45,000 a day. The company responded by suspending downloads of its software and selling all of its assets, including its name, to an Australian firm. The following March, however, the Amsterdam Court of Appeal overturned the trial court's ruling, emphasizing the facts that (1) the KaZaA service could be used to exchange jokes, Microsoft Word files, photographs, and real-estate listings as well as MP3 recordings; (2) KaZaA had no effective way of differentiating lawful from unlawful exchanges; and (3) shutting down KaZaA would not prevent the people who already possessed copies of the pertinent software from continuing to use the network. In December, that decision was upheld by the Dutch Supreme Court.[85]

In April of 2003, Judge Wilson of the Central District of California proved similarly unreceptive to the suits brought in the United States by the record companies, music publishers, and film studios against Grokster and StreamCast. Both of those services, he insisted, are commonly used for non-infringing purposes—ranging from "distributing movie trailers" to "sharing the works of Shakespeare" to locating "computer software for which distribution is permitted." Moreover, the relatively decentralized structure of the networks used by the services meant that they had little control over their subscribers' behavior:

> Plaintiffs appear reluctant to acknowledge a seminal distinction between Grokster/StreamCast and Napster: neither Grokster nor StreamCast provides the "site and facilities" for direct infringement. Neither StreamCast nor Grokster facilitates the exchange of files between users in the way Napster did. Users connect to the respective networks, select which files to share, send and receive searches, and download files, all with no material involvement of Defendants. If either Defendant closed their doors and deactivated all computers within their control, users of their products could continue sharing files with little or no interruption.

In light of these circumstances, Judge Wilson ruled, it could not fairly be said that the services "materially contributed to the infringing activity of another" (a condition essential to liability for contributory copyright infringement) or had "the right and ability to supervise the infringing conduct" (a condition essential to liability for vicarious infringement). To be sure, Wilson insisted, much of the conduct of the Grokster and Morpheus subscribers was unlawful. But the services themselves could not be held legally responsible for that conduct.[86]

The siege is far from over. As of this writing, Judge Wilson's ruling concerning Grokster and Morpheus is on appeal, and the record industry has recently opened another front against KaZaA in Australia. At least for the time being, however, the companies have managed to repel the copyright owners' assaults.[87]

The most recent entrant into the file-sharing industry is Freenet. Designed by Ian Clark, an Edinburgh University student passionately committed to free communication on the Internet, Freenet purports to offer its users complete anonymity. Clark explains:

> Most P2P applications today were not designed to hide the identities of their users. Their goal was primarily to insulate the operators of the P2P networks from the actions of their users, and they have been reasonably successful in this regard. I draw comfort from the fact that systems like Freenet exist which do maintain the anonymity of users and can therefore continue to ensure users'

freedom of communication. I don't particularly care for people whose only desire is to get music without paying for it, but Freenet can't protect the rights of political dissidents without also protecting file-swappers. It is an inevitable side effect of Freenet's design.[88]

Freenet is substantially less user-friendly than the FastTrack services or even Gnutella. Largely as a result, it remains relatively unpopular and has not yet faced the fury of the copyright owners.[89]

Despite the declarations by Judge Wilson and others that use of the decentralized systems to share copyrighted files was clearly illegal, consumers continued to do just that with ever greater frequency. An excellent snapshot of consumers' habits was provided by a study conducted in the spring of 2003 by the Pew Research Center. The crucial findings of the study are reproduced in Table 3.1.[90]

Some of these findings are unsurprising—that the propensity to download is inversely correlated with age, and that people with more Internet experience are more likely to download files than people with less. Others are more intriguing—that men download somewhat more often than women; that blacks and Hispanics are more likely to download than whites; and that the propensity to download is inversely correlated with income (although the latter finding is probably a function of the age factor). But the most important figures are contained in the top line: the percentage of American Internet users who downloaded music was just as high in early 2003 as it had been in February of 2001, the heyday of Napster. Because the population of Internet users grew during the interim, the absolute number of downloaders was even higher. Specifically, as of early 2003, approximately thirty-five million American adults engaged in the activity. Other polls (some of which included children as well as adults) conducted at roughly the same time suggested that the total number of downloaders was even higher—forty or even sixty million. Wendy Seltzer of the Electronic Frontier Foundation puts these figures in harsh perspective: "We have more Americans using file-sharing than voted for the President."[91]

One additional finding in the Pew Report is perhaps even more striking: as of early 2003, "67 percent of Internet users who download music" reported that they "do not care about whether the music they have downloaded is copyrighted," leaving only 27 percent who reported that "they do care," and 6 percent who reported that "they don't have a position or know enough about the issue." The percentage disinterested in the legal status of their activity was higher than ever before. And, not surprisingly, it was highest among the youngest group of downloaders.[92]

In the late spring of 2003, the record companies, frightened by these

TABLE **3.1.** *Music Downloading Demographics*

Percentage of each group of Internet users who download music

	July–August 2000	February 2001	March–May 2003
All adults	22	29	29
Men	24	36	32
Women	20	23	26
Whites	21	26	28
Blacks	29	30	37
Hispanics	35	46	35
Age cohorts			
18–29	37	51	52
30–49	19	23	27
50 or older	9	15	12
Household income			
Under $30,000	28	36	38
$30,000–$50,000	24	31	30
$50,000–$75,000	20	29	28
$75,000 or more	15	24	26
Educational attainment			
Less than high school	38	55	39
High school graduate	25	31	31
Some college	25	32	33
College degree or more	15	21	23
Internet user experience			
Less than six months	20	27	26*
Six months to one year	20	25	26*
Two to three years	24	28	29
Three years or more	22	33	59

SOURCE: Pew Internet and American Life Project Surveys, March–May 2003.
NOTE: Margin of error is ± 3 percent. * represents music downloaders who have been online for less than one year.

trends, abruptly changed tactics. Until then, the companies had tried to stop file sharing by shutting down the services that facilitated it, but had refrained from attacking the individuals who engaged in the practice. Why? Partly because suits against individuals seemed like "a teaspoon solution to an ocean problem." And partly because suing your customers is ordinarily considered bad business practice. Apparently concluding that they now had no other choice, the companies announced that they would bring "thousands" of copyright-infringement suits against people who used the services to trade MP3 files.[93]

To do so, they first had to learn the identities of the individuals who were using these services to share music. Getting the IP numbers they used while exchanging files was relatively easy (unless they happened to be Freenet subscribers). Agents of the record companies merely signed up for the file-sharing services and then used them to identify other subscribers who were either offering to share large numbers of copyrighted songs or who were downloading large numbers of songs. Rarely, however, would those subscribers identify themselves by their full, true names. Thus, to determine their identities, the record companies needed the help of their Internet service providers (ISPs), which typically kept logs of which of their subscribers were using particular IP numbers at particular times. Most ISPs were reluctant to provide this information—at least in part because a reputation for revealing such data might frighten away customers. But a provision of the Digital Millennium Copyright Act seemed to empower the record companies to force the ISPs to disgorge the information even before they initiated lawsuits. Specifically, section 512(h) permitted a copyright owner to obtain from the clerk of a federal court a subpoena, which would require the named ISP to reveal the identity of a person alleged to have infringed his or her copyright.[94]

Relying on this provision, the record companies began to serve subpoenas on a wide variety of ISPs, ranging from large commercial providers to the operators of university networks. Some initially refused to comply. The most vigorous resistance was mounted by Verizon, which contended that the pertinent statutory provision only applied to ISPs accused of storing or controlling infringing material on their own computers—or that, if the provision applied more broadly, it was unconstitutional. Both arguments, however, were rejected by a federal trial court. Reluctantly, most ISPs began to turn over the requested data. (When they returned to campus in the fall of 2003, students were solemnly informed during their orientation programs that their universities, if asked by the record companies, would be obliged to reveal their identities.)[95]

Armed with this information, the record companies began filing suits against individuals—first in a trickle, then at an accelerating pace. The targets were diverse—ranging from a twelve-year-old girl in New York City to a Yale professor. Facing potentially enormous liability (up to $150,000 in statutory damages for each illegally copied work), most defendants succumbed quickly. In settlement agreements, they typically agreed to pay the record companies between $2,000 and $17,500, to refrain from similar behavior in the future, and to say nothing in public inconsistent with their acknowledgments of wrongdoing.[96]

It was apparent from the beginning that the record companies could not hope to identify and sue all of the individuals who have been making use of the file-sharing services to trade songs. Rather, the companies hoped that a relatively few suits would curb the practice in two ways. First, through deterrence. Even a small chance of having to pay a very large amount in damages might be enough, they hoped, to discourage most Internet users from engaging in the practice. Second, through education. In particular, the companies hoped that parents and university administrators, who for years had largely ignored what their wards were doing with their computers, would get more involved—and, specifically, would make clear to them their rights and obligations under copyright law.

As of this writing, it is not yet clear that either tactic will work. In December of 2003, the trial-court ruling upholding the record companies' use of section 512(h) to learn the identities of file-sharers was overturned by a federal Court of Appeals, forcing the companies to turn to more cumbersome and time-consuming methods. Large numbers of students, figuring that their odds of getting caught are smaller than their odds of getting hit by a bus, are continuing to download just as often. Some have tried to reduce their profiles by disabling the switch in their file-sharing software that makes the contents of their hard drives available to the world. Others, less cavalier, are gravitating toward services that offer them greater privacy. Usage of Freenet, the existing service that offers users the greatest anonymity, is rising fast (so fast, in fact, that the system at least briefly was overloaded). Similar systems are likely to spring up like toadstools. For example, Earth Station Five—a company recently founded in the West Bank by a group of "Jordanians, Palestinians, Indians, Americans, Russians and Israelis"—offers users "the anonymity and privacy of Freenet without the hassle." "Resistance is futile," trumpets its Website. Meanwhile, many parents, pressed for the first time to discuss the ethics of file sharing with their kids, are discovering that they don't know what to say. Why, exactly, is it permissible to use a VCR to copy a copyrighted television program, but not to use a computer to copy a copyrighted song? (The answers have been outlined in the preceding pages, but they are neither obvious nor easily explained to skeptical teenagers.)[97]

In short, the battle continues. Complete victory by either side is an unattractive prospect. If the copyright owners succeed in shutting down the file-sharing services, the public will lose the most efficient and convenient system for distributing recorded entertainment ever devised. If the companies fail, the current mechanisms for compensating artists (imperfect as they may be) will further deteriorate, and, sooner or later, the production of music and movies will decline. Both trajectories are grim.

CD Burning

CD burners are devices that enable users to copy digital sound recordings (or other materials) onto compact discs. Versions suitable for business use became available in the United States during the early 1990s. The first model suitable for personal use, capable of making recordings at four times the original's playback speed, hit the consumer market in 1995, carrying a suggested retail price of $995. By 2003, versions capable of making copies at fifty-two times playback speed were available for as little as $40. Unlike digital audiotape recorders (considered earlier in this chapter), CD burners were eagerly accepted by consumers. By 2002, 120 million had been purchased and installed in the United States. Today, the large majority of personal computers come with such a device already installed.[98]

CD burners are used for a wide variety of purposes. Many consumers employ them to reproduce discs they have purchased—either to have backup copies on hand in case the originals are damaged or to have extra copies for use in their cars, offices, bedrooms, and so on. Others use the machines to make copies of discs owned by their friends, thus avoiding the cost of purchasing them themselves. (Both of my daughters have larger collections of copied CDs than they do collections of store-bought CDs.) Still others use their burners for so-called "format-shifting"—for example, copying downloaded sound recordings stored on the hard drives of their computers onto CDs, which they can then play in their cars or portable "discmen," or copying their older vinyl albums onto more durable and versatile CDs. A few of the drives are used by commercial pirates, who make many copies of commercial CDs and then sell them on the black market. (This is not so common in the United States, but ubiquitous in some other countries.) Some people use the drives to prepare copies of recordings suitable for use in teaching materials, parodies, and so on. Last but not least, some people employ them not to copy sound recordings at all but to make backup copies of other sorts of data housed on their computers.[99]

The legal statuses of these different uses vary considerably. Making copies of copyrighted sound recordings for use in teaching materials, scholarship, or parodies is almost certainly lawful under the fair-use doctrine. At the opposite extreme, the preparation of black-market CDs is clearly unlawful. The status of the common practice of duplicating commercial CDs for one's friends is not so clear; probably, however, it's illegal. (It clearly constitutes a violation of section 106 of the copyright statute, which gives copyright owners the exclusive right to reproduce their works. For the reasons explained earlier in this chapter, CD burners embedded in personal computers do not qualify as "digital audio recording devices," and thus my daughters' behavior is not immunized by the Audio Home Recording Act. Finally, because their behavior undoubtedly causes them to purchase fewer commercial CDs and thus impairs the normal market for the recordings contained therein, it probably does not qualify as a fair use. Bottom line: it's unlawful.) Format-shifting and the making of backup copies, because they do not impair the normal market for commercial CDs, are more likely to pass muster.

Most of these assessments remain tentative, however, because, with the exception of commercial piracy, the record companies have never sought, through litigation, to stop these behaviors. For several years, the companies tacitly tolerated all noncommercial uses of CD burners. When, in 2001, they decided that these behaviors had to be curbed, they looked for aid not to law but to technology. Beginning with Charley Pride's album *A Tribute to Jim Reeves*, they began to embed in their commercial CDs technologies designed to prevent them from being reproduced.

So far, there does not exist a single, standard CD copy-protection system. Rather, several systems, each developed by a different firm, have been employed at different times. All of them exploit somehow the differences between the error-correction technologies employed by ordinary CD players and the more sophisticated error-correction technologies employed by CD-ROM drives, which are used to "rip" the data that the CD burners then reproduce. But they do so in different ways. For example, the "Key2Audio" scheme, developed by the Digital Audio Disc Corporation, uses a hidden signature applied to the master copy of a commercial disc that prevents its offspring from being played on personal computers. The "Safe-Audio" scheme, developed by Macrovision and TTR Technologies, deliberately adds errors to commercial CDs—mistakes sufficiently small that they can be ignored by ordinary CD players but sufficiently large that they create audible pops and clicks in unauthorized copies. The "Cactus Data Shield" scheme, developed by the Israeli firm Midbar, includes in commercial CDs extra data falsely labeled as "music"; when copied onto another disc, that data, read as music, disrupts the sound. Finally, the "MediaCloQ" scheme, developed by Sunn-Comm, disguises the table of contents of a commercial CD, so that CD-ROM drives cannot locate the tracks to copy.[100]

In 2002 and 2003, employing one or another of these systems, the record companies began to release ever larger percentages of their products in forms that resisted reproduction. Initially, for reasons that remain unclear, they employed this strategy most often in Europe. But recently, it has been spreading in the United States.

Some consumers, insisting that they have a right to copy CDs, fought this change in marketing strategy. Enterprising souls discovered that some of the early schemes could be evaded relatively easily—for example, by using a black magic marker to obscure copy-protection information located in the outermost ring on a commercial CD or by holding down the Shift key on the keyboard to prevent copy-protection software stored on a commercial CD from being loaded into one's computer. As the schemes become more sophisticated, however, circumvention will become harder. And both the distribution and the use of software capable of unlocking the new CDs will be curtailed by the fact that such circumvention violates the Digital Millennium Copyright Act.[101]

For the large majority of consumers who lack the skill, time, or disrespect for the law necessary to evade the copy-protection systems, the new-style CDs have two major disadvantages. First, they prevent consumers from engaging in several activities that are either clearly or probably lawful. Second, because the encryption systems work by introducing errors into the stored musical files, CDs equipped with them commonly function less well than traditional CDs. Many are unplayable in DVD players, CD-ROM drives, portable players, and even some regular audio CD players. Some cause computers to crash. And analysts fear that damage to the discs from ordinary wear and tear, when added to the deliberately introduced errors, will cause them to begin to skip or otherwise malfunction sooner than "clean" CDs. In other words, not only can't you make backups of these discs, but also the discs themselves will fail faster.[102]

A few consumers have sought through litigation to curtail the distribution of the new CDs. In an early suit, Karen DeLise succeeded in forcing the manufacturer and distributors of the encrypted Charley Pride CD to relabel it (warning consumers of its limitations) and to provide refunds to any consumers dissatisfied with the product. A much broader class-action suit, alleging that the distribution of copy-protected discs violates a California consumer-protection statute and a variety of common-law doctrines, is currently pending in California court. Meanwhile, Philips Electronics, the owner of several patents on CD technology, has been complaining that the new discs do not comport with industry standards. Pressures of these various sorts may compel the record companies to label their encrypted products more clearly and, perhaps, even to stop referring to them as "compact discs." But the new products are here to stay.[103]

Enhanced PVRs

A personal video recorder (PVR) is essentially a digital version of a video-cassette recorder (VCR). Like a VCR, it is designed primarily to record (and then replay) films and television shows broadcast either over the airwaves or through satellite or cable systems. Unlike a VCR, it stores those recordings in digital form, typically on a hard drive. Some PVRs, such as TiVo and ReplayTV, are stand-alone units. Others are offered as accessories by satellite or cable services, such as Dish Network and Time Warner Cable. Still others, like Microsoft's Windows XP Media Center Edition, are embedded in personal computers designed specifically to serve as media and entertainment hubs.[104]

Most PVRs have features that make them substantially more powerful and flexible than VCRs. Their digital storage systems facilitate the recording of large numbers of programs. Purchasers of PVRs typically subscribe to guide services that assist them in selecting programs they would like to watch. Some of the machines will even pick programs for you, predicting your tastes on the basis of what you have recorded in the past. All permit viewers to "pause" or "replay" programs that they are watching "live."

Such systems first became available to consumers in 1999. Although highly praised by reviewers, they did not penetrate the consumer market quickly. The reasons for their slow adoption include cost (the stand-alone units currently sell for between $120 and $1,000), their apparent complexity and the corresponding difficulty of explaining their core features, and consumers' reluctance to commit to yet another monthly bill for a guide service. Consumers who did take the plunge, however, typically became passionate devotees of the technology. "Almost everyone who has [a PVR] becomes sort of a religious convert. They say it's a life-altering change, and there's no going back." Michael Powell, chairman of the FCC, has gone so far as to describe the PVR as "God's machine." The fervor of these reactions and the recent introduction of PVR functionality built into cable packages with no initial purchase cost lead most analysts to predict that consumers' hesitation to buy them will soon break down. By the end of 2003, they will likely have been installed in 4.3 million American households; by the end of 2005, in 17.6 million; and by 2007 in 38.9 million.[105]

The film studios were uneasy from the beginning concerning ways in which these devices might erode their revenue streams, but the aura of the *Sony* decision discouraged the studios from attacking the manufacturers and distributors of PVRs. In *Sony*, you will recall, the Supreme Court had declared that the manufacture and distribution of VCRs did not constitute contributory copyright infringement—on the ground that the use of those devices to time-shift broadcast programs, although a violation of section 106 of the Copyright Act, was nevertheless excusable as a fair use and that therefore the machines were manifestly "capable of a substantial non-infringing use." At the time (1984), there was considerable doubt concerning the wisdom of the decision. (Indeed, the Supreme Court Justices divided five to four on the issue.) In the ensuing years, however, the *Sony* ruling came to be widely viewed as sensible—even (in Judge Posner's words) "prescient." The close resemblance of the first-generation PVRs to VCRs suggested to the studios that a contributory-infringement lawsuit against the manufacturers of the former would probably fail.[106]

In 2001, the introduction of a new style of PVR changed their minds. The 4000 and 5000 series of ReplayTV machines contained two features that seemed to the studios new and especially dangerous. The "Commercial Advance" function enabled consumers to instruct their machines to skip all advertisements when playing a recorded program. The "Send Show" function enabled consumers to send to other Replay owners, via broadband connections, copies of recorded shows. The first of these features, the studios believed, would seriously impair the willingness of advertisers to pay to place ads in broadcast programs, which in turn would erode the license fees that the studios could charge the broadcasters. (The same claim, remember, was made in the *Sony* case, but now the studios believed that the threat was much more serious.) The second feature would undercut subscriptions to "premium" cable channels, rentals from video stores, and license fees paid by second-tier channels. (Why sign up for HBO, take a trip to Blockbuster, or watch TNT if a fellow Replay owner is willing to send you copies he or she has recorded of *Sex and the City* and *Law and Order*?)[107]

In the summer and fall of 2001, these concerns prompted four separate groups of studios and networks to file suit against SonicBlue, the company that had recently purchased ReplayTV for $40 million. The plaintiffs argued that the activities enabled by the new features constituted unlawful reproductions and distributions of their copyrighted programs, unprotected by the fair-use defense, and thus that the manufacture and sale of the machines constituted contributory infringement. These claims were by no means obviously correct. There was evidence that PVRs were having less impact on advertising revenues than the studios feared. The versatility of the new machines arguably would attract *more* viewers, some of whom would not avoid ads. The "Commercial Advance" function was not so different from features available on state-of-the-art PVRs. And SonicBlue could and did point to various noninfringing activities enabled by the "SendShow" function, such as transmitting home videos and photos to one's friends. In response, the plaintiffs expressed skepticism concerning the importance of these beneficial impacts and alternative, lawful uses—and, more ominously, suggested that the *Sony* doctrine might have to be reconsidered to take into account the dangers created by digital technology.[108]

The stage was thus set for a potentially far-reaching analysis, not only of the legality of enhanced PVRs, but also of the proper shape of copyright law in the new technological environment. Unfortunately, SonicBlue lacked the resources necessary to fight the battle up through the courts. In March of 2003, it declared bankruptcy. The following month, it sold Replay to Digital Networks North America. The new owner decided that discretion was the better part of valor and removed the features that had provoked the studios' and networks' ire.[109]

To sum up, eight times in the past thirteen years, an innovation—capitalizing in some way upon the new digital storage and playback technologies and the communicative power of the Internet—has offered consumers better or more convenient access to recorded entertainment. In each instance, the people that stood to lose from widespread deployment of that innovation fought back—through litigation, through law reform, or with technological countermeasures. Not all of these cycles have run their course. But so far, in each case the resisters have in the end prevailed.

There are no villains in this story. In seeking to protect their companies' sources of revenue, the resisters were merely doing their jobs. Nevertheless, from the standpoint of society at large, the net result has been disastrous. Most of the mechanisms upon which we continue to rely for distributing audio and video recordings are outmoded and inefficient. To the already large transaction costs associated with those mechanisms we have added huge litigation expenses. Partly as a result, the prices paid by consumers for access to entertainment remain unnecessarily high. Digital-rights-management systems, reinforced by legal bans on encryption circumvention, prevent consumers from making creative uses of the recordings to which they do gain access, impeding semiotic democracy. And tens of millions of Americans, frustrated by the foregoing costs and restrictions, regularly violate the law— an unstable and culturally corrosive state of affairs.

In short, we have thus far failed to redeem the promise of the new technologies. The remaining chapters of this book explore some ways in which we might do so.

4 Taking Property Rights Seriously

"No black flags with skull and crossbones, no cutlasses, cannons, or daggers
identify today's pirates. You can't see them coming; there's no warning shot
across your bow. Yet rest assured the pirates are out there because today
there is plenty of gold (and platinum and diamonds) to be had. Today's
pirates operate not on the high seas but on the Internet, in illegal CD
factories, distribution centers, and on the street. The pirate's credo is still
the same—why pay for it when it's so easy to steal? The credo is as wrong
as it ever was. Stealing is still illegal, unethical, and all too frequent in
today's digital age. That is why RIAA continues to fight music piracy."

Website of the Recording Industry Association of America.[1]

"There is no difference between pocketing a CD in a Tower Records
and downloading copyrighted songs from Morpheus. Theft is theft."

*Speech by Representative Howard L. Berman to the Computer
and Communications Industry Association, July 25, 2002.*[2]

Language like this is commonly used by representatives or defenders of
the industries adversely affected by the new distribution technologies. In addition to "piracy," "stealing," and "theft," unauthorized use of those technologies is often likened to "trespasses" and "takings." Implicit in this vocabulary is an important claim: that a copyright is a property right, and thus
that infringement of a copyright is equivalent to the seizure, destruction, or
invasion of a piece of property.

Some of the time, those who deploy this language seem to take the position that the legal system already treats copyrights just like property rights in
tangible things. More often, however, they appeal to the equivalence of copyrights and property rights in arguing for legal reform. In various ways, they
point out (accurately) that the law does not yet accord the owners of intellectual property as much protection as it accords the owners of tangible property. The law should be modified, they claim, to eliminate that disparity—giving copyright owners the rights and respect they are due as property owners.

There are at least three reasons to be skeptical of this line of argument. First, the vocabulary used by the industry representatives is of relatively recent origin. For most of American (and world) history, copyrights, like patents, were more likely to be referred to as "monopolies" than as property rights. Second, as we saw in Chapter 2, in many respects copyrights behave differently from property rights. To take just one example, property rights last forever; copyrights last only for limited periods of time. Such differences in scope are clues that sharply different social purposes are at work in the two fields. Third, property rights typically pertain to objects that are either unique or scarce, whereas copyrights, like patents, pertain to intangible interests that could, in the absence of legal intervention, be made available to everyone simultaneously. It is far from obvious that legal rules appropriate for managing resources of the first type would also be appropriate for managing resources of the second type.[3]

We will return to these three arguments in subsequent chapters. For the purposes of this chapter, however, you are asked to ignore them—and at least provisionally to take seriously the claims of the industry representatives that copyrights and property rights are alike, and that the law should recognize their parallelism. What sort of legal system—and what sort of entertainment industry—would emerge if we fully accepted those arguments?

Two related considerations justify trying to answer this question. First, an important set of legislative proposals, currently being debated both inside and outside Congress, is founded in large part on the contentions that copyright infringement is just like theft and that the law should strive equally hard to prevent or punish both. Before deciding whether to adopt those proposals, it would be helpful to know where they are likely to lead us. Second, the contention of Pragmatist philosophers that public policies should be assessed first and foremost by their consequences has considerable appeal in this context. If acceptance of the analogy between copyrights and property rights would have beneficial social effects, perhaps we should ignore our doubts concerning the premises on which that analogy rests.

A Sketch of Property Law

What, then, would entertainment law look like if it were reformed to parallel as closely as possible "regular" property law? To answer that question, we need at least a rough idea of the contours of "regular" property law. Fortunately, we won't need the sort of fine-grained understanding that a lawyer specializing in this field enjoys. But a sense of the major principles is essential.

Rights

Right at the outset, we confront a fork in the analytical road. Should we focus on the law of "personal property," which governs moveable objects, or the law of "real property," which governs land and objects (like buildings) attached to land? The fact that audio and video recordings are mobile might seem to suggest that the law of personal property would be more relevant. But, for two reasons, we'll take the second route. First, the law of real property is better developed and will offer us more useful analogies when considering possible reforms of the copyright system. Second, the protections the law affords land tend to be stronger than the protections it affords moveable objects. Thus, using the law of real property as our template will suggest a more sweeping set of changes to the copyright system. (We can always, if we think those changes are too radical, adopt a subset.)

What rights, then, are encompassed by ownership of a piece of land and the buildings that rest upon it? As one might imagine, there are several. Among the more important and stable of the "sticks" in what is conventionally called the "bundle" of the landowner's entitlements are the following:

- A right to "use" the premises
- A right of "quiet enjoyment"—in other words, a right not to be subjected to "unreasonable" noises, odors, bright lights, and so on from adjacent parcels
- A right to give, sell, or bequeath the land to others
- A right to keep other people out.[4]

The last of these entitlements—commonly called the "right to exclude"—is generally considered the most important. In the eighteenth century, it took center stage in William Blackstone's famous and influential paean to private ownership: "There is nothing which so generally strikes the imagination, and engages the affections of mankind, as the right of the property; or that sole and despotic dominion which one man claims and exercises over the external things of the world, in total exclusion of the right of any other individual in the universe." Two centuries later, Felix Cohen placed similar weight on the right to exclude in his pithy definition of private property: "[T]hat is property to which the following label can be attached: 'To the world: Keep off X unless you have my permission, which I may grant or withhold. Signed: Private Citizen. Endorsed: The state.'" Of the many ways in which state and local governments may interfere with property rights, the one that the courts consider most serious is curtailment of the right to exclude. So, for example, if a municipal government imposes a strict new zoning regulation on a sector of a city, thereby sharply reducing the value of the land in the area, it probably will not have to compensate the owners of the tracts for the economic injuries they sustain—whereas, if the government authorizes a cable television company to pound a few nails in the walls of apartment buildings in order to install its wires, it probably will have to pay the owners of the buildings for the unwanted "invasion" of their premises, despite the fact that the economic value of the damage is minimal. The primacy that the law accords the right to exclude can also be observed in popular culture. Nonlawyers, when asked what aspect of land ownership is most fundamental, typically point to the ability of the owner to keep others out.[5]

In the Anglo-American legal system, the physical zone over which a landowner exerts such powerful control includes not merely the surface of the parcel but also the earth below it and the air above it. Again, Blackstone:

> Land hath also, in its legal signification, an indefinite extent, upwards as well as downwards. *Cujus est solum, ejus est usque ad coelum*, is the maxim of the law; upwards, therefore no man may erect any building, or the like, to overhang another's land: and, downwards, whatever is in a direct line between the surface of any land, and the centre of the earth, belongs to the owner of the surface; as is every day's experience in the mining countries. So that the word "land" includes not only the face of the earth, but every thing under it, or over it.[6]

Thus, digging a tunnel under someone's land or entering a cave that lies beneath it is just as much a violation of the owner's rights as walking across it.[7]

Finally, a landowner's right to exclude encompasses, not only a right to prevent other people from intruding, but also a right to prevent other people from projecting physical objects into his or her space. Thus throwing a Frisbee through the air above a privately owned tract or allowing livestock to wander onto it would both be considered unlawful.

What happens if someone without permission invades a landowner's domain? In a wide variety of ways, the law will assist the owner in expelling and punishing the intruder. First, a court, applying the doctrines of "ejectment" and "trespass," will, at the request of the owner, both throw the entrant out and force him or her to pay monetary damages for the invasion.

That the owner should be able to invoke both of these remedies may seem obvious, but in fact is unusual in the universe of legal remedies for noncriminal misconduct. The victims of most kinds of injuries are able through the court system to collect money to compensate them for their losses, but not to insist that the wrongdoers turn over to them objects that they have wrongfully withheld. Suppose, for example, that I make a contract with a Honda dealership to buy a particular red Accord sitting in the dealer's lot. I promise to pay the dealer $15,000 as soon as I've obtained a loan from the bank; the dealer in return promises to sell me the car at that price. Three days later, I return to the dealership with the money in hand. The dealer tells me that, soon after I left, someone else offered him $16,000 in cash for the car, and that he has decided to sell it to that person. As one might imagine, the law under such circumstances will allow me to collect from the dealership enough money to compensate me for my injury. Indeed, I will be able to collect enough money to protect my "expectation interest" in the contract—in other words, the financial benefit of my bargain. For example, if I cannot now obtain an equivalent car elsewhere for less than $17,000, the courts will force the dealer to pay me $2,000—which, when combined with the $15,000 I obtained from the bank, will enable me to obtain a substitute for the car I originally wanted. But suppose that I want the specific car that the dealer agreed to sell me. It's still sitting in the lot. Will the courts force the dealer to make good on his original promise and sell it to me for $15,000? No. Unless there is something unique about the car, I am only able to collect damages.

The way that legal scholars describe this state of affairs is to say that, ordinarily, contractual rights are protected only by a "liability rule." That phrase means that a representative of the state will compel the wrongdoer to pay the victim a sum of money. In this particular case, the representative is a court, and the amount of money is determined by the magnitude of the plaintiff's expectation interest. But liability rules sometimes confer this responsibility on administrative agencies and sometimes use other criteria to determine the magnitude of the award. The crucial characteristic of a liability rule is that it enables the victim only to obtain money, not to insist that the wrongdoer turn over a specific object to the victim or perform a specific action.

Some legal rights enjoy a higher level of protection, known among legal scholars as a "property rule." Not surprisingly, the premier example of this class of specially favored rights is ownership of land. To illustrate, suppose that, for investment purposes, I buy for $100,000 a vacant tract in eastern Montana. Three years later, I visit the area and find that, after my purchase, squatters moved onto the parcel, built a house, and began cultivating crops. I demand that they leave. They refuse. Suppose, further, that a functionally identical parcel of equal size, located immediately adjacent to my land, is currently on sale for $120,000. If the law treated this situation like the broken contract, a court would compel the intruders to pay me $120,000, which would enable me to buy the adjacent parcel and thus would restore me to the financial position I was in before the intrusion—but would not compel them to surrender possession of my original tract. In the eyes of the law, however, this situation is not like a broken contract. Property is special. Every piece of land, it is sometimes said, is presumed to be unique. That attitude prompts the legal system to provide landowners a much more generous set of remedies than the victims of broken contracts. So, in our hypothetical case, a court at my request would compel the intruders to tear down their structures, restoring the land to its original condition; pay me the fair rental value of the parcel for the period in which they occupied it; and, most important, leave. If they threatened to reenter, the court would issue an injunction, forbidding them to do so.

The special legal status of property rights goes further. Breaches of contracts are not crimes. Deliberate invasions of property, by contrast, typically are. In almost all states, an intentional unauthorized entry upon fenced or otherwise enclosed land, or upon unenclosed land conspicuously posted with signs excluding the public, constitutes criminal trespass. This has two practical implications. First, a landowner does not have to bear the cost and inconvenience of enforcing her legal rights. She may call the police. Thereafter, agents of the state—the police and a prosecutor—will carry the ball. (The landowner may eventually have to testify in the criminal proceeding, but that is a relatively minor burden.) Second, the penalties for crimes are commonly more severe than the penalties for so-called "civil" wrongs. People who deliberately invade the land of others must pay fines that ordinarily exceed the value of any damage they cause; in extreme cases, they are imprisoned.[8]

Indeed, not only does criminal law forbid deliberate invasions of private property, but in most American jurisdictions, it also criminalizes the possession of certain kinds of devices used to invade property. Section 11.46.315 of the Alaska statutes is typical:

(a) A person commits the crime of possession of burglary tools if the person possesses a burglary tool with intent to use or permit use of the tool in the commission of
  (1) burglary in any degree;
  (2) a crime referred to in AS 11.46.130(a)(3); or
  (3) theft of services.
(b) As used in this section, "burglary tools" means
  (1) nitroglycerine, dynamite, or any other tool, instrument, or device adapted or designed for use in committing a crime referred to in (a)(1)-(3) of this section; or
  (2) any acetylene torch, electric arc, burning bar, thermal lance, oxygen lance, or other similar device capable of burning through steel, concrete, or other solid material.
(c) Possession of burglary tools is a class A misdemeanor.

Finally, under some circumstances, the law permits landowners to use "self-help" to enforce their rights. Not so with broken contracts. For example, I may not walk into the Honda dealership, leave a check for $15,000 on the counter, and forcibly take the car I was promised. But, if a neighbor's tree grows so that its roots encroach upon my property or its branches overhang my house, I may simply cut them off. And if a trespasser refuses to leave my premises, I may throw him or her out.[9]

Limitations

It should by now be apparent that real property rights are highly favored by the law. Both the entitlements accorded to landowners and the remedies available to landowners when their entitlements are violated are generous. However, property rights are not unqualified. Blackstone's characterization of a right to land as "absolute dominion" over it was an exaggeration even at the time he wrote, and is surely so today. Every one of a landowner's rights is subject to important limitations and exceptions.

For example, myriad rules and regulations curtail landowners' freedom to "use" their premises. Fire and building codes limit what they can build and how. Zoning ordinances limit what businesses (if any) may be conducted on the premises. The common-law doctrine of "nuisance" forbids landowners to engage in activities that seriously annoy their neighbors. As millions of nostalgic suburbanites can attest, even the privilege of burning leaves in the fall has been eliminated in most jurisdictions.

Landowners' rights to "quiet enjoyment" are similarly curtailed. They may insist that their neighbors not engage in behavior that would "unreasonably" disturb an average person. But, if a particular landowner happens to be especially sensitive to sound or light or smoke, he or she cannot stop the neighbors from emitting moderate amounts of them.

Many people think that a property owner's power to convey that property to others—during the owner's lifetime or upon his or her death—is absolute. But, in fact, it too is subject to important limitations designed either to enforce moral obligations or to protect the public interest. For example, the property owner is not permitted in a will to disinherit his or her spouse and is discouraged in various ways from disinheriting his or her children. And there are limits to the property owner's power to place conditions on the use of the property once it's out of his or her hands. For example, a landowner may not forbid someone to whom he or she gives or sells the property to convey it to someone else. And, landowners may not control too far into the future (very roughly speaking, past the age of majority of their grandchildren) who will inherit their property.

Even the right to exclude—the most celebrated stick in a landowner's bundle of entitlements—is subject to important limitations. For example, the right to the column of air above his or her tract is no longer absolute. The portion of that column above "minimum safe altitudes of flight" prescribed by the Federal Aviation Administration (one thousand feet in "congested areas"; five hundred feet in most other zones) is now subject to "a public right of freedom of transit in air commerce." In other words, planes may fly through it, even if the landowner objects. In many jurisdictions, landowners' abilities to exclude livestock are tempered by "open range" laws; unless they erect and maintain fences around their holdings, they cannot object if animals belonging to other people wander on. A traveler on a public road adjacent to a tract of private property, confronting an obstacle (a snowdrift, a fallen tree), may if necessary walk or drive onto the adjacent land to get around the obstacle. Other kinds of emergencies will similarly suspend a landowner's right to keep others out. Finally, the owner of a farm who employs migrant workers and houses them on his or her tract may not exclude healthcare experts or lawyers who wish to speak to the workers.[10]

The remedies that a landowner or the state may deploy to protect the right to exclude are also frequently qualified. For example, as a close reading of the Alaska statute (quoted earlier) reveals, possession of burglary tools is not, by itself, a crime. Only possession "with intent to use or permit use of the tool in the commission of" specific other crimes is illegal. The statutes of other states typically contain similar limitations.[11]

The remedy that is most sharply limited is self-help. When expelling a trespasser, a landowner is entitled to use only so much force as is absolutely necessary, under the circumstances, to remove him or her. The landowner may not use methods likely to cause death or serious bodily injury—unless the trespasser also threatens the landowner's personal safety, thus triggering the right of self-defense. Nor may a landowner install on his or her property devices that would cause trespassers serious injury—such as spring guns or high-voltage electric fences.[12]

A final limitation on the privilege of self-help is well illustrated by the famous case of *Ploof v. Putnam*. Mr. Putnam owned an island in Lake Champlain. Mr. Ploof was sailing on the lake with his wife and children, when a sudden storm arose. To save his boat, Ploof without permission moored it to the defendant's dock. One of Putnam's employees refused to allow the boat to remain at the dock and cast off the mooring lines. The boat was then driven by the wind onto a nearby shore. The boat was destroyed and Ploof and his family injured. The Supreme Court of Vermont ruled that Putnam must compensate Ploof for his various injuries. In the court's view, the emergency justified Ploof in committing what would otherwise have been a trespass (tying up to the dock without permission). Putnam was thus obliged to permit the plaintiff to remain there. Had the boat, by banging up against the dock, caused injury to the pilings, Ploof most likely would have been obliged to compensate Putnam for the damage. But Putnam was not entitled to expel Ploof to prevent possible damage to his possessions.[13]

The general principle latent in this decision is that the exceptions that the law carves out of landowners' right to exclude curtail not only their ability to call upon the courts and the police to expel intruders but also the privilege to employ their own efforts to halt or prevent intrusions. On the same principle, the owner of a tract of land located near an airport, annoyed by the sound of planes taking off, would not be permitted to construct a fifteen-hundred-foot tower solely to discourage aircraft from flying through his or her airspace. Nor might the owner of a farm on which migrant workers are living use guard dogs or fences to prevent labor organizers from entering. In sum, the privilege of self-help applies when and only when the landowner could invoke the aid of the state to keep others out.[14]

It's worth pausing for a moment to consider the reasons for this parallelism. It surely would be possible to organize the legal system along different lines. As legal theorist Wesley Hohfeld pointed out many years ago, one can imagine a system of rules in which each of two people interested in the same resource (Hohfeld's odd example of such a resource was shrimp salad) would have a "privilege" to try to seize it for him- or herself, but neither had a "right" to invoke the aid of the state to prevent the other from seizing it. Similarly, in this context, one could imagine a regime of property law that authorized intruders to enter private property under specific circumstances, but also authorized landowners to use self-help to repel the intruders. Indeed, one might justify such a regime on the ground that, just because the state has decided not to expend its scarce judicial and police resources in barring certain kinds of entrants from private land doesn't mean that the owners should be prevented from devoting their own resources to keeping the entrants out. Why does our own legal system eschew this approach?[15]

Two reasons seem to be at work. First, it would likely lead to expensive and potentially violent "arms races." Landowners would build higher fences; entrants would carry higher ladders. Landowners would deploy ever fiercer dogs; entrants would carry ever more powerful canine anesthetics.

Second, the rules of property law have evolved over centuries through the efforts of courts (and occasionally legislatures) to strike balances between important competing interests: on one hand, the many social and economic benefits that accrue when parcels of land (and hunks of other resources) are entrusted to the custody of individual owners; on the other hand, the serious harms that would arise if those owners did not sometimes subordinate their own desires to the needs of the public. The catalogue of exceptions to landowners' right to exclude consists of situations in which lawmakers, over time, have come to view interests of the latter sort as predominant. Landowners' concern that their docks not be damaged by unwanted visitors during storms has been deemed less important than sailors' personal safety. Landowners' desire to keep noisy planes out of their airspace has been deemed less important than providing the public safe and convenient air travel. And so forth. In sum, the line drawn by the law between owners' interests in keeping the public off their premises and the public's interest in entering those premises is neither arbitrary nor justified merely by the scarcity of judicial resources. Rather, it reflects the accretion over many years of lawmakers' judgments concerning which of those interests deserves primacy in which circumstances. It would make no sense to permit landowners with sufficient determination, money, and firepower to override those judgments through the use of "self-help."

Refashioning Rights to Digital Entertainment

Many of the rights and duties created by the law of real property find close analogues in the law of copyright. For example, copyrights, like rights to land, are both alienable and divisible. I am permitted to sell my tract in Montana to my neighbor, bequeath it to the Sierra Club, or divide my interests in it among two or more people (for example, by giving it to my wife for the period of her life and thereafter to my two children). Similarly, I may sell my copyright in the folk song I composed to a music publisher, bequeath it to my university, or divide my rights to it among two or more assignees. The exclusive rights enjoyed by a landowner are also echoed—albeit imperfectly— by the exclusive rights associated with a copyright. Thus, just as landowners may "use" their premises more or less how they please and may deny others access to the premises, copyright owners may reproduce, adapt, or publicly perform their works and may forbid others to engage in those activities. Finally, the many exceptions, designed to protect various public interests, that the law carves out of landowners' rights are paralleled by the many exceptions, such as the fair-use doctrine, that the law carves out of copyrights.

That said, the spokesmen for the record companies and movie studios are right in observing that in significant respects copyrights currently are protected less generously than real property rights. Five differences in their scope are most glaring. If we wished to place copyright owners on a par with landowners, each of these disparities would need to be corrected.

Public Performances

First, the owners of the copyrights in sound recordings still do not enjoy a general right to control performances of their works. Until 1996, anyone was free without permission to perform a sound recording publicly. Thus, as we saw in Chapter 2, when radio stations broadcast musical recordings, they were obliged to pay the music publishers who held the copyrights in the *compositions* embodied in those recordings, but were not obliged to pay the record companies that held the copyrights in the recordings themselves. In Chapter 3, we then saw how the advent of Webcasting prompted Congress to give the record companies a partial public-performance right—by forbidding unauthorized broadcasts in the form of digital audio transmissions. From the record companies' standpoint, that reform was of course better than nothing, but still did not give them the rights they believed they were due. In the companies' view, just as a landowner may forbid anyone to drill for oil on his premises, regardless of the technology the driller might employ, so the owner of the copyright in a sound recording ought to be able to forbid anyone to perform it publicly, regardless of the method by which the performance is transmitted. If we wished to model copyright law as closely as possible on the law of real property, we should accede to their long-standing demand.

Compulsory Licenses

The second major difference in scope concerns the remedies available to landowners and copyright owners. Recall that rights to land are protected (appropriately enough) by "property rules." In contrast to the holders of contract rights, who ordinarily can only collect monetary damages when their rights are violated, property owners can demand both damages for past harms and injunctive relief against future invasions of their exclusive entitlements. Put differently, landowners are almost never forced to surrender their rights for a price determined by the state. Rather, to enter or use their premises, nonowners must secure their permission, typically by paying a freely negotiated fee. And if landowners are sufficiently attached to their tracts that they are unwilling to permit access to them for any price, they may refuse to negotiate and simply deny entry.

In these respects, the owner of a copyright is more like the holder of a contract right than a landowner. As we saw in Chapters 2 and 3, the current law of copyright contains many so-called "compulsory licenses." In other words, copyright owners are forced in many circumstances to acquiesce in nonpermissive uses of their creations, so long as the users pay fees set by an administrative agency. For example, a musician is permitted to make a "cover" of my copyrighted composition without my permission provided he or she pays me 8 cents for each copy made of his or her version. Public broadcasting stations are permitted to play my song in the course of non-commercial broadcasts so long as they pay me a modest administratively determined fee. The same goes for jukebox operators who include recordings of my song in their machines and for cable systems and satellite carriers that receive over-the-air broadcasts containing my song and relay them to subscribers. Even the recently created right of the owners of copyrights in sound recordings to control digital audio transmissions of their works is burdened with a compulsory license. Thus, as we saw in Chapter 3, Webcasters are currently free to make noninteractive broadcasts of copyrighted sound recordings over the Internet, provided they abide by some administrative regulations and pay the copyright owners .07 cents for each listener who hears each song.

If we took seriously the claim of the record companies and movie studios that they deserve legal protections no worse than those of real property owners, we would eliminate all of these compulsory licenses. Copyright owners, like landowners, would be free to determine the terms, if any, on which they would grant access to their property. Thus, for example, if a PBS station, jukebox operator, or cable system wanted to make use of my composition, it would have to pay a price set by me, not by the state. And all Webcasters would have to pay the record companies freely negotiated fees to use their material.

Would strengthening the rights of copyright owners in this fashion mean that, in the future, each time someone wished to make use of a musical composition, sound recording, or film, he or she would have to request permission from its owner? Almost certainly not. Billions of individualized deals of this sort would have to be struck each day. The cost of making those arrangements would be prohibitive. Copyright owners, recognizing as much, would most likely set up private licensing organizations very similar to ASCAP and BMI (whose operation we studied in Chapter 2). Webcasters, jukebox operators, and other intermediaries would obtain blanket licenses from the new organizations, just as radio stations currently obtain blanket licenses from ASCAP and BMI. The net result would resemble the current situation in many respects—but would differ in one crucial way: the new private licensing organizations, guided by and acting on behalf of the copyright owners they represented, rather than a government agency, would determine the license fees that users must pay.

Criminal Sanctions

The third difference between the protections enjoyed by landowners and those currently enjoyed by copyright owners pertains to the role played by the criminal justice system. A person who walks past the "Keep Out" signs posted on the edge of my land triggers all of the private rights we have discussed thus far. But he or she also violates the law of criminal trespass. The result is that I don't have to expend the time, money, and energy necessary to bring a private lawsuit against the intruder, recover damages, secure an injunction against future entries, and so on. I can simply call 911. The police will come and arrest the intruder, and the courts will subsequently impose upon him or her a criminal sanction—a fine or, in extreme cases, imprisonment. Awareness of those penalties deters most potential trespassers from entering my land in the first instance. In short, public law powerfully reinforces my private rights.

In theory, copyrights are also buttressed by criminal sanctions. Title 17, section 506(a) of the United States Code provides the following:

> Any person who infringes a copyright willfully either
> (1) for purposes of commercial advantage or private financial gain, or
> (2) by the reproduction or distribution, including by electronic means, during any 180-day period, of 1 or more copies or phonorecords of 1 or more copyrighted works, which have a total retail value of more than $1000, shall be punished as provided under section 2319 of title 18, United States Code.

Section 2319, in turn, sets forth ranges of potential penalties for violations of these two provisions. The upper bounds of those ranges are formidable: repeat offenders of subsection 1 can go to jail for up to ten years, and repeat offenders of subsection 2 can go to jail for up to six years. In addition, defendants face the "forfeiture and destruction . . . of all infringing copies or phonorecords and all implements, devices, or equipment used in the manufacture of such infringing copies or phonorecords."

In two respects, the power of this provision has recently been increased in response to the growing frequency of copyright infringement over the Internet. First, subsection 2 was added to the statute in 1997 to catch people who engage in widespread infringement but who don't make a profit from their activities. (The trigger for the change was a judicial ruling that the operator of a bulletin-board service who distributed copyrighted software for free over the Internet could not be convicted under subsection 1, because his activities were not "for commercial advantage or private financial gain." The amendment to the statute designed to plug this gap was known as the

"No Electronic Theft Act.") Second, the United States Department of Justice has recently begun to devote more resources to the detection and prosecution of intellectual-property crimes. Until the mid-1990s, copyright infringement was virtually never prosecuted. In 1995, the growing frequency of violations, particularly over the Internet, prompted the Justice Department to establish the Computer Crime and Intellectual Property Section. Since then, rates of prosecution have increased significantly.[16]

Despite these reforms, however, the criminal copyright statute remains much weaker, in practice, than the law of criminal trespass. Three limitations deprive it of most of its apparent force. First, the Federal Sentencing Guidelines, as applied, sharply reduce the potential penalties for violating the statute. Even large-scale commercial pirates rarely receive significant jail time.

Second, only "willful" copyright violations can result in criminal liability. To be sure, in order to convict a person of *any* crime, the prosecution must prove that it was in some sense intentional. For example, a conviction for criminal trespass ordinarily requires proof that the defendant entered the property deliberately (getting thrown involuntarily from your horse onto someone's lawn will not expose you to criminal sanctions) and that the defendant had reason to know the owner of the land did not want him there (hence the requirement that unenclosed land be posted with "No Trespassing" signs). But a conviction for criminal copyright infringement requires more. The prosecution must show that "the defendant knew that his acts constituted copyright infringement or, at least, knew that there was a high probability that his acts constituted copyright infringement." At least one court has held that the result is to excuse someone who has an honest and good-faith belief that his or her actions were lawful. This heightened state-of-mind requirement would make it more difficult to prosecute people who download music and movies from the Internet—many of whom (at least until recently) have believed that they have both moral and legal rights to share recordings online.[17]

Finally, despite the increased interest of the Justice Department in intellectual-property crimes, the amount of government resources available to detect and prosecute violations of section 506(a) is tiny compared to the amount available to detect and prosecute trespasses on land. Hundreds of thousands of local police, state prosecutors, and state and local judges can be called upon to punish intrusions upon private property. Vastly fewer FBI agents, federal prosecutors, and federal judges can be called upon to punish copyright infringement. The activities of home, noncommercial copyists are especially unlikely to trigger law enforcement. (Virtually no one any longer credits the multicolored warnings that appear at the beginning of every home video that the FBI will get you if you misuse the tape.)

If we took seriously the claim that copyrights deserve the same protection as real property rights, we would eliminate each of these impediments to effective enforcement. We would modify section 506(a) by increasing the actual sanctions that violators could expect and lowering the state-of-mind requirement to match the kind of "general intent" that suffices for a criminal-trespass conviction. Most important, we would dramatically augment the law-enforcement resources available to detect and punish violators.

Strategically, the most important targets for such an intensified campaign would be the people who, as we saw in Chapter 3, knowingly permit their computers to be used as "supernodes" in the modern peer-to-peer file-sharing networks. With modest detective work, they could be identified. There are relatively few of them; thus the courts would not be overwhelmed with cases. And the volume of copyrighted material that they "distribute" almost certainly would satisfy the requirements of subsection 2 of the statute. A few well-publicized prosecutions, followed by even short periods of imprisonment, would undoubtedly go far toward discouraging people from serving as supernodes in the future. And that, in turn, could cripple at least the currently dominant versions of the P2P networks.

Burglary Tools

The fourth respect in which copyrights are protected less generously than rights to land involves the legal treatment of devices used to violate the law. Property law, as noted earlier, is buttressed not just by the law of criminal trespass but also by state laws forbidding the possession of objects commonly used to commit trespasses. Copyright law currently contains a few analogous provisions, but each has limitations. As we saw in Chapter 2, the doctrine of "contributory copyright infringement" has been construed by the courts to forbid the manufacture and sale of equipment that facilitates copyright infringement—but only if the equipment is not capable of substantial noninfringing uses. As we saw in Chapter 3, the Digital Millennium Copyright Act prohibits manufacturing or "trafficking in" devices that circumvent technological protections for copyright owners, but that rule is best understood as a supplement to copyright owners' power of "self-help" (a topic to which we will turn shortly). The spokesmen for the recording and movie industries argue that they need and deserve more—that we should find some way to block the sale and possession of the technological "swords" that the Internet pirates are using to raid the ships transporting copyrighted material.

How? One way, of course, would be to criminalize the distribution or possession of general-purpose computers. But no one is suggesting that we go that far. It would be the equivalent of forbidding the distribution or possession of crowbars, on the theory that they are sometimes used to break into homes.

A more plausible strategy would be to forbid the sale or possession of computers (or other devices capable of receiving or manipulating digital files) that did not contain a combination of hardware and software that would prevent them from being used in ways inconsistent with copyright law. Various legislative proposals based on this general idea have been introduced in Congress during the past few years. The most recent version, known as the Consumer Broadband and Digital Television Promotion Act (CBDTPA), would forbid the sale or transportation in interstate commerce of any "digital media device" (defined quite broadly) that did not contain "standard security technologies" prescribed by the Federal Communications Commission. Those "technologies" would be designed (either by a consortium of "representatives of digital media device manufacturers, consumer groups, and copyright owners" or, if they fail, by the commission itself) so as to track closely the contours of copyright law. For example, they would prevent the machines in which they were embedded from reproducing and distributing copyrighted recordings—but would permit users to make "personal copies" of broadcast programming "for lawful use in the home" and would also "take into account the limitations on the exclusive rights of copyright owners, including the fair use doctrine." (The proposal has many other details, but we need not explore them here; by the time this book appears, some other iteration will undoubtedly have supplanted this particular version.)[18]

Many observers have doubts that it is possible to design security systems that mimic so nicely the judgments of the federal courts concerning what sorts of uses of copyrighted material are lawful and what sorts are not. But the representatives of the record and movie industries, enthusiastic backers of the proposal, apparently think that it's feasible. Let's assume, for the purposes of this analysis, that they are right. If so, then the proposal would seem to have much to recommend it. It would prevent people from engaging in illegal activity—and only illegal activity. More to the point, it would provide an ancillary reinforcement for copyright law analogous to—indeed, even more precise than—the reinforcement that the prohibition on burglary tools provides to property law.

Self-Help

The fifth and final way in which the entitlements enjoyed by landowners and copyright owners currently diverge involves their privileges to engage in self-help. Recall that the law permits landowners to expel intruders from their premises. However, their privilege to do so is qualified in important respects. They may not use more force than is necessary to oust unwanted entrants and, in any event, may not use deadly force. And they may not rely on self-help to repel or oust persons whose entry onto their premises would be excused by one of the many public-regarding exceptions to the right to exclude. If, like Mr. Putnam, they ignore this limitation, they will be liable for any injuries the would-be entrants suffer.

Copyright owners argue with some force that they should enjoy similar privileges to protect their property. The context in which they have made this argument most forcefully involves the systems currently being developed by the recording industry to disrupt the operation of peer-to-peer systems. Frustrated by their inability thus far to halt through litigation the growth of unauthorized P2P distribution of sound recordings, the record companies recently began using "technical countermeasures" to discourage the file-sharers. To date, the most popular of these has been "spoofing"—the practice of flooding P2P systems with files that appear to be popular songs but that, when downloaded and played, turn out to contain either silence, garbled versions of the songs in question, or lectures concerning the evils of copyright infringement. A less common and more controversial tactic is "interdiction," which consists essentially of denial-of-service attacks on persons offering copyrighted songs on P2P networks. Software firms hired by the record companies are in the process of developing even more aggressive techniques. These include "freezing" (programs that lock the computers of file-sharers for minutes or even hours), "silencing" (programs that scan hard drives for pirated sound recordings and delete them), and even programs designed to delete noninfringing files found on file-sharers' computers.[19]

In the current legal system, "spoofing" is probably lawful. However, the legal status of the other strategies is more doubtful. Substantial arguments can be made that they violate both the federal Computer Fraud and Abuse Act and state wiretapping laws. Worries on this score have made the record companies hesitant to deploy them.[20]

Should they be lawful? Opinions vary widely. Commentators concerned with consumers' rights or with privacy of course argue no. At the opposite extreme, Senator Orrin Hatch recently suggested in a hearing of the Senate Judiciary Committee that antipiracy self-help measures ought to be permitted even if they destroyed a "pirate's" computer (a comment he later retracted).

In a somewhat more moderate vein, Representative Howard Berman once introduced in Congress a bill that would have immunized copyright owners for "disabling, interfering with, blocking, diverting, or otherwise impairing the unauthorized distribution, display, performance, or reproduction of his or her copyrighted work on a publicly accessible peer-to-peer file trading network," so long as such disruptive activities did not "damage the property of a P2P file trader or any intermediaries, including ISPs."[21]

Does the law of real property offer us any guidance in determining who is right? If our goal, to repeat, were to mimic the privileges available to landowners, then the unqualified power advocated (at least briefly) by Senator Hatch would plainly be excessive. Granting copyright owners the right to destroy pirates' computers would be analogous to empowering a landowner to use deadly force to expel a trespasser. Representative Berman's proposal seems, at first glance, much more promising. Its general spirit—to authorize copyright owners to use only so much "force" as is reasonably necessary to protect their copyrighted material—seems consistent with the spirit of real property law. And Berman's bill even contained a provision that would have enabled persons harmed through unnecessarily aggressive self-help measures to recover damages from the companies that deployed them—a remedy closely analogous to the one enjoyed by Mr. Putnam.

In one crucial respect, however, Berman's bill would have to be amended to sustain the parallelism with property law: technological self-help measures could not be deployed with impunity in circumstances in which copyright law would not forbid peer-to-peer exchanges. For example, as we saw in Chapter 3, Judge Posner recently suggested that using a system like Aimster to "space-shift" MP3 files—in other words, to transfer them from one's home computer to one's office computer—might well be justified on the basis of the fair-use doctrine. To track the corresponding doctrine in real property law, Berman's "safe-harbor" proposal would have to be modified so as to exclude technological countermeasures that blocked such legitimate activities. Designing such an intelligent self-help device would not be an easy task, to be sure. But we don't allow landowners to expel all intruders, just because it is sometimes difficult to differentiate rustlers from travelers who are avoiding snowdrifts.

With this one major qualification, it seems that the record companies (and Representative Berman) could fairly invoke the analogy to property law in advocating an expansion of the rights of copyright owners. That same analogy, however, suggests that, in another respect, the ability of creators and their assignees to rely upon self-help to shield their works has already been extended too far and should be pruned back. Specifically, through the use of encryption, copyright owners currently exercise control over their works far greater than copyright law would allow.

Here are some examples. The fair-use doctrine, as we have seen, privileges many unauthorized uses of portions of songs, movies, and books for the purposes of parody, criticism, and teaching. By encasing the publicly circulated copies of their recordings in technological wrappers that prevent recipients from copying or redistributing them, copyright owners can make such uses impossible or at least more difficult. The law also sets a time limit on the duration of copyrights—currently, the life of the author plus seventy years for most works. After that date, anyone is free to make any use he or she wishes of the formerly copyrighted material. But, by encrypting all copies of their creations, the copyright owners can extend the effective duration of their entitlements indefinitely. Finally, the protection of copyright law is currently not available for intellectual products that do not embody a minimal level of "originality." (Thus, for example, one cannot copyright the "white pages" of a telephone directory, on the theory that an alphabetical, nonselective list of names and numbers is not sufficiently creative.) Yet, through the use of encryption, the creators of such materials can, in effect, secure many of the protections that copyright law deliberately withholds from them.

When compared to the structure of real property law, this combination of rules is surprising and troubling. For two reasons, remember, we don't permit landowners to cast adrift boats moored during emergencies at their docks or to repel planes passing through their airspace. First, to permit landowners to employ self-help in such circumstances would lead to dangerous and expensive "arms races." Second, the limitations on real property rights are thought to be just as important as the rights themselves, and landowners should not be able to override them. Why, then, do we permit copyright owners, through self-help, to control a much wider set of activities than copyright law would enable them to reach?

Two possible answers come to mind. First, we have discovered an alternative way of preventing "arms races." Specifically, the Digital Millennium Copyright Act, discussed at length in Chapter 3, forbids the manufacture and use of encryption circumvention devices. (It's as if we permitted farm owners employing migrant workers to build high fences to exclude labor organizers and then forbade labor organizers to purchase or use ladders.) This seems, at best, an incomplete justification. At most, it addresses only the first of the two reasons why we expect the privilege of self-help to track the right to exclude.

The second possible answer is more plausible: the reason why we give copyright owners so much latitude in engaging in self-help is that we realize that "theft" is rampant and that the law of copyright law has proven ineffective to stop it. The Internet, seen from this angle, is like a stereotype of the Wild West. The relatively few sheriffs in the region are incapable of controlling the many bandits. To achieve some semblance of law and order, we encourage ordinary landowners to arm themselves, and we tolerate the excesses that inevitably accompany vigilante justice. Though rarely put so bluntly, thoughts of this general sort were in the air when the Digital Millennium Copyright Act was adopted and are still occasionally expressed by representatives of the record companies and movie studios.

If this is indeed the justification for the worrisome structure of the current rules concerning self-help, it invites two responses. First, if the law of copyright could be strengthened, we would have less need for vigilantes. Several of the recommendations outlined above for enhancing the protections available to copyright owners would seem to serve that role. In particular, harsher and more frequently applied criminal sanctions would go a long way toward deterring illegal uses of copyrighted material. Adoption of those recommendations would thus permit us to cut back copyright owners' privileges to employ self-help.

Second, even if we were unable or unwilling to reinforce copyright law, we could curb *excessive* forms of self-help. One way to achieve this would be to legalize the manufacture or use of circumvention technology when it is applied to encryption systems that do not respect the traditional exceptions to copyright protection, such as the fair-use doctrine. A more dramatic way —applying the principle of real-property law illustrated by the *Ploof* case— would be to impose sanctions upon copyright owners who use encryption to prevent others from making lawful uses of their creations.[22]

Is this technologically feasible? Is it possible to design an effective encryption system that respects the traditional privileges of the users of copyrighted materials? The representatives of the record and movie industries seem to think so—as evidenced by their support for initiatives like the CBDTPA, which, as we just saw, envisions the development of a standard security system that would respect users' rights. Some commentators concur. Dan Burk and Julie Cohen, for example, have proposed an elaborate regime that would first require copyright owners who wished to obtain the benefit of the anticircumvention rules to build into their encryption programs "automatic fair use defaults based on customary norms of personal noncommercial use" and then would permit a person unsatisfied by those defaults to apply for permission to a government agency, which, if it were convinced that the requested activity was lawful, would issue the applicant a "key" unlocking the security system. Complex, to be sure, but in their judgment workable.[23]

In short, it seems that it would be possible, albeit in some contexts difficult, to trim copyright owners' powers of self-help so that they could be exercised only in circumstances authorized by copyright law. If, as the representatives of the record and movie industries have urged, we truly wanted to
place copyright owners on a par with landowners, such an adjustment
would seem just as important as the expansions of the copyright owners' entitlements discussed previously in this section.

Effects

So far, we've been engaged in a thought experiment: What would the
copyright system look like if it were modified to parallel as closely as feasible
the law of real property? The primary justification for taking this analytical
path was the hypothesis that altering the legal infrastructure in this way
would facilitate the emergence of an improved entertainment industry. It's
now time to test that hypothesis. Suppose that the changes outlined above
were implemented. How would the world of recorded entertainment change?

For reasons that will become apparent, it makes most sense to approach
this question in two stages. In the first, we'll temporarily exclude from our
analysis one component of the cluster of reforms we've addressed—namely,
the legal requirement that consumer electronic devices be designed so as to
prevent them from being used in ways inconsistent with copyright law. In
the second, we'll add that one element to the mix.

So, to review, we're imagining that the laws pertaining to the distribution and use of audio and video recordings would be modified in the following respects: the various compulsory licenses that currently riddle copyright law would be eliminated; copyright owners of all sorts would enjoy
unqualified rights to control public performances of their works; the criminal penalties for copyright infringement would be substantially strengthened; and copyright owners would be authorized to use "self-help" to prevent consumers from reproducing, distributing, or gaining access to their
works when and only when copyright law would forbid such activities.
What would be the impact of adoption of this raft of reforms?

Opening the Market for Authorized Downloads

The most important effect would likely be a dramatic increase in the
availability of audio and video recordings over the Internet. For several years,
the record and movie companies have hesitated to make the bulk of their

collections available online out of a fear that unauthorized duplication of those materials not only would prevent the companies from making a profit from their online operations but also would corrode their traditional markets. For the reasons explored in the first half of this book, that anxiety seems justified. Increasing the legal protections for copyright owners to match those of real property owners would go far toward alleviating the companies' fear. Supplementing the civil remedies provided by copyright law with a credible threat of criminal sanctions—and the resultant suppression of peer-to-peer file-sharing services—would likely be especially influential. The deployment of legalized technological countermeasures—such as "spoofing" and "interdiction"—would further reduce the convenience of P2P file sharing. Piracy would not stop altogether, of course. Some degree of unauthorized duplication and distribution of recordings would undoubtedly continue to occur. But moderate amounts of "leakage" would not prevent the companies from making a profit. (Witness the continued strength of the software industry, despite the fact that, even in the United States, piracy rates continue to hover around 25 percent.) What the companies have long sought, reasonably enough, is a decent level of copyright protection. The outlined reforms would provide them that.[24]

How, more precisely, would the companies likely respond to the improvement in the legal environment? In the music industry, we would probably see a dramatic increase in the repertoires of recordings that the companies made available for permanent download through online services, such as MusicNet, the iTunes Music Store, and the resurrected Napster. Attracted by those offerings and discouraged by the diminished availability of "free" music online, consumers would likely flock to the legitimate services. (Polls taken during the heyday of the original form of Napster suggested that most consumers would be willing to pay modest fees for access to online music; now they would have no choice.) As we saw at the end of Chapter 3, the lawsuits recently filed by the RIAA against individual file-sharers have already diminished unauthorized P2P traffic somewhat and boosted usage of the authorized, for-fee sites. Adoption of the reforms sketched above would likely accelerate both trends sharply.[25]

Similar services would quickly emerge for films. Assured that, by making high-quality digital copies of movies available to consumers, they would not be shooting themselves in the feet, the studios would likely begin selling copies online or through cable and satellite systems. Instead of renting or buying VHS tapes or DVDs, consumers would be able to download movies to large hard drives in their computers or set-top boxes.

Pervasive Encryption

To date, most of the companies that have begun selling recordings online have used technical protection measures—commonly known as "digital rights management" (DRM) systems—to limit the ways in which consumers can use those recordings. For example, iTunes currently uses a relatively mild DRM system, known as "FairPlay," that controls as follows the ways in which a musical "track" downloaded from the system may be employed:

- The track may be copied to any number of iPod portable music players.
- The track may be played on up to three authorized computers.
- The track may be copied to a standard CD audio track any number of times. (The resulting CD has no DRM and may be reconverted to MP3, but this will aggravate the sound artifacts of encoding, since the resulting sound file will have been encoded twice.)
- A particular playlist within iTunes containing a FairPlay track can only be copied to a CD up to ten times before the playlist must be changed.[26]

The systems used by most other services—such as MusicNet—are substantially more restrictive.

Once the legal reforms outlined in this chapter were in place, would online distributors of music and films continue to rely on such technological shields? They wouldn't have to. For the reasons sketched above, the strengthened legal rights and increased opportunities for self-help would be sufficient to support a viable market even in unencrypted recordings—MP3 files, movies in DivX format, and so on. But three considerations would incline the companies to continue to employ DRM systems.

First, they would be able thereby to reduce further the amount by which the new market "leaked." To be sure, the technological shields would be no more leak-proof than the legal barriers. As we saw in Chapter 3, every encryption system that the companies have deployed to date has been "hacked," and even the most enthusiastic proponents of technological controls concede that a hack-proof system, even if it could be devised, would be too expensive to embed in billions of audio and video recordings. (Remember that we are ignoring, for the time being, technological shields built into the machines that copy or play those recordings.) But the fact that digital rights management would not be perfect does not mean that it would not be useful, from the companies' standpoint. The Digital Millennium Copyright Act, already in place, inhibits at least to some extent the distribution of technology capable of disabling encryption systems. And most people lack the skill, time, or determination to develop hacking technology themselves. The result: the majority of consumers, as Jonathan Zittrain suggests, would, like sheep, respect the technological barriers. A minority would not. Some, for fun, would strip the DRM codes out of the recordings distributed by the authorized services. (Indeed, hackers are already doing this with iTunes recordings.) But the legal reforms discussed in this chapter would curtail circulation of those illicit versions. In short, the companies would see technological protections and enhanced legal protections as complementary. Even in combination, they would not be perfect. But together they would keep the "piracy" rate lower than either could alone.[27]

The second consideration is that digital rights management would enable the companies to offer recordings in different forms to groups of potential customers with different tastes. For example, consumers who wished to watch a movie straight through once and only once could be offered—for a low price—a version that, like the old *Mission Impossible* tapes, self-destructed at the end. Consumers who wished to watch the movie multiple times but who had no interest in transforming it could be offered—for a moderate price—a version that lasted forever but could not be disassembled or reproduced. Consumers who wished to try their hands at modifying the film could be offered—for a high price—a version susceptible to editing using Final Cut Pro or other software. And so forth.

The third consideration (latent in the foregoing example) is that technological usage limitations would facilitate price discrimination. (We'll address that topic in considerably more detail shortly.)

A fourth consideration points in the opposite direction. To comply with the guideline developed in the previous section, the companies would have to build into their technological fences gates that would allow users to engage in "fair uses" and other activities privileged under copyright law. Designing and maintaining those gates could be difficult and expensive. Though troublesome, from the companies' standpoint, this requirement would likely not be sufficient to offset the other three factors.

In sum, for various reasons, in the new legal environment consumers would have access to many authorized Websites (and similar cable services) offering for modest prices an enormous variety of audio and video recordings, most of which would be subject to some kinds of digital rights management. Would this be a good thing? In many respects, clearly yes. For the reasons explored in Chapter 1, large cost savings would be reaped. Over half of the price of a CD or DVD is attributable to the cost of making it and getting it from the manufacturer to the consumer. In the new environment, those expenses would disappear. The new distribution system would also be vastly more convenient. No more waiting for the CDs to arrive from Amazon. No more trips to the video store. No more late fees. No more scowls when you tell your children that all of the available copies of the most recent animated film have been rented or purchased by other customers. At any time, you could instantly and lawfully obtain a clean copy of any sound recording or any movie ever made—in a format and for a fee that suits your tastes and your budget.

Who Benefits?

A worry: what would prevent the record and movie companies from appropriating all of the cost savings? The ways in which the record companies, in particular, have responded to analogous revolutions in the past are certainly cause for concern. The shift in the music industry from shellac "78"s to long-playing vinyl albums had at least one major benefit: the new containers were much less likely to break during shipment. Yet the record companies continued to deduct "breakage" costs from musicians' royalties— thus, in effect, keeping all of the economic benefit of the new technology for themselves. (Indeed, as we saw in Chapter 2, some still do so today, despite the fact that CDs are virtually unbreakable.) Another example: compact discs are easier to store and ship than records and cost little to make. Yet the transition during the 1980s from records to CDs as the dominant way of distributing sound recordings resulted in an increase, not a decrease, in the cost of an "album." The ongoing antitrust investigations into the record industry may, in the end, reveal the source of companies' remarkable power to appropriate the benefits of such technological advances—and might even force the companies to disgorge some of their gains. But in the meantime, we should perhaps not be so sure that the companies would pass along to musicians and consumers the economic advantages of online distribution. Nor, in view of the similar degree of concentration in the film industry, should we be confident that the studios would pass along to consumers the large potential gains of online distribution of movies.[28]

This is indeed cause for concern, but another factor goes some distance toward addressing it. Remember from Chapter 1 that other technological changes during the past decade have been loosening the big companies' grip on their respective industries. This is especially true of music. The costs of making high-quality sound recordings have recently dropped dramatically. The traditional, payola-ridden radio-based system for alerting consumers to new music is rapidly being displaced by new Internet-based marketing and promotional mechanisms. And demand for online music has been primed by Napster and its successors. All of these developments reduce the dependence of musicians on the major record companies. All that remains to set them free is a reliable business model—a way in which they can earn money by making their music available to customers directly.

The reforms outlined in this chapter would provide that model. Joshua Redman could, if he wished, set up a Website offering his recordings for sale. Initially, the setup would likely be straightforward: twenty-five cents per song, in whatever compression format you wish. (More complex arrangements will be considered in a moment.) Most of his fans, knowing that the recording could not be obtained more cheaply elsewhere, would buy the authorized versions. For a typical twelve-track "album," customers would pay $3.00, a sixth of the cost of a studio-produced CD. Redman would of course earn $3.00. Large sales at that level, even after deducting the (modest) fee charged by the operator of the server, would provide him an income substantially greater than he currently enjoys.

To be sure, not all of the money would remain in his pocket. To generate those sales, Redman would have to pay other people first to help produce his recordings and then to promote them. In the old world, those costs would have been borne (at least initially) by the record company with whom he had a contract. In the new world, Redman would foot the bills. But the rapidly declining costs of digital production technology and the increased efficiency of the Internet-based promotion systems available in this altered environment would keep those expenses at moderate levels.

In short, a new business model, made possible by the reinforcement of copyrights, would improve the lots of both artists and consumers.

Streaming

So far we've been focusing on downloading—the distribution of recordings by creating permanent copies on customers' machines. What about streaming? In particular, how in the music industry would the proposed reforms affect the emerging world of Webcasting? In some respects, the impact would likely be beneficial. Certainly, the compulsory licensing systems that currently organize that world leave much room for improvement. Robert Merges offers a general theoretical explanation of why. Efforts by government agencies to set the prices that intermediaries must pay for the right to use intellectual property, he argues, are typically plagued by three difficulties: the agencies lack effective ways of gathering the information necessary to estimate accurately the value of the rights at issue; the prices they set are hard to adjust in response to changing market conditions; and such regimes induce the players in the affected industries to spend large amounts of money seeking to influence the government decisionmakers. As we saw in Chapter 3, the manner in which the rates for nonsubscription, noninteractive Webcasting were recently set lends considerable credence to Merges's contentions. Eliminating compulsory licenses in the Webcasting industry and elsewhere would most likely trigger the creation of private collective rights societies along the lines of ASCAP and BMI. Those organizations would probably, as Merges indicates, be simpler, less expensive, and more responsive to the rapidly evolving industry. A clear improvement.[29]

Yet another, unexpected benefit would accompany the replacement of liability rules with property rules. Controversy currently swirls around how some of the new Internet-based distribution technologies should be classified, using copyright law's traditional taxonomy of entitlements. For instance, streaming audio or video recordings over the Internet typically results in the temporary storage in a "buffer" on the recipient's computer of portions of the recording. Should that activity be treated as a "public performance" of the recording, a "reproduction" of it, or an "incidental digital phonorecord delivery"? Another example: Should the delivery of downloadable files to many consumers simultaneously be treated as a "public performance" or merely the "distribution" of "reproductions"? The reason why the answers to such questions matter is that each of these terms corresponds to a different compulsory licensing system. Thus the manner in which each activity is classified determines who makes how much money. Efforts to answer the questions are currently absorbing the time and energy of several teams of lawyers—an unmitigated social waste. Under a property-based regime, such questions would be irrelevant. Copyright owners would issue (most likely through intermediaries of the sort sketched by Merges) all-purpose licenses to businesses (like Webcasters) that wished to make use of their creations. The license fees would be negotiated, taking into account the benefits to both licensors and licensees of allowing particular activities to go forward. Exactly which set of copyright entitlements are implicated by each activity would have no bearing on either the owners' willingness to issue the licenses or the magnitude of the fees.

So far, so good. But, again, we confront a cause for worry. As mentioned in Chapter 3, during the recent CARP proceeding, an expert witness testifying for the record companies argued that, if the companies were able to set Webcasting license fees without interference from the government, it would be rational for them deliberately to select levels high enough to force approximately two thirds of the existing Webcasters out of business in the near future. By pruning the weaker firms in this way, the record companies would make the Webcasting industry as a whole more profitable—and would make it easier for them in the end to buy up the survivors, achieving thereby a level of vertical integration resembling the movie industry in the early twentieth century. The reforms outlined in this chapter would make it possible for the record companies to pursue such a strategy. Indeed, they would not have to wait for the high fees to scorch the existing set of enterprises. They could simply use their new property rights to refuse to grant public-performance licenses to any independent Webcasters, instantly limiting Webcasting services to their own in-house ventures.

Though perhaps rational from the companies' standpoint, this approach would be disastrous from the standpoint of society at large. As we saw in Chapter 1, a large, independent, variegated Webcasting industry has many social benefits. It offers consumers a diverse array of music. It offers amateur Webcasters opportunities for creativity. And it provides musicians ways of alerting the public to their creations more capacious than the radio network. All of these advantages would be forfeited if the record companies first reduced and then took over the system.

Some comfort may be drawn from the declining market power of the major record companies in the new environment. If, for the reasons sketched above, musicians increasingly cut loose from the "majors" and began selling their recordings on their own, Webcasters would be much less vulnerable. To be sure, the musicians, who would now own strengthened copyrights in their own recordings, could if they wished either refuse to grant public-performance rights to the Webcasters or charge exorbitant fees. But the musicians stand to gain, not lose, from the cultivation of a vibrant Webcasting industry. So they would be far more likely to wield their newfound power in socially productive ways. In sum, the restructuring of the recording industry might eventually shield the Webcasters from predatory practices of the record companies. But, in the short run, Webcasting would most likely suffer from the reforms outlined in this chapter.

Fair Use

Other, even more serious disadvantages of the property-based model reinforce the worries just mentioned. The easiest to see are the flaws of the mechanism, outlined earlier, for preserving opportunities for fair uses of copyrighted materials in the new legal and technological environment. To review, we can expect that copyright owners in this altered environment would rely not merely on their strengthened rights under copyright law, but also on digital rights management to protect copies of their creations from unauthorized reproduction and distribution. That strategy risks closing off the socially important opportunities, traditionally shielded by the fair-use doctrine, for creative and critical uses of copyrighted materials. To preserve those opportunities—and to maintain parity between copyright owners and landowners—we examined various ways in which digital rights management systems could and should be regulated or qualified. The most ambitious and promising of those proposals was the one outlined by Professors Burk and Cohen. But even they acknowledge that their system would be far from perfect. In particular, it would be worse in two respects than our current situation:

> First, it would not foster the full degree of spontaneity enjoyed by fair users in non-digital media. Even a well-designed set of automatic defaults will not permit every use that a court might deem fair. Even a streamlined Internet-based procedure for obtaining keys will inhibit spontaneity and will impose transaction costs that users of non-digital media need not incur . . . Second, and more important, the proposal . . . protects privacy, not anonymity. Traditional fair users have enjoyed both. There is no central (or distributed) database containing their names and contact information. . . . In sum, the proposal is a second-best solution designed to make the best of a bad situation.[30]

In combination, Burk and Cohen acknowledge, these two unavoidable flaws would chill many of the creative and critical uses to which unencrypted copyrighted materials are currently susceptible. Adapters and critics of music and films would obviously suffer—as would all of the rest of us deprived of access to their adaptations and commentaries.

Creativity would be inhibited by other aspects of the system as well. Recall that section 115 of the current copyright statute permits any musician to make a "cover" of a musical composition that has already been recorded and distributed to the public, provided that he or she pays the owner of the copyright in the composition a modest administratively determined fee. It is because of this provision that the public is able to hear so many different versions of popular and jazz compositions. Section 115—like all other compulsory licenses—would be eliminated by the slate of reforms considered in this chapter. In the future, composers or their assignees would be free to determine how much they would charge for permission to make covers of their creations—or to refuse permission altogether. Would they grant permission? Maybe. But two factors suggest that the number of licenses issued would diminish. First, the fees would undoubtedly rise, and some cover artists could not pay them. Second, some musicians who compose and perform their own songs would probably wish to prevent other renditions from displacing their own.

The second of these factors illustrates a more general danger of the property-based model. The revenue that the owner of any kind of resource (whether a parcel of land or a song) can earn by granting someone a license to use his or her possession in a particular way is often substantially less than the total social benefits of the activity in question. This is especially likely when the activity would generate significant positive "externalities"— in other words, when it would benefit third parties in ways that the putative licensee cannot charge for. For example, a parody of a copyrighted song is likely to provide the public benefits (in the form of amusement and topics of conversation) that substantially exceed the profit that the parodist could make and thus the maximum license fee that the parodist could pay the copyright owner. The same is true when a government wishes to lay a public road across a tract of private land; for political reasons, the government would be unable to charge (either in tolls or in taxes) anywhere near as much as the benefits that would be reaped by subsequent users of the road. In situations of these sorts, the social benefit of the activity in question may exceed the owner's reservation price (the minimum amount that he or she would accept in return for allowing the activity to go forward), which in turn may exceed the maximum license fee that the person wishing to engage in that activity could pay. Under such circumstances, an owner who has the right to forbid the activity in question will demand a prohibitively high fee, and a socially valuable activity (that is, one whose aggregate benefits exceed its aggregate costs) will be blocked. To avoid such an outcome, it is common (though surely not universal) for the law to force the owner to grant permission—either for free (as in the case of parody) or for an administratively determined fee (as in the case of the road). Many of the compulsory licensing systems discussed in Chapter 2 that course through entertainment law have arisen to deal with situations of just this type. By eliminating those compulsory licenses—or by enabling copyright owners to evade them through encryption—we would surely increase the frequency with which socially optimal licenses were not granted.[31]

Price Discrimination

The last and the most complex of the likely effects of the proposed raft of reforms concerns the increased opportunities that they would provide copyright owners to engage in price discrimination. In Chapter 2, we discussed this issue briefly, when considering the "windowing" system used by film studios to increase their revenues. It's now time to explore the topic in more depth.

First, some background. Roughly speaking, price discrimination refers to the practice of charging different consumers different prices for access to the same good or service. Somewhat more precisely, it means charging different consumers different prices when the variation cannot be explained by differences in the costs of the versions of the good or service that is supplied to them. A traditional example of price discrimination is the practice of airlines to offer discounts to customers who "stay over" at their destinations for a Saturday night. The cost to the airline of supplying the service in question—the various expenditures necessary to carry a person in a plane from, say, Boston to San Francisco and back—is the same regardless of whether the passenger stays in San Francisco for a day or a week. The only reason for varying the price is to extract higher fares from people who are able and willing to pay more (in this case, business travelers, most of whom have expense accounts), without pricing out of the market people who are able and willing to pay less (in this case, tourists).[32]

Price discrimination increases a seller's profits. Why, then, don't all sellers engage in it? The main reason is that, with rare exceptions, price discrimination is only feasible when the seller both has some degree of market power and is able to discourage "arbitrage." Market power exists when there are no readily available, equally satisfactory substitutes for the good or service that the seller is offering. Arbitrage occurs when a customer who purchases a good or service at a low price is able to resell it (typically at a profit) to someone who otherwise would be obliged to pay a high price for it. To illustrate, the manufacturer of a patented drug for which there are no generic substitutes enjoys considerable market power. It can raise the price of the drug well above the cost of producing it without losing significant market share. But unless it can prevent purchasers of its products from reselling them, it will have trouble engaging in price discrimination. For example, if it charges low prices to customers in Mississippi and high prices to customers in New York (on the theory that the residents of those states are able and willing to pay different amounts), arbitrageurs will buy truckloads of the cheap versions in Mississippi and resell them in New York, preventing the manufacturer from collecting a premium from the New Yorkers. By contrast, arbitrage is not a serious problem for sellers of ice-cream cones. (The product is simply too perishable for arbitrageurs to buy them at low prices and resell them at higher prices.) But ice-cream parlors (at least in major cities) lack market power. If a particular store decided to charge higher prices to people wearing business suits or designer glasses (on the theory that they are able and willing to pay more), wealthy potential customers would simply go to another store on the next block.

Economists conventionally divide price discrimination into three types. In so-called "first-degree" price discrimination, the seller seeks to ascertain exactly how much each buyer is able and willing to spend for a good or service and then to charge him or her accordingly. Not surprisingly, this is the most lucrative of the varieties, but the conditions that make it possible are rare. "Second-degree" price discrimination occurs when the seller does not know how much different potential buyers are able and willing to pay, but induces them to reveal their resources or preferences, typically by offering them different versions of the good or service. For example, the price of a business-class ticket from Boston to California usually is approximately triple the price of a coach-class ticket (even without the Saturday-night discount). The separation of the two classes and the corresponding price differential cannot be explained by the difference in the airline's costs (the extra seat size and better food in business class). Rather, it is designed to induce price-insensitive flyers (typically wealthy tourists and business travelers with large expense accounts) to reveal themselves. "Third-degree" price discrimination occurs when the seller knows enough about the universe of potential buyers to separate them into classes corresponding roughly to their ability and willingness to pay, and then to charge each class a different price. Student or senior-citizen discounts are perhaps the most obvious examples. Enough context; now back to the problem at hand.[33]

The owners of copyrights in entertainment products often enjoy some degree of market power. (Fans of Bruce Springsteen's songs typically regard the compositions and recordings of all other musicians—even those as close as John Mellencamp—as imperfect substitutes. The same goes for Steven Spielberg's or Spike Lee's movies.) Some of the time, those copyright owners are also able to prevent arbitrage. (The primary variable here is the extent to which the first-sale doctrine prevents the owner from controlling resale or rental of copies of his creation.) The net result is that, in the current legal environment, copyright owners are *sometimes* able to engage in price discrimination.

Two important examples we saw in Chapter 2. The owners of the copyrights in films commonly engage in temporal price discrimination—first milking the market of especially eager or wealthy viewers by charging high license fees to first-run theatres (which, in turn, charge substantial fees for admission), then gradually releasing the film at diminishing prices in a series of secondary markets. Similarly, performing rights organizations, acting on behalf of music publishers, commonly charge high blanket-license fees to radio stations operating in large markets and lower fees to stations in smaller markets.

Adoption of the reforms outlined in this chapter would increase dramatically the scale and precision of the price-discrimination schemes that copyright owners could employ. Two of the legal changes would be especially important in this regard. First, the reinforcement of encryption and other digital rights management systems both would enable copyright owners to charge consumers whenever their works are used in a particular way and would frustrate arbitrage, by preventing consumers from reselling digital copies. Second, the elimination of compulsory-licensing systems would give owners much more flexibility in setting the fees that different groups of consumers and intermediaries would have to pay for access to their products.[34]

In this altered legal and technological environment, a wide variety of price-discrimination regimes would likely emerge. A relatively simple one would entail adjusting the prices of the different versions of a recording to reflect differences among their respective groups of consumers. For example, remember the hypothetical case, discussed a few pages ago, in which a movie studio offered for download two versions of a film: the first in a format that could not be altered and the second in a format suitable for editing using commonly available software. If, as seems likely, persons interested in the latter format are less price-sensitive than persons interested in the former, the studio could and should charge a much higher price for the latter—even though, because it contains fewer technological restrictions, it would probably be cheaper to produce.

Here's a somewhat more complex variation on the theme: Suppose that, instead of paying a one-time fee of 25 cents for a recording of a Joshua Redman song, I were allowed to download the song for free, but each time I played it, my player sent a signal (through either a wired or a wireless Internet connection) back to the intermediary who distributes Redman's music, which in turn charged my credit card a "micropayment" (say, .01 cents). (In effect, like the harp in *Jack and the Beanstalk*, the recording would periodically report back to its owner where it was and what was being done to it.) The pricing system could be even more refined: the amount of the micropayment could vary with the character, quality, and cost of the sound system on which I played it:

- .001 cents for a "walkman" or "Rio"
- .002 cents for a boombox
- .003 cents for an ordinary car stereo
- .004 cents for a luxury car stereo
- .005 cents for an ordinary home stereo
- .01 cents for a high-end home stereo

- .5 cents for a mid-sized public sound system (the sort of thing that a band performing at a wedding would use to play recorded music to the guests in between their sets)
- 10 cents for a concert-hall-sized public sound system

The purpose of these gradations would be to differentiate among users on at least two axes: how much benefit they were getting from each performance, and how much they could pay. Video recordings could be monitored in the same way, with the micropayments varying with the size, character, and quality of the screen on which they were displayed.

Yet another strategy—which could be used either instead of or in combination with the one just outlined—would rely upon information concerning the wealth and tastes of potential users. As suggested above, such information can sometimes be inferred from the groups to which users belong. For example, students and senior citizens typically earn below-average incomes. It would thus be rational for suppliers of entertainment products to charge members of those groups less than average prices. By contrast, people whose zip codes correspond to wealthy suburbs typically enjoy above-average incomes; suppliers could charge them more. Even more precise discrimination could be achieved if suppliers had access to data concerning the habits of individual customers. People who fly often to Europe (as revealed by their frequent-flier records) or who commonly buy swordfish for dinner (as revealed by their grocery-store discount-card records) ordinarily are able and willing to spend more for entertainment than people who don't. If suppliers could obtain those records and match them with specific customers, they could fine-tune the prices they charged.

Techniques of these sorts would plainly benefit copyright owners, enabling them to make much larger profits. Would they also benefit society at large? In two respects, yes. First, they would expand access to recorded entertainment. Currently, poor consumers cannot buy many compact discs, attend many first-run showings of movies, or subscribe to "premium" cable channels. The price-discrimination strategies outlined above would enable suppliers of entertainment products to identify such "low-margin" consumers and offer them discount prices. The suppliers would gain; they would reach new customers without eroding their existing markets. The recipients would gain; they could now afford many more entertainment products. Finally, to the extent that society at large has an interest in equalizing its citizens' access to informational products, we would all benefit. (Price discrimination does not have such uniformly benign effects in all settings. But the strong correlation in this particular market of consumers' wealth and their ability to pay for the product at issue, combined with the precision of the sorting systems enabled by the altered legal environment, would likely lead to this happy outcome.)

The second respect is related. As indicated, the suppliers of recorded entertainment already engage in some forms of price discrimination. But many of the existing systems are clumsy and socially costly. For example, the sequential release of movies (first in theatres, later in video stores, later on television, and so on) is an example of second-degree price discrimination. High-margin customers are offered (for a relatively high price) an "optimal" version of the product—specifically, a high-quality performance in a theatre at the time when they are most eager to see it. Lower-margin customers are offered (for lower prices) inferior versions—specifically performances months or years after they would most like to see it. The studios could, if they wished, eliminate this disparity, simply by making movies available in video stores and on television at the same time they are performed in theatres. As suggested in Chapter 2, the only reason the studios don't do so is to enable them to separate their customers into segments, based roughly on their ability and willingness to pay. In this respect, the studios' marketing strategy is no different from that of a laser printer manufacturer, offering customers two versions of its product—a regular version, for a high price; and an identical model containing a "go-slow" chip that cuts its speed in half, for a lower price. Price-discrimination techniques of this sort have obvious social disadvantages: they deprive many consumers of optimal versions of goods and services. By contrast, many of the techniques outlined earlier involve third-degree price or even first-degree discrimination. Instead of offering consumers artificially differentiated versions of products and relying on them to sort themselves, the suppliers of entertainment would gather data about their customers—either directly or by inferring their tastes and incomes from their other purchasing decisions—and then use that data to offer them identical products at different prices. The net effect would be to approximate more closely the ideal of "perfect" price discrimination. From a social-welfare standpoint, this represents a clear improvement.[35]

Sadly, these benefits would pale in the face of three other pernicious effects. The first is cultural. As Wendy Gordon has suggested, the world outlined above would have a distressingly granular feel. Each time you listened to a song or watched a movie, you would know that a tiny meter, attached to your credit card or bank account, was whirring. Each time you bought a lobster in an upscale grocery store, you would know that your "consumer profile" was being adjusted—and that, next week, the prices you paid for all entertainment products would be one notch higher. Awareness of these effects would likely make you more calculating. Also, perhaps, less altruistic.

Conscious that you are paying for each bit of entertainment you consume, you might be less inclined to "give back" freely to the culture the fruits of your own imagination. To most people, such a world seems unattractive.[36]

Second, creative and critical uses of entertainment products would likely suffer in this new environment. As indicated above, suppliers would most likely charge higher prices to people who wished to modify their products or incorporate them in other works. Cover artists, rap artists (who rely on digital sampling), and ordinary consumers who just like to "play around" with recordings, would all pay substantially higher fees. This price rise, plus inevitable imperfections in the rate-setting mechanisms, would sometimes place access to digital products beyond the financial means of such second-tier creators. Society at large, consequently, would lose the benefit of their derivative products, and opportunities for semiotic democracy would be curtailed. (Again, price discrimination does not invariably have this result. If conjoined with a substantial expansion of the fair-use doctrine, it could operate quite differently. But the system of reforms outlined in this chapter does not include such offsetting safe harbors.)[37]

Finally, when added to the many other opportunities to make money considered in this chapter, the ability to engage in precise price discrimination would radically increase the incomes of the creators of music and movies. The result would be a massive transfer of wealth from consumers to producers—much more than necessary to offset the losses that the producers are currently suffering or are likely to suffer in the future. That effect seems troubling in its own right. In addition, it would exacerbate the problem discussed at the end of Chapter 2—in which the large and highly visible incomes of "star" performers draw inefficiently large numbers of aspirants into the music and movie businesses. If that problem is bad now, it would become worse in the altered legal and business environment.

Eroding "End to End"

Let's take stock. In this first (and longer) stage of our analysis, we have considered the likely response of the entertainment industry to the following slate of reforms: the elimination of compulsory licenses; the creation of an unqualified public-performance right for sound recordings; a substantial strengthening of the criminal penalties for copyright infringement; and expansion of copyright owners' authority to use "self-help" to prevent consumers from reproducing, distributing, or gaining access to their works (specifically, when and only when copyright law would forbid such activities). These changes, we've concluded, would likely have several beneficial effects.

They would lead to large cost savings, increase sharply the availability to consumers of clean, authorized versions of audio and video recordings, enable more musicians to break free of the major record companies and make their music available directly to the public, and stimulate the emergence of private collective-rights societies more efficient and flexible than the extant government agencies. Unfortunately, these advantages would be accompanied by some regrettable effects. Creative and critical uses of audio and video recordings would be curtailed, the cost savings might redound to the benefit of the record companies and studios rather than consumers, and copyright owners would employ price-discrimination schemes that, in this particular setting, would on balance be socially pernicious. On the whole, this combination of features seems far from ideal, but superior to our current state of affairs.

Now add one variable to the equation. Suppose that, in addition to the reforms we've mapped thus far, Congress adopted a statute similar to the proposed Consumer Broadband and Digital Television Promotion Act, discussed earlier. In brief, such a law would forbid the manufacture and distribution in the United States of electronic devices that failed to recognize and enforce usage restrictions embedded in digital recordings by the owners of the copyrights therein. How would that alter the picture we have sketched thus far?

In the short run, its impact would be slight. None of the devices currently installed in American households contains such copyright-enforcing technology. Recent polls suggest that most consumers find such technology unattractive and would be reluctant to purchase compliant devices. Thus, until the existing stock of computers, set-top boxes, CD and DVD players, and so on either broke or became obsolete, the record and movie companies would reap only modest benefit from this reform.[38]

In the long term, however, the effect of this change would be enormous. Most observers think that a statute of this sort would be far more effective in controlling consumers' behavior than would digital rights management. Very few consumers possess the skills to circumvent hardware-based protections of this sort. Thus, once the existing machines collapsed or were superseded, the "piracy" rate would likely drop to near zero.

From the standpoint of the record companies and film studios (and perhaps from the standpoint of the creators they represent) that prospect is obviously attractive. All of the beneficial effects of the set of reforms we have considered thus far would be amplified. But a "technological lockdown" of this sort would have one other effect that would swamp these gains.

The hazard can be seen most clearly when set against the backdrop of one of the fundamental principles on which the Internet was built. Twenty years ago, Professors Jerome Saltzer, David Reed, and David Clark referred to that principle as "end-to-end" architecture. Professors Mark Lemley and Larry Lessig summarize it as follows:

> The e2e argument organizes the placement of functions within a network. It counsels that the "intelligence" in a network should be located at the top of a layered system—at its "ends," where users put information and applications onto the network. The communications protocols themselves (the "pipes" through which information flows) should be as simple and as general as possible.[39]

This structure has two major benefits. First, it's durable. It was originally designed to be resistant to a nuclear attack. Nowadays, we may care more that it is relatively (not perfectly) resistant to "cyberterrorism." Second, it fosters creativity. Tim Wu explains:

> The principle amounts to a salutary delegation of the coding power in the Internet structure to the designers of applications. It grants the maximum possible application autonomy, giving to the application writers the freedom to achieve application goals in whatever manner they see fit, and innovate whenever and however they like. And at the same time, by confining the network itself to simple functions of broad usage, the design avoids blocking out future applications unknown or unpredictable at the time of design.

The history of the Internet provides ample support for this hypothesis. The rates of technological and commercial innovation on the Net have been extraordinary. Many of its major applications—including electronic commerce, "instant messaging," and Internet telephony—were unforeseen at its inception. The utility and popularity of those applications, in turn, have sustained its phenomenal global growth.[40]

The key idea, to repeat, is that the center of the Internet (the systems by which data is packaged and the channels though which it flows) should be simple and open, while its edges (the computers connected to it and the applications that run on those computers) should be characterized by variety, experimentation, and freedom.

This structure is currently being eroded in various ways. Perhaps the most serious threat, as Lemley and Lessig argue, consists of the increasing power of the suppliers of cable-based broadband Internet service to control the information and entertainment delivered to consumers through the portions of the pipes that they oversee. The proliferation of firewalls and nation-specific content "filters"—for example, those designed to keep information about democracy off the computer screens of Chinese residents or information about sex off the screens of Saudi Arabian residents—threatens the structure in a different way.

The proposal of the record and movie companies that manufacturers of electronic equipment be obliged to embed encryption systems in their products threatens the principle from yet a third angle. If adopted, it would limit the technological options available to the manufacturers. Even more seriously, it would limit the versatility of the machines they make available to the public, which in turn would curtail purchasers' ability to experiment with new Internet applications. That the next generation of computers could not be employed to reproduce copyrighted recordings may not be so terrible. Much more worrisome, however, would be the design features that would be necessary to prevent the owners of the computers from reconfiguring them to circumvent those constraints. What sorts of new applications would be forestalled by those features? We don't know. And that's precisely why we should eschew this strategy.

To sum up, the proposal that, to protect the revenues of the music and movie industries, we mandate the inclusion of copyright-protection systems in electronic devices seems a manifestly bad idea—to be avoided if at all possible. If that one plank were removed, the raft of reforms that would result from taking more seriously the "property" rights of the copyright owners has much to recommend it. The world it would generate, though flawed, would be an improvement over the one we currently occupy. The next two chapters consider ways in which we could do even better.

5 Online Entertainment as a Regulated Industry

Private property rights, as we saw in Chapter 4, are always qualified with exceptions and limitations designed to protect the public interest. Likewise, all industries are to some extent controlled by governments—in the sense that firms participating in them must abide by myriad rules designed to protect the environment, shield their workers from injury, afford those workers fair opportunities to organize, ensure the viability of their pension plans, and so on. That said, some industries are subject to qualitatively different levels of supervision. In those fields—conventionally known as "regulated industries"—the government typically controls much more extensively who enters the business, what goods or services they provide, and what prices they charge.[1]

As we saw in Chapters 2 and 3, the entertainment industry for many decades has been influenced powerfully by a detailed system of copyright laws—and, during the past fourteen years, the complexity of those rules has increased. Nevertheless, some observers think that the industry is not yet regulated enough—that the major players have excessive economic and cultural power and too often abuse it. Adoption of the reforms outlined in Chapter 4, by further strengthening the entitlements of copyright owners, would amplify the critics' concerns and strengthen the case for intensified governmental involvement.

This chapter takes the tack the critics suggest. It asks: What would a more heavily regulated entertainment industry look like? What would be its merits and demerits?

Background

In the second and third quarters of the nineteenth century, railroads spread over the United States, rapidly becoming the primary mode of transporting both people and goods long distances. As the industry matured, however, it was increasingly characterized by practices considered by many Americans to be abusive. On segments where there existed only one railroad (typically short-haul, intrastate "spur" lines), prices were often perceived to be exorbitantly high. On segments where two or more railroads competed for customers (typically long-haul, interstate "trunk" lines between major cities), prices were lower but varied sharply among types of customers. Specifically, large-volume shippers commonly received heavy "discounts," and shippers of low-value goods (like coal or lumber) typically paid much less than shippers of high-value goods (like clothing). In the mid-nineteenth century, state railroad commissions were established in hopes of curbing these practices, but their effectiveness was limited by (among other things) their lack of jurisdiction over interstate shipments. In 1887, Congress sought to remedy this gap (and perhaps to protect the railroads from overly aggressive state commissions) by establishing the Interstate Commerce Commission. A series of subsequent federal statutes steadily expanded the power of the commission to ensure that railroad rates and practices (first interstate and eventually even intrastate) were just, reasonable, and nondiscriminatory. During the early twentieth century, the regulatory strategy pioneered by the railroad commissions was extended to other sectors of the transportation industry (ocean shipping, trucking, and finally aviation), the communications industry (telegraphs and telephones), and public utilities (electricity and natural gas).[2]

Until approximately 1975, each of these fields conformed to what Joseph Kearney and Thomas Merrill have helpfully described as the traditional regulatory model. Each industry sector was "managed" by a single federal administrative agency (sometimes working in concert with analogous state agencies). The typical agency wielded its power in four ways. First, it required firms to offer customers standardized packages of services and forbade them to discriminate among similarly situated customers in the pricing of those packages. For example, the early state railroad commissions sought to prohibit the forms of discrimination among types of shippers just described. Later, the Federal Communications Commission (FCC) encouraged telephone companies to offer customers, for a flat fee, an integrated combination of services—including local access, wiring inside their homes, and telephone equipment—and to forbid them to obtain any component of the combination elsewhere. Second, the typical agency regulated the prices that firms within the industry could charge—usually through periodic, massive administrative proceedings that evaluated firms' past investments and current costs and then reviewed their proposed tariffs to ensure that the firms were able to earn a "reasonable" rate of return but could not make "excessive" profits. Third, the agency regulated the entry of new firms into the industry. In wielding that power, the agency usually did not seek to maximize competition; on the contrary, the preservation of either a monopoly or an oligopoly was often thought entirely consistent with the public interest. New "certificates" permitting entry were ordinarily granted only if the existing firms were not providing the public "adequate" service. Fourth and finally, the agency permitted, even required, firms to use "cross-subsidies" to ensure that all groups of potential customers could afford the service in question. For example, telephone companies and public utilities were encouraged to charge urban customers substantially more than the cost of providing them service, in order to offset the higher costs associated with rural customers, and for similar reasons to charge businesses more than residential customers.[3]

In the last quarter of the twentieth century, this traditional regulatory model fell into disfavor. A few of the industries that had been managed on this basis (most notoriously, aviation) were truly "deregulated"—in the sense that the relevant administrative agency was abolished, and virtually all of the constraints on the behavior of participating firms were lifted. More commonly, however, an industry remained regulated, but according to new principles. Now firms were encouraged to develop novel packages of services and to price them at different levels for different types of customers. (In a few sectors, such as telecommunications regulation, a vestige of the traditional commitment to "universal service" survived, but now that goal was supposed to be achieved not through cross-subsidies latent in uniform prices but through the imposition of more visible and uniform "fees" on most customers in order to reduce the prices paid by favored groups.) Similarly, price regulation was curtailed. The rates charged by firms that enjoyed so-called "natural" monopolies in particular areas or aspects (for example, suppliers of local telephone service and carriers of natural gas and electricity) remained tightly regulated. But outside those zones, the agencies sought to keep prices down not through regulation but through greater competition, which they sought to stimulate in three ways. First, the agencies abandoned their traditional restrictions on entry into the industries and thus increased the number of competitors. Second, they required firms enjoying strategic power to "unbundle" the packages of services they offered their customers in order to foster competition in sectors of the industry "upstream" or "downstream" of the bottlenecks they controlled. For example, local telephone companies were required by the FCC to permit their customers to obtain long-distance telephone service or "customer premises equipment" (phones, answering machines, and so on) from unaffiliated firms. Similarly, large natural-gas suppliers were required by the Federal Energy Regulatory Commission to unbundle the gas itself, the service of transporting it through pipelines, and the service of storing it, thus fostering competition in each of those areas. Third, firms with strategic power were sometimes required to provide "interconnection" services to competitors. For example, electric transmission companies were obligated "to permit third parties to transmit electricity over the companies' lines (a practice known as 'wheeling'), and to do so under terms and conditions no less favorable than those offered to the transmitters' own generating affiliates." In extreme cases, firms in key positions were forbidden to enter closely related markets and even required to provide their products or services "at cost" to rivals, which could then "resell" them to customers.[4]

Kearney and Merrill summarize as follows the spirit of this new model: "Under the new paradigm, the regulator plays a far more limited role. Instead of comprehensively overseeing an industry in order to protect the end-user, its principal function is to maximize competition among rival providers, in the expectation that competition will provide all the protection necessary for end-users. . . . In effect, the agency becomes a limited-jurisdiction enforcer of antitrust principles, applying a version of the 'essential facilities' doctrine in a single industry."[5]

Our final example of a "regulated industry" is quite different in character. In the United States, the relations between landlords and residential tenants have never been managed by a single administrative agency. However, during the past quarter century, they have been subjected to a level of governmental control even greater than that found in the fields of transportation, telecommunications, and public utilities. The most sweeping of the constraints is the so-called "implied warranty of habitability." Residential tenants are deemed entitled to a decent place to live. What does "decent" mean in this context? Roughly speaking, a place that conforms to the local housing code. If a landlord fails to keep an apartment up to this standard, a tenant has a variety of remedies. In most jurisdictions, he can withhold rent payments, repair the defective condition himself and deduct the cost from his rental payments, or collect damages from the landlord. These rights are typically said to be "nonwaivable." In other words, even an explicit agreement by the tenant in the lease that he will be satisfied with an apartment that does not meet the pertinent standards of habitability, or he will be responsible for making the repairs necessary to keep the place habitable, will be ignored by the courts. Finally, a landlord may not retaliate against the tenant for asserting these rights—for example, by evicting him or refusing to renew his lease.

A variety of other rules supplement this central obligation on the part of landlords. For example, in many cities, rent-control ordinances limit the amounts that landlords may charge tenants—or, less harshly, limit the rates at which landlords may increase rents. "Condo-conversion" statutes frequently forbid landlords to oust tenants in their buildings in order to sell off the apartments as condominiums. Last but not least, landlords are forbidden to take into account, when selecting tenants or providing them benefits, a wide variety of "suspect" criteria—race, gender, ethnicity, religion, handicap status, and so on.

The historical forces that prompted these particular industries to be subjected to especially high levels of governmental control and that subsequently reshaped the regulatory regimes imposed on them are extremely complex. Among the factors were the shifting interests (or perceived interests) of the firms within each industry, their customers, and their suppliers—as well as the rise and fall during the past 150 years of various economic and political theories. But stepping back, as we must, from the details of the story, we can discern five related concerns that help account for the special status of these fields and that continue to color the legal systems under which they operate.

The first and most obvious is the proposition that, unless constrained, the holders of market power will use it to make more money than they deserve or need. As the previous chapter suggested, the term *market power* is conventionally defined as the ability of either a buyer or a seller within a given market to exert significant influence over either the quantity of goods or services traded in that market or the prices at which they are exchanged. In a competitive market, no individual seller or buyer enjoys such power. At the opposite extreme is a monopoly, in which one firm controls the production or distribution of a good or service for which there are no substitutes (such as the holder of the patent on a drug uniquely capable of curing a particular fatal disease)—and thus enjoys complete freedom in determining how much of the good or service will be made available and the price at which it will be sold. Most real-world situations involve more moderate amounts of market power—such as where there are decent but not perfect substitutes for the good or service controlled by a particular firm, or where the production and distribution of a good or service is controlled not by a single firm but by a small set of firms (oligopoly). For centuries, it has been understood that a person or company enjoying market power will be inclined to wield it so as to earn unusually large profits, and it has been widely thought that (with some exceptions we will consider in the next chapter) such conduct is both economically inefficient and socially undesirable.

Those convictions go far to explain why the industries surveyed in this section have been singled out. Most of them are characterized by concentrations of market power. The traditional way in which government responded to such a concentration was to limit the prices that the participating firms could charge. More recently, as we've seen, regulators have come to rely, where possible, on a different strategy: forcing the firms in the industry to behave in ways that facilitate the entry into the business of rivals and thus better approximate the condition of perfect competition.

The second factor is that, since the late nineteenth century, American lawmakers have taken the view that certain industries, though privately owned, are "affected with a public interest" and thus are properly subject to greater than usual levels of public control. The criteria that determine whether a particular industry falls into this basket have never been entirely clear, but the list supplied in 1923 by Chief Justice Taft is probably as good as any.[6]

> Businesses said to be clothed with a public interest justifying some public regulation may be divided into three classes:
>
> (1) Those which are carried on under the authority of a public grant of privileges which either expressly or impliedly imposes the affirmative duty of rendering a public service demanded by any member of the public. Such are the railroads, other common carriers and public utilities.
>
> (2) Certain occupations, regarded as exceptional, the public interest attaching to which, recognized from earliest times, has survived the period of arbitrary laws by Parliament or Colonial legislatures for regulating all trades and callings. Such are those of the keepers of inns, cabs and grist mills.
>
> (3) Businesses which though not public at their inception may be fairly said to have risen to be such and have become subject in consequence to some government regulation. . . . In nearly all the businesses included under [this third heading], the thing which gave the public interest was the indispensable nature of the service and the exorbitant charges and arbitrary control to which the public might be subjected without regulation.[7]

In class #1, businesses owe their existence to some special governmental act—such as the grant of an exclusive right to operate a bridge at a particular location. In class #3, Taft seems to be saying, the good or service supplied by the industry is a necessity rather than a luxury, and thus the public at large has an especially strong interest in its continued availability at reasonable prices. (Class #2 seems purely historical in character.) Either circumstance, it has been thought, warrants—as a matter of policy and as a matter of constitutional law—greater than usual governmental control over the conduct of private enterprises.[8]

The third of the five impulses that have caused these particular industries to be regulated especially tightly is a worry that they are especially prone to noxious forms of "discrimination." The kinds of discrimination at stake—and thus the foci of the enhanced regulations—have varied. In the context of landlord-tenant relations, the activity that government has sought to prevent is differential treatment of members of historically disadvantaged groups—blacks, women, handicapped persons, and so on. By contrast, the early railroad commissions sought to curb "discrimination" of a very different sort—in which small-scale or local shippers were charged rates much higher than large-scale or long-distance shippers. In the field of telecommunications, the concern has been that customers would be charged sharply different rates for access to the network; even if those differences were justified by variations in the cost of providing them service, they were thought to be socially pernicious. Underlying these divergent conceptions of "discrimination" are different versions of the notoriously ambiguous ideal of "equality." Some are rooted in modern Liberalism. Some are more closely connected to late-nineteenth-century Populism. Some echo concerns prominent in the eighteenth century that residents of rural areas enjoy rights and opportunities equal to city dwellers. The theme common to all is the notion that, in certain fields, it is both especially likely and especially troublesome that people would not enjoy equal access to an important good or service.[9]

The fourth factor is more technical. In certain markets, it has been feared, some players have disproportionate "bargaining power" and thus are able to take advantage of others. Sometimes, by "bargaining power" people mean "market power"—in which case this factor is just a restatement of the first one. But another, equally important meaning of "bargaining power" is disproportionate access to information or the capacity to process it effectively. In addition to the industries we have already surveyed, examples of markets that are widely thought to be characterized by such inequality are home mortgages and insurance. In both, a large number of relatively unsophisticated consumers confronts a small number of highly sophisticated suppliers. In the absence of governmental intervention, the former would frequently get duped—and would not realize it until too late. In some settings, this "informational asymmetry" can be remedied simply by conditioning the enforceability of deals upon full disclosure of all relevant data. Thus, for example, we require mortgagors, before we permit them to enter into binding contracts, to read and sign many documents alerting them to just how much they will be paying over the course of their loans and how severe would be the penalties for default. But sometimes this mandatory-disclosure strategy is impracticable—either because the information in question is too voluminous or complex, or because cognitive biases of various sorts impede the ability of the vulnerable parties to process that information properly. In the context of residential housing, for example, we fear that tenants will be willing to sign unwise leases no matter how fully their onerous terms are explained. The same goes for high-interest secondary mortgages and forfeiture clauses in credit sales of consumer goods. In such contexts, the only option is to regulate the content of the bargains that people may strike.[10]

The last and most controversial of the impulses that have defined and shaped this field is sometimes referred to as "paternalism." With respect to some goods or services, lawmakers believe that they know better what is in the long-run best interest of consumers than do the consumers themselves. Again, the residential housing market provides the best illustration. The nonwaivable character of the implied warranty of habitability is justified at least in part on the ground that, although some tenants may think they would be better off spending their meager incomes on food, cars, or entertainment than on decent apartments, lawmakers know better. The harshness of such a judgment can be mitigated by rephrasing it in the philosophic language of "future selves": when, many years later, the tenants forbidden to accept lousy apartments discover the many benefits to themselves and their children of habitable living spaces, they will thank "us"—just as will middle-aged survivors of motorcycle crashes who were forced by the government to wear helmets in their youths. But such analytical maneuvers are often thin disguises for a blunter posture: people frequently don't know what's good for them, and government must then limit their (contractual) freedom for their own good.[11]

Applications to Entertainment

Many people react with dismay or derision to the suggestion that government should regulate music and movies the same way it regulates natural gas. In part, this response derives from a general suspicion, common these days, of government regulation of any sort. It may also be connected to the fact that the most visible ways in which government officials recently have sought greater control over the entertainment industry have entailed efforts to tame its content—to reduce the levels of violence in films, to purge rap music of misogynist lyrics, and so on—efforts that to many observers seem threatening to freedom of expression. Most broadly, the response draws upon the view that music and films are not "products" or "services"; they are forms of art. And the last thing anyone wants is governmental control over art.

These objections will be difficult to overcome. In the end, they may carry the day. But, just as I asked you in Chapter 4 to suspend temporarily your skepticism concerning the analogy between copyright and real property rights, here I will ask you to suspend temporarily your unease concerning the prospect of increased regulation of entertainment—to test fairly the hypothesis that the lessons we have learned from 150 years of managing the transportation, communications, and energy industries might help us solve the current crisis involving digital music and the looming crisis involving digital movies. We'll begin by reviewing the five concerns, discussed in the previous section, that have defined and shaped the traditional "regulated industries" and asking which are relevant to entertainment.

The first of the circumstances that has traditionally triggered high levels of government regulation has been a concentration of market power. In both the music and the film industries, this condition can readily be found. Five record companies currently produce and distribute 83 percent of the recorded music sold in the United States. If mergers currently proposed or pending are approved and completed, the number of dominant firms may soon shrink to three. Similarly, the largest four film distributors control 66 percent of the North American market, while the largest seven control 90 percent of the market. In both fields, economies of scale (particularly with respect to distribution) create high barriers to entry. In both, the dominant firms have often collaborated in developing marketing strategies and setting prices. In the music industry, "tacit coordination" by the "majors" has created a situation in which the wholesale prices of CDs and singles rarely vary by more than a few cents across companies. In the film industry, since the 1930s, the relationship among the "majors" has ranged from "tacit collusion" to a full-blown cartel. Periodic efforts to use the antitrust laws to separate the players have had only modest long-term effects. Moments of genuine price competition stand out because they are exceptional. For instance, in early September of 2003, Universal (the largest of the record companies) suddenly announced that it would slash the prices of its CDs by 25 to 30 percent. Commentators asked reasonably, if Universal were capable of making such a dramatic cut and still earning a profit, why hadn't competition among the record companies forced prices down before? In sum, both industries are fairly characterized as "oligopolies."[12]

What about the second of the factors that traditionally have prompted governmental intervention? Would it be appropriate to describe entertainment as an industry "affected with a public interest"? At first glance, it

appears to have little in common with the traditional members of that class
—grain elevators, railroads, and the like. On reflection, however, both of the
criteria highlighted by Chief Justice Taft's definition of the class do indeed
seem to be present. First, the production and distribution of music and film
is heavily dependent on a prior grant of a "special privilege" by the government—namely, copyright. In most other industries, competitors are free to
copy one another's products. In the world of entertainment, such competition is deliberately suppressed. In other words, people and organizations
that create songs and films for which, in the minds of consumers, there are
no good substitutes are granted, by the government, artificial monopolies in
their reproduction and distribution—precisely the circumstance that Taft
suggested warranted greater than usual governmental control over private
enterprises.

The other criterion is more slippery. Can recorded entertainment be fairly
characterized as a "necessity"? It's surely not as essential to a decent life as
housing, heat, and electricity. Many people have long done without it. It
would thus seem the paradigmatic case of a "luxury." Remember, however,
our discussion in Chapter 1 of the cultural significance of music and film.
Recordings permeate our lives. In 2004, Americans will spend, on average,
roughly 852 hours watching broadcast television, 821 hours watching cable
and satellite television, 74 hours watching videotapes and DVDs at home, 12
hours watching films in movie theatres, 995 hours listening to the radio, and
244 hours listening to recorded music in other formats. That's a total of
2,998 hours—or approximately 8 hours a day, 365 days a year. (By way of
contrast, during 2004, Americans will spend, on average, roughly 145 hours
[24 minutes per day] reading newspapers, 101 hours [17 minutes per day]
reading magazines, 86 hours [14 minutes per day] reading books, and 103
hours [17 minutes per day] playing video games.) Not surprisingly, songs
and films color our conversations and our self-images. The increasing spread
of digital technology, by making it even easier to gain access to recordings,
will only enhance their cultural power. Critics of the amount of attention being devoted these days by both the news media and politicians to the record
business sometimes point out that, compared to most other industries (say,
textiles or biotechnology), it's tiny—generating a mere $12 billion in domes-
tic sales. True enough, but its cultural importance vastly exceeds its economic clout. The bottom line: for many Americans today—and increasingly
for people in other cultures—recorded entertainment has come to seem just
as important as food and heat. It is thus plausible for a second, independent
reason to treat the processes by which audio and video recordings are generated and distributed as an industry "affected with a public interest."[13]

By contrast, the third factor—the prevalence of noxious discrimination—until very recently had little relevance to the entertainment industry. Purchasers of sound recordings traditionally have faced none of the types of discrimination discussed above. Purchasers of all races and both genders could buy recordings at the same price. Except perhaps for the members of "record clubs," no one obtained quantity discounts. And no variations in the cost of providing people access to recordings disadvantaged subsets of purchasers. To be sure, some amount of discrimination among consumers could be found in the film industry. As explained in Chapter 2, the studios have long practiced temporal price discrimination in the marketing of their products—first releasing films at high prices in theatres, later at lower prices in video stores, later at still lower "prices" on television. But this practice was not generally seen as abusive. Buyers of tickets at theatres rarely complained that it was unfair to charge them so much more than the consumers who, a few months later, rented the same movie at Blockbuster.

Soon, however, this situation will change. For the reasons outlined in the previous chapter, the combination of sophisticated digital-rights-management systems, legal prohibitions on the circumvention of those systems, and the increased availability of data concerning the ability and willingness of specific consumers to pay for entertainment will make possible the implementation of highly refined price-discrimination schemes. The seller of an audio or video recording will know a great deal about you—the artists you most like, the amount of your "disposable income," your patience for and skill at haggling or bargain-hunting—and the price at which the seller offers the recording to you will reflect that knowledge. As suggested in Chapter 4, many observers react to this prospect with fear and loathing. In short, in the near future, the apparent need for government regulation to curb undesirable forms of "unequal treatment" in the entertainment industry will surge.

The factor with the relevance to the entertainment industry easiest to see is information asymmetry. As early as 1942, Judge Jerome Frank could remark, when arguing for a statutory interpretation that would protect songwriters from their own shortsighted decisions, "We need only take judicial notice of that which every schoolboy knows—that usually, with a few notable exceptions . . . authors are hopelessly inept in business transactions and that lyricists . . . often sell their songs 'for a song.'" Countless anecdotes from the recording industry make clear that performers, typically, are just as uninformed and inept as composers. Stories of young soloists or groups entering into long-term recording contracts from which they make little or no money are legion. More is involved here than the superior skill and experience of the record companies in negotiating deals; the vulnerability of the artists is reinforced by the fact that, as we saw in Chapter 2, the typical recording contract provides that the performer's income will be subject to myriad "deductions," the calculation of which is left to the record companies' accountants. In making those calculations, the accountants often show extraordinary creativity. The informational disadvantages of artists are not quite so severe in the film industry. As we saw in Chapter 2, the most prominent actors and directors, often represented by shrewd agents or lawyers, have considerable bargaining power. And most second-tier players are represented by unions. But it is still widely and accurately believed that, when cutting deals, the producers and studios usually have the upper hand.[14]

The final factor, as mentioned above, is the most controversial. Some readers will find entirely unacceptable the proposition that increased regulation of a given industry is justified by the fact that consumers of the product or service in question are not as good as government officials in determining their own best interests. But let's assume, for the time being, that the criterion is legitimate. Is it applicable to entertainment? The argument of Chapter 1 suggests yes. As noted there, among the many benefits of the new technologies for creating and distributing recordings is the potential for a dramatic increase in semiotic democracy—the ability of "consumers" to reshape cultural artifacts and thus to participate more actively in the creation of the cloud of cultural meanings through which they move. In the context of collaborative, interactive computer games, many consumers are already beginning to recognize and exploit those opportunities. Thus far, however, very few consumers of music or film have seen the possibilities for engagement in the creative process. If, as Chapter 1 argued, such engagement would be good for them—would enable them to live richer lives—then it may be necessary for the law (that is, the government) to regulate the entertainment industry in ways that keep such opportunities alive.

In sum, all five of the concerns that have traditionally been invoked to justify greater-than-usual levels of governmental involvement in the structure or operation of an industry are already applicable to the entertainment business or will soon be. Not all of these concerns will seem compelling to all readers. (The last, in particular, is likely to leave some readers cold.) But, in combination, they make a strong case for treating the production of audio and video recordings as a regulated industry.

Additional support for this proposal may be found in the fact that, although most observers are unaware of it, the entertainment industry is already regulated in many respects. For example, as we saw in Chapter 2, the fees that copyright owners may collect from many types of consumers of their products are controlled to varying degrees by administrative agencies or courts. The fees that the owners of copyrights in musical compositions may collect from noncommercial public broadcasting stations or the operators of jukeboxes are determined (in the absence of voluntary agreements) by arbitration panels. The rates and contractual terms that ASCAP and BMI may demand from organizations that wish to "perform" compositions within their collections are subject to supervision by a "rate court." The fees that record companies must pay composers and music publishers when they make and distribute "mechanical" copies of compositions are set through an administrative proceeding. The amounts that cable and satellite systems must pay to the owners of the copyrights in the audio and video programming transmitted through their systems are heavily regulated. And, as we saw in Chapter 3, the amounts that noninteractive Webcasters must pay to the owners of copyrights in sound recordings are now periodically reset by arbitration panels.[15]

But it is not just the prices that copyright owners may charge that the government oversees; it also limits in various ways the contractual freedom of participants in the industry. For example, the authors of most types of copyrighted materials (including songs and motion pictures) after certain periods of time may "terminate" any previous assignments of their rights to other parties. This power is nonwaivable. In other words, the courts will ignore contractual provisions purporting to surrender it. The avowed purpose of these termination rights (like that of the renewal rights they replaced) is to protect authors to some degree against their own folly. One of the few types of copyrighted works to which the termination right does not apply are works for hire. However, as we saw in Chapter 2, the same concern that musicians will foolishly sign away their rights in perpetuity prompted Congress to deny work-for-hire status to sound recordings. (A few years ago, the recording industry quietly secured an amendment of the copyright statute reversing that rule. The ensuing torrent of criticism prompted Congress to change the rule back quickly.)[16]

Finally, copyright law on occasion dictates how revenue streams of particular sorts are to be distributed. The only provision of this sort in the American copyright statute is section 114(g), which specifies that, of the money paid by noninteractive Webcasters for the right to broadcast sound recordings over the Internet, 45 percent must be paid to featured artists, 2.5 percent to nonfeatured musicians, 2.5 percent to nonfeatured vocalists, and 50 percent to the companies holding the sound-recording copyrights. But similar provisions may be found in the copyright laws of other countries. For example, a Greek statute provides that the pertinent portion of the revenues collected through a tax on recording equipment and blank tapes must be divided among the various contributors to audio or video recordings as follows: 55 percent to the authors, 25 percent to the performers, and 20 percent to the producers. What's the point of these provisions? Why not let the various parties sort out among themselves their respective shares? Implicit in such statutes is the (plausible) belief that, left to their own devices, the most vulnerable groups of artists would end up with little. Consequently, the government intervenes on their behalf.[17]

In short, entertainment is already regulated in significant respects—but not as thoroughly as the industries reviewed in the first section of this chapter. The increasing relevance of all five of the factors that traditionally have justified heightened governmental involvement in a field of private enterprise suggests that we should consider tightening the controls on music and film. The argument for moving in this direction would be especially strong if we adopted the set of reforms discussed in Chapter 4, most of which were designed to strengthen the rights of copyright owners. Why? Because, as our analysis of those reforms showed, their beneficial effects (facilitating the emergence of a "legitimate" online market in audio and video recordings) would be offset at least in part by some serious dangers of abuse. The most natural way of preventing copyright owners from abusing their newly enhanced entitlements would be, of course, by forbidding them to exercise them in particular ways.

Components of a Regulatory Scheme

The previous section argued for the presumptive desirability of a regulatory regime for recorded entertainment, but did not indicate what such a regime would look like. Now's the time to get down to details. In constructing a list of possible regulations, we should keep two things in mind: the set of probable misuses of enhanced copyright entitlements identified at the end of Chapter 4, and the kinds of restrictions that have proven effective in curbing analogous practices in other industries. That methodology points toward five zones of possible regulatory action.

Opening Bottlenecks

Recall that one of the central strategies of the style of regulation that has come to dominate in the United States during the past quarter century is to prevent firms with strategic power from wielding it in ways that inhibit competition in sectors of the industry "upstream" or "downstream" of them. That strategy would have many potential applications to the online distribution of recorded entertainment. For example, many observers fear that if nonpermissive file sharing were suppressed, and authorized download services such as iTunes flourished, the range of musical recordings available to consumers would shrink. Why? Because the major record companies, seeking to maximize their revenues, would insist that the new sites carry only material from the companies themselves. (An alternative route to the same undesirable situation supposes that the authorized services gain sufficient market power themselves that they, like Walmart and Best Buy today, are able to charge large fees for virtual "shelf space"—fees that only the major record companies could afford.) To prevent this outcome, we could compel all download services to carry in their catalogues every sound recording that any copyright owner submits to them, and forbid them to discriminate among suppliers either in the prices they charge to consumers for different songs or the percentage of the purchase price turned over to the copyright owner. (To illustrate, if iTunes offers consumers a four-minute Grateful Dead recording for $1 and, for each download, pays Warner Bros. 50 cents, it must offer consumers my four-minute ballad for $1 and, for each download, pay me 50 cents.) The same principle would be applied to Websites offering films for download.[18]

Adoption of this strategy would have two related benefits. First, it would foster greater competition among potential creators of recorded entertainment. Second, it would promote diversity in the forms of entertainment available to consumers—one of the long-standing goals, you will recall, of government regulation in the closely related field of telecommunications regulation.

For similar reasons, we could forbid the record companies to leverage their power in the market for sound recordings into control over the market for interactive Webcasting. Currently, the record companies are required to make their recordings available to *noninteractive* Webcasters for governmentally determined fees. But they are free to demand whatever fees they wish from Webcasters who want to stream music to consumers "on demand." Some observers think that the companies are abusing this power. A relatively nonintrusive solution to the problem would be to impose on the record companies the equivalent of a "most-favored-nation" duty. In other words, they must offer to all interactive Webcasters deals as generous as the deals they offer to their most favored commercial partners. Again, the result would be both to foster competition among Webcasters and to enrich the array of material available to the public.[19]

In the future, the general principle that underlies these two examples could be extended to other aspects of the industry. Whenever one or a few firms acquire strategic power over a particular aspect of the creation or distribution process, we would compel it or them to behave in ways that preserve or increase competition in adjacent aspects.

Resisting "Integration"

The approach just outlined has a potential flaw, however. Suppose—to return to the Webcasting example—that all five record companies responded to the "most-favored-nation" rule by refusing to license their catalogues to any independent interactive Webcasters, instead setting up their own "in-house" on-demand streaming services. (If they acted in concert, they might run afoul of existing antitrust laws. But if each set up its own service—or if they divided into two clumps as they did when establishing MusicNet and Pressplay—they could avoid that particular hazard.) Plainly, both competition and diversity would suffer.

One possible retort is that musicians unaffiliated with the major record companies could respond to such a lockout by setting up their own interactive Webcasting services—and thus make their own material available to the world over the Internet. True enough, but consumers, when deciding which on-demand streaming system(s) to sign up for naturally gravitate toward the sites offering the largest percentages of the material they want to listen to. That inclination would make it very hard for nonaffiliated interactive services to compete effectively.

For guidance in dealing with this danger—and similar risks in analogous contexts—we might look to the history of telecommunications regulation. Since the 1930s, the Federal Communications Commission has sought to increase the diversity of both radio and television programming available to American consumers. The commission's conception of diversity has included, among other things, variety among the viewpoints represented in broadcast programs and the continued availability of shows attentive to local news and concerns. The commission has used three different tools in trying to achieve this end. First, it has forbidden any one company to own or control an excessive number of media outlets. For example, the National Television Ownership Rules have limited the number of stations that a single company may own nationwide, the Local Ownership Rules have limited the number of television stations within a given local market that may be commonly owned, and the Cross Ownership Rules have limited the number of outlets of different sorts (television stations, radio stations, and newspapers) that may be commonly owned within a given market. Second, the commission adopted so-called Prime-Time Access Rules (PTARs), forbidding television stations affiliated with the major networks to broadcast more than three hours of network-produced programming during the four-hour prime-time slot, in hopes of providing a "healthy impetus to the development of independent program sources, with concomitant benefits in an increased supply of programs for independent (and, indeed, affiliated) stations." Third, also in hopes of preserving the viability of independent stations, the commission adopted so-called "Fin/Syn" rules, forbidding the television networks to syndicate network-produced programs on independent stations or to purchase syndication rights to programs that they had obtained from outside producers.[20]

In recent years, the dramatic expansion of the range of programming caused by the spread of cable and satellite services, combined with growing hostility toward government management of the media and increased receptivity to the need to promote greater efficiency in the broadcast industry (sentiments manifested most clearly in the Telecommunications Act of 1996), has prompted the commission to reduce sharply the stringency of these controls. The Fin/Syn rules were first softened and then, in 1993, repealed altogether. The PTARs were repealed in 1995. And the media-concentration rules have been steadily softened. To be sure, the government has not abandoned its pursuit of "diversity" altogether. For example, it continues to forbid a merger among the top four television networks and to ban any one network from acquiring so many stations that it could reach more than 45 percent of the national television audience. And, the most recent move by the commission to weaken even further the Local Ownership Rules provoked a backlash in the Congress. But the modern trend has plainly been toward deregulation.[21]

The emergent market for the distribution of audio and video recordings over the Internet, however, differs from television and radio broadcasting in a crucial respect. Most of the FCC's recent deregulatory initiatives have been powered by its finding that the market for the production of broadcast programming is no longer concentrated—and, indeed, is becoming increasingly competitive. By contrast, in recent years, the markets for the production and distribution of audio and video recordings have become increasingly concentrated—and, for the reasons outlined previously, the strengthening of the copyrights of the dominant firms is likely to accelerate that trend. Thus diversity-enhancing rules of the sort pioneered by the FCC, though less and less appropriate in the context of television and radio broadcasting, may be just what we need to foster competition and diversity in recorded entertainment.

Following are some possible examples. An extreme (but effective) response to the evasive maneuver described at the outset of this subsection would be to forbid record companies to own or operate interactive or noninteractive Webcasting services. A less severe rule (modeled on the media-concentration regulations) would forbid the record companies to own or operate more than 50 percent of interactive or noninteractive services. In conjunction with the "most-favored-nation" principle discussed above, the latter rule would ensure the availability to consumers of unaffiliated Webcasters offering comprehensive collections of recordings—because to set up their own systems, the record companies would have to offer equally favorable licenses to an equal number of independent companies. Similar rules would govern the relations between the major film studios and services offering on-demand access to movies.

The most draconian variation on this theme would draw inspiration from the now-defunct PTARs. Noninteractive Webcasters (the Internet equivalent of radio stations) might be required to include in their programming a certain percentage of recordings produced by musicians unaffiliated with the major record companies. The result, of course, would be to force the virtual disk jockeys to be more imaginative in their programming and to increase dramatically the ability of independent musicians to reach large audiences. At this point, however, such a dramatic move is probably unnecessary. As Chapter 1 showed, the range of material available on independent Webcasting stations is already extraordinary. For the foreseeable future, all we would need to do in order to preserve the diversity of recordings available to the public is to ensure that the independent stations can survive and flourish. The less intrusive regulations outlined above should be sufficient to do the job.

Mandatory Distribution of Revenues

Suppose that, like Jerome Frank, we were persuaded that most of the primary creators of recorded entertainment—composers, performers, and actors—lacked the knowledge, experience, or skill necessary to defend their interests effectively when negotiating with the primary intermediaries. Suppose, further, that we concluded that no amount of mandatory disclosure (documents telling them precisely how biased are the contracts they are asked to sign) would prevent them from behaving foolishly. What might we do?

One response, suggested by section 114(g) of the current copyright statute, would be to dictate the shares of the revenues generated by specific uses of copyrighted recordings that must go to specific groups of contributors—and then forbid the relevant parties to alter those shares by contract. For example, loosely tracking the regime currently applicable to noninteractive Webcasting, we might require that the money paid out by on-demand Webcasting services or authorized download services be distributed as follows:

17 percent to the composers of the recordings; 17 percent to the music publishers holding the copyrights to the compositions; 30 percent to the musicians featured on the recordings; 2 percent to the nonfeatured musicians; 2 percent to the nonfeatured vocalists; and 32 percent to the companies holding the sound-recording copyrights.

Application of the same principle to the film industry would be both more difficult and less imperative. As Chapter 2 showed, a much more complex array of people participate in the creation of the typical movie than participate in the creation of the typical song. Determining a formula that fairly took into account their relative contributions would be very hard. In addition, "star" actors and directors plainly already have sufficient bargaining power and do not need the aid of a mandatory distribution scheme. Against this backdrop, regulation of the allocation of shares of the revenues generated by the online distribution of films, if appropriate at all, would have to be less detailed than the scheme applicable to music. For example, one might imagine a rule specifying the minimum percentage that goes to all contributors to the venture other than the producer, director, and lead actors.

An incidental advantage of systems of this sort is that, if made public, they might help reduce the complacency with which consumers currently engage in unauthorized downloading of recordings. Nowadays, most consumers pay little heed to solemn statements from the RIAA and MPAA that unauthorized downloads hurt their favorite artists—in large part, because they think that very little of the money that record companies and studios collect through legitimate distribution channels actually ends up in artists' pockets. (In 2003, public-service announcements interspersed among the previews shown in American movie theatres depicted set designers and other minor participants in the filmmaking industry pleading with the audience to stop downloading films. In most theatres, such ads elicited laughter from the audience. Why? Because most moviegoers simply don't believe that a reduction in downloading would redound to the benefit of set designers.) If consumers knew that if they paid a modest sum to obtain online a copy of a song or film, the true creators of it would earn a specified share of that sum, they might be more willing to do so.

Prohibit Price Discrimination

Chapter 4 showed how and why, in the new informational environment, companies holding the copyrights in movies or songs for which there are no close substitutes are likely, especially if we reinforce their legal and technological powers, to engage in more aggressive forms of price discrimination. In other words, they will gather information concerning the ability and willingness of specific consumers (or groups of consumers) to pay for access to their works, and will vary their prices accordingly. Consumers who live in good neighborhoods, have little leisure time, have shown themselves to be price-insensitive in the past, or love recorded entertainment will pay substantially more than consumers who don't fit into these categories. And each purchasing decision will alter a consumer's profile—and thus change the prices that are offered to him or her in the future. Chapter 4 also concluded, at least provisionally, that this practice, although it has some substantial economic and social advantages, on balance is culturally corrosive and should be prevented.

In selecting a mechanism for meeting this danger, we should pay heed to the history of the Robinson-Patman Act, the primary vehicle by which antitrust law has sought in the past to limit price discrimination. Enacted in 1936, that statute ostensibly forbids sellers "either directly or indirectly, to discriminate in price between different purchasers of commodities of like grade and quality." That sweeping prohibition, however, is qualified by many additional requirements and exceptions. For example, price discrimination is forbidden only where the effect thereof "may be substantially to lessen competition or tend to create a monopoly in any line of commerce, or to injure, destroy, or prevent competition with any person who either grants or knowingly receives the benefit of such discrimination, or with customers of either of them." Discrimination is allowed when justified by differences in the costs of manufacturing or delivering commodities to different customers or by the "imminent deterioration of perishable goods." And so forth. These supplementary provisions, in combination, make the statute notoriously complex and unpredictable. Partly as a result, the two agencies charged with enforcing the statute—the Federal Trade Commission and the Department of Justice—have over the years shown less and less interest in detecting and punishing instances of price discrimination. Currently, the statute is virtually a dead letter.[22]

If we wish to avoid the fate of the Robinson-Patman Act, we will need a narrower and simpler rule. The following might do the job: "It shall be unlawful at the same time to offer different prices to two or more potential purchasers of identical copies of an audio or video recording, or identical performances thereof." Such a rule would permit sellers and streamers of recordings to raise or lower their prices, so long as such changes affected all customers. It would also permit them to offer customers different versions of the same recording at different prices—for example, a copy of "The Return of the King" that expires in a week for $5 and a copy of the same film that expires in a month for $10. But it would prevent them from engaging in the practices that many observers find noxious—for example, charging consumers who watched "The Fellowship of the Ring" two or more times higher prices for access to "The Return of the King" than consumers less enamored of Tolkien and Peter Jackson.

Price Regulation

All of the forms of governmental intervention considered up to this point could fairly be considered supplements to the set of reforms proposed in the previous chapter. In other words, they could all be understood as devices to ensure that copyright owners do not exercise their enhanced entitlements in ways inconsistent with the public interest. By contrast, the fifth and last of the possible regulations we will examine cannot be considered supplementary in the same sense; rather, it runs directly counter to the spirit of Chapter 4. One of the main proposals set forth in that chapter was that we jettison the "liability rules" currently applicable to many of the interests enjoyed by the owners of copyrights in audio and video recordings, replacing them with "property rules." The practical implication of such a shift would be that the government would cease regulating the prices that copyright owners could charge for access to their works. We now consider the opposite possible reform: instead of eliminating the zones of copyright law currently covered by compulsory licenses, expand them. Specifically, extend price regulation to cover all methods of distributing digital recordings over the Internet.

For the reasons outlined in Chapter 4, such a move would be risky. As Robert Merges has shown, administrative agencies have trouble acquiring the information necessary to engage in sensible price regulation, often fail to respond appropriately to changes in market conditions, and stimulate socially wasteful "rent-seeking" behavior by both the firms they regulate and the consumers on whose behalf they purport to act. So why venture down this well-trodden but thorny path? Chapter 4 also identified the main reason we should consider doing so: at least for a few years, until recording artists and filmmakers are able (by capitalizing on newly available methods for distributing their works directly to consumers over the Internet) to break free of the major record companies and studios, the latter organizations will continue to enjoy substantial market power. The structural devices outlined in this chapter may not be sufficient to prevent them from using that power to raise prices to exorbitant levels. Thus, the only way of preventing them from engrossing all of the large potential economic gains made possible by the new technology may be to fall back upon the oldest technique in the regulatory handbook: limiting what they can charge.[23]

The question immediately arises: how should the maximum prices be set? Guidance in answering that question may be obtained from a survey of the ways in which compulsory-licensing provisions previously have been framed.

A good example of a system to avoid is the original version of section 115, which (you will recall) governs the fee that the owners of copyrights in musical compositions may charge firms (typically record companies) that make "mechanical copies" of those compositions. Between 1909 and 1978, the fee was set by Congress. Not surprisingly, it did not change—remaining at 2 cents per song per copy for most compositions. Virtually all observers agree that, by the 1970s, that figure was far too low.[24]

At the opposite extreme is the standard employed in section 114(f)(2)(B) to govern the fees that must be paid to the record companies by noninteractive Webcasters. The Copyright Arbitration Royalty Panels charged with setting those fees are instructed "to establish rates and terms that most clearly represent the rates and terms that would have been negotiated in the marketplace between a willing buyer and a willing seller." As we saw in Chapter 3, the first panel to interpret that statutory standard attempted to approximate the amount that the record companies would have charged Webcasters in the absence of any statutory control—thereby forfeiting most of the economic and cultural benefits of a compulsory royalty. The net result, as one might expect, was a rate that was too high—forcing many Webcasters out of business and prompting the Librarian of Congress and ultimately Congress itself to override the panel's ruling.[25]

In between these two poles lies the standard set forth in section 801(b), which governs the current version of the section 115 "cover" license, the fees paid by jukebox operators, and the rates paid by certain "preexisting" services for the right to make digital audio transmissions of sound recordings. Arbitration panels governed by this provision are instructed to select rates that will achieve the following objectives:

(A) To maximize the availability of creative works to the public;
(B) To afford the copyright owner a fair return for his creative work and the copyright user a fair income under existing economic conditions;
(C) To reflect the relative roles of the copyright owner and the copyright user in the product made available to the public with respect to relative creative contribution, technological contribution, capital investment, cost, risk, and contribution to the opening of new markets for creative expression and media for their communication;
(D) To minimize any disruptive impact on the structure of the industries involved and on generally prevailing industry practices.[26]

If not "just right," this intermediate rule at least seems sensible, identifying most of the factors that, in the course of this chapter, we have suggested ought to be advanced by a system of government regulation. (Not all of the copyright owners whose activities are governed by this standard are happy with it—but that, of course, is to be expected.)

Two considerations suggest that that system of price regulation, if adopted, ought not be permanent. First, increased competition in the music and film industries may soon eliminate the need for price controls. Second, as Professor Merges observes, once in place, such regulatory regimes are very hard to dislodge—even after they have plainly outlived their usefulness. Thus, a "sunset" provision—perhaps of three years—would seem to be in order.[27]

Institutional Design

So far, we have left vague the identity of the arm of government that would be charged with setting and adjusting these regulations. Various branches might be assigned the job. Congress could specify the pertinent regulations itself—as it did, for example, in the Robinson-Patman Act. Another possibility would be to give the courts more regulatory authority. As mentioned above, a court already has supervisory responsibility, pursuant to a consent decree, over the "blanket-license" fees charged by ASCAP. That responsibility conceivably might be extended to the license fees charged by copyright owners of all sorts for all kinds of reproductions and performances of audio or video recordings over the Internet. But neither of these options is especially attractive. Congress, as noted above, cannot be expected to amend rules frequently to respond to changes in technologies and market conditions. And the courts lack the expertise, time, and information-gathering capacities to do the job responsibly.

Once Congress and the courts have been eliminated, the only plausible remaining candidate for the job (at least within the American system of government) is an administrative agency. Congress might define with broad strokes the kinds of regulations it wished to impose on the entertainment industry, delegating to the agency the task of filling in (and periodically modifying) the details. Alternatively, Congress might give the agency broad authority—for example, responsibility to manage the business of online distribution of recorded entertainment so as to promote "public convenience, interest, or necessity."[28]

Either of these approaches, but especially the latter, carries risks of its own. Administrative agencies, particularly when given expansive powers, can set off on regulatory larks, imposing rules that would not have been approved by the elected representatives of the people. Even more seriously, administrative agencies are vulnerable to "capture" by the industries they are supposed to be regulating. There exists no single, reliable vaccine to either disease, but over the course of the twentieth century, we have developed a series of mechanisms designed to reduce the incidence and severity of the infections. Agencies can be required to consult broadly before adopting regulations and to provide rational responses to critics of their initiatives. They can be structured to remain as "independent" as possible, both of the political party currently in control of the executive branch and of the private firms they are supposed to be supervising. And their rules and decisions can be subject to periodic review by the courts, to ensure that they are founded on defensible findings of fact and fall within the agencies' statutory authority.[29]

One agency that, because of its expansive powers and important portfolio, has been subjected over the years to especially close scrutiny and supervision is the Federal Communications Commission. Rather than construct a new administrative agency to handle the entertainment industry, we might simply add recorded entertainment to the topics already managed by the FCC. Alternatively, we might restructure the current Copyright Office so as to more closely resemble the current version of the FCC, and then add to its existing portfolio the responsibilities outlined in this chapter. That would require, among other things, replacing (or complementing) the Register of Copyrights with a group of five commissioners, serving staggered five-year terms, appointed by the president and confirmed by the Senate. The result would be both to increase the autonomy of the office and to enhance its capacity and inclination to engage in the delicate task of formulating an appropriate body of regulations.[30]

Selecting the right administrative agency to handle the task, structuring it appropriately, and subjecting it to a sensible level of judicial review would help a good deal in reducing the dangers created by giving any governmental body this much power. But institutional precautions of this sort can only go so far. In the end, much would hinge on the qualifications and commitments of the people who were appointed to run the agency. If conscientious, informed, nonpartisan, and uninterested in currying favor with potential future employers in the private sector, they could use the tools canvassed above to great effect. If they lacked those traits, they might do more harm than good.

Summing Up

When assessing its merits and demerits, the set of legal reforms considered in this chapter is best viewed alongside the set considered in the last chapter. The two arguments fit together as follows:

In Chapter 4, pursuit of the analogy between copyrights and real property rights suggested several ways in which the entitlements currently enjoyed by the owners of copyrights in audio and video recordings might be enhanced (as well as a few ways in which they might be curtailed). The adoption of that package of recommendations would make possible an important set of new business models, which, in turn, would improve in several respects the manner in which recorded entertainment is created and distributed. Specifically, the availability of clean, authorized copies of audio and video recordings would increase dramatically; many more musicians would be able to make their music available directly to the public; and private collective-rights societies, more efficient and flexible than the extant government agencies, would assume responsibility for processing the myriad licensing transactions between copyright owners and the people who wanted access to their works. But these benefits would be accompanied by several unfortunate effects: at least initially, the dominant intermediaries would use their enhanced powers to drive out potential competitors and to line their pockets, creative and critical uses of audio and video recordings would be curtailed, and copyright owners would employ socially undesirable forms of price discrimination. The most radical of the initiatives considered in Chapter 4—mandatory inclusion of copyright-protection systems in electronic devices—would also threaten the "end-to-end" design principle upon which the Internet was founded.

In this chapter, we first explored some general considerations suggesting that it would be plausible to treat the entertainment industry as a "regulated industry," and then examined a list of specific ways in which the already substantial legal constraints on copyright owners' freedom might be tightened further. The primary purpose of those regulations would be to curb the likely abuses by copyright owners of the enhanced entitlements that Chapter 4 would provide them—using tools already developed (typically through painful processes of trial and error) in other regulated industries.

In view of the way the two inquiries were conducted, it should come as no surprise that an entertainment industry built upon a combination of Chapters 4 and 5 would be even better than an entertainment industry built upon Chapter 4 alone. Specifically, it would be characterized by more competition in more sectors of both the music and film markets, by greater diversity in the products and services made available to the public, by lower prices, by less price discrimination, and by greater fairness in the distribution of the revenues generated by the industry among the many people who contribute to it. However, serious problems would remain. None of the regulations considered here would alleviate the dampening effect of effective encryption systems on critical and transformative uses of audio and video recordings or the regrettable erosion of the end-to-end principle. Finally, the transaction costs associated with running such a complex regulatory regime, added to the already substantial costs of ensuring compliance with the enhanced entitlements prescribed in Chapter 4, would be dauntingly high.

Can we do better? Chapter 6 makes one more run at the problem.

Imagine that I own a rocky promontory on the coast of Maine. A submerged reef extends from my land a half mile seaward. Mariners have trouble seeing the reef, especially at night or when it's foggy. As a result, ships have been running aground on the reef for centuries. Even today, small pleasure craft lacking sophisticated electronic navigation equipment frequently hit it in the summer months. Some are seriously damaged, and a few are wrecked.

One evening, after I've helped to extricate yet another smashed sailboat from the rocks, a friend suggests to me, "You know, you ought to build a lighthouse on the point. A bright light would warn boats to steer clear. If each boater paid you even a fraction of the benefit of the signal to him, you could make a tidy profit." We discuss the possibility for a bit. All aspects of the plan make sense, except one: we can't figure out how I could charge the beneficiaries of the lighthouse. My friend suggests making a deal with a nearby charter company, which rents boats to sailors unfamiliar with the local waters—who in turn run aground especially often. But such a contract would cover only a portion of the cost of the lighthouse. And once I made the light available to the company's customers, I couldn't prevent all other sailors from making use of it for free. In short, we can't envision a profitable business model. Stymied, we abandon the idea.

This parable, familiar to economists, illustrates what they refer to as the problem of "public goods." They point out that a small number of socially valuable products and services have the following two related characteristics: First, they are "nonrivalrous." In other words, enjoyment of them by one person does not prevent enjoyment of them by other persons. Second, they are "nonexcludable." In other words, once they have been made available to one person, it is impossible or at least difficult to prevent other people from gaining access to them. Goods that share these features are likely to be produced at socially suboptimal levels. Why? Because potential suppliers of them, like me, recognize that they would not be able to recover from consumers the costs of producing them. Besides lighthouses, things that fall into this category include roads, national defense, inventions, and recorded entertainment.[1]

For centuries, governments have sought in various ways to counteract the danger that public goods will be underproduced. Looking back over the historical record, we can see that their efforts have taken five forms. First, they sometimes supply such goods themselves. Navigational aids and national defense are the clearest examples. Today, throughout the world, virtually all lighthouses and armies are supplied by governments, rather than by private parties. Some kinds of inventions are also generated in this way. In the United States, for example, much innovation in the fields of aerospace, agriculture, and medicine comes from government laboratories operated by the National Aeronautics and Space Administration, the Department of Agriculture, and the National Institutes of Health, respectively.

Second, governments sometimes pay private actors to produce public goods. In the United States, the grants given to artists by the National Endowment for the Arts and the grants given to private universities and individual researchers by the National Institutes of Health exemplify this approach.[2]

Third, governments sometimes issue *post-hoc* prizes or rewards to persons and organizations that provide public goods. The lure of such rewards is intended to offset, in whole or in part, the disincentive to produce them in the first instance. Reward systems have been employed in various countries in various industrial contexts. For example, the British government offered a prize of £20,000 to the first person to invent a chronometer that would enable mariners to measure longitude accurately—on the condition that the inventor make his or her creation freely available for public use. In the 1950s, the governments of the Soviet Union and the People's Republic of China experimented with various reward systems to stimulate innovation. And the American government employs a reward system to encourage innovations relating to atomic energy. A long line of political and economic theorists— from James Madison to Steven Shavell and Tanguy van Ypersele—have argued that such systems should be employed more broadly.[3]

Fourth, governments sometimes protect the suppliers of public goods against competition, typically by granting them exclusive rights to make their products available to the public. For example, in the nineteenth century, American state governments would commonly authorize a private company to build a road, bridge, or canal; empower the company to charge tolls; and (most important) guarantee that no competitive transportation system would be built for a prescribed period of time. Patent law rests on a similar strategy: inventors are given exclusive rights for twenty years to "make" or "sell" objects embodying their inventions. Those rights enable the patentees—provided that there are no good substitutes for their creations—to charge consumers high enough prices both to recoup the costs of their training and inventive activity and to earn a profit.

Fifth and finally, governments sometimes assist private parties in devising or deploying devices that increase the "excludability" of such goods— and thus enhance the ability of producers to charge consumers for access to them. The most familiar example of this strategy is trade-secret law. It is sometimes possible for companies to sell innovative products (for example, new soft drinks or software programs) without revealing the inventions that underlie them (the chemical formulae for the drinks or the source code for the programs). So long as the companies take "reasonable precautions" to maintain the secrecy of their innovations, the law will lend them a hand, by forbidding competitors to ferret out the innovations through "improper means." The same principle supported the statutes adopted by some American states that forbade a particular type of reverse engineering of vessel designs, thereby compelling competitors to use more circuitous ways of learning and replicating the dimensions of novel boats.[4]

Each of these strategies has disadvantages. The first three all invest government with the power to determine which people or projects to fund or reward and thus create, to varying degrees, the danger that government will wield that power unwisely or repressively. The fourth raises the prices that both consumers and subsequent creators must pay for access to public goods, thus reducing consumer welfare and potentially impeding cumulative innovation. The fifth suffers from the same difficulty and, in addition, may foster unnecessarily expensive (and thus socially wasteful) ways of replicating innovations. Which then is best? It varies entirely by context.[5]

For decades, the primary approach used by most governments in the world to stimulate the production of music and movies has been a variant of the fourth strategy. Copyright law—supplemented, in some countries, by the associated law of "neighboring rights"—has protected composers, performers, and filmmakers against competition in the reproduction, adaptation, distribution, and performance of their creations, thus enabling them to raise the prices they charge consumers and licensees. The resultant profits have provided a crucial stimulus for creativity. As we saw in Chapter 2, the various business models that were built upon this legal foundation had some flaws, but until recently they worked reasonably well. Certainly, they generated an enormous stream of entertainment products. As we saw in Chapter 3, during the 1990s a spate of technological innovations destabilized this approach. The rapidly increasing popularity of digital recording and storage systems, the improvement of compression technologies, and the communicative power of the Internet made it ever harder for artists and their assignees to enforce their rights under copyright law. Near the turn of the century, the resultant threats to established business models prompted the American government (as well as governments in other countries) to turn their attention to the fifth strategy. The producers of entertainment (and other informational products) were given extensive legal protections against the circumvention of encryption and other private access-control systems. As we saw, this shift in strategy increased somewhat the ability of producers to shield their creations from unauthorized reproduction and thus protected their income streams, but it had other, substantial drawbacks: curtailment of traditional "fair use" privileges; high transaction costs; and, most important, frustration of the opportunities for semiotic democracy latent in the new technologies.

The growing disadvantages of strategies four and five suggest that we should consider a fundamental change in approach. Specifically, this chapter proposes that we replace major portions of the copyright and encryption-reinforcement models with a variant of the third strategy—a governmentally administered reward system. In brief, here's how such a system would work. A creator who wished to collect revenue when his or her song or film was heard or watched would register it with the Copyright Office. With registration would come a unique filename, which would be used to track transmissions of digital copies of the work. The government would raise, through taxes, sufficient money to compensate registrants for making their works available to the public. Using techniques pioneered by American and European performing rights organizations and television rating services, a government agency would estimate the frequency with which each song and film was heard or watched by consumers. Each registrant would then periodically be paid by the agency a share of the tax revenues proportional to the relative popularity of his or her creation. Once this system were in place, we would modify copyright law to eliminate most of the current prohibitions on unauthorized reproduction, distribution, adaptation, and performance of audio and video recordings. Music and films would thus be readily available, legally, for free.

Painting with a very broad brush (details will come later), here would be the advantages of such a system. Consumers would pay less for more entertainment. Artists would be fairly compensated. The set of artists who made their creations available to the world at large—and consequently the range of entertainment products available to consumers—would increase. Musicians would be less dependent on record companies, and filmmakers would be less dependent on studios, for the distribution of their creations. Both consumers and artists would enjoy greater freedom to modify and redistribute audio and video recordings. Although the prices of consumer electronic equipment and broadband access would increase somewhat, demand for them would rise, thus benefiting the suppliers of those goods and services. Finally, society at large would benefit from a sharp reduction in litigation and other transaction costs. The ensuing sections of this chapter describe this system in more detail and explore its merits and demerits.

Logistics

Registration

Essential to such a system would be a way of tracking digital copies of songs and movies. This might be achieved by inserting into the original version of each work a unique and durable digital fingerprint, which would then be replicated in each copy of the original. The barcodes now routinely placed on packages of food in the United States enable grocery stores to process sales quickly, to manage their inventories, and (most ominously), by correlating sales with customers' "discount cards," to keep track of what individual people are eating. In the near future, radio frequency identification (RFID) tags, buried in food packages and other consumer goods, will make the process even easier. Digital fingerprints could enable comparable tracking of entertainment products. A mechanism of this sort would probably be both feasible and effective. Some of the technology left over from the failed SDMI project, discussed in Chapter 3, could probably be harnessed for this purpose. But it would be expensive and, for reasons discussed below, unnecessary.[6]

A simpler approach would rely upon a centralized registration system. A musician or filmmaker who wanted to be paid when others made use of his or her creation would send a copy of it to a government agency, which would store the copy and provide, in return, a unique registration number. The creator would insert that number into the filename of the copy of the recording that he or she made available to the world. Following are some details:

What government agency? You could imagine creating a new administrative agency for this purpose, but the Copyright Office already runs, quite effectively, a registration system that could be modified slightly to fill this function.

Would there be a registration fee? Yes, a fee large enough to make the registration system self-financing. But the simplicity of the mechanism would keep that fee at modest levels.

Would each creator be obliged to register his or her creations? No. Unlike cars, songs and films could be unlicensed. Creators who wished for whatever reason to dedicate their products to the public domain could do so.[7]

How would you submit your registration? Over the Internet, of course.

What would a registration number look like? Probably a series of letters and numerals, preceded and followed by an identifier of some sort. Example: #4m8sp6owxi#. (There exist over three quadrillion unique sequences of ten letters and numerals, which should be plenty for the foreseeable future.)

How much information concerning the content of the material contained in a recording should the registrant be required to supply? Only so much as would be useful to the administrators of the system when deciding how much to pay the registrants of different recordings. For reasons explored in detail below, it would be both feasible and sensible for the administrators, when calculating payments, to differentiate between audio and video recordings and among recordings of different lengths. By contrast, it would do them little good to know whether an audio recording contained opera or rap music—or whether a video recording contained a western or a comedy. Accordingly, registrants would be required to indicate whether their submission consisted of a song or a film and how long it was, but nothing more.

The person or institution entitled to register a recording would be the copyright owner. Thus, for the reasons outlined in Chapter 2, the registrant of a video recording of a film would typically be the producer or the studio. The registrant of an audio recording of a song would typically be the performer or the performer's assignee. In addition, the registrant of an audio recording would be required to specify the owner of the copyright in the underlying musical composition. The forms for both types of work would permit designation of more than one author—when and only when they qualified as "joint authors" under the copyright statute. In short, the new system would leave in place the current legal standards for determining who is the author of a creative work—just as it would the current system of contracts and customs by which "authors" compensate other people and organizations who participate in the creation or marketing of entertainment products.[8]

This feature means that, sometimes, there would arise disputes over who is the rightful copyright owner of the work underlying a particular recording. To handle such disputes as efficiently as possible, the Copyright Office should be empowered to create a formal "opposition" procedure closely analogous to the procedure currently used by the Patent and Trademark Office to handle challenges to trademark registrations. Decisions in such proceedings could be appealed to the federal courts.

What about recordings that incorporate portions of other recordings—rap songs that contain "samples" of other copyrighted recordings, movies that contain excerpts of other movies, and so on? To gather the information necessary to compensate fairly both the creator of the incorporated work and the creator of the incorporating work, the form would require each registrant to indicate how much of the material contained in the submitted recording had been taken from other registered recordings. A precise accounting would be unnecessary. Rather, the registrant would pick among five ways of characterizing the proportion of the recording that had been taken from others—none; a small amount (less than 5 percent); some (5 to 50 percent); most (50 to 95 percent); all or almost all (95 to 100 percent)—and then list the registration numbers of the works incorporated in whole or in part. Because these figures would be determined quantitatively (by dividing the duration of the incorporated material by the duration of the composite recording) rather than qualitatively (assessing how important to the final product was the incorporated material), they would be relatively easy to determine. However, some registrants would be tempted to underreport the extent of their reliance on others' work. To deter such behavior (and to encourage others to detect and challenge it), we might provide that proof of underreporting would result in all of the revenue that the registrant would have earned through the system being diverted to the registrant of the recording from which the underreported material was taken.[9]

Figure 6.1 is a sample of a registration form that could be used to gather the data of these various sorts.

Determining Aggregate Compensation Levels

To run the system, the government would need to raise money. How? Through taxation. That much seems clear enough. Two harder questions remain: How much money would the government be obliged to raise? And what would it tax?

Name:

Email address:

Street address:

The recording you are registering is a:

☐ Sound recording

☐ Video recording

If the recording you are registering is a recording of a musical composition, indicate the owner of the copyright in the underlying composition:

How much (measured by duration) of the material in the recording you are registering consists of material taken from other registered recordings:

☐ None

☐ Less than 5%

☐ Between 5% and 25%

☐ Between 25% and 50%

☐ Between 50% and 95%

☐ Between 95% and 100%

Indicate the registration numbers of the recordings from which you derived material and the duration of each:

FIGURE **6.1.** *Registration Form.*

To answer the first question, we need first to determine the amount of money the government would be distributing to creators. That sum, plus the administrative costs of the system, is the amount that would have to be collected. Any of several different principles might be employed to determine how much creators receive. The choice of principle will make a large difference in the cost and operation of the system, so it's important to be clear at the outset concerning the governing criterion.

One possible approach would strive to give creators the full social value of their creations—or, more precisely, the full social value of their creations minus the money that they are able to make through other channels. What is the full social value of an entertainment product? An economist would say that it's the sum of the "consumer surplus" and the "producer surplus" that could be reaped from making it available to the public. That, in turn, is equal to the total amount that consumers (including other creators who wished to improve upon or adapt it) would be able and willing to pay for access to the product—up to the point where the marginal cost of producing an additional copy equals the marginal benefit reaped from it—minus the costs of producing that number of copies. More crudely, it's the total benefit that all members of society could reap from the product.

A criterion of this sort seems to underlie the most recent and sophisticated analysis of reward systems as alternatives to intellectual property systems—the paper, mentioned above, by Steven Shavell and Tanguy van Ypersele. In the view of those authors, "the optimal reward equals the expected surplus over the distribution of possible demand curves." The authors contend that, if the rewards given to inventors are less than that amount, "there will be an inadequate incentive to invest" in research. If the rewards exceed that amount, "there will be an excessive incentive to invest" in research.[10]

Should we use this guideline when reshaping the music and film industries? For two reasons, the answer seems to be no. First, it would be extremely expensive. The cost of reproducing and distributing digital copies of songs and movies is very low, and the total amount that consumers in the aggregate would pay for access to those copies is very large. The difference between those two figures would be an enormous sum. It would be very difficult, for political reasons, to impose taxes large enough to raise that much money.

Second, as Arnold Plant and Glynn Lunney have shown, awarding the creators of intellectual products the full social value of their creations would seriously distort the system of incentives that shape people's choices of professions. Most workers do not reap the full social value of their efforts. Schoolteachers, civil-rights activists, and university-based research scientists, for example, all confer on society gains that vastly exceed their incomes.

Enabling musicians and filmmakers to reap everything they have sown, without transforming comparably the systems by which workers of all other types are compensated, would exacerbate the problem discussed at the end of Chapter 2—in which too many people wait tables in New York and Los Angeles, waiting for the big break, while too few prepare to become teachers.[11]

A radically different approach would abandon the quest to create an optimal pattern of incentives, and would instead strive, through the distribution of government rewards, to give creators what they *deserve*. This may have been what British reformer Robert MacFie had in mind when he urged giving inventors, as an "honorarium," "what is fair, considering utility, cost of preliminary trials, originality, probability of others making the same discovery, etc." This criterion seems unpromising for a different reason. Natural-rights theorists, from John Locke to Robert Nozick, have struggled with little success for centuries to determine the "just" proportion between a person's efforts and the reward he or she reaps. It seems implausible that, in designing a reward system to handle the new technological environment, we could succeed where they have failed.[12]

A final criterion would be harder to defend on theoretical grounds but more practical: make creators, as a group, whole. More specifically, we could use the new reward system to compensate creators and their assignees for the losses they have suffered—and will likely suffer in the immediate future—as a result of being deprived of their ability to enforce their copyrights in the new technological environment. The attitude underlying this approach is the same one that prompted Fritz Machlup to remark, famously,

> If we did not have a patent system, it would be irresponsible, on the basis of our present knowledge of its economic consequences, to recommend instituting one. But since we have had a patent system for a long time, it would be irresponsible, on the basis of our present knowledge, to recommend abolishing it.[13]

In the same spirit, it would seem wisest, when replacing the current copyright system with a system of government rewards, to begin by holding more-or-less constant the aggregate amount by which creators are currently compensated—and only to make adjustments, up or down, to their collective incomes when we have better information about the likely effects of such changes.

What would application of this criterion entail in practice? It's impossible to say with precision given the limited amount of data available to us at present. The relevant numbers would have to be determined by an administrative agency after an extensive fact-gathering process. For the reasons outlined in Chapter 5, the best candidate for the job would likely be a new, quasi-independent arm of the Copyright Office, the judgments of which would be subject to meaningful review by the Court of Appeals for the D.C. Circuit.

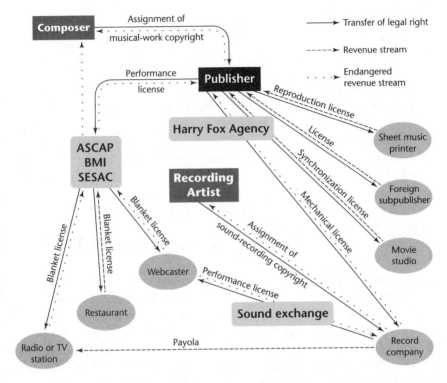

FIGURE 6.2. *Endangered Revenue Streams in the Music Industry.*

Following is a discussion of the kind of accounting that the Copyright Office would have to conduct. As you will see, many of the estimates that we will deploy are soft. The purposes of the analysis are merely to illustrate the methodology that the office would have to employ and to suggest that a reward regime founded on this approach would be practicable.

Let's start with the music industry. In Chapters 2 and 3, we examined the various streams of revenue that currently flow to the owners of copyrights in musical compositions and sound recordings. Shown with dotted lines in Figure 6.2 (a variant of Figure 3.1) are the channels that would likely be constricted by elimination of the current prohibitions on the reproduction, distribution, and performance of audio recordings over the Internet.

Implicit in this chart is a prediction that three business models would be corroded. The first—and by far the most important—is sales by record companies of CDs and tapes. As revenues from that source diminished, all of the streams of income that flow "upward" from the record companies would also shrink. A second, less certain effect would be diminution of the audiences (and therefore the advertising revenues) of radio stations, as consumers came to rely increasingly on the superior, ad-free offerings available through the Internet. If that occurred, the public-performance royalties paid by the stations (which, in turn, are tied to their gross revenues) would also diminish. Finally, and least important, the small payments that are currently being made by the Webcasters to the music publishers and record companies would disappear, not because the Webcasters would go out of business, but because nonpermissive streaming would now be lawful.

In estimating the magnitude of these changes, it seems fair to use as our baseline the year 2000, approximately the moment when album sales began to fall off under the pressure of the technological changes. (Indeed, adoption of that date is generous, because a healthy economy led to unusually high levels of consumption of entertainment products.) During that year, sales of CDs, tapes, and records in the United States earned the record companies gross revenues of approximately $7.35 billion (53 percent of $13.868 billion in total retail sales).[14]

What percentage of this income would the companies lose if we permitted unlimited copying of sound recordings? Plainly, that figure would increase over time and eventually might approach 100 percent. For the immediate future, however, the percentage would be significantly less. Neil Netanel, relying upon careful empirical work by Stan Liebowitz, estimates that the companies would lose no more than 20 percent of their sales revenues through unlimited noncommercial file sharing. That number does not correspond exactly to what we are seeking, insofar as it contemplates legalizing only a subset of the activities that our new system would permit. However, for the immediate future, it seems a plausible figure. Since 2000, declining sales of albums have cost the recording industry a total of 18 percent of their revenues. The extent to which the slump in sales was caused by file sharing and CD burning is currently a hotly contested issue. Against that backdrop, to project a loss of 20 percent during the first year in which the new system were in operation thus seems, again, generous—recognizing, of course, that this number would have to be revised (presumably upward) as consumers' behavior changed.[15]

Twenty percent of $7.35 billion is $1.47 billion. To determine the actual injury suffered by the record companies, we would have to deduct from that figure the amounts that they would save as their sales declined. Approximately 15 percent of the record companies' gross revenues is currently devoted to manufacturing costs—the costs of producing CDs and cassettes, packaging them, preparing the artwork, and shipping them to distributors. A decline of $1.47 billion in revenues would thus be partially offset by a savings of $221 million in manufacturing costs. The net loss would thus be

$1.249 billion. It is possible, as Brett May and Marc Singer suggest, that the companies would also experience savings in "overhead" (as their operations shrank) and variable marketing costs (by taking advantage of the increased efficiency and precision of Internet-based marketing). But again, we will take a conservative line and, for the time being, not assume any reduction in those expenditures. (May's and Singer's projections—along with some analogous predictions made in Chapter 1—will have greater bite when we're ready to predict how this system would change over time).[16]

The record companies are not the only copyright owners we need to worry about. Also injured by declining sales of CDs and tapes are the music publishers, the holders of the copyrights in the compositions embodied in those products. In 2000, total American phono-mechanical license fees were $691 million. A 20 percent reduction in sales would thus cost them $138 million. This affects our accounting in two, roughly offsetting ways. First, it requires us to add to the total amount that we would be obliged to raise in taxes a sum of $138 million, tentatively earmarked for the music publishers. Second, it requires us to reduce the $1.249 billion tentatively earmarked for the record companies by $145 million—the amount that they would save in mechanical royalties as a result of their declining sales. (The difference between the two figures represents the 5 percent bite that the Harry Fox Agency typically takes out of those royalties.)[17]

Our final figures: $1.104 billion for the owners of the copyrights in sound recordings; $138 million for the owners of copyrights in musical compositions.

The second of the three sources of injury arising from free Internet-based reproduction, distribution, and performance of audio recordings would be smaller but not trivial. Radio stations would suffer in this new world, because a wider variety of better-quality, ad-free music would now be obtainable for free on the Internet. How much would their incomes decline? It's impossible to say at this point. The stations have not to date complained that Webcasting has eroded their markets, and consumers would probably not suddenly abandon altogether their favorite disk jockeys. So let's guess, wildly, that the stations' revenues would decline 5 percent in the first year in which this new system were in place—expecting that they would decline more sharply in the future. (To repeat, this and all other estimates made in this section would be reevaluated, using financial data submitted by the relevant parties, by the Copyright Office. Our goal here is just to outline the methodology and identify "ballpark" numbers.) What would be the corresponding injury to the owners of the copyrights in musical works? In 2000, total public-performance royalties paid by radio stations in the United States were $292 million. Five percent of that amount would be approximately $15 million. Added to the loss of $138 million they would suffer from declining record sales, this would produce a total injury to the owners of musical-works copyrights of $153 million.[18]

For two reasons, we can safely ignore for the purpose of our accounting the last of the three potential sources of injury. First, in our baseline year, the license fees paid by Webcasters were trivial compared to the other figures we are considering. Second, as we saw in Chapter 3, the reason why the record companies pressed (successfully) for a right to collect those fees was to compensate them for diminution in their sales of CDs and tapes. The system we are constructing provides them an alternative (indeed, substantially more generous) way of recouping those losses.

As rough as these numbers are, the numbers for the film industry are even rougher. Legalizing the reproduction, distribution, and performance over the Internet of digital versions of movies would likely adversely affect, in the near term, three of the many streams of revenue upon which the studios currently depend: sales and rentals of videotapes and DVDs; cable and satellite television licenses; and pay-per-view licenses. Figure 6.3 (a variant of Figure 2.3) highlights these sources of injury.

The first of the threatened sources of revenue is the biggest. In 2000, sales and rentals of videotapes and DVDs generated income at the retail level of $21.856 billion. $7.8 billion (approximately 36 percent) of that money ended up in the coffers of the studios.[19]

Revenues attributable to distribution through subscription cable and satellite services—such as HBO, Showtime, and the Movie Channel—are harder to estimate. During 2000, total spending on such services was approximately $7.314 billion. Roughly two thirds of that amount ($4.876 billion) was retained by the operators of the local cable franchises, and one third ($2.438 billion) went to the services themselves. A significant portion of the latter sum was paid to the studios in license fees, but exactly how much is hard to determine, in part because the major cable channels were owned by the same conglomerates that owned the studios themselves. Until we can obtain better data on this front, we'll assume that 50 percent of the money ($1.219 billion) was earned by the studios.[20]

The smallest but fastest growing of the three revenue streams is pay-per-view. In 2000, the total amount spent by Americans for pay-per-view movies was $1.426 billion. Absent more refined data, we'll assume that 40 percent of that amount ($570 million) went to the studios.[21]

Now comes the softest part of the analysis. In the immediate future, what would likely be the adverse impact upon these revenue streams of le-

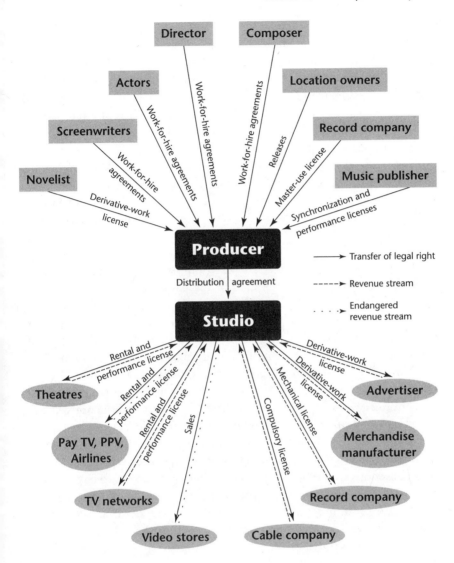

FIGURE 6.3. *Endangered Revenue Streams in the Film Industry.*

galizing the reproduction and distribution of digital video files? Three related circumstances suggest that that adverse impact would be substantially
less (in percentage terms) than the harms sustained by the music industry.
First, transmitting even compressed video files over the Internet takes a long
time, even through broadband connections, and storing those files requires
vastly more hard-disk space than is required for audio files. Second, relatively

few consumers currently own the equipment necessary to collect, store, and project digital video files. Third, the motion picture industry has not made a colorable claim that, up to this point, its revenues have been materially undermined by unauthorized Internet distribution. Together, these factors suggest that our estimate of near-term harm should be much lower than the 20-percent figure we used for the music industry. A 5 percent figure is more plausible. (When ascertaining this number the Copyright Office would, of course, rely less on seat-of-the-pants reasoning.)

Putting these various estimates together, to offset the likely injuries sustained by the owners of copyrights in movies, we would need, in the first year, approximately 5 percent of ($7.8 billion plus $1.219 billion plus $570 million), which comes to $479 million. Added to the $153 million and $1.104 billion we would need to make whole the owners of copyrights in musical works and sound recordings, this produces an aggregate figure of $1.736 billion.

We're not quite done. To this sum would have to be added the cost of creating and running a new branch of the Copyright Office. How much would that be? A useful point of reference is the cost of running ASCAP, the largest private American performing rights organization. In 1998, ASCAP's overhead expenses were 16 percent of its collections. Would the Copyright Office be more or less efficient? Different factors point in different directions. Its collections would be approximately four times those of ASCAP, enabling it to enjoy economies of scale. On the other hand, it would be a government agency—and those, as Robert Merges emphasizes, are generally less efficient intermediaries than are private organizations. In addition, start-up costs would be substantial. It seems likely that the latter factors would predominate. Let's then adopt a conservative estimate: 20 percent of the office's collections would be devoted to administrative costs. To pay copyright owners $1.736 billion, it would thus have to raise in taxes $2.170 billion. Last but not least, that number would have to be adjusted for inflation. For that purpose we'll use (for simplicity) the Consumer Price Index for the past three years plus a rough projection of likely inflation during 2004. The net result: $2.389 billion.[22]

That's a large figure. To be sure, the federal government routinely spends even larger amounts on related projects. The annual budget for NASA, for example, is currently about $15 billion per year, and the National Science Foundation distributes about $5 billion per year in research grants. Still, $2.389 billion is a lot of money.[23]

In a few pages, we'll consider where such a daunting sum might come from. Before taking up that question, however, it's important to acknowledge that the criterion that we have been employing thus far (and that would guide the Copyright Office in making much more precise estimates of the harms suffered by copyright owners) can help us only during a transitional period. The question of how much money would be necessary to put copyright owners, collectively, in the same position they would have occupied in the old technological and legal universe would become, over time, ever harder to answer and would make less and less sense as a guideline. Periodically (presumably annually) the office would be obliged to recalibrate the amount of money it needed to collect and distribute. On what basis would it make those adjustments?

Gradually, a more ambiguous and controversial criterion could and should come to dominate the agency's decisionmaking. In rough terms, the emergent goal would be the public interest. Slightly more precisely, the office would strive to determine the amount of money that, when distributed to creators, would sustain a flourishing entertainment culture. The best way to answer that question would be iteratively—through frequent, modest adjustments of the tax rates, followed by studies of the impact of each change. If, in a given year, the entertainment industry seemed starved, the office would enrich the mixture a bit. If it seemed flush, the office would constrict a bit the flow of money.

The judgments underlying these adjustments would be unavoidably impressionistic. The aspiration of the office would not be to increase the flow of money to musicians and filmmakers until it produced what economists would describe as the socially optimal output of entertainment products. For the reasons sketched above, fidelity to that criterion would be prohibitively expensive and would draw an excessively large number of workers into the entertainment industry. Instead, the office would strive to select a level of aggregate reward sufficient to provide consumers a rich array of entertainment products. In pursuing this goal, its staff could and should estimate the rewards, other than income attributable to the distribution of recordings, available to musicians and filmmakers—including nonmonetary benefits (the various sources of gratification available to participants in the entertainment industry) and the revenues that they could earn from live performances. Plainly, the larger those supplementary rewards, the smaller must be the pot of money collected through taxes. But more important than these essentially predictive sources of information would be the office's judgments concerning the quantity and quality of the recordings currently being produced and the observed impact of its most recent adjustments on the production of new products.

Would judgments of this sort involve the exercise of discretion? Certainly. Can any government agency be trusted to wield this power responsibly? We'll take up that question in the next section. Before then, however, we have many other logistical issues to consider.

Taxation

The two and a half billion dollars a year necessary to run this system might be raised in one of two ways. First, we might increase slightly the federal income tax. Currently, approximately 87 million households pay federal income taxes in the United States. If the increased tax burden were spread evenly over that population, each household would pay an additional $27 per year. If, more plausibly, the burden were distributed in accordance with the rates those taxpayers are already paying, then taxpayers with higher incomes would pay somewhat more than that amount, while taxpayers with lower incomes would pay less than that amount.[24]

This approach would have two major advantages. First, it would be efficient. The relevant tax increases could be implemented without incurring any significant additional administrative costs. Nor would the relevant tax base have to be reevaluated in future years.

The other advantage is more subtle but equally important: a slight increase in the income tax would probably result in less distortion of the behavior of people subject to the tax than would any alternative system of financing. To be sure, the income tax does distort behavior. Specifically, it causes people to work less (in other words, to substitute leisure for the consumption of goods purchased with income). However, two circumstances, together, suggest that that effect should not trouble us unduly. First, most (though not all) economists estimate that the economic costs to which it gives rise—so-called "deadweight losses"—are moderate in scale. Second, as Louis Kaplow has shown, those losses are mitigated if the tax is imposed in order to pay for a public good (such as stimulating the production of entertainment products) that directly benefits the persons paying the tax. In the extreme case, if the incidence of the tax exactly matches the incidence of the benefits of the public good, people will behave no differently at all. Could we achieve such a perfect match between the amount by which each person benefited from increased access to music and film and the additional amount that he or she paid in taxes? Of course not. But the facts that the benefits of the system would vary roughly with income (that is, the greater one's income, the greater one's ability, by buying more or better entertainment equipment, to take advantage of the new distribution and consumption technologies) and that an increase in the federal income tax would be progressive suggest that the benefits and burdens of the increased tax burden would be roughly aligned, and thus that its distortionary effects would be modest. As we will see, the most plausible alternatives to the income tax would likely have more serious impacts on the behavior of the people to which they are applied.[25]

This approach does, however, have one equally substantial disadvantage:

it would likely be politically unpopular. Several overlapping objections would almost certainly be deployed by opponents. One line of resistance would emphasize the fact that the rough alignment noted in the preceding paragraph would be just that—rough. Many people who pay significant income taxes would not benefit from the new compensation system—because they lack either the equipment or the inclination to download or stream recorded entertainment. To be sure, this is a common situation. (For example, childless homeowners reap no benefit from the local public schools, but help pay for them through their real-estate taxes.) But many voters consider such misalignments unfair and would resist creating more of them. A second, related objection is that the monies raised through an income tax, ostensibly to provide a fund for the creators of entertainment, could easily be diverted to other purposes. In the United States, this worry is not especially common. When the possibility of a tax-subsidized alternative compensation system is broached in developing countries, by contrast, this objection is routinely raised. A third line of resistance would find a more receptive audience in the United States. Critics would point out, accurately, that significant portions of the funds distributed through the system would be used to compensate the creators of kinds of material that many taxpayers find offensive. That fact would provoke angry questions: My tax dollars support pornography? Misogynist rap music? Violent movies? Some years ago, analogous objections contributed to the corrosion of the National Endowment for the Arts. The proposed system—vastly larger and more visible—would likely draw even more fire.

The second of the two ways in which the funds might be raised would be through a tax on the goods and services used to gain access to music and film. This is the approach advocated by Neil Netanel in his pioneering article exploring the possibility of an alternative compensation system for the music industry. Following Netanel's lead, we might identify four categories of devices and services suitable for taxation: (1) equipment used to make copies of digital recordings; (2) media used to store such copies; (3) services used to gain access to the Internet, either to download files or to stream recordings; and (4) peer-to-peer systems or other services used to share files.[26]

Exactly what sorts of things fit into each of these categories would, of course, change over time, and one of the responsibilities of the Copyright Office would be to reassess, periodically, how digital entertainment is obtained, stored, and played. Following is a discussion (again, offered purely for illustrative purposes) of what such an analysis, conducted today, might reveal. With respect to each potential tax target, we will estimate the current volume of retail sales. Then, at the end, we will calculate the tax rate that would be necessary to raise, from this base, enough revenue to fund the proposed system.

Currently, the most prominent of the copying devices are CD recorders—including stand-alone units and, more important, the CD burners commonly sold these days as components of personal computers. In 2001, sales of such devices in the United States generated revenue at the retail level of $684 million. We'll assume, conservatively, that in 2004 (the first year in which our proposed system could be implemented), that figure will be the same.[27]

Less visible than CD burners but likely soon to be equally important are personal video recorders (PVRs). Included in this group are separate machines, like TiVo and Replay, as well as devices that accompany satellite or cable receivers. Although sales of PVRs during the past few years have been nowhere near as furious as analysts originally predicted, they are now rising fast. The most plausible current projections of PVR ownership by American households are those made recently by the Yankee Group. They estimate that, in 2003, 3.8 million U.S. households owned PVRs; in 2004, the number will be 7.8 million; in 2005, 13 million; and in 2006, 19.1 million. Note that the difference between the total number of machines projected to be in use in 2004 and the total number in 2003 is 4 million. PVRs currently cost approximately $200. Thus, if the Yankee Group is right, retail sales of PVRs will generate in 2004 approximately $800 million in revenue. In addition, purchasers must pay approximately $10 per month ($120 per year) for access to the accompanying services. The owners of the 3.8 million extant machines will thus be paying an additional $456 million for service. Assuming that sales of new machines during 2004 are spread evenly over the course of the year, buyers of those machines would, during the year, spend on service an additional $240 million. Grand total: $1.496 billion.[28]

The most obvious targets in the second category—media used to store digital recordings—are blank CDs. Approximately 1.7 billion were sold in the United States in 2002, up 30 percent from the previous year. A conservative estimate of 2004 sales would be 2 billion. At roughly 50 cents apiece, that would generate retail sales of $1 billion.[29]

In the same category are MP3 players. Their primary function is to store (and then perform) sound recordings. The vast bulk of material housed on them consists of copyrighted songs. At least 1.7 million were sold in 2002, and sales are expected to rise by at least 20 percent a year for the next four years. (Sales of iPods alone reached 216,000 in the last quarter of 2002.) Such devices cost between $150 and $500. Assuming, conservatively, a mean price of $250, retail sales of the devices in 2004 would be $612 million.[30]

These are only the currently most popular storage systems. Many other, more esoteric devices are already on the market—and will likely become more widespread in the future. For example, the Hewlett-Packard "Digital

TABLE **6.1.** *U.S. Internet Access Accounts, 2000–2004.*

	Millions of households with				
	Dial-Up Modem Access	Cable-Modem Access	DSL Access	Wireless or Satellite Access	Total Internet Access
2000	38.7	3.3	1.5	0	43.5
2001	42.5	7.2	3.5	0.2	53.4
2002	39.8	11.3	6.8	0.3	58.2
2003	37.3	14.9	9.0	0.5	61.7
2004	34.8	18.0	10.8	1.4	65.0

Entertainment Center de100c," which retails for about $1,000, "offers a 40Gb hard drive that can store more than 750 CDs-worth of music, which can be surfed via remote control either on the device display or through a television menu." As such systems multiply, the corresponding sources of tax revenue would increase sharply. For the time being, however, we will exclude them from our calculus.[31]

The most important of the potential tax targets consists of Internet access services. The most efficient way of gaining access to digital entertainment is through the Internet. In addition, peer-to-peer file sharing—the activity that copyright owners claim has eroded their revenues most severely —is entirely dependent on the Internet. For both reasons, it seems appropriate to secure a substantial portion of the revenue necessary to run the proposed system from ISPs.

Taxing ISP access has another, practical advantage: it is very difficult for a resident of the United States to gain access to the Internet through a foreign ISP. (It would be possible to do so through a dial-up modem account, but the long-distance telephone charges would be prohibitive.) Thus, American consumers would be unable to avoid a tax imposed on domestic ISPs by obtaining service from foreign providers.

Now comes a critical choice: Should taxes be imposed on both modem-based and broadband accounts or only on the latter? Some numbers may help us in answering. In Table 6.1, Veronis Suhler Stevenson provides estimates of the growth of consumer Internet access accounts in the United States during the past five years.[32]

So which of these groups should we tax? Arguments in favor of taxing subscriptions of all types are

- The resultant tax rate would of course be lower.
- It's possible to download digital files through any type of ISP account.
- If we taxed only broadband subscriptions, we would discourage people from shifting from dial-up to broadband service, causing inefficient distortions in the ISP market.

Arguments in favor of limiting the tax to broadband services (cable, DSL, wireless, and satellite systems) are[33]

- Most methods of obtaining recordings over the Internet are inconvenient without broadband access. Downloading audio files over a dial-up account is time consuming, and downloading video files is almost prohibitively time consuming. Decent-quality streaming also requires broadband speed. As a result, the large majority of file sharing is currently done by Internet users with broadband access.
- Limiting the tax to broadband services would enable persons who use the Internet only to send email, buy products, or "surf" the Web for information to opt for dial-up accounts and thereby avoid the tax.

On balance, the latter set of arguments seems stronger, but not overwhelmingly so.

The most plausible projections of broadband subscription revenues in the United States in 2004, along with estimates of total revenues in previous years, are shown in Table 6.2.[34]

Note that, in 2004, total consumer spending on all forms of broadband access is expected to be approximately $16.456 billion.

The final tax target consists of Internet-based services that assist consumers in locating or sharing audio and video recordings. At present, the most obvious members of this class are the decentralized peer-to-peer file-sharing services. Their incomes are not large, but are not trivial either. In 2002, the company that owns Morpheus, for example, reportedly collected $5.7 million in revenues. Fitting such things into the overall tax scheme would be tricky for two reasons. First, unlike the suppliers of all of the goods and services considered thus far, they make money not by charging consumers directly but through various advertising and promotional schemes. In this respect, they resemble the network television systems discussed in Chapter 2. Consumers end up paying for the services provided by both, but by buying

TABLE **6.2.** *U.S. Broadband Subscription Revenues, 2000–2004.*

	Average Annual Subscription			Total Spending (millions)			
	Cable-Modem	DSL	Wireless and Satellite	Cable-Modem	DSL	Wireless and Satellite	Total Broadband
2000	$488	$720	—	$1,612	$1,080	—	$2,692
2001	$493	$618	$540	$3,551	$2,163	$108	$5,822
2002	$498	$600	$546	$5,627	$4,080	$164	$9,871
2003	$505	$602	$550	$7,527	$5,422	$275	$13,224
2004	$508	$606	$553	$9,137	$6,545	$774	$16,456

the advertised products, rather than by paying the companies directly. This feature makes it awkward merely to plug their revenues into the overall "tax base" for the new scheme. Second, a substantial portion of their revenues are derived (indirectly) from consumers outside the United States. Thus, determining the portion of their incomes appropriately subject to taxation in the United States is both important and difficult. Both factors would require careful attention when designing and periodically readjusting the proposed taxation system. For the time being, however, the small amounts of money at stake (compared with the other sources of revenue we are considering) justify bypassing these complexities and excluding from our overall calculations the funds that might be raised from this source.[35]

Putting these various figures together, the projected total tax base in 2004 would be $0.684 billion plus $1.496 billion plus $1 billion plus $0.612 billion plus $16.456 billion, for a total of $20.248 billion. What tax rate would then be necessary to raise $2.389 billion in revenue? 11.8 percent.

Because it would be applied to a smaller population, this approach would generate per-person tax burdens significantly larger than an income-tax increase. Hardest hit would be broadband subscribers. (Not directly. Administratively, the most sensible approach would be to impose the tax on the ISPs that provide broadband services. But the ISPs would of course raise their subscription rates to offset the tax.) How much, in the end, would the subscribers be obliged to pay? In 2004, the average monthly broadband subscription fee (weighted by the numbers of customers using the various types of service) will be approximately $45.43. Assuming that the ISPs passed through to consumers the entire amount of the tax, that average fee would rise by $5.36 per month ($64.33 per year), to a total of $50.79 per month ($609.48 per year).[36]

As one might expect, the advantages and disadvantages of this second approach mirror those associated with income taxes. On the positive side, a tax on products and services of the sort described above would likely be more popular than an income tax increase. It would be (and would be perceived as) more voluntary—in the sense that one could choose not to purchase the goods or services subject to the tax. In addition, objections of the form, "I don't want my tax dollars supporting smut," would be less salient. The tighter fit under this system among (1) each person's purchases of entertainment-related equipment and services, (2) his or her consumption of entertainment products, and (3) the magnitude of the tax he or she would pay would strengthen the retort: "Your tax dollars don't support smut unless you consume smut; they only support the creators of the entertainment products that you yourself watch and listen to."

On the negative side, this approach would be much more cumbersome and expensive. An administrative agency would be obliged to conduct a new survey annually of the devices and services that enable people to gain access to digital recordings and to recalibrate accordingly the tax rates. Collecting the tax would also be costly. And the visibility of all of these activities would be a constant irritant to people troubled by the idea of governmental involvement in the production and distribution of entertainment.

Finally, a tax on devices and services would likely give rise to more serious distortions of consumers' behavior than would an income tax. For example, some broadband subscribers who dislike both music and movies (in other words, who pay for cable or DSL subscriptions to have convenient access to ecommerce, email, online databases, and the like, not to download or stream entertainment) would be sufficiently price sensitive that they would cancel their subscriptions rather than pay the higher fees caused by the new tax. Similarly, some individuals and companies who use generic blank CDs to back up their data rather than to record music would, when confronted with a 6-cents-per-disc price jump, buy fewer discs—and thus run greater risks of data loss. These effects are clearly unfortunate.

Distortions of the sorts just described could be reduced somewhat if, instead of taxing all devices and services at the same rate, we employed a technique that economists refer to as "Ramsey pricing" (named after the economist who popularized it). The question that this technique was first developed to answer is: What pricing scheme by a multiproduct monopolist would maximize social welfare subject to a profit constraint? (That question was most commonly asked by administrative agencies, like those discussed in Chapter 5, attempting to regulate in socially responsible ways the prices charged by multiproduct monopolists.) The answer: The markup on the marginal cost of each product should be inversely proportional to the price elasticity of demand for that product. Adapting that approach to the problem before us, we would make the tax rates applicable to the various devices and services used to gain access to recorded entertainment inversely proportional to the elasticity of demand for each. Suppose, for example, that consumers saw portable MP3 players as essential to their lifestyles; even a sharp increase in their price would not materially erode sales. By contrast, consumers were much less attached to personal video recorders (like TiVo or Replay); even a modest increase in their price would cause many consumers to rent DVDs instead. We would then tax the MP3 players heavily and the PVRs lightly. This technique, systematically applied, would indeed reduce the distortionary effect of a tax on devices and services. But the pattern of levies it generated would likely be troublesome for other reasons. Consumers would end up paying much more for things they considered "necessities" and only modestly more for things they considered "luxuries." And, at best, this maneuver could only mitigate the problem of behavior distortion, not eliminate it altogether.[37]

In short, each of the two major tax options has merits and demerits. If an income tax were (or became) politically viable, it probably would be the better of the two approaches. Until then, we would likely have to rely on a tax on devices and services, despite its imperfections.

Measuring Value

The principle on which this pot of money would be distributed among the registrants of audio and video recordings would be the same one that underlies the current system: consumer sovereignty. Somewhat more specifically, our objective would be to make each artist's share of the pot proportional to the total value that, during a given year, consumers derived from his or her creations.

Three separate considerations justify continued adherence to this criterion. First, it would provide appropriate signals to musicians and filmmakers. Only if they know what consumers desire—and know that the sizes of their own incomes depend upon the extent to which their products satisfy those desires—will they be induced, collectively, to produce an optimal mix of music and movies. Second, it would be fair. At least in the view of most Americans and Western Europeans, distributive justice requires giving each person in a collective enterprise (whether it be a project, an industry, or a society) a share of its fruits proportional to his or her contribution to the venture. Applied in this context, that belief justifies adjusting artists' rewards to match their relative contributions to consumers' enjoyment of entertainment products. Finally, it would avoid relying on the judgments of government officials concerning which entertainment products are meritorious and which are not—a system that would invite censorship and political bias.[38]

Currently, to determine the value that consumers place upon a given entertainment product, we use the price system. In other words, we use consumers' willingness and ability to pay for access to a given product as an indicator of how much they value that product. Under the proposed alternative compensation system, that familiar tactic would be unavailable. One of the system's central features is that consumers would not pay anything (in cash, anyway) for access to entertainment. How then do we gauge the value to them of particular songs and films?

A good (although, as we will see, not perfect) technique would be to count the frequency with which each song or film was enjoyed. Consumers, we can expect, will gravitate toward the products that give them the most pleasure. By observing what they are listening to and watching, we can get a decent sense of what they value. (In effect, something like a price system is at work here. Consumers are paying with their time for particular products. Put differently, the cost to them of watching a particular film is the associated opportunity cost—the pleasure they could reap from watching a different film or engaging in some other activity.)

Would we need to observe and record *every* instance in which someone listened to a song or watched a movie? No. Our goal, remember, is to estimate the *relative* value to consumers in the aggregate of each entertainment product. For that purpose, neither a comprehensive count nor perfect accuracy is essential, just a system for determining, roughly, the relative popularity of registered songs and films.

It would be easy to construct such a system for streamed recordings. Noninteractive Webcasters could be required to provide the Copyright Office records indicating which recordings (identified by their registration numbers) they broadcast at what times—and approximately how many listeners used their services at various times during the day. (As we saw in Chapter 3, Webcasters are already required to collect such data. The proposed reward system would leave that accounting requirement undisturbed. The only difference is that Webcasters would now not be obliged to pay fees to copyright owners.) Interactive Webcasters—that is, Websites that stream music or movies to individuals "on demand"—would similarly keep track of the number of times they supplied to a consumer each registered recording.[39]

Rates of CD burning would also be reasonably easy to estimate. Sales data for prerecorded CDs, combined with periodic surveys to determine (1) the frequency with which discs of particular genres get copied (presumably lower for classical music than for hip-hop, for example) and (2) the total number of times discs of each genre typically get played, would enable us to predict with sufficient accuracy the consumption rates of particular sets of recordings. As DVD burning becomes more common, a similar technique would be used to estimate the consumption of movies originally distributed in DVD format.

Unfortunately, counting consumptions of downloaded recordings would be harder. Counting the downloads themselves would be straightforward: Websites that make audio or video files available for download could be required to keep track of the number of times each was copied. Similarly, peer-to-peer file-sharing services could be required to provide data concerning the frequency with which particular recordings (each one bearing a unique registration number in its filename) were transmitted through their systems. (The Napster litigation [discussed in Chapter 3] made clear that the gathering of such data is feasible. KaZaA has already volunteered to collect such information and make it available to an appropriate government agency. All of the other file-sharing services could be required to do so—as a condition of immunization from liability for copyright infringement.)

The trouble is that the figure we care about is not the total number of times each recording is copied, but the frequency with which each recording is listened to or watched. Three circumstances make it dangerous to try to derive the latter figure from the former. First, many consumers currently use file-sharing systems to try out music. The ubiquity of this practice is suggested by a study conducted during the early years of Napster by a group of AT&T researchers. Of approximately eight thousand MP3 recordings downloaded through the system by students at Oberlin College during a two-month period in 1999, more than 15 percent were listened to only once, more than 50 percent were listened to less than once (meaning that the downloader began playing the song but concluded, even before it was finished, that he or she didn't like it), and more than 10 percent were never listened to at all. Less than 10 percent of the downloaded songs were played more than four times. Casual conversations suggest that this practice is less common today; file-sharers are more adept at locating and downloading only songs they want to keep. But even if the percentage of songs sampled and discarded has dropped considerably, we should be wary of assuming that, just because a recording has been transmitted through a file-sharing system, someone is regularly watching or listening to it.[40]

The second circumstance also pertains more to music than to film. Ideally, we would like to know how often each recording is listened to, not how many people like it barely enough to keep a copy of it in their collections. If consumers store on their hard drives just as many Doobie Brothers songs as Eric Clapton songs, but play the latter ten times as often, we would want to pay Clapton ten times as much. Counting downloads plainly will not enable us to do this. To be sure, the present system for compensating artists suffers from the same distortion. In the new regime, however, the problem would be worse because consumers, undeterred by the high cost of a complete set of Doobie Brothers CDs, are more likely to have the entire collection gathering virtual dust on the virtual shelves of their computers.

The third problem is that a system of counting downloads would make it discouragingly easy for unscrupulous people to "game" the system. In the simplest version of this tactic, artists could program their computers to download their own registered songs or films continuously, deleting each copy as soon as it was saved. Many more complex schemes can be imagined. Originally, I thought that "ballot-stuffing" of this sort could be kept to manageable levels (though of course not eliminated entirely) by disregarding multiple downloads to a single IP number and by penalizing people who were found to have engaged in such deliberate deception. But I have now been persuaded—largely by vigorous online debate of this issue—that such checks would be ineffectual. As Aaron Swartz notes, "MIT has 16.5 million Internet addresses which a clever student could download the song from, racking up billions of downloads without causing an unusual number of copies from any single address. The student could do it completely anonymously, from an innocuous laptop anywhere on the MIT campus and so could avoid any penalties you tried to impose."[41]

In short, if we want to know how frequently people actually consume downloaded recordings, we need some mechanism other than a raw count of the number of copied files. What could we use?

The option that currently seems most promising would be sampling. Both the strengths and the weaknesses of this technique are well illustrated by the business practices of Nielsen Media Research, the dominant supplier to television networks and local stations of data concerning the number of households that watch particular broadcasts—data that both the stations and advertisers, in turn, rely upon when setting advertising license fees. To gather that data, Nielsen pays rotating, medium-sized samples of households, chosen to be representative of the population as a whole, to report what they watch. The methods by which such reports are made vary. The roughly five thousand households that form the national sample use "People Meters"—sophisticated set-top boxes that keep track not only of the channel to which each television is tuned but also of who within each household is watching the television at a given time, and then automatically transmit that information to Nielsen. The roughly five hundred households that form the sample for each of the fifty-five major local markets use a combination of less sophisticated set-top boxes plus paper diaries, in which viewers record by hand their consumption habits. Finally, the households that constitute the samples for the smaller local markets rely exclusively on paper diaries.[42]

Overall, this system works remarkably well. Most studies have concluded that the Nielsen estimates of viewing habits are fairly accurate. Nevertheless, the system has three characteristics that reduce its precision. First, the members of the sampled households have to do something in order to register their viewing choices. The burden is slight with respect to the People Meters, but substantial with respect to the paper diaries. Awareness of that burden causes several problems. Some households—especially wealthy households relatively insensitive to monetary incentives—selected by Nielsen to participate in the samples refuse to do so. Within households that do agree to participate, some members refuse or neglect to register their viewing choices. Young and minority viewers apparently are especially likely to opt out. Finally, constant reminders that their choices are being recorded gives rise to a "conditioning" effect, in which viewers alter their behavior in order to affect the aggregate ratings. The second troublesome characteristic of the system is that viewers—particularly those dependent on diaries—can misreport what they watch. Sometimes they do so inadvertently. At the end of the week, when they fill out the forms, they remember the popular well-advertised shows they saw and forget the marginal shows. Sometimes they do so semi-deliberately—for example, by "forgetting" to report pornographic or juvenile programs. The third of the limitations of the system is that the size of the samples is too small. They may have been adequate ten or twenty years ago, when viewers' choices were more limited. But as the programming available through cable and satellite systems has become increasingly diverse, the ability of the system to reflect accurately consumers' choices has declined.[43]

The Nielsen sampling approach could be adapted for use in an alternative compensation system. Specifically, the Copyright Office could randomly select a set of entertainment consumers who were willing to allow the office to monitor what they actually listen to and watch. The imperfections of the Nielsen model could be avoided (or at least mitigated) through the following, related adjustments. First, the process of gathering data concerning consumers' habits could and should be automated. Software—distributed as "plugins" for playback devices or bundled with peer-to-peer file-sharing applications—would automatically record the registration numbers of the songs and films that sample members heard and watched (all the way through) and periodically transmit that information to the office. Sample members thus would experience no inconvenience and would have few opportunities to misreport their choices.

Next, the size of the sample employed by the Copyright Office would have to be vastly larger than the sizes of the samples used by Nielsen. This would be essential to enable reasonably accurate estimates of the frequency with which each member of an enormous array of songs and films were being consumed. It would be feasible because of the low cost of the automated reporting system.

A final, important constraint on the design of a sampling system: to persuade a representative set of households to permit their consumption patterns to be monitored, one would have to provide them credible assurances of privacy. In other words, they would have to be persuaded that the data the Copyright Office gathered concerning the frequency with which they watched particular films or listened to particular songs would be aggregated when determining the amounts of money paid to artists, would be discarded after each monthly accounting, and would not be made available to any other public or private entity. If, but only if, the Copyright Office could credibly make such a promise, many people would probably be willing to volunteer. After all, the effect of agreeing to participate is that one's favorite artists would get compensated. But the assurances of privacy would be essential. Otherwise, anyone at all uneasy about making their entertainment choices public would refuse to participate. Unless privacy lovers are perfectly representative of the population at large in their tastes in music and film (unlikely), the result would be distortion of the consumption count.[44]

A system of this sort would avoid the bulk of all three of the kinds of distortion that would afflict simple download counts. Would it be perfect? No. It would still be possible for artists, if they were selected for inclusion in the sample, to set their computers to play their own recordings endlessly (while they were at work), thereby artificially inflating estimates of the popularity of their works. But because the system would only count songs that have been played all the way through, the number of such "false positives" would be limited—and the resultant distortion of the consumption estimates would be tolerable. If a significant number of sample members persisted in this practice, the Copyright Office might modify its guidelines to curb it. For example, it might adopt a rule that no more than three "plays" of a given song and no more than one showing of a given movie within a twenty-four-hour period would be counted. (A minor, probably acceptable side effect of this constraint would, of course, be underpayment of the Beatles if some sample members truly did want to listen to "Yellow Submarine" continuously for eight hours a day.)

To sum up, the most plausible way of estimating the relative values to consumers of downloaded registered recordings would be to use a large-scale sampling system that automatically detects and records what persons willing to participate in such a regime are actually watching and listening to, and that aggregates such reports to prevent government officials from learning the consumption choices made by specific participants. The difficulties associated with this issue should not be underestimated. In particular, worries concerning the temptations to "game" the system justifiably loom large in the criticisms that have been made of all compulsory licensing systems. But the sampling approach seems sufficient to avoid the most serious of the known sources of distortion. Two other factors provide additional sources of solace. First, the large majority of consumers would try to make the system work, not to break it. After all, by disguising their true consumption patterns, they would not change the amount they paid in taxes; they would only prevent their favorite artists from getting their fair shares. Second, this task will get easier over time—as people increasingly consume recorded entertainment not by replaying permanent copies of recordings but through interactive streaming, which prevents far fewer logistical challenges.

Systems of the sorts described above would go far toward providing us information concerning the relative value to consumers of entertainment products. However, even a perfect count of consumption patterns would neglect two important factors—which, if possible, we should strive to take into account. The first is differences in the duration of works. Generally speaking, longer recordings provide more value to consumers than shorter recordings. The former keep people entertained longer than the latter. Viewed from another angle, the former demand from consumers more of their scarce time than the latter; the fact that consumers are willing to pay that price is indicative of the greater value they derive from the former. Various aspects of the laws and business models that currently govern the entertainment industry reflect sensitivity to this variable. A CD containing three twenty-minute recordings costs the same as a CD containing fifteen four-minute recordings. In effect, the copyright owner of the former earns more per song than the copyright owner of the latter. The mechanical royalties paid to the composers of songs (discussed in detail in Chapter 2) also vary with the duration of the resultant recordings. The current rate is 8 cents for recordings up to five minutes in length, and 1.55 cents per minute (or fraction thereof) for longer recordings. Thus, the composer of a song captured in a twenty-minute recording receives from the record company 31 cents for each copy made and distributed, while the composer of a song captured in a four-minute recording receives approximately one quarter of that amount. Pricing practices with respect to video recordings are not so consistent, but duration does matter to some extent. For example, a DVD or tape containing a short children's film or documentary typically costs less to rent or buy than a DVD or tape containing a feature-length film.

An alternative compensation system could and should incorporate this variable even more precisely. If we wished to give it a great deal of weight, we would multiply the number of times each registered work was listened to or watched by its duration when determining the share of the tax revenues to which each registrant was entitled. (Remember that we collected on the registration form the data necessary to make such adjustments.) But that may be going too far. Is a fifteen-minute version of "Stairway to Heaven" really worth three times as much to listeners as a five-minute Beatles song? Polls and studies of consumer behavior, conducted by the Copyright Office, might suggest a more modest multiplier. The main point is that some adjustment for duration would seem warranted.

Would the result be to induce all musicians to make long songs and all producers to create long films? No. The same forces that constrain the length of recordings today—cost pressure and awareness of consumers' tastes and attention spans—would offset the lure of larger per-consumption fees.

The second factor we risk neglecting is variation in the intensity of the pleasure consumers get from different works. For all three of the reasons outlined at the start of this section, we would want, if possible, to pay more to the creators of recordings that give consumers intense satisfaction than to the creators of recordings that please them less.

With respect to music, this variable is likely to be captured reasonably well in our consumption counts. If I like song number 1 a good deal, I am likely to listen to it often. If I like song number 2 less well, I am likely to listen to it less often. A determination of how frequently a given song is heard will thus be a reasonably good guide to the intensity of the pleasure consumers get from it. Even in the context of music, however, this correlation will be imperfect. Suppose, for example, I play recordings by Roy Hargrove and Branford Marsalis equally often, but the former I use as background music, while the latter engage my full attention. The greater value to me of Marsalis's music will not be captured in a consumption count.

With respect to movies, consumption data will be an even poorer indicator of consumers' experiences. To be sure, if I love a film, I may watch it more than once. But, of the large majority of films that I watch only once, some will give me a great deal of enjoyment, others relatively little. Refining our estimates of the relative value of different films to consumers would require us somehow to take such variations into account. To be sure, the present system does not. I cannot demand a rebate if, upon emerging from a theatre, I feel that the film I just watched was mediocre. Nor do I ordinarily tip the studio after watching what I consider a great film. But that the present system is crude in this respect does not mean that we should accept similar imperfection in the proposed regime.

So, would it be possible to take intensity of enjoyment into account? The most obvious of the possible mechanisms for doing so would be to ask consumers. In other words, a system based on consumption rates could be supplemented (or, conceivably, replaced) by a voting system. Several scholars exploring the possibility of an alternative compensation system for digital entertainment have considered schemes of this general sort. For example, in the spring of 2003, a small group of lawyers, academics, and musicians met at the Banff Centre for the Arts to continue a conversation begun the previous fall at the Blur Workshop on Power at Play in Digital Art and Culture concerning possible ways of compensating artists whose works are downloaded through peer-to-peer technologies. One of the participants, Jamie Love, subsequently reported the fruits of their discussions in a document known as the "Blur/Banff Proposal." Among its principal features is the following suggestion:

> To counter the dangers of government control over allocations, or the lack of legitimacy of elites to allocate funds, there was a proposal that listeners themselves could directly or indirectly decide who received funds. Listeners would not avoid the compulsory licensing fee, but they would decide who would receive the money. There were several variations on this theme including proposals that listeners would choose artists directly or intermediators that supported musicians.
>
> The role of the intermediaries was discussed at length. There were after all, lots of areas where buyers or sellers now choose intermediators for various tasks. For example, companies who sell stocks choose exchanges to list shares, and the various exchanges compete against each other for the public's trust. The more the exchange is trusted, the more access to investor support.
>
> It was proposed that intermediaries would compete against each other, offering listeners different alternatives for how the money would be distributed. In this model, each intermediator could propose very different systems, and listeners would decide (and continually re-evaluate) where to put their money,

effectively choosing the groups that did the best job in supporting artists. Anything would be possible. For example, an intermediator might propose to:

1. Give all the money to performances of a specific genre of music, such as African music, American jazz, or performances of classical music
2. Ensure that 15 percent of the revenue supported retired blues artists that are down on their luck
3. Allocate all money on the basis of the volume of downloads
4. Allow the listeners to directly allocate fees to specific artists.[45]

A system of this sort would indeed enable us to track more precisely the values that people place upon digital works. Under such a system, for example, Marsalis would get more of my money than Hargrove.

Voting would not merely enable consumers to identify and reward music they really like, but it would also enable them to express preferences of other sorts. As some of the examples set forth in the Blur/Banff Proposal suggest, consumers might decide to divert flows of money from artists that they like to hear or watch to artists that they deem "deserving"—for example, because they were pioneers in a particular field or because they are especially needy. Among other things, this power might help to offset what the Blur/Banff discussants refer to as "the Britney effect"—the unfortunate tendency, discussed in Chapter 2, for "most of the money [to go] to a handful of famous artists, making them fabulously wealthy while other artists barely eke out an existence."[46]

Another potential advantage of such a system is identified by Peter Eckersley. A voting mechanism would likely require simple pieces of hardware and software, which in turn could be configured so as to frustrate ballot-stuffing, a phenomenon that, as we have seen, threatens a usage-based system.[47]

These benefits are considerable, but they are offset by some serious worries. The simplest is that it is notoriously difficult to induce people to vote. Many Webcasters, for example, currently ask their listeners to "rate" the songs that are streamed to them; few listeners take the trouble to do so.

A different sort of worry involves the criteria that consumers might employ when casting their votes. "Giv[ing] all the money to performances of a specific genre of music, such as African music" seems unobjectionable, even commendable. But what if consumers used their power to reward musicians they found physically attractive or personable? One of the features of the current entertainment industry that many artists find noxious is the need they feel to present an attractive persona—through music videos, magazine photos and interviews, and so on—in order to sell records or films. A voting system might increase rather than reduce that problem—and thus exacerbate, rather than alleviate, "the Britney effect." Yet another possibility, identified by Eugene Volokh, is that consumers would vote, not for the musicians whose music they most liked, but for political causes. I might decide to devote all of my share of the tax revenues to the National Rifle Association, owner of the copyright in "The Second Amendment Blues," or the Sierra Club, owner of the copyright in "Tree-Sitting Chants."[48]

Such an outcome would be unfortunate for two separate reasons. First, it would divert money from the entertainment industry to politicians or lobbying organizations—one of the things that opponents of alternative compensation systems most fear. Second, it would introduce static into the signals that we are trying to provide musicians and filmmakers—indications of the kinds of recordings that consumers like to hear and watch. On balance, therefore, it seems that the hazards of voting systems exceed their potential benefits.

Is there any other way in which we could measure more sensitively the intensity of consumers' likes (and dislikes)? One possibility, suggested by Steve Shavell, would be to observe the ways in which consumers behave when confronted with the same or similar products in other contexts. For example, from the fact that tickets to the opera commonly cost more than tickets to rock concerts, we might infer that opera provides its devotees more intense satisfaction. Similarly, from the fact that Universal Music recently lowered the suggested retail price of all of its CDs—except those in its classical collection—from $18 to $12, one might infer that classical music is more valuable to its listeners than music of other genres. And so forth. These inferences would then be used to adjust the payments made to the registrants of recordings that fell into each category—for example, to give registrants of opera more per consumption than the registrants of rock.

At one, very high level, use of this technique seems to make good sense. When deciding how much of the pot to distribute to the registrants of movies and how much to distribute to the registrants of sound recordings, it's probably wise to look for guidance, at least for the immediate future, to the ways in which consumers in the aggregate have behaved in the recent past. Specifically, we can and should assume that the relative amounts that consumers spent during the past few years on movies and music fairly reflect the difference in the value they derived, in the aggregate, from those very different forms of entertainment. This guideline, in conjunction with the "make-whole" principle on which the system is founded, argues for maintenance of the shares each sector enjoyed before the new technologies began to undercut their markets. Thus, if our rough estimates of the magnitude of the injuries sustained by each group of copyright owners proved accurate, the Copyright Office in 2004 would divide up the pie as follows: $527 million ($479 million, adjusted for inflation) to the owners of copyrights in films; $168 million ($153 million, adjusted for inflation) to the owners of copyrights in musical compositions; and $1.214 billion ($1.104 billion, adjusted for inflation) to the owners of copyrights in sound recordings.

Past this point, however, the technique seems highly problematic for three reasons. First, as the foregoing examples suggest, it would be possible to employ this method only to differentiate *types* of recordings (opera versus rock music; action movies versus comedies; and so on), not to differentiate individual songs and films. Determining the relevant categories—and then deciding how to classify individual recordings—would be hard, costly, and controversial. (Are Jackie Chan films best described as action movies, comedies, or something else entirely?) Second, the difficulty of making choices of these sorts would create opportunities for government officials to indulge their biases concerning the relative merits of various types of entertainment —one of the primary hazards of an alternative compensation system. Finally, adoption of this approach would forfeit one of the great advantages of an alternative compensation system as compared to a market system. In the former, unlike the latter, the menu of entertainment products made available to the public would reflect fairly the preferences of all consumers of digital entertainment and would not be tilted toward the tastes of the rich, who are able and willing to pay more for their songs and films.

Once again, therefore, it seems that a technique for tracking more carefully the intensity of consumers' desires, though intriguing, has more costs than benefits. We would be better off relying on the imperfect approach outlined above: a simple consumption count, adjusted to take into account differences in the duration of songs and films.

Derivative Works

It is increasingly common these days for audio and video recordings to incorporate portions of other recordings. The proposed system would make it possible to divide the stream of revenue attributable to such a derivative or composite recording among the various contributors to it. How exactly the division should be made should be left to the Copyright Office. But some illustrative cases may be helpful in identifying general principles that could guide the office in formulating detailed guidelines:

Digital Sampling. Rap musicians frequently take snippets of other songs and rework them into new recordings. (For the reasons explored in Chapter 2, when unauthorized this activity is illegal under current copyright law, but is common nevertheless.) Because the bulk of the creative contribution to the final recording comes from the rap musician, it seems appropriate to give him or her the lion's share of the resultant revenue. That intuition is consonant with (and may reflect) a rough-and-ready utilitarian calculus: giving the original creator a small portion of the revenue would increase incentives for creating works suitable for sampling without eroding substantially the incentives to produce rap music. It also seems fair—using as our guide the criterion of distributive justice outlined above. What formula would serve these ends? Because the sampled sounds typically constitute only a small portion of the final recording, distributing revenue in proportion to the relative durations of the old and new material would seem to do the trick. As always, precision is not essential. The approximations solicited in Question 7 of the registration form would be sufficient.

Expurgated films. Chapter 1 described the increasingly common practice of preparing and distributing versions of commercially released films from which violent or sexually explicit material has been deleted—and argued that, though of questionable legality under current copyright law, this activity is socially valuable and should be encouraged. How should the revenues attributable to the consumption of such expurgated versions be distributed? All of the material in such recordings has been derived from the original copyrighted film. (Thus the registrant would have checked the last box in Question 7.) Under these circumstances, it would seem fair—and would preserve appropriate incentives for filmmaking—to give the bulk of the revenue to the owner of the copyright in the original film. But not all; the expurgator deserves a reward, and we would want to provide incentives for expurgation. A 75 percent/25 percent split would seem roughly right—the exact numbers to be left to the discretion of the Copyright Office.

Mash-ups. What should happen when an artist combines an audio recording, a video recording, and some new material to create a novel work (of the sort described in Chapter 1)? Suppose, to make the problem concrete, that the new material consisted of more than 5 percent of the final recording, so the registrant thereof checked the next-to-last box in Question 7. The same considerations discussed in the preceding example seem germane. The only difference is that the owners of the copyrights in the underlying audio and video recordings would split (roughly) 75 percent of the resultant revenue stream, leaving the remainder to the masher. (Could the owners of the copyrights in the audio and video recordings object? Not if they had registered their works in the system. The implications for "moral rights" of this feature of the model will be reconsidered shortly.)

So far, we have considered only one layer of derivative works. But once such a system were in place, one would expect to see multiple layers—mash-ups of expurgated films and rap recordings, and so on. Would the system continue to allocate to each contributor to the final work his or her fair share? Yes, but only up to the point past which the administrative costs associated with tracking each contribution and distributing the resultant money made it senseless to do so. Modern computer technology would place that point well down the road. But, again roughly speaking, once the chain of derivative works became long enough that the share attributable to one of the contributors to an early link dipped below 1 percent, he or she would cease receiving any revenue.[49]

Merits and Demerits

Almost (but not quite) everyone would benefit from adoption of this system. The most direct beneficiaries would be consumers. To see how and how much, bear in mind that the average American household currently spends approximately $470 per year on purchases, rentals, and subscription access to audio and video recordings. In addition, the members of the average household also "pay" a large (although difficult to calculate) amount for access to recordings on radio and television by listening to or watching advertisements they would rather not hear or see. Against this backdrop, consider how, in the first year of its operation, the proposed regime would affect the three major subsets of consumers.[50]

- The group that would benefit most dramatically consists of the 30.2 million households that, in 2004, will already have both computers and broadband access. The new tax would increase their subscription fees during the first year by $64. But in return, they would now have convenient ad-free access to unlimited amounts of recorded entertainment for no additional charge. Assuming, plausibly, that they formerly spent at least average amounts on music and films, they would be far better off.
- The 34.8 million households that, in 2004, will be connected to the Internet but lack broadband subscriptions would have three choices. They could (A) subscribe to a cable-modem or DSL service, which would increase their annual costs for Internet access from approximately $221 to approximately $609 per year—a jump of $388—and thereby reap the full benefits of the new system; (B) rely upon their dial-up modems and obtain, for no additional

cost, ad-free recorded entertainment less conveniently and rapidly than they could through broadband service; or (C) simply continue to buy recorded entertainment in the old-fashioned ways. Options A and B would leave them better off; option C would leave them no worse off.[51]

- The 44.5 million households that, in 2004, will still not be connected to the Internet would probably end up, on balance, in more or less the same position. They too would still be able to gain access to entertainment in the traditional fashions—buying CDs, renting and buying videotapes, listening to commercial radio, watching commercial television, and so on. In that sense, they would not be injured. They might reap an ancillary benefit from the creation of the new regime: for reasons we will consider shortly, the variety of music and movies in public circulation would likely increase. On the other hand, at least some of those new products would probably only be available online—and thus would be beyond their reach. Bottom line: they would be unlikely to suffer net harm and might even gain.

To be sure, some consumers would have to buy new kinds of electronic equipment to take full advantage of this new system. But Americans are already buying personal computers—the most expensive component of an Internet-based entertainment system—at extraordinary rates for reasons entirely unrelated to obtaining music and movies. Most of the other possible components are not especially costly. And consumers who made the shift would no longer need to buy (and repair) the gadgets necessary to handle the old formats: CD players, VCRs, DVD players, and so on.

From the standpoint of consumers, the new regime would have other advantages as well. Because the marginal cost of entertainment would now be close to zero, they could listen to and watch as many songs and films as they wanted. Using the language of economics, the net result would be a substantial diminution in "deadweight loss" and a corresponding increase in "consumer surplus." Using a less technical vocabulary, the result would be a major change in the "feel" of music and film. We would come to experience recorded entertainment of all sorts the way we now experience the material available on the radio and television. It would be always available, and would seem free. The difference is that the quality and variety of that "free" content would rise sharply and would not be larded with advertisements.

Another major change is that, within the portion of the entertainment market governed by the new system, price discrimination would be eliminated. No longer would consumers be separated into classes, differentiated on the basis of their ability and willingness to pay for recordings. Now, all consumers would pay the same (low) amount—through taxes on electronic products and services—for audio and video recordings. Should we applaud that effect? For obvious reasons, consumers would benefit. But what about society at large? You will recall that the closing sections of Chapter 4 suggested that, on balance, the sorts of refined price-discrimination schemes made possible by effective encryption systems would be inferior, from a social-welfare standpoint, to the combination of monopoly pricing and second-degree price discrimination practiced by record companies and movie studios today. That conclusion is debatable. But there is no question that uniform, marginal-cost pricing would be better, from a social-welfare standpoint, than either of those strategies.

Finally, as compared either to the current state of affairs or to the reform proposals considered in Chapters 4 and 5, the proposed regime would have a large additional advantage for consumers: they could do whatever they wanted with the digital recordings they received. Neither technological nor legal impediments would interfere with their ability to modify to their hearts' content the songs or movies that came into their hands. The potential for semiotic democracy—of the sort considered in detail in Chapter 1—would be enormous.

Artists of all sorts would also benefit in two ways from the new system. First, their incomes would be protected from corrosion. Second, they would enjoy greater artistic freedom and financial independence. The latter effect is easiest to see—and probably would be greatest—with respect to musicians. Chapters 1 and 2 showed how and why most performing artists suffer in the current music industry. Until recently, they could only hope for fame and fortune by entering into long-term contracts with the major record companies. The terms of those contracts typically were onerous. The net result was that only a few stars, heavily promoted by their companies, prospered. Recently, a decline in the costs of musical production has encouraged a growing number of artists to break free of those arrangements and set up shop on their own. But the absence of a plausible business model for selling their recordings directly to fans has limited the number of such defections. The proposed regime would expand the opportunities sharply. In the new environment, musicians could create (at modest cost) their own recordings, set up Websites, and offer their wares to the world at large. Consumers would not pay for the recordings directly. Rather, the musicians would receive royalties through the government—the magnitude of which would depend on the popularity of their music.

An important side effect would be a substantial increase in the variety of recordings available to the public. For the reasons sketched in Chapter 2, the range of entertainment products generated by the major suppliers has been declining recently. The number of films released annually in the United States has been stable in recent years, but many observers think that the variety has been diminishing. Similar narrowing has occurred in the music industry. If distribution by the major intermediaries—record companies and studios—is no longer the only way of profitably providing recorded entertainment to consumers, one can expect the set of suppliers and the kinds of things they supply to increase radically.

In addition, the proposed system would help us to reconcile two goals long considered to be in conflict—facilitating cumulative innovation, and ensuring that pioneers are adequately compensated. Situations involving tensions between those two aspirations arise in many economic and cultural contexts. X develops a new form of air brake for trains and patents his or her invention; Y adds a feature to X's invention, producing a substantially superior braking system. X's novel combines an unusual and intriguing plot with mediocre writing; Y, a better writer, creates a second, more readable novel using the same plot. X develops the first user-friendly computer program for managing spreadsheets; Y develops a functionally superior program with a user interface identical to X's. In each of these instances, we wish to provide X sufficient legal rights to encourage potential pioneers in the future to produce analogous breakthroughs and then to make them available to the public—but also to prevent X from exercising those rights in ways that interfere with the ability of others to improve upon their breakthroughs.

The tools that copyright law provides for dealing with situations like this were reviewed in Chapter 2: the "substantial similarity" test; the "derivative works" doctrine; the fair-use doctrine; and the exclusion of copyright protection for "methods of operation." Those tools have three defects. First, they are notoriously vague. For example, as we saw in Chapters 2 and 3, each instance in which an improver like Y claims that his creation should be deemed a "fair use" of X's copyrighted work must be resolved on an ad-hoc basis by a court. This process is expensive and often unpredictable. Second, the doctrines are poorly designed to identify and excuse *improvements* upon prior works, rather than mere consumptions of prior works. Finally, these doctrines are capable of generating only one of two outcomes with respect to a given controversy. Either Y's work is deemed an infringement of X's work, in which case Y must pay X a freely negotiated fee for the right to use X's creation, and X may, if he or she wishes, refuse to grant permission at any price—or Y's work is not deemed to be an infringement of X's work, in which case Y is free to distribute his or her improvement to the public and X gets no share of the proceeds. The analogous doctrines in patent law—the rules governing "equivalents," "reverse equivalents," and "blocking patents"—are only slightly more supple.[52]

For these purposes, the proposed compensation system would work better than either copyright or patent law on many dimensions. As the previous section showed, the creators of composite entertainment products (such as rap music, expurgated movies, and "mash-ups") would, in their registration forms, identify the copyrighted works that they had incorporated into their own products and the total duration thereof. Using that data and some formulae, the revenue stream attributable to each composite product would be divided among the various contributors to it in rough proportion to the relative magnitudes of their contributions. The result would be a cheap, predictable, easily administered system in which both pioneers and improvers are appropriately compensated. As entertainment products that build overtly upon other entertainment products become ever more common and important, this advantage of the proposed system would loom ever larger.

So, artists would benefit financially from the new regime, would become less dependent on a few intermediaries to distribute their recordings, and would enjoy much greater freedom to incorporate into their own products other artists' creations. All to the good. But what about those artists whose creations are appropriated without permission—the director whose masterpiece is sanitized; the singer whose signature recording is incorporated into a motion picture whose message the singer considers loathsome; and so on? Under current copyright law, they (or their assignees) would be able to block the preparation of such derivative works. Under the proposed alternative compensation system, they could not. (They'd make money when the modified forms are distributed, but could not block either their creation or their distribution.) For some artists, the prospect of such a loss of control over the manner in which their works are presented to the public is horrifying.[53]

They might find some solace in two aspects of the system—one legal, the other technological. First, the proposed regime would leave untouched the rules of trademark law that forbid deceiving consumers concerning the sources of goods and services. Thus, for example, it would violate the Lanham Act to distribute to the public an expurgated version of a Spielberg movie without making clear that it differed from the version Spielberg originally created. (To avoid this legal hazard, one would expect expurgators to insert into the initial credits for their movies disclaimers of the general sort: "This film has been modified from its original version. Sexually explicit language and scenes have been deleted. The creator and copyright owner of the original version are not responsible for these changes.") Second, the Copyright Office registry upon which the new regime would be based would be made available to the general public on the Internet. The result is that any consumer could easily ascertain the composition of any registered audio or video recording—what other recordings it incorporated and how much original material had been added to them. Together, these features would reduce to a minimum the danger that a consumer would mistakenly give a composer, performer, or filmmaker either too much or too little credit for a given work.

Nevertheless, it remains true that artists would, under this regime, lose a good deal of the control they exercise under American copyright law over what happens to their works once they enter the public arena—and that some artists would find that loss painful. A blithe response would point out that this (and only this) aspect of the new regime would be voluntary, insofar as the privilege to make derivative works only applies to audio and video recordings registered in accordance with the new scheme. Thus, artists truly appalled at the prospect of losing creative control could simply refuse to register their recordings and would thereby retain the entitlements they currently enjoy under section 106(2) of the Copyright Statute. But that would not be a fair retort. The new system, if it worked, would be far superior to the existing regime as a mechanism for distributing entertainment products. If they wished to make money or to reach large audiences, most artists would likely feel compelled to use it.

A more severe response would be to assert that, in the new digital environment, musicians' and filmmakers' interests in the integrity of every copy of their recordings are no longer (if they ever were) worthy of protection. After all, artists of many other sorts are obliged to tolerate revisions and reconstructions of their works. An architect, for example, cannot prevent the owner of one of his buildings from making whatever "alterations" to the structure he wishes—or from subsequently reselling the altered structure to someone else. The rights of a cabinetmaker are similarly limited. Both of those examples involve unique works of art. The interest of a musician or filmmaker in blocking the modification and subsequent redistribution of one among millions of duplicates of his creations seems demonstrably weaker. Finally, and perhaps more important, whatever modest weight the right of integrity might have in this context is more than offset by the competing value of semiotic democracy—of enabling the public at large to participate more actively in the construction of their cultural environment.[54]

A reader unconvinced by this argument might find congenial an ingenious approach suggested by Jamie Boyle. If we wished to preserve some degree of protection for moral rights under the new regime, we might create a separate track within the system for artists reluctant to expose their works to mash-ups, sampling, parodies, and so on. By checking a box on the registration form, registrants could retain the entitlements they currently enjoy to control the preparation of derivative works (entitlements qualified, of course, by the fair-use doctrine). Electing this option would have a price; by checking the box, registrants would agree to be paid only, say, two thirds of the amount to which they would otherwise be entitled under the system. The foregone funds both would discourage artists from taking this tack cavalierly and would roughly compensate the artists who did not choose this option for the diminution in the stock of materials upon which they could draw in the future.

Who else might have cause for complaint? The manufacturers, distributors, and retailers of the containers currently used to store audio and video recordings plainly would. The largest cost savings in the proposed system result from cutting them out. It's thus not surprising that their businesses would be undermined. One could expect Tower Records and Blockbuster to close more stores, and CD and DVD makers to cut back their operations.

The big players in the existing system—the record companies and studios—would not be injured initially. On the contrary, for a few years at least, the proposed regime would help them by replacing the revenues they lose to Internet activities with money transmitted through the Copyright Office. Their longer-term fate, however, would be more in doubt. Marketing and promotion would remain crucial functions in the brave new world. Because the income of a copyright owner would, as before, depend upon the popularity of his or her creations, stimulating consumer demand for a particular song or film would continue to be important. In one scenario, the record companies and studios could capitalize on their marketing experience and power to remain vital and profitable in the new environment. In another scenario, however, they would be outperformed by newer, leaner enterprises, better able to develop and exploit the different kinds of marketing tactics enabled by the Internet. It would all depend upon the flexibility of the existing companies.

What about the manufacturers of consumer electronics and the suppliers of broadband access? Under the second of the two taxation options discussed above, their products would be subject to substantial taxes. Wouldn't that undermine their businesses? Perhaps. But the levies would not be exorbitant—far less, for example, than are imposed on alcohol, cigarettes, and gasoline. More important, the new system would make their products far more valuable to consumers and would thus increase demand for them. The creation of an alternative compensation system would also eliminate the need for rules—like the CBDTPA and the "broadcast flag" system discussed in Chapter 4—that restrict their freedom in designing their systems. Thus, on balance, they would be better, not worse off.

Finally, society at large would benefit in various ways from the shift to such a regime. The most obvious is that total transaction costs would decrease. There is substantially less law in this model than in any of the models considered in previous chapters. Many of the doctrinal questions that stimulate litigation under the current system—and that would persist in the regimes described in Chapters 4 and 5—would be irrelevant. Should the creation of a temporary buffer accompanying the streaming of an audio or video recording be considered a "public performance," a "reproduction," both, or neither? Should Launch.com be considered an "interactive" or "noninteractive" Webcaster? Millions of dollars currently turn on the answers to such questions. In the proposed system, they would be irrelevant. The results: fewer disputes, fewer lawyers, less social waste. The costs of enforcing rules would also drop sharply. As we saw in Chapter 3, the resources devoted by content providers and society at large to policing violations of copyright law have been rising fast in the past decade. Under the proposed model, they would largely disappear. Nor would content providers bear the costs of developing and deploying encryption systems. To be sure, the proposed regime would not be free. We have estimated, conservatively, that administrative costs during the start-up period would absorb 20 percent of the new tax revenues. But compared with the costs associated with all of the plausible alternatives, that drain would be modest.[55]

At least as important as these economic advantages of the proposed regime would be elimination of the widespread lawbreaking fostered by the current regime. In the spring of 2003, approximately thirty-five million Americans were downloading digital entertainment from the Internet without permission. After the RIAA began its highly publicized campaign to locate and sue individual downloaders, that number dropped sharply. But by the end of the year, at least eighteen million Americans were still engaged in the activity. A side effect (or perhaps the primary purpose) of that campaign has been to increase sharply the percentage of the population that acknowledges the illegality of this behavior. Yet millions continue to do it. That so many people are knowingly violating the law is culturally unhealthy. The reforms outlined in Chapters 4 and 5 would reduce the number of violators considerably, but many people would continue to evade the enhanced legal and technological defenses of copyrights. Even the most optimistic advocates of those reforms concede that they would generate situations analogous to our current efforts to suppress the use of "recreational" drugs. The proposed regime would enable us to avoid this unfortunate state of affairs altogether. Downloading, copying, and performing audio and video recordings would be lawful—indeed, encouraged by the owners of the copyrights in those materials.[56]

So far, the proposed system looks pretty good. To be sure, we have already discussed two substantial problems to which it would give rise. First, under both of the two plausible taxation options, the fit between the set of people who benefit from the new regime and the set of people who would pay for it would not be perfect—and that misalignment would cause some degree of unfairness and some distortion of consumers' choices. Second, unless tempered with the no-derivative-works option discussed above, it would undermine artists' control over the manner in which their creations are presented to the public. But, with these reservations, the system has many substantial attractions. We're not quite done, however. Two other aspects of the proposal create serious cause for concern.

The more obvious is that the proposed regime would confer on a government agency—most likely, the Copyright Office—a substantial amount of discretionary power. For the reasons explained above, the office would have no control over which artists within each entertainment category received which shares of the pot of revenue allocated to their genre. But the office would determine the total amount of money paid in royalties and the portions given to each type of copyright owner. Moreover, the office would make those determinations on the basis of an unavoidably vague criterion: sustaining a vibrant and flourishing entertainment culture.

To give any institution that much power is problematic. To be sure, we often do it. For example, the National Institutes of Health, the National Science Foundation, the Federal Communications Commission, the Food and Drug Administration, and the Securities and Exchange Commission all enjoy as much or more discretionary authority and shape equally important aspects of our collective lives. But it's nevertheless always cause for concern.

It's especially problematic to give this much power to a government agency that would be subject to strong pressure from representatives of the groups who stand to be affected by its decisions. The RIAA and MPAA are extraordinarily effective lobbying organizations, capable for example of recently persuading Congress to adopt the Copyright Term Extension Act, a statute widely believed to be economically misguided. Wouldn't they be able to turn this new system to their advantage?[57]

This danger is real, but is at least mitigated by two factors. First, the procedural precautions and the appellate mechanism discussed in Chapter 5 would reduce somewhat the vulnerability of the Copyright Office. Second, as was suggested above, the economic power of the primary extant intermediaries (the record companies and studios) may diminish under the new regime. Rather than confronting a tension between a concentrated and well-funded interest group and a dispersed community of consumers, the Copyright Office would, reasonably soon, be called upon to balance the needs of consumers against the needs of a similarly dispersed community of artists. Striking that balance would be difficult, and the office's judgment would not be tightly constrained by the criteria and methodology we have outlined. But at least the office's judgment would be less likely to be distorted by an imbalance in the power of the various constituencies it serves.

The final disadvantage is that a system of the sort outlined in this chapter—a tax-and-royalty regime instituted only in the United States—would leak across national boundaries. French musicians and filmmakers who registered their recordings with the American Copyright Office would be compensated, out of tax funds collected from American consumers, when those recordings were heard and watched by American consumers. But American musicians and filmmakers would receive nothing when their recordings were heard or watched by French citizens. This effect would likely make American taxpayers justifiably resentful. To be sure, American creators under such a regime would not be significantly worse off than they are at present. In the new world, as in the existing one, it would be illegal, under French copyright law, for French citizens to download American songs and films from the Internet without permission. In the new world, as in the present one, many French consumers would ignore the pertinent legal prohibitions and would fill their hard drives with American entertainment. So the new system would not *hurt* American producers. But it would also do nothing to strengthen their positions vis-à-vis "foreign pirates." In this respect, it would be less desirable than the set of legal and technological defenses outlined in Chapter 4, which would have the effect of limiting the availability of unauthorized audio and video recordings in other countries as well as in the United States.

To sum up, the advantages of the system include:

- For consumers—large cost savings, more convenient access to more diverse programming uncontaminated by advertisements, freedom from price discrimination, and greater opportunities to participate in the creative process;
- For artists—a reliable source of income, greater freedom in selecting the intermediaries to distribute their work, and expanded opportunities to draw upon existing recordings when making new ones;

- For the manufacturers of electronic equipment—increased demand for their products and the elimination of constraints upon the design of their devices;
- For society at large—a sharp reduction in the costs associated with enforcing copyright law plus elimination of the culturally unhealthy practice of widespread lawbreaking;

Its disadvantages include:

- Cross-subsidies and associated distortions of consumers' behavior;
- Erosion of artists' ability to control the public presentations of their works (unless the system contains a second track for artists hostile to the reconfiguration of their creations);
- The hazards of administrative discretion and "rent-seeking";
- Leakage across national boundaries.

Overall, though not perfect, this seems the best of the models we have considered in this book.

The Life Cycle of the System

As we've seen, many things would have to happen to get this system off the ground. The Copyright Office would have to be revamped. The registration system would have to be designed and implemented. Congress would have to authorize new taxes. If Congress opted for a tax on devices and services, rather than an increase in the income tax, the Copyright Office would have to conduct extensive hearings to develop data much more detailed and reliable than I have been able to offer here concerning the size and shape of the tax base and the amount of money necessary to offset the injuries that would be sustained by copyright owners as a result of being deprived of their traditional sources of revenue. Once all these pieces were in place, the federal copyright statute would have to be amended to permit consumers to engage in a host of activities that are currently illegal.

What, more specifically, would the necessary revisions of the copyright statute encompass? You will recall, from Chapter 2, that section 106 currently grants the owners of copyrights in musical compositions, sound recordings, and motion pictures an extensive set of exclusive rights. Sections 107 through 118 balance that grant with many exceptions and limitations. Once the regime described in this chapter were operational, Congress could and should add a new provision to the list of exceptions. The new provision (call it section 107A) would permit the following:

- Reproduction of a musical composition, sound recording, or motion picture for noncommercial purposes (that is, consumption, not resale);
- Preparation of a derivative work of a sound recording or motion picture registered pursuant to the new scheme, provided that the derivative work is also so registered before it is made available to the public[58];
- Distribution of a sound recording (including a musical composition embodied therein) or motion picture via the Internet;
- Public performance of a sound recording (including a musical composition embodied therein) via a digital audio transmission;
- Public performance of a motion picture via a digital video transmission.

These "safe harbors" correspond, as one might expect, to the methods of accessing and enjoying digital entertainment that the counting and sampling systems described above are designed to track and that determine how the new tax revenues are to be distributed.

A crucial ancillary issue: What would be the role, if any, for digital rights management in this new environment? That issue has three dimensions. First, would a copyright owner be permitted to register an audio or video recording formatted so as to limit the ways or number of times in which it could be copied or altered (such as the sound recordings distributed by Apple through its iTunes Music Store) and then collect money from the government when those recordings were reproduced or performed in ways permitted by the copy-protection system (such as streamed by a Webcaster)? Second, would a copyright owner be permitted to register an unencrypted version of a particular recording but also to distribute to the public, presumably for fees, encrypted versions of the same recording? Third, if a copyright owner opted out of the system entirely, releasing only an encrypted version of his or her recording, would he or she be able to invoke the protections of section 1201 of the Digital Millennium Copyright Act to discourage consumers from "hacking" the encryption system? The answer to none of these questions is obvious; with respect to each, reasonable arguments could be made on both sides. On balance, however, the best answers seem to be the following.

On the first issue, no. One of the main aspirations of the new regime is to foster semiotic democracy and more broadly to free consumers and artists to reproduce, modify, and redistribute recordings. Permitting copyright owners to impose partial restraints on their creations would limit our achievement of that end.

With respect to the second issue, it would seem sensible, at least until the new regime had proven its effectiveness, to permit copyright owners to adopt such a hybrid marketing strategy—for example, to sell copy-protected CDs while simultaneously registering and distributing for free via the Internet unencrypted MP3 versions of the same songs. Certainly, the preservation of this option would help reduce copyright owners' hostility to the adoption of the regime.

For much the same reason, it would seem unnecessary—at least at first—to withdraw audio and video recordings from the protection of the DMCA. Let skeptical musicians and filmmakers continue to use technological self-help measures to restrict access to their creations—and let them continue to call upon the aid of the legal system to protect those measures from hackers. If the new regime is as efficient as we have argued, the skeptics will soon discover that it is simpler, cheaper, and more profitable to register their recordings with the Copyright Office and rely upon distribution of royalties from the government for their source of income.

Those, then, are the primary statutory adjustments that would be necessary to launch the new regime. Unfortunately, that's not the end of the story. Adoption of the proposed section 107A would necessitate amendment of two treaties to which the United States is a signatory: the Berne Convention and the Agreement on Trade-Related Aspects of Intellectual Property Rights (commonly known as TRIPS). Article 2 of the former extends copyright protection to all "literary and artistic works," including "musical compositions" and "cinematographic works." Articles 9, 11, and 12 grant to the "authors" of such works the power to control their "reproduction," "public performance," and "alteration." Article 9 of the TRIPS Agreement, in turn, requires member countries to "comply with Articles 1 through 21 of the Berne Convention."[59]

Unless modified, these treaty provisions would seem to forbid the curtailment of copyright law necessitated by the proposed regime. With respect to recordings of musical compositions, Article 13 of the Berne Convention allows signatory nations some flexibility: "Each country of the Union may impose for itself reservations and conditions on the exclusive right granted to the author of a musical work, . . . but all such reservations and conditions . . . shall not . . . be prejudicial to the rights of these authors to obtain equitable remuneration which, in the absence of agreement, shall be fixed by competent authority." It is conceivable that this escape hatch might be sufficient to authorize, vis-à-vis music, the displacement of copyright law with the new reward system. But no such discretion is permitted with respect to cinematographic works. The bottom line: before implementing the proposed regime, the United States would have to obtain a modification of the Berne Convention.

What about domestic law? Would the United States Constitution interfere in any way with the creation of such a regime? It is conceivable that the holder of the copyright in a musical work, sound recording, or motion picture might challenge the proposed abrogation of his statutory entitlements as a "taking" of "property" without "just compensation" in violation of the Fifth Amendment. But such a claim would almost certainly fail. The Fifth Amendment is indeed applicable; intellectual-property rights—including copyrights—are shielded by the Constitution against uncompensated expropriation. But the expropriation effected by the new regime would not be uncompensated. On the contrary, the proposed system is explicitly designed to protect creators, as a class, against injury.

That may well be true, our hypothetical challenger might respond, but not every individual copyright owner would come out equally well under the new regime as he or she would under an unmodified copyright system. Doesn't a particular owner disadvantaged by the transition have a constitutional claim? The courts would likely reject such an argument, relying for precedential support on the failure of an analogous constitutional challenge, during the early twentieth century, to state statutes displacing the increasingly creaky tort system for compensating the victims of industrial accidents with the more efficient administrative mechanism of workmen's compensation.[60]

So much for the establishment of the regime. Once in place, it would begin, quickly, to evolve. The advantages—in terms of cost and convenience—of obtaining audio and video recordings over the Internet would entice growing numbers of consumers to buy the equipment and subscribe to the services necessary to participate in the system and simultaneously to reduce their expenditures on CDs, videotapes, and DVDs. The resultant reduction of the revenues flowing to copyright owners through traditional channels would, in turn, compel the Copyright Office to increase the volume of royalty payments. Would taxes rise? In the aggregate, certainly. If the method by which the money was raised were an income tax, then the increase in aggregate taxes over time (almost certainly at a rate faster than the growth of the population) would also generate an increase in per-capita taxes. The figure mentioned earlier—$27 per household, on average—would obtain only during the first year. The number would be larger in each subsequent year, until such time as virtually all audio and video recordings were distributed under the auspices of the new regime.

How high might the taxes go up? Would there ever come a point at which consumers would be paying more, on average, in taxes for access to entertainment than they currently pay under a market-based system? No. The new regime would be substantially more efficient than the present one for several independent reasons. First, it would eliminate the many costs associated with manufacturing and distributing containers (CDs, DVDs, and so on). Second, for the reasons sketched in Chapter 1 and emphasized by May and Singer in their analysis of Internet distribution, the overhead costs and marketing expenses of the major intermediaries would diminish under the proposed regime—in ways that the Copyright Office could and would take into account when making its annual adjustments of royalty and tax rates. Third and finally, the legal costs and R&D expenditures currently borne by copyright owners would decline sharply. (One would expect, for example, the litigation departments of the RIAA and MPAA to shrink rapidly and the budgets for projects like SDMI and P2P spoofing and interdiction virtually to disappear.) Again, those savings would be reflected in the annual accountings conducted by the Copyright Office and thus would mitigate tax increases.[61]

A reprise of the calculations outlined earlier in this chapter lends credence to that blanket prediction. Assume that, instead of displacing 20 percent of the distribution systems currently employed in the record industry and 5 percent of the analogous systems in the film industry, the new regime displaced 100 percent of both. Ignore, for the time being, the potential savings, just mentioned, in overhead, marketing, legal expenses, and encryption. Finally, assume, conservatively, no increase in the size of the population over which the taxes would be spread. How much would the average household have to pay in income taxes in order to run the expanded system? Approximately $254 per year—roughly half of the amount they are currently paying. Note that this is a worst-case scenario; almost certainly, for the reasons just outlined, the number would be lower.[62]

What if the money were raised, not through an income tax, but through a tax on devices and services? Again, the aggregate tax burden would of course rise over time. But the rate of increase would be partially offset by growth in the number of households purchasing the equipment and services necessary to take advantage of the new system. Indeed, on the assumption that the new regime would fully displace the old one only when close to 100 percent of American households had broadband access, the average tax burden per household under this approach would actually be lower than under the income-tax approach (simply because the total number of households in the United States is larger than the number that pay federal income taxes). Specifically, using the worst-case assumptions set forth, each household would pay, on average, $202 per year—or $16.84 per month—in combined taxes on their Internet subscriptions and purchases of various entertainment-related devices. (Unlike the income tax, these levies would not be imposed on a progressive basis. In other words, poor households would pay approximately the same amounts as wealthy households.)[63]

If successful, the system might expand over time to cover other forms of digital entertainment. The distribution of electronic books, for example, could easily be brought within its ambit. The electronic-games industry is a bit different, but might be folded into the system with some adjustments. These additions would require a further increase in tax rates, of course, but the benefits of the regime would expand correspondingly.

One change in the structure of the system may be forced by technological advances. At some point in the near future, Americans may cease to gain access to the Internet through individualized ISP accounts. Some other business model may emerge to enable consumers to take advantage of the rapidly developing technologies for connecting to the Internet through wireless networks. If so, running the system through taxes on devices and services— the most important of which are broadband subscriptions—would no longer be feasible. At that point, Congress would have no choice but to change to an income tax. Such a shift would be fair, insofar as, by then, the large majority of taxpayers would be beneficiaries of the regime. For the reasons sketched above, it would reduce administrative costs. And, by then, it might even be politically acceptable.

Finally, the success of the system might prompt countries other than the United States to institute similar systems. Each would impose taxes on its own residents' ISP subscriptions and purchases of electronic equipment. Each would establish a registration system, permitting copyright owners from every country to register audio and video recordings. (Ultimately, these separate national offices might be superseded or supplemented by a global registry for digital works.) Using schemes like those already outlined, each country would estimate the relative frequency with which those recordings were consumed by its residents—and would then distribute its tax revenues accordingly, to both domestic and foreign registrants. An interlocking set of national regimes of this sort would cure the third of the three major disadvantages of a tax-and-royalty system noted in the previous section—namely its tendency to leak across national boundaries. All of the national regimes would continue to leak, of course. But the leaks would occur in both directions—and would fairly reflect the extent to which consumers within one country were relying for their entertainment on works created by artists in other countries.

Coda: An Entertainment Coop

There are many advantages to a governmentally administered alternative compensation system of the sort outlined in this chapter. But what if no government were willing, at least initially, to institute such a system? Could it be created without state aid? In other words, could a voluntary analogue to such a regime be constructed in the shadow of current copyright law? Yes. If successful, such an enterprise could serve as a demonstration project—reassuring skeptical legislators of the feasibility of a more comprehensive, compulsory, tax-based regime. Alternatively, if successful enough, it might survive indefinitely without governmental aid. This final section sketches such a system, then considers its strengths and limitations.

The registration process for obtaining a unique identification number for a digital version of an audio or video recording would be virtually identical. The form the copyright owner filled out and the process of filing it would be the same. The registration process would differ in only two respects. First, instead of the Copyright Office, the registrar would be a private organization—which (for reasons to be explored shortly) we will call The Entertainment Coop. Second, the registration form would include one additional line: "By registering this work, I authorize all members of The Entertainment Coop to reproduce it for noncommercial purposes, to distribute it to other members, to modify it, to distribute to other members copies of the modified version, and to perform it publicly to other members via a digital audio or video transmission—so long as I am compensated in accordance with the rules and regulations of the coop." In other words, through a license agreement, the registrant would effect the same suspension of copyright law that, in the compulsory regime, would be achieved through law.[64]

By contrast, the source of the funds necessary to run the system would be different. Instead of taxes, the money would come from subscription fees. In other words, if and only if an individual consumer wished to participate in the system, he or she would pay a flat monthly sum. How much? Initially, it would be quite low. As the array of works available through the system increased, the fee would gradually rise—until the monthly payments roughly matched the levels of taxation discussed earlier in this chapter.

The simplest way to collect such fees would be for the coop to enter into partnerships with Internet service providers. The ISPs would, in turn, offer their customers two plans: a regular subscription, and a premium subscription that would carry with it membership in the coop. The difference between the prices charged for the two plans would be the current subscription fee for the coop, plus a small margin to induce the ISP to participate. (An especially important subset of ISPs for this purpose would be college and university networks.) Each premium subscriber would receive a password, which would provide him or her access to the various channels (described below) through which registered entertainment products would be made available. The passwords would be changed frequently to reduce unauthorized access to those channels.

Like the Copyright Office under a compulsory alternative compensation system, the Entertainment Coop would maintain a publicly available directory of all registered recordings and their corresponding registration numbers. But the coop could and should also provide its members several additional services. First, the coop would maintain on its servers—or, more plausibly, on a variety of servers run by other organizations licensed by the coop—copies of all registered recordings (in a variety of formats), which members could download to their own computers upon submitting their passwords. Next, the coop would license Webcasters to stream registered recordings to coop members. Some of those streams would be noninteractive —like the History Channel or the collection of Webcasters currently housed under the umbrella of Live365.com. Some would be interactive, providing streams of audio and video recordings to users on demand. Many of those services would be free. For access to others (especially interactive ones), members would likely have to pay a fee—but a small one, because the services themselves would not be paying the coop for the content they would be distributing. Finally, the coop would provide its members a variety of informational services—discussion boards, reviews of recently registered films and music, devices (like Gigabeat or MusicMatch, discussed in Chapter 1) that would assist members in finding recordings or services likely to match their tastes or needs.

The management of some of these services would be top-down. For example, a "disk jockey" interested in Webcasting progressive jazz would obtain from the coop a license to use any of the recordings in the coop registry. (The "price" of that license, as indicated above, would be merely a commitment to limit access to the Webcast to coop members.) The "disk jockey" would then select the sequence of cuts, perhaps add some commentary and some recorded interviews with musicians, and begin streaming.[65]

But other services could and should be organized on a bottom-up basis. For example, the selection of recordings included in some of the noninteractive Webcasts would be made, collaboratively, by their respective listeners or viewers—in other words, by subsets of the coop members. The best model for the mechanism that would make this possible is the pioneering Website "Slashdot." Yochai Benkler summarizes as follows the pertinent aspects of the system:

Billed as "News for Nerds," Slashdot primarily consists of users commenting on initial submissions that cover a variety of technology-related topics. The submissions are typically a link to an off-site story, coupled with some initial commentary from the person who submits the piece. Users follow up the initial submission with comments that often number in the hundreds. . . .

Slashdot implements an automated system to select moderators from the pool of users. Moderators are selected according to several criteria: They must be logged in (not anonymous), they must be regular users (average users, not one-time page loaders or compulsive users), they must have been using the site for a while (this defeats people who try to sign up just to moderate), they must be willing, and they must have positive "karma." Karma is a number assigned to a user that primarily reflects whether the user has posted good or bad comments (according to ratings from other moderators). If a user meets these criteria, the program assigns the user moderator status and the user gets five "influence points" to review comments. The moderator rates a comment of his choice using a drop-down list with words such as "flamebait" and "informative." A positive word increases the rating of a comment one point and a negative word decreases the rating one point. Each time a moderator rates a comment, it costs the moderator one influence point, so the moderator can only rate five comments for each moderating period, which lasts for three days. If the user does not use the influence points within the period, they expire. The moderation setup is designed to give many users a small amount of power— thus decreasing the effect of rogue users or users with poor judgment. The site also implements some automated "troll filters," which prevent users from sabotaging the system. The troll filters prevent users from posting more than once every sixty seconds, prevent identical posts, and will ban a user for twenty-four hours if the user has been moderated down several times within a short time frame.

The system is powerful and popular. Tens of thousands of people serve as volunteer editors. Hundreds of thousands read the posted stories and comments. Its rating and filtering system is widely recognized as a success.[66]

As Todd Larson suggests, a system of this general sort could be adapted for use in the Webcasting context. A group of coop members interested in a particular genre—say, samba or "alternative country"—could form a group dedicated to managing a noninteractive stream of music of that sort. Each member could submit recordings. Using a variant of the Slashdot mechanism and software, other group members would rate submitted recordings —and rate their fellow members' evaluations. Members' rating power would rise or fall depending on the extent to which their judgments found favor with their compatriots. Whether—or how often—recordings were included in the Webcast would then be determined by their weighted ratings. Any coop member, not just the participants in the club, could listen to the stream. Similar techniques might be employed to generate and sort reviews of newly registered recordings and Gigabeat-style guides for members seeking to expand their entertainment horizons.[67]

The mechanisms that the coop would use to measure the relative frequency with which registered recordings were consumed by its members would closely resemble the mechanisms that the Copyright Office would employ in a compulsory system. Suppose, for example, that Joshua Redman submitted his next set of jazz recordings. He would receive a unique registration number for each track. The operators of each of the Websites where the recordings were posted would then periodically report the number of times they had been downloaded. More important, software distributed for free to all coop members would periodically "call the mothership" to report the number of times the downloaded tracks—and all other registered recordings—had been listened to (from beginning to end). Similarly, Webcasters operated or licensed by the coop would report the number of times each track was streamed and the approximate size of the audience for that stream.

The simplest way of disbursing the funds collected through the system would be to employ exactly the same usage-based approach described earlier as the most attractive mechanism for distributing tax revenues. But the voluntary character of the coop might make more palatable some of the voting mechanisms discussed (and criticized) previously in this chapter. For example, one could imagine organizing the system so that a portion of the funds (how large a portion will be considered shortly) was distributed on the basis of relative consumption data, while the remainder was distributed on some other basis.

It would probably make most sense to organize the system as a nonprofit corporation. Its charter would set forth the design features described above. It would be administered by a traditional board of directors. In practice, however, the organization could and should function as a special kind of cooperative society. To see how and why requires some background.

There are two main kinds of cooperative enterprises. Producer cooperatives consist of firms owned and operated by the people who supply the labor or the raw materials for the products that the firm sells. The profits of such an enterprise are typically shared among its members. The most famous of these consist of the enterprises clustered in Mondragon, Spain, but others (such as traditional law firms) are scattered through modern capitalist economies. Consumer cooperatives consist of clusters of people who regularly buy a particular type of goods (such as groceries or hiking equipment) who band together to buy the goods in bulk (thereby getting better prices) and more generally to "defend and promote consumers' interests." Typically, they redistribute to their members (in the form of "dividends") the amount by which the members' contributions exceed the costs of the enterprise. Consumer cooperatives come in various shapes and sizes, but the ones that flourished in the United States in the 1960s and 1970s had an additional feature: the coop members, typically working together as volunteers, assumed many of the functions ordinarily performed by employees of retailers—selecting products, negotiating with suppliers, packaging products, stacking shelves, and serving as cashiers. Crucial to the success of most enterprises of both sorts is a spirit of cooperation, of common commitment to an enterprise (and sometimes a cause). In addition, most enterprises of both sorts are to some extent steered by their members—meaning that some of their rules and decisions are determined by their members, voting either directly or through representatives.[68]

Our proposed Entertainment Coop would incorporate some (though not all) features of traditional cooperatives of both types. The suppliers of the registered recordings would not own the enterprise, but, like the contributors to a producer cooperative, they would share its profits. Partly as a result, one could expect them to strive to nourish the enterprise—by encouraging their fans to participate, by exhorting other artists to sign up (thus helping to produce a critical mass of recordings), by providing interviews or other material for the ancillary informational services, and so on. Like the members of (American-style) consumer cooperatives, the members of the Entertainment Coop would help to shape and distribute its products—by participating, as volunteers, in Slashdot-style rating systems that would help determine what recordings were delivered to other members. An increasing percentage of the participants in the enterprise would perform both roles: they would combine material drawn from the stock of registered recordings with their own material to generate derivative works, which they in turn would register. Thus, over time, the distinction between contributors and consumers would blur.

Would the Entertainment Coop, like some traditional cooperatives, be run democratically? In other words, would its contributors or members have any say in its policies? Among the reasons for structuring the organization so as to provide them that opportunity is that it would reinforce its participatory, communitarian ethos—likely one of its main attractions. But there are hazards along this path. For example, contributors might be inclined to exercise their voting power so as to limit expenditures on the kinds of services described above and thus maximize the percentage of the organization's revenues that ended up in their own pockets. (Producer cooperatives are notoriously vulnerable to this particular disease.) Thus, if democratic procedures were incorporated into the organization, checks and balances and "constitutional" constraints analogous to those that stabilize the American system of representative government should also probably be included. For example, one might embed in the charter of the organization a provision, immune to revision through the votes of the members, that two thirds of the coop's profits must be distributed on the basis of the relative popularity of the registered recordings. One might further specify that, with respect to the distribution of the remaining one third, deviation from the relative-popularity criterion would occur only upon the affirmative consent of majorities both of the contributors and of the consumer members.[69]

A voluntary organization of the sort just sketched would have many of the advantages of a compulsory, tax-based alternative compensation system. In addition, it would be a good deal less controversial—precisely because it would be voluntary. Who could persuasively object to the formation of a new funding and distribution agency, whose success or failure would depend entirely upon whether individual artists and consumers thought it superior to the existing agencies?

Such an organization would, however, be less good than a compulsory regime in two ways. First, it would leak. Sooner or later, despite the password protections on the coop-affiliated Websites and streams, the files made available to coop members would find their way into peer-to-peer systems unaffiliated with the coop and accessible to the world at large. When the files were shared in that environment (illegally), the artists would not receive any compensation. Knowing this, why would artists be willing to participate in the system? In part because they would be no worse off than they are under the present regime—in which "ripped" versions of their recordings are already available on the peer-to-peer networks. In part, because they would gain a new stream of revenue—the volume of which would gradually increase as the number of subscribers rose. And in part, because they would gain thereby the right to make creative use of the digital products submitted to the coop by other artists. Nevertheless, in this respect, a voluntary regime would plainly be worse than a compulsory, tax-based regime, which would not be subject to any "leakage."

Second, it would be both crucial and difficult, as was suggested parenthetically above, to persuade enough musicians and filmmakers to sign up for the system in order to provide a sufficiently large stock of recordings to attract consumers. After all, the coop would have to compete with the a-la-carte for-profit distribution services, such as the iTunes Music Store and the new Napster, each of which can already offer consumers several hundred thousand recordings. To be sure, the coop would have other advantages.

Unburdened by the transaction costs associated with micropayments, its prices would be lower than those of the commercial sites. And many consumers would likely be attracted by the image of an organization that promised to distribute to its contributors all of the amount by which its revenues exceeded its operating costs. But these attractions would only go so far. In the end, the coop could survive only if very large numbers of artists signed on.

How might that be achieved? One strategy would be for a consortium of public and private actors to prime the pump. As it happens, in Brazil, something of that sort is already occurring. A group of scholars and musicians, led by Ronaldo Lemos and Joaquim Falcao, with the crucial support of Gilberto Gil, the Brazilian minister of culture, has begun to build a digital library of Brazilian music, to be called Canto Livre. To date, the organizers have focused most of their attention on gathering recordings sufficiently old that the copyrights in them have expired. (In Brazil, old music enjoys greater respect and popularity than it does in the United States.) With respect to that material, no one needs to be compensated when copies are deposited in the library and made available to the world. Soon, however, they will begin to offer the owners of the copyrights in more recent recordings fees in return for contributing their creations to the pot. Where will the money necessary to provide those incentives and then run the system come from? Initially, from a government agency (Financiadora de Estudos e Projetos, the Brazilian equivalent of the National Science Foundation) and from private and state-owned corporations, whose generosity has been stimulated by commitments from the national government to afford them partially offsetting tax exemptions. But Minister Gil has made clear that, soon, the library must stand on its own feet, financially. How might it do so? Through the formation of a voluntary, subscription-based entertainment coop of the sort outlined in this section. Efforts to launch such a venture have already begun.[70]

We thus end where we began—not in the United States, the jurisdiction that has occupied our attention for most of this journey, but in Brazil. In 2000, the popularity of the Napster system in that country was an indicator of the character and severity of the crisis about to overwhelm the music and film industries. In 2004, cultural and political conditions there may provide us, fortuitously, an opportunity to test one of the most promising solutions to that crisis. Stay tuned.

Appendix: Where Does the Money Go?

As of this writing, the suggested retail list price of a typical compact disc in the United States is approximately $18. In whose pockets does that money end up?

Answering that question proves to be surprisingly difficult. The Recording Industry Association of America does not make the relevant financial data publicly available,[1] so we are obliged to rely on other, less direct sources of information. The most detailed and probably the most reliable is an article on the subject published by Brett May and Marc Singer in the *McKinsey Quarterly*.[2] May and Singer report that the wholesale price of "a new-release CD by a major label" in 2001 was approximately $10. To that amount, a retailer would add a markup of between $2 and $6. For the purpose of calculating the cost components of an undiscounted CD, we will use the latter figure. Where the $10 collected by the record company ends up varies significantly. Somewhere between $1.50 and $4.00 goes to overhead; between $1.50 and $3.00 goes to marketing; $1 goes to the manufacturer of the disc; $1.40 goes to the distributor; and between $1.50 and $3.00 is paid to artists in the form of royalties or advances, leaving the record company a profit that falls somewhere between $3.10 and -$2.40. If we pick the middle of each of those ranges, we get the cost allocation shown in Table A.1.

In *This Business of Music Marketing and Promotion*, Ted Lathrop and Jim Pettigrew Jr. provide a rougher—but reasonably similar—breakdown. They report that, of the $17.99 retail price of a CD, $5.40 (30 percent) typically goes to the retailer, and $3.60 (20 percent) typically goes to the distributor. The first figure is somewhat lower than the number provided by May and Singer; the second somewhat higher.[3]

TABLE A.1. *May and Singer CD Cost Allocation Figures.*

	Cost (dollars)	Percentage of Retail Price	Percentage of Record Company's Cost
Retailer	6.00	37.5	
Distributor	1.40	8.7	
Record company			
Overhead	2.75	17.2	32
Marketing	2.25	14.1	26
Manufacturer	1.00	6.2	12
Artist royalties	2.25	14.1	26
Profit	0.35	2.2	4
Total	16.00	100.0	100

The numbers supplied by Neil Strauss in a 1995 article in the *New York Times* are slightly different: "Currently, when a CD is sold, 35 percent of the retail price goes to the store, 27 percent to the record company, 16 percent to the artist, 13 percent to the manufacturer and 9 percent to the distributor."[4] Notice, in Strauss's accounting, that the artist's share and the manufacturer's share are both somewhat higher than in the May and Singer accounting. The latter difference may reflect the fact that the cost of manufacturing a CD (and paying license fees to the holders of the patents on the relevant technologies) has declined somewhat since 1995.

Benjamin Compaine and Douglas Gomery, in *Who Owns the Media?*, rely upon a 1996 *Washington Post* article to provide a roughly similar breakdown of the cost of a typical CD (Table A.2).[5]

Notice that Compaine and Gomery disaggregate the category conventionally referred to as "Artists' Royalties," separating it into "Songwriter Costs" (mechanical royalties paid to the music publisher, which are not subject to recoupment), "Performer Costs" (royalties actually paid to the recording artists), and "Recording Costs" and "Producer Costs" (which are conventionally "recouped" from the recording artists' contractual share).

Putting these various estimates together (giving extra weight to more recent estimates and more credible sources), we generate the approximate cost breakdown shown in Table A.3.

TABLE **A.2.** *Compaine and Gomery CD Cost Allocation Figures.*

	Cost (dollars)	Percentage of Record Company's Cost
Disc and package	1.10	13
Recording costs	.30	3
Producer costs	.35	4
Songwriter costs	.65	8
Performer costs	.80	9
Artist pensions	.10	1
Music video production costs	.25	3
Advertising and promotion	.65	8
Amortizing new artist development	1.40	16
Other	.85	10
Managers and lawyers	.20	2
Operating profit and executive salaries	2.00	23
Distribution	1.15	
Retailer's rent	.75	
Retailer's labor costs	.90	
Other retail costs	.95	
Retailer's profit	-.41 to 3.59	
Total	11.99 to 15.99	100

As a coda, it is worth noting that the sources of the retail prices of CDs in a few other countries are not wildly dissimilar. In Canada, the pertinent numbers are as shown in Table A.4.[6]

The only figure that stands out as significantly different from the comparable number in the American market is the 22 percent that goes to the distributor.

UMG provides the following breakdown of the wholesale costs of an average hit CD in Italy: "royalties 28 percent, marketing 15 percent, royalties to authors' society SIAE 10.5 percent, recording costs 8 percent, pressing 8 percent, distribution 7.5 percent and administration and overheads 23 percent."[7]

TABLE **A.3.** *Consolidated CD Cost Allocation Estimate.*

	Cost (dollars)	Percentage of Retail Price[a]	Percentage of Record Company's Cost
Retailer	7.00	39	
Distributor	1.50	8	
Record company			
Overhead	2.57	14	27
Artist and repertory	0.95	5	10
Marketing	1.52	8	16
Manufacturing	1.42	8	15
Performer royalties[b]	2.09	12	22
Composer royalties	0.76	4	8
Profit	0.19	1	2
Total	18.00	100	100

[a] Rounding error explains why these percentages add up to 99 percent.
[b] Refers to the share ostensibly due to the recording artist. Ordinarily, the various costs associated with making the master recording and some of the costs associated with marketing the recording will be "recouped" from this amount.

TABLE **A.4.** *CD Cost Allocation in Canada.*

	Cost (dollars)	Percentage of Retail Price
Retailer	5.95	30
Record company	6.17	31
Manufacturer	1.00	5
Distributor	4.39	22
Artist royalties	1.31	7
Producer	0.44	2
Songwriter	0.69	3
Total	19.95	100

Reference Matter

Notes

Contained in several of the notes set forth below are resources that may be found on the Internet. The Internet addresses for those sources have all been checked as of March 1, 2004. By the time this book appears in print, however, some will likely have been changed or eliminated. Readers who wish to find sources that have become unavailable for this reason can locate them in an "archive" view of the Internet, available at http://web.archive.org.

Introduction

1. See Amanda Lenhart and Susannah Fox, "Downloading Free Music: Internet Music Lovers Don't Think It's Stealing," *Pew Internet & American Life Project's Online Music Report*, September 28, 2000, http://www.pewinternet.org/reports/pdfs/PIP_Online_Music_Report2.pdf, 6; and "Poll Suggests that Home PC Users Favor Napster's Arguments," *Tech Law Journal*, July 27, 2000, http://www. techlawjournal .com/intelpro/20000727.asp. More recent polls suggest that, despite the subsequent decision of the Court of Appeals in the *Napster* case, these numbers remained high or even rose until the summer of 2003. See "Majority of Americans Agree that Downloading Free Music from the Internet Will Increase," February 22, 2001, http://www .intersearch.tnsofres.com/press/releases/violations.htm; and P. J. McNealy, "Digital Consumers: Are They 'Fair Users' or Copyright Pirates?," Gartner/G2 Research, October 14, 2002, http://www.gartnerg2.com/rpt/rpt-1002-0184.asp (password required). For a careful analysis of the poll data, see Lior Jacob Strahilevitz, "Charismatic Code, Social Norms, and the Emergence of Cooperation on the File-Swapping Networks," *Virginia Law Review* 89 (2003): 505, 542–47. Preliminary evidence suggests that the litigation campaign against individual file-sharers—an initiative launched during the summer of 2003—has caused these numbers to decline significantly.

2. This theme is explored in more detail in William Fisher, "The Significance of Public Perceptions of the Takings Doctrine," *Columbia Law Review* 88 (1988): 1774, 1780.

3. The figures concerning declining record sales have been derived from Recording Industry Association of America, "2002 Yearend Market Report on U.S. Recorded Music Shipments," http://www.riaa.com/news/marketingdata/pdf/year_end_2002.pdf; and International Federation of the Phonographic Industry (IFPI), *The Recording Industry in Numbers*, 10th ed. (2003): 24. For the popularity of KaZaA, see "More than 72 Percent of the U.S. Online Population Uses Internet Applications," Nielsen/NetRatings, November 2002, http://www.nielsen-netratings.com/pr/pr_021218.pdf, Table 1. Other reports concerning the impact of unauthorized file sharing on commercial record sales include Larry Dignan, "Study: Kazaa, Morpheus Rave On," *CNET News*, August 14, 2002, http://news.com.com/2100-1023-949724.html; Lorraine Ali and Vanessa Juarez, "Hit or Miss," *Newsweek*, January. 20, 2003, 73–75; "Special Report: CD-R Piracy," *IFPI Network* 8 (October 2001): 12; Neil Strauss, "Behind the Grammys, Revolt in the Industry," *New York Times*, February 24, 2002, section 4, 3; and Lynette Holloway, "Despite a Marketing Blitz, CD Sales Continue to Slide," *New York Times*, December 23, 2002, C9.

4. Estimates of U.S. box-office receipts during the past few years can be found in Motion Picture Association, Worldwide Market Research, "U.S. Entertainment Industry: 2002 MPA Market Statistics," http://www.mpaa.org/useconomicreview/2002/2002_Economic_Review.pdf, 3–4. The other facts and figures set forth in this paragraph are derived from "MPAA Snooping for Spies," *Wired News*, July 22, 2002, http://www.wired.com/news/politics/0,1283,54024,00.html; Ian Fried, "Apple Adds DVD Burner to PowerBook," *CNET News*, August 28, 2002, http://news.com.com/2100-1040-964708.html; Bill Howard, "Burn DVDs on Your Notebook —Finally!" *PC Magazine*, December 19, 2002, http://www.pcmag.com/article2/0,4149,794893,00.asp; and "How Can I Make Copies of My DVD Movies or Games?" in "The DVD Recordable FAQ—Your Top-10 DVD-Burning Questions," http://americal.com/cgi-bin/smart_cart2.cgi?page=dvd-r-faq.html&cart_id=2084018_20145#faq_1.

5. See, for example, Michelle Kessler, "Hollywood, High-Tech Cross Swords Over Digital Content," *USA Today*, June 25, 2002; Bob Keefe, "Download Debate; PC Makers Support Sharing of Music, Movies," *Atlanta Journal and Constitution*, April 18, 2002; "Time to Choose Sides or Get Left Behind," *Broadband Networking News*, Vol. 12, No. 4, February 10, 2002; "Technology and Record Company Policy Principles," http://www.bsa.org/usa/policyres/7_principles.pdf; Declan McCullagh, "Antipiracy Détente Announced," *CNET News*, January 14, 2003, http://news.com.com/2100-1023-980633.html; Declan McCullagh, "Copyright Truce Excludes Key Voices," *CNET News*, January 15, 2003, http://news.com.com/2100-1023-980671.html?tag=fd_lede2_hed; and "Unexpected Harmony," *The Economist*, January 23, 2003.

Chapter 1

1. In 1990, 11.7 million LP albums, 442.2 million prerecorded analog cassettes, and 266.5 million audio CDs were shipped to (and not returned by) U.S. dealers. In

1995, those numbers were 2.2 million, 272.6 million, and 722.9 million, respectively. In 2000, they were 2.2 million, 76.0 million, and 942.5 million, respectively. See Recording Industry Association of America, "1999 Yearend Statistics and 2000 Yearend Statistics," http://www.riaa.com/news/marketingdata/facts.asp. The percentage of American households that own analog VCRs rose steadily from 1980 (2.4 percent) to 2001 (91.2 percent). Between 2001 and 2002, it fell very slightly, to 91 percent. By contrast, the percentage of households that own DVD players is still rising fast: in 2000, it was 12.7 percent; in 2001, 23.5 percent; in 2002, 36.4 percent; see Motion Picture Association of America, "U.S. Entertainment Industry: 2002 MPA Market Statistics," http://www.mpaa.org/useconomicreview/2002/2002_Economic_Review.pdf, 29–31. Personal video recorders have only recently begun to make significant inroads into the consumer market. In 2001, they were installed in only 0.6 million American households; in 2002, 1.8 million; in 2003, 3.8 million. But the combination of strong consumer interest and declining prices will likely cause them to spread rapidly. The Yankee Group predicts that by 2006, 19.1 million households will have them; see Aditya Kishore, "The Death of the 30-Second Commercial," *The Yankee Group Report: Media and Entertainment Strategies*, August 2003, 6. (I am grateful to the Yankee Group for permitting me to refer to these figures, which are ordinarily reserved for the use of their clients.) The projections of Veronis Suhler Stevenson are more conservative, but still contemplate that PVR penetration will increase at a compound annual rate of 24.6 percent during the near future. See Veronis Suhler Stevenson, *Communications Industry Forecast*, 17th ed. (Media Merchant Bank, July 2003), 274. In 2001, 71 million VHS tapes were sold to U.S. dealers for rental purposes and 566 million for resale to customers; in 2002, those numbers declined to 50 million and 433 million, respectively. In 2001, 37 million DVDs were sold to U.S. dealers for rental purposes and 345 million for resale to customers; in 2002, those numbers rose to 69 million and 633 million, respectively. In 1999, there were twelve digital cinema screens in the United States; in 2000, there were 31; in 2001, 45; in 2002, 124. See MPAA, "U.S. Entertainment Industry: 2002 MPA Market Statistics," 24, 30.

2. Stephen M. Kramarsky, "Copyright Enforcement in the Internet Age: The Law and Technology of Digital Rights Management," *DePaul University Journal of Art and Entertainment Law* 11 (2001): 1, 5.

3. Kramarsky, "Copyright Enforcement in the Internet Age," 6; *Universal City Studios, Inc. v. Reimerdes*, 111 F.Supp.2d 294, 313 (S.D.N.Y. 2000); Trevor Marshal, "Open Source Video: The Web Video Turf Wars," Byte.com, September 11, 2000, http://www.byte.com/documents/s=446/byt20000905s0004/. DivX must be differentiated from DIVX, an entirely unrelated proprietary system developed by Circuit City, used between 1998 and 1999 to make video recordings distributed on DVDs expire after prescribed periods of time. For a concise account of the rise and fall of the system, see "A Short History of the DIVX Home Video System," http://www.the-doa.com/Pages/DoaDivxHistory.html.

4. See Oliver Masciarotte, "All Right, Mr. DeMille, I'm Ready for My Close-Up," *Mix*, September 2002, 10; "Goodbye to the Video Store," *The Economist*,

September 21, 2002; Glenn Fleischmann, "Store 80 Gigs on Your Network with a No-Fuss File Server," *New York Times*, December 26, 2002.

5. These data are derived from a survey of 106,211 American households conducted by the Gartner/G2 consulting firm during the fourth quarter of 2003.

6. See Veronis Suhler Stevenson, *Communications Industry Forecast*, 306–7; United States Department of Commerce, *A Nation Online: How Americans are Expanding Their Use of the Internet*, February 2002, http://www.ntia.doc.gov/ntiahome/dn/, 5–6. To generate the percentages listed in the text, I needed to know, of course, the total number of households in the United States in each year. That information proves to be surprisingly hard to obtain. The most recent projections by the Census Bureau (available at *Projections of the Number of Households and Families in the United States: 1995 to 2010*, http://www.census.gov/prod/1/pop/p25-1129.pdf, 5) are badly out of date. So, instead I have used the following:

- For 2000: 105,480,101 (taken from *Households and Families: 2000*, Census 2000 brief, September 2001, http://www.census.gov/prod/2001pubs/c2kbr01-8.pdf)

- For 2001: 106,428,857 (taken from U.S. Census Bureau, "2001 American Community Survey Profile, 2001 Supplementary Survey Profile," http://www.census.gov/acs/www/Products/Profiles/Single/2001/SS01/Tabular/010/01000US1.htm)

- For 2002: 107,366,878 (taken from U.S. Census Bureau, "2002 American Community Survey Profile," Table 1: General Demographic Characteristics, http://www.census.gov/acs/www/Products/Profiles/Single/2002/ACS/Tabular/010/01000US1.htm)

- For 2003: 108,424,184 (a projection, based on the assumption that the number of households increased between 2002 and 2003 at the same rate as the population as a whole—0.985 percent)

- For 2004: 109,508,425 (a projection, based on the assumption that the number of households will increase between 2003 and 2004 at the same rate that the Census Bureau currently predicts the population as a whole will increase—1 percent [See http://www.census.gov/Press-Release/www/releases/archives/population/001632.html.])

These estimates will be used throughout the book.

7. *A Nation Online*, 11, 14–15, 16. One can still find mild gender differences within a given age cohort. Specifically, "[w]omen, from approximately age 20 to age 50, are more likely to be Internet users than men. From about age 60 and older, men have higher rates of Internet use than women."

8. See United Nations Conference on Trade and Development, *E-Commerce and Development Report*, 2003, http://www.unctad.org/en/docs//ecdr2003_en.pdf; and *A Nation Online*, 5.

9. See Fredric Dannen, *Hit Men: Power Brokers and Fast Money Inside the Music Business* (New York: Vintage Books, 1991), 64.

10. Beau Brashares, "15 MB of Fame: A Music Industry Insider (and Law School Student) Gives His Perspective on How the Net Will, and Won't, Improve the Lives of Artists," http://cyber.law.harvard.edu/events/netmusic_brbook.html#_Toc475699199.

11. See Dick Weissman, *The Music Business: Career Opportunities and Self-Defense* (New York: Three Rivers Press, 1997), 61–63.

12. Dannen, *Hit Men*, 61.

13. The anecdote concerning Clive Davis and Janis Joplin is from Dannen, *Hit Men*, 76. The quotation is from Geoffrey P. Hull, *The Recording Industry* (Needham Heights, MA: Allyn and Bacon, 1998), 135–36. The ways in which producers get paid are discussed in Chapter 2.

14. See Hull, *The Recording Industry*, 162–64, 249–52.

15. See Hull, *The Recording Industry*, 140–46; Rick Carr, "TechnoPop," aired on National Public Radio in September and October, 2002, http://www.npr.org/programs/morning/features/2002/technopop/index.html.

16. Sadly, Gigabeat.com is no longer in operation. It was purchased by Napster and then sank in the maelstrom created by Napster's demise. See Michael Bartlett, "Gigabeat Says It's the Future of Music Delivery," *Newsbytes*, January 24, 2001; Nancy Gondo, "Sick of the Same Old Song? Try These Sites," *Investor's Business Daily*, April 3, 2001. But similar (albeit not quite so good) services, relying on software rather than employees to predict customers' desires from their current musical tastes, have since become available. See, for example, MusicMatch, http://www.mmguide.musicmatch.com/. Many more are likely to emerge soon.

17. The advantages (to consumers) of the sampling system are explored in detail in Stan Liebowitz, "Policing Pirates in the Networked Age," *Policy Analysis*, May 15, 2002, http://www.cato.org/pubs/pas/pa-438es.html, text accompanying note 32.

18. See John Stuart Mill, "On Liberty," reprinted in *The Philosophy of John Stuart Mill*, ed. M. Cohen (New York: Modern Library, 1961) 252–57.

19. See Andrew Rodgers, "'Phantom Edit' Deletes Jar Jar Binks," *Zap2it*, June 4, 2001, http://www.zap2it.com/movies/news/story/0,1259,—-6903,00.html; "Mystery of Star Wars Phantom Edit," BBC News, June 7, 2001, http://news.bbc.co.uk/1/hi/entertainment/film/1375742.stm; Daniel Kraus, "The Phantom Edit," Salon.com, November 5, 2001, http://dir.salon.com/ent/movies/feature/2001/11/05/phantom_edit/index.html; "The Phantom Edit," *Wikipedia*, http://en.wikipedia.org/wiki/The_Phantom_Edit; and Pete Howel, "When Movie Fans Make the Final Cut," *Toronto Star*, August 25, 2002, D6. For a Website discussing the merits of the modified version and the legitimacy of creating it, see http://forum.onecenter.com/phantomedit/.

20. See "Introducing Final Cut Pro 4," http://www.apple.com/finalcutpro/; and Los Angeles Final Cut Pro User Group, http://www.lafcpug.org/.

21. Information concerning Gotuit TV may be found at http://www.gotuit.com. Reader beware: my enthusiasm concerning the system may be affected by the fact that I have given business advice to the company.

22. The contest description can be found at http://ftp.archive.org/html/contest01/contest.htm. The entries can be downloaded from http://ftp.archive.org/html/contest01/gallery.htm.

23. J. D. Biersdorfer, "Making Your Own Music, Even if You Can't Play a Note," *New York Times*, December 12, 2002; Rick Carr, "TechnoPop" (quoting Steve Albini). On the proliferation of small-scale Webcasters (and their vulnerability to rising license fees), see Dawn C. Chmielewski, "KPIG Snuffs Web's 1st Online Radio Simulcast," *Mercury News*, July 18, 2002; John Borland, "New Bill Would Save Small Webcasters," *CNET News*, July 26, 2002, http://news.com.com/2100-1023-946642.html. The history of Webcasting in considered in more detail in Chapter 3.

24. The phrase "semiotic democracy" originates in the writings of John Fiske. See *Television Culture* (London: Methuen, 1987), 236, 239. Treatments of the idea by legal scholars include Jack M. Balkin, "Digital Speech and Democratic Culture: A Theory of Freedom of Expression for the Information Society," *New York University Law Review* (forthcoming), http://papers.ssrn.com/sol3/papers.cfm?abstract_id=470842; Rosemary J. Coombe, "Objects of Property and Subjects of Politics: Intellectual Property Laws and Democratic Dialogue," *Texas Law Review* 69 (1991): 1853; Rosemary J. Coombe, "Author/izing Celebrity: Publicity Rights, Postmodern Politics, and Unauthorized Genders," *Cardozo Arts & Entertainment Law Journal* 10 (1992): 365; Rosemary J. Coombe, "Publicity Rights and Political Aspiration: Mass Culture, Gender Identity, and Democracy," *New England Law Review* 26 (1992): 1221; Rochelle Cooper Dreyfuss, "Expressive Genericity: Trademarks as Language in the Pepsi Generation," *Notre Dame Law Review* 65 (1990): 397; David Lange, "At Play in the Fields of The Word: Copyright and the Construction of Authorship in the Post-Literate Millennium," *Law & Contemporary Problems* 55 (1992): 139; Joseph P. Liu, "Owning Digital Copies: Copyright Law and the Incidents of Copy Ownership," *William and Mary Law Review* 42 (2001): 1245, 1328–30; Michael Madow, "Private Ownership of Public Image: Popular Culture and Publicity Rights," *California Law Review* 81 (1993): 125; Neil Weinstock Netanel, "Copyright and a Democratic Civil Society," *Yale Law Journal* 106 (1996): 283; and Sudakshina Sen, "Fluency of the Flesh: Perils of an Expanding Right of Publicity," *Albany Law Review* 59 (1995): 739, 752–55. The John Wayne example comes from Madow, "Private Ownership," 144.

25. The data showing declining unit sales of sound recordings in the United States through 2002 were derived from the International Federation of the Phonographic Industry (IFPI), *The Recording Industry in Numbers*, 10th ed. (2003), 24. The data for 2003 were derived from Recording Industry Association of America, "2003 Yearend Market Report on U.S. Recorded Music," http://www.riaa.com/news/newsletter/pdf/2003yearEnd.pdf. The numbers supplied by the RIAA for the years 2000–2002 are almost, but not quite, identical to those used by the IFPI. For reasons persuasively presented by Stanley Liebowitz, I am excluding from these indicators of the adverse impact of unauthorized copying the continued decline in sales of "singles." See Liebowitz, "Will MP3 Downloads Annihilate the Record Industry? The Evidence So Far," in *Advances in the Study of Entrepreneurship, Innovation, and Economic Growth*, ed. Gary Libecap (Greenwich, CT: JAI Press, 2003), 8–9, http://wwwpub.utdallas.edu/liebowit/knowledge_goods/records.pdf.

26. See Motion Picture Association of America, "U.S. Entertainment Industry: 2002 MPA Market Statistics," 3–4, 7–8; Veronis Suhler Stevenson, *Communications*

Industry Forecast, 17th ed. (Media Merchant Bank, July 2003); Harold L. Vogel, *Entertainment Indusry Economics: A Guide for Financial Analysis*, 5th ed. (Cambridge: Cambridge University Press, 2001), 62 (showing the declining relative importance of theatrical revenues and the rising relative importance of home-video revenues); and Rick Lyman, "A Fat Increase at the Box Office: A Record Year, but Reasons for Caution Amid Hollywood Riches," *New York Times*, December 30, 2002, B1.

27. Janis Ian, "The Internet Debacle—An Alternative View," *Performing Songwriter Magazine*, May, 2002, available at http://www.janisian.com/article-internet _debacle.html.

28. See Liebowitz, "Policing Pirates in the Networked Age."

29. See Paul-Jon McNealy and George Shiffler, "Downbeat U.S. Economy Is Not the Cause of Music Industry's Blues," Gartner/G2 Study, November 2002. There is also substantial, though not conclusive, support for the hypothesis that consumer spending on movies is similarly "contracyclical." In other words, it rises (at least during the early stages of) recessions and falls during times of prosperity. See Vogel, *Entertainment Industry Economics*, 5th ed., 44–45; J. M. Nardone, "Is the Movie Industry Contracyclical," *Cycles* 33 (April 1982): 77 (summarizing research by Dr. Albert Kapusinski).

30. Janis Ian, "The Internet Debacle—An Alternative View."

31. The colorization debate is well reviewed in Note, "Motion Picture Colorization, Authenticity, and the Elusive Moral Right," *New York University Law Review* 64 (1989): 628. For a summary of the CleanFlicks litigation and Spielberg's comment on it, see "G-Rated Revolutionary," *People*, February 17, 2003.

32. These themes and trends are examined in Steven Cherensky, "A Penny for Their Thoughts: Employee-Inventors, Preinvention Assignment Agreements, Property, and Personhood," *California Law Review* 81 (1993): 595, 646–53; Edward J. Damich, "The Right of Personality: A Common-Law Basis for the Protection of the Moral Rights of Authors," *Georgia Law Review* 23 (1988): 1; Justin Hughes, "The Personality Interest of Artists and Inventors," *Cardozo Arts & Entertainment Law Journal* 16 (1998): 81; Justin Hughes, "The Philosophy of Intellectual Property," *Georgetown Law Journal* 77 (1988): 287, 330–65; Jeffrey Malkan, "Stolen Photographs: Personality, Publicity, and Privacy," *Texas Law Review* 75 (1997): 779; Margaret Jane Radin, "Property and Personhood," *Stanford Law Review* 34 (1982): 957; and Madhavi Sunder, "Authorship and Autonomy as Rites of Exclusion: The Intellectual Propertization of Free Speech in *Hurley v. Irish-American Gay, Lesbian, and Bisexual Group of Boston*," *Stanford Law Review* 49 (1996): 143, 156–58.

33. Justin Hughes, "'Recoding' Intellectual Property and Overlooked Audience Interests," *Texas Law Review* 77 (1999): 923, 941, 955.

Chapter 2

1. Under the law of some American states, it is possible to acquire a copyright in an oral work—in other words, in a work not (yet) "fixed" in a tangible medium of expression. See *Nimmer on Copyright* (Dayton, OH: Matthew Bender, 2003),

§2.02. However, because that option has little bearing on the music or film industries, we will ignore it for the purposes of our discussion, concentrating instead on federal copyright law, which does require "fixation."

2. 17 U.S.C. §109(a). The relationship between the first-sale doctrine and price discrimination will be discussed in considerably more detail in Chapter 4.

3. 17 U.S.C. §109(b). For the origins of the rule, see H.R. Rep. No. 987, 98th Cong., 2d sess. (1984).

4. For explication of the tangled history that resulted in the treatment of all of these acts as "performances," see *Nimmer on Copyright*, §8.18.

5. 17 U.S.C. §110.

6. 17 U.S.C. §118. Nowadays, this function is performed, not by the Copyright Royalty Tribunal, but by Copyright Arbitration Royalty Panels, convened by the Librarian of Congress.

7. 17 U.S.C. §116A. The clarity of this system was disrupted by the adoption in 1988 of a statute implementing in the United States the Berne Convention for the Protection of Literary and Artistic Works. (The Berne Convention is the primary multilateral copyright treaty, but the United States, for various reasons, had long delayed joining it.) Because the Berne Convention does not permit compulsory licenses for nonbroadcast public performances (such as jukebox performances), Congress grudgingly "encouraged" copyright owners and jukebox operators to negotiate license fees voluntarily or to submit them to arbitration. If such voluntary undertakings failed, however, the compulsory licensing system remained in place.

8. For a thorough description of the state of this system as of 1990, see Paul Goldstein, *Copyright: Principles, Law, and Practice* (Boston: Little Brown, 1989 and 1990 Pocket Part), Vol. I, 638–67.

9. 17 U.S.C. §119.

10. H.R. Rep. 1476, 94th Cong., 2d sess. (1976), 65 (quoting *Report of the Register of Copyrights on the General Revision of the U.S. Copyright Law* 24 [1961]).

11. *Campbell v. Acuff-Rose Music*, 510 U.S. 569 (1994).

12. The case was eventually settled. See "Acuff-Rose Settles Case with Rap Group," *The Commercial Appeal (Memphis)*, June 5, 1996.

13. For an argument that *one* of the functions of the fair-use doctrine is to facilitate uses of copyrighted materials that otherwise would be blocked by transaction costs, see Wendy J. Gordon, "Fair Use As Market Failure: A Structural and Economic Analysis of the Betamax Case and Its Predecessors," *Columbia Law Review* 82 (1982): 1600. For an argument that that is the *exclusive* function of the doctrine, see Tom W. Bell, "Fair Use v. Fared Use: The Impact of Automated Rights Management on Copyright's Fair Use Doctrine," *North Carolina Law Review* 76 (1998): 557.

14. The relevant literature is large. Here are a few of the pertinent works: William Fisher, "Reconstructing the Fair Use Doctrine," *Harvard Law Review* 101 (1989): 1659; Mark A. Lemley, "The Economics of Improvement in Intellectual Property Law," *Texas Law Review* 75 (1997): 989; Pierre Leval, "Toward a Fair Use Standard," *Harvard Law Review* 103 (1990): 1105; Robert Merges, "*Are You Mak-*

ing Fun of Me? Notes on Market Failure and the Parody Defense in Copyright," *American Intellectual Property Law Association Quarterly Journal* 21 (1993): 305; Gideon Parchomovsky, "Fair Use, Efficiency, and Corrective Justice," *Legal Theory* 3 (1997): 347; and Lloyd L. Weinreb, "Fair's Fair: A Comment on the Fair Use Doctrine," *Harvard Law Review* 103 (1990): 1137.

15. Some of these provisions have been plucked from the contract recommended by the Songwriters Guild of America, which can be found on the SGA Website: http://www.songwriters.org/thecontract2.htm. Others consist of terms that Don Passman (perhaps the most experienced of entertainment lawyers) urges songwriters to try, if possible, to bargain for. See Donald S. Passman, *All You Need to Know About the Music Business* (New York: Simon & Schuster, 1991), 209–25.

16. For a discussion of "controlled compositions"—and the complications that arise when one of two coauthors records a composition—see Geoffrey P. Hull, *The Recording Industry* (Needham Heights, MA: Allyn and Bacon, 1998), 132–33.

17. See 37 CFR 255.3.

18. For one view on the matter, see Robert P. Merges, "Contracting into Liability Rules: Intellectual Property Rights and Collective Rights Organizations," *California Law Review* 84 (1996): 1293, 1308–16.

19. See Passman, *The Music Business*, 212–13. This is the one exception to the customary rule, noted previously, that the songwriter is paid 50 percent of the licensing revenues reaped by the publisher.

20. See Stanley M. Besen, Sheila N. Kirby, and Steven C. Salop, "An Economic Analysis of Copyright Collectives," *Virginia Law Review* 78 (1992) 383, 385.

21. See M. William Krasilovsky and Sidney Shemel, *This Business of Music*, 6th ed. (New York: Billboard Books, 1990), 196–216. Not all restaurants are obliged to obtain such licenses. For analysis of the evolution of the rules that determine which do and which don't, see *Nimmer on Copyright*, §8.18. Recently, those rules were revised still further by the Fairness in Music Licensing Act of 1998. For a critical analysis of that statute, see *Nimmer on Copyright*, §8.18[C][2][b].

22. For a more detailed explanation of the systems (currently) employed by ASCAP to measure the frequency with which songs are broadcast and then to allocate revenues among the copyright owners thereof, see "How You Get Paid at ASCAP," http://www.ascap.com/about/payment/paymentintro.html.

23. See Stanley M. Besen and Sheila Nataraj Kirby, *Compensating Creators of Intellectual Property: Collectives that Collect* (Santa Monica: Rand Corp., 1989); Besen, Kirby, and Salop, "An Economic Analysis of Copyright Collectives," 390–407; Ruth Charles, "ASCAP—A Half Century of Progress," *Bulletin of the Copyright Society of the U.S.A.* 11 (1964): 133; and Merges, "Contracting into Liability Rules," 1328–40.

24. For a detailed analysis of the terms of typical subpublishing contracts, see Passman, *The Music Business*, 199–205. Although the arrangement described in the text governs most of the ways in which American compositions are exploited in other countries, one of the streams of revenue follows a slightly different path. Typically, the songwriter's share of public-performance royalties, in contrast to the pub-

lisher's share, is paid by the foreign PRO, not to the subpublisher, but instead to the American PROs (ASCAP, BMI, and SESAC), which then pay the writer, thus bypassing the domestic music publisher altogether. See Passman, 200. For simplicity, this nuance is ignored in Figure 1.2.

25. If Smither were assisted in creating the recording by a record producer (or, more plausibly, by a sound engineer employed by a producer), he would have to share the copyright in the recording with the producer. See *Nimmer on Copyright*, §210[A][3]. Adelphi would then be obliged to secure assignment of the producer's copyright interest as well as Smither's. For simplicity, this complication is ignored in the text.

26. 17 U.S.C. §114(b).

27. The cost of producing a high-quality master for an album varies with the genre. Jazz and hip-hop albums are generally cheaper to produce than rock albums, for example. But $150,000 is a decent approximation. See Hull, *The Recording Industry*, 126, 138.

28. For a discussion much more thorough than I can provide here of the likely terms of their deal—and where those terms came from—see Passman, *The Music Business*, 55–166; and Krasilovsky and Shemel, *This Business of Music*, 6th ed., 3–23. For a typical contract, see "Recording Artist Agreement (Exclusive)," available on the CD-ROM Supplement to Krasilovsky and Shemel, *This Business of Music*, 8th ed. (2000).

29. What's an "album"? In 1990, as the CD was displacing the LP vinyl record and the cassette as the primary vehicle for distributing music, that term was (as one might expect) in flux. However, it was conventionally defined as a collection of "eight to twelve [musical] selections, with approximately thirty-five minutes of playing time." Passman, *The Music Business*, 144.

30. For discussions of the origins of this seemingly odd way of defining the contract term, see Passman, *The Music Business*, 94–96. The sixth edition of Krasilovksy and Shemel, *This Business of Music*, 8, suggests that record companies in 1990 still adhered to the traditional practice of defining the contract term as one year plus options to renew. The seventh edition, published in 1995, however, acknowledges that the system described in the text had displaced it. Passman's discussion of the rationale for and timing of the shift seems more persuasive.

31. See Passman, *The Music Business*, 83. Krasilovsky and Shemel, *This Business of Music*, 6th ed., 4, suggest that the percentages that can be obtained by each type of artist may be slightly lower than those reported by Passman.

32. See Passman, *The Music Business*, 83, 104–14; Krasilovsky and Shemel, *This Business of Music*, 6th ed., 51.

33. See Passman, *The Music Business*, 65, 138–39; Krasilovsky and Shemel, *This Business of Music*, 6th ed., 5. In 1990, it cost an average of $1.40 (about 15 percent of the typical SRLP [for a mid-level artist] of $9) to manufacture a cassette and $2.55 (about 16 percent of the typical SRLP of $16) to manufacture a CD; see Harold L. Vogel, *Entertainment Industry Economics: A Guide for Financial Analysis*, 1st ed. (Cambridge: Cambridge University Press, 1990), 144. The second of these

numbers would soon decline precipitously; by 1994, it cost an average of $0.60 to manufacture a CD; see Harold L. Vogel, *Entertainment Industry Economics*, 3rd ed. (Cambridge: Cambridge University Press, 1994), 143.

34. As of 1990, most record companies had discontinued use of this particular ruse, but artists were not, as a result, getting paid more. Rather, those companies had merely shifted to the more straightforward practice of paying artists royalties on only 85 percent of the records sold. See Passman, *The Music Business*, 65–68.

35. Other formats subject to this additional discount include digital audiotapes (which will be discussed in Chapter 4) and "audiophile recordings." As one might imagine, by far the most important financially were CDs. See Passman, *The Music Business*, 138–40.

36. Passman, *The Music Business*, 69–70, suggests that, by 1990, the majority of record companies had abandoned use of the maneuver, but Geoffrey Hull, writing in 1998, and Krasilovsky and Shemel, in the seventh edition of their treatise (published in 1995), indicated that some companies still employed it. See Hull, *The Recording Industry*, 129; Krasilovsky and Shemel, *This Business of Music*, 7th ed., 4. Because of the uncertainty concerning its usage, this particular deduction will not be invoked when, soon, we calculate the royalties that Smither would likely earn from his recording of my song.

37. See Passman, *The Music Business*, 69–71.

38. See Passman, *The Music Business*, 74–75.

39. See Passman, *The Music Business*, 123–26.

40. If a sound recording is a "work for hire," then the musicians and producer who created it cannot exercise their statutory rights to terminate their assignment of their copyrights to the record company after thirty-five years. The termination rights just mentioned pertain only to recordings produced during 1978 and afterward. Thus, this issue will become live only in 2013. For reasons too complex to explore here, it was uncertain prior to 1999 whether any or all sound recordings embodied in collections (like CDs) could fairly be characterized as works for hire. In 1999, the record companies sought to resolve the issue in their favor, by persuading Congress to add an ostensibly "technical" amendment to an unrelated bill, making clear that sound recordings were eligible for work-for-hire status. The ensuing popular outcry prompted Congress to repeal the amendment quickly. The net result is that the effect of the "boilerplate" work-for-hire language found in most recording contracts remains uncertain. For a careful exploration of this issue, see *Nimmer on Copyright*, §5.03[B][2][a][ii].

41. In 1990, the large majority of recordings sold by American record companies were in the form of cassettes or CDs. A total of approximately 442 million of the former and 286 million of the latter were purchased—roughly a 60-40 breakdown. See Recording Industry Association of America, "1990–1999 U.S. Manufacturers Unit Shipments and Value Chart," http://www.riaa.com/news/marketingdata/facts.asp. The corresponding SRLPs are derived from Passman, *The Music Business*, 64, 139. The calculations set forth in Table 2.1 are patterned on those supplied in Passman, *The Music Business*, 88.

42. This system, the net effect of which is to leave little money in the pockets of most recording artists, is certainly not limited to the world of folk music, nor has it changed significantly since 1990. See Lola Ogunnaike, Laura Holson, and John Leland, "Feuding for Profit: Rap's War of Words; In Rap Industry, Rivalries as Marketing Tools," *New York Times*, November 3, 2002.

43. See Fredric Dannen, *Hit Men: Power Brokers and Fast Money Inside the Music Business* (New York: Vintage, 1991), 13–17; Lauren J. Katunich, "Time to Quit Paying the Payola Piper: Why Music Industry Abuse Demands a Complete System Overhaul," *Loyola of Los Angeles Entertainment Law Review* 22 (2002): 643; and Kerry Segrave, *Payola in the Music Industry: A History, 1880–1991* (Jefferson, NC: McFarland, 1994), 166-221.

44. A "motion picture" is defined by the copyright statute as "an audiovisual work consisting of a series of related images which, when shown in succession, impart an impression of motion, together with accompanying sounds, if any"; see 17 U.S.C. §101. One implication of this definition is that the soundtrack is considered part of the film and is not governed by the special rules, discussed previously in this chapter, that regulate sound recordings.

45. When two or more people contribute to the production of a film, they may specialize in different aspects of the job—hiring the "talent," securing financing, arranging logistics, and so on. Those various roles sometimes elicit different labels—"Executive Producer," "Line Producer," and so on. It was once possible to glean from those designations information concerning the nature of each person's job. But they have come to be used so promiscuously that such inferences are no longer reliable. See David Lees and Stan Berkowitz, *The Movie Business* (New York: Vintage, 1981), 5–7. I am grateful to Jeremy Williams and Jared Jussim for clarifying these issues.

46. 17 U.S.C. §101.

47. For some of the complications, see Alex Alben, "Future Technology Clauses and Future Technologies: Legal Roadblocks to New Media Uses Along the Information Super Highway," in Donald E. Biederman, Edward P. Pierson, Martin E. Silfen, Jeanne A. Glasser, Robert C. Berry, and Lionel S. Sobel, *Law and Business of the Entertainment Industries*, 3rd ed. (Westport, CT: Praeger, 1996): 668, 669–71.

48. See Biederman et al., *Law and Business of Entertainment*, 606–7; and Tim Connors, "Beleaguered Accounting: Should the Film Industry Abandon Its Net Profits Formula," *Southern California Law Review* 70 (1997): 841, 845–63. The Websites for the three guilds are: www.wga.org; www.dga.org; www.sag.org. For a survey of the kinds of "participation" deals that major actors and directors may demand, see Vogel, *Entertainment Industry Economics*, 1st ed., 104–13. For an illuminating account of the typical struggle over onscreen credits, see Lees and Berkowitz, *The Movie Business*, 3–20.

49. This practice is detailed in Mark Litwak, *Dealmaking in the Film & Television Industry: From Negotiations to Final Contracts* (Los Angeles: Silman-James Press, 1994), 31–60.

50. The numbers set forth in the text have been derived from the Motion Picture Association of America. See "U.S. Entertainment Industry: 2002 MPA Market Sta-

tistics," http://www.mpaa.org/useconomicreview/2002/2002_Economic_Review.pdf, 17. For descriptions of the seven majors as of 1990 (as well as of several smaller companies that operated in their shadow), see Vogel, *Entertainment Industry Economics*, 2nd ed., 35–37; Ronald V. Bettig and Jeanne Lynn Hall, *Big Media, Big Money: Cultural Texts and Political Economics* (Lanham, MD: Rowman & Littlefield, 2003), 47–55.

51. For a more thorough discussion of the stages in the typical financing arrangement, see Vogel, *Entertainment Industry Economics*, 2nd ed., 64–70. Jared Jussim (Executive Vice President, Intellectual Property Division, Sony Pictures) provides the following helpful account of the kinds of inquiries that inform a studio's decision whether to approve a project: "A Studio does not decide to make a motion picture and then throw money at it. Prior to the time that a motion picture is 'greenlighted,' a study is made as to who is the audience for that film, how much it is anticipated it will earn in each media and market, foreign and domestic, in which the motion picture will be released, from a worst-case scenario to a reasonably optimistic forecast, and how much must be expended to release and promote the motion picture in that market, securing that level of earnings. The expenses for each such forecast are then subtracted from the anticipated earnings, and the result will tell you how much can be expended to produce that motion picture. As is indicated, this forecast is made over several 'slices' of anticipated earnings. Decisions as to whether to produce that particular motion picture are based on whether a picture of that genre, with that cast etc., can reasonably be expected to earn that level of receipts as is needed to break even, and hopefully earn a profit. Do the Studios make pictures that call for a greater risk? Of course. Do the Studios not make pictures that look like sure-fire winners? Of course. But this type of analysis does govern their thinking."

52. *Twentieth-Century Fox Film Corp. v. MCA, Inc.*, 715 F.2d 1327 (9th Cir. 1983); *Metro-Goldwyn-Mayer, Inc. v. American Honda Motor Co., Inc.*, 900 F. Supp. 1287 (C.D. Cal. 1995).

53. See *Nimmer on Copyright*, §3.07; Naomi Abe Voegtli, "Rethinking Derivative Rights," *Brooklyn Law Review* 63 (1997): 1213, 1218–32.

54. The cases are *Columbia Pictures Industries, Inc. v. Redd Horne, Inc.*, 749 F.2d 154 (3rd Cir. 1984); *Columbia Pictures Industries, Inc. v. Aveco, Inc.*, 800 F.2d 59 (3rd Cir. 1986); and *Columbia Pictures Industries, Inc. v. Professional Real Estate Investors, Inc.*, 866 F.2d 278 (9th Cir. 1989).

55. For detailed discussions of theatrical licenses (including some other kinds of deals not relevant here) see Biederman et al., *Law and Business of Entertainment*, 607–8; Vogel, *Entertainment Industry Economics*, 2nd ed., 75–76.

56. For the data concerning the growing power of the theatre chains, see Vogel, *Entertainment Industry Economics*, 2nd ed., 35. By 2001, the proportion of American screens controlled by the major chains had increased from 35 percent to 65 percent. See Harold L. Vogel, *Entertainment Industry Economics*, 5th ed., (Cambridge: Cambridge University Press, 2001), 42. For recognition of the studios' desire to keep the theatres afloat, I am indebted to Jeremy Williams and Shelley Presser.

57. Vogel, *Entertainment Industry Economics*, 2nd ed., 74. A slightly different

account of the character and timing of the windows through which the typical film is released may be found in Bruce M. Owen and Steven S. Wildman, *Video Economics* (Cambridge, MA: Harvard University Press, 1992), 30 (Table 2.2), which in turn relies on "A Survey of the Entertainment Industry," *The Economist*, December 23, 1989, 5.

58. The calculations the studio executives make in selecting and timing their various windows is, of course, far more complex than this simple example would suggest. For some of the factors, see Owen and Wildman, *Video Economics*, 26–63.

59. For more thorough discussions of the price-discrimination function of the "window" system, see Vogel, *Entertainment Industry Economics*, 5th ed. (2001), 83, 352; Owen and Wildman, *Video Economics*, 27–29, 37.

60. Goldstein, *Copyright: Principles, Law, and Practice*, §6.1.

61. *Sony Corp. of America v. Universal City Studios*, 464 U.S. 417 (1984).

62. See RIAA, "1990–1999 U.S. Manufacturers' Unit Shipments and Value Chart," http://www.riaa.com/news/marketingdata/facts.asp; *Copyright Industries in the U.S. Economy: 1993 Perspective* (prepared for the International Intellectual Property Alliance by Economists Incorporated) (Washington, D.C. 1993), Table 10. A slightly lower figure for domestic sales—$6.8 billion—is reported in Dannen, *Hit Men*, 15.

63. The figures pertaining to the total number of major films released in the United States and the total American box-office revenues were derived from "U.S. Entertainment Industry: 2002 MPA Market Statistics," http://www.mpaa.org/useconomicreview/2002/2002_Economic_Review.pdf; and Vogel, *Entertainment Industry Economics*, 5th ed., 52–55 (Figure 2.4). The number of films released by smaller companies was derived from MPAA Worldwide Market Research, *2001 U.S. Economic Review*, "Films Released," http://mpaa.org/useconomicreview/2001Economic/sld009.htm. (The major films accounted for approximately 95 percent of box-office admissions and revenues. See Vogel, *Entertainment Industry Economics*, 2nd ed., 44 note b.) The breakdown of the sources of revenue for the film industry was derived from Vogel, *Entertainment Industry Economics*, 2nd ed., 52 (Figure 2.7). (Vogel also includes an entry for licenses generated by "made-for-TV movies" ($2 billion), but because that pertains to an aspect of the industry outside the scope of my concern in this book, I have excluded it from the total.)

As the text indicates, most of these numbers had been rising for some time. Somewhat more specifically, the same sources just cited enable us to compare along the following axes the states of the industry in 1980 and 1990: In 1980, 161 films were released in the United States by the major studios; in 1990, 169. In 1980, 233 films were released in the United States by studios of all sorts; in 1990, 410. In 1980, U.S. theatrical admissions were 1,022,000,000; in 1990, 1,189,000,000. In 1980, U.S. box-office revenues were $2,748,500,000; in 1990, $5,021,800,000. In 1980, the major studios' domestic theatrical license revenues were $1,183,0000,000; in 1990, $2,100,000,000. In 1980, the major studios' foreign theatrical license revenues were $911,0000,000; in 1990, $1,200,000,000. In 1980, the major studios' home-video revenues were $280,000,000; in 1990, $5,100,000,000. In 1980, the major studios' pay-cable license revenues were $240,000,000; in 1990, $1,100,000,000. In 1980, the major studios' network-TV license revenues were $430,000,000; in 1990, $100,000,000. In 1980, the major studios' foreign-TV revenues were $100,000,000; in 1990, $1,000,000,000. In 1980, the major studios' syndication revenues were $150,000,000; in 1990, $600,000,000. Adding the last six sets of figures together, in 1980, the major studios' total licensing revenues (excluding made-for-TV films) were $6,042,500,000; in 1990, $16,221,800,000.

Notice that there were two exceptions to the upward trends during this ten-year period: the studios' income from network TV licenses declined, and the total number of major films released in the United States was roughly constant. The significance of the last fact will be considered at the end of this chapter.

64. For the argument that payola may be efficient, see R. H. Coase, "Payola in Radio and Television Broadcasting," *Journal of Law and Economics* 22 (1979): 269. For an analysis of the sources of inefficiency in the modern system of independent promotion, see J. Gregory Sidak and David E. Kronemyer, "The 'New Payola' and the American Record Industry: Transactions Costs and Precautionary Ignorance in Contracts for Illicit Services," *Harvard Journal of Law and Public Policy* 10 (1987): 521, 537–46.

65. See Robert H. Frank and Philip J. Cook, *The Winner-Take-All Society* (New York: Penguin, 1996); Comments by Robert Frank in "The Wages of Stardom: Law and the Winner-Take-All Society: A Debate," *University of Chicago Law School Roundtable*, 6 (1999): 1, 2–3; F. M. Scherer, "The Innovation Lottery," in Rochelle Cooper Dreyfuss, Diane Leenheer Zimmerman, and Harry First, eds., *Expanding the Boundaries of Intellectual Property* (New York: Oxford, 2001), 3, 12–13.

66. Sherwin Rosen, "The Economics of Superstars," *American Economic Review* 71 (1981): 845. Scherer's data concerning "the attention posterity has paid" to classical composers is consistent. See "The Innovation Lottery," 13–14.

67. For descriptions, as of 1990, of the major record companies—and of the "minimajor" and "major-distributed independent" companies that operate under their wings—see Passman, *The Music Business*, 1st ed., 55–59; Dannen, *Hit Men*, 112.

68. See Biederman et al., *Law and Business of Entertainment*, 603.

69. See Vogel, *Entertainment Industry Economics*, 2nd ed., 72; and Litwak, *Dealmaking in the Industry*, 165–202.

70. See Biederman et al., *Law and Business of Entertainment*, 606–7. In this respect, the compensation system of the American film business loosely resembles that of American professional football. The number of professional "players" vastly exceeds the number of aspirants. (The number of players on Division-I college teams who would, if they could, subsequently play in the National Football League dwarfs the number who do.) But the incomes of those who do make the grade are generous. The stars, of course, earn extraordinary salaries, but the journeymen are also more than adequately compensated. See Frank and Cook, *The Winner-Take-All Society*, 81–82. For this analogy, I'm grateful to Jeremy Williams.

71. See Frank and Cook, *The Winner-Take-All Society*, 101–23.

72. See Scherer, "The Innovation Lottery," 17–18.

73. The numbers on the music industry are derived from Dannen, *Hit Men*, 112. For discussions of the associated long-term reduction in music variety, see Renee Graham, "Pop Music," *Boston Globe*, February 23, 2003; and Joan Anderman, "The Music Business: What's Next?," *Boston Globe*, February 23, 2003. The numbers on the film industry are derived from "U.S. Entertainment Industry: 2002 MPA Market Statistics," http://www.mpaa.org/useconomicreview/2002/2002_Economic_Review.pdf, 9, 10, 17, 19–20, 23. The fact that the total numbers of major film releases in the United States in 1980 and 1990 were virtually identical is somewhat misleading; that figure has fluctuated significantly over the past three and a half decades. But the overall trend has been roughly flat. See Vogel, *Entertainment Industry Economics*, 5th ed., Figure 2.3. Similarly, while the total number of films released in the United States by all studios varied wildly between 1950 and 2000, the overall trend was roughly flat. See MPAA Worldwide Market Research, *2001 U.S. Economic Review*, "Films Released," http://mpaa.org/useconomicreview/2001Economic/sld009.htm.

Chapter 3

1. See Aaron L. Melville, "The Future of the Audio Home Recording Act of 1992: Has It Survived the Millennium Bug?," *Boston University Journal of Science and Technology Law* 7 (Summer 2001): 372, 376–77; and Lawrence J. Glusman, "It's My Copy, Right? Music Industry Power to Control Growing Resale Markets in Used Digital Audio Recordings," *Wisconsin Law Review* 1995 (1995): 709, 714. A few miscellaneous facts concerning the genesis of this format: The first CD player retailed for more than $1,000. The first generation of CDs were priced between $20 and $25. Billy Joel's *52nd Street* was the first album released in CD format. CDs were manufactured to hold seventy-four minutes of music because Beethoven's *Ninth Symphony* is seventy-four minutes long.

2. See Rob Gilde, ed., "DAT-Heads Frequently Asked Questions," SolOrb, http://www.solorb.com/dat-heads/FAQ; and Lewis Kurlantzick and Jacqueline E. Pennino, "The Audio Home Recording Act of 1992 and the Formation of Copyright Policy," *Journal of the Copyright Society of the U.S.A.* 45 (Summer 1998): 497, note 8 (citing N. Jansen Calamita, "Note: Coming to Terms with the Celestial Jukebox: Keeping the Sound Recording Copyright Viable in the Digital Age," *Boston University Law Review* 74 (1994): 505, 515).

3. On the controversy surrounding the status of home taping, see *Elektra Records Co. v. Gem Electronics Distribs., Inc.*, 360 F. Supp. 821, 824 (E.D.N.Y. 1973) (arguing that "Congress was particularly concerned with combating extensive pirating of phonograph records and tapes and clearly did not intend to extend coverage of the bill to at least two types of usages of protected recordings: (1) library uses and (2) home recordings."); Melville B. Nimmer, "Copyright Liability for Audio Home Recording: Dispelling the Betamax Myth," *Virginia Law Review* 68 (1982): 1505, 1506 (arguing that "[T]here is not and never has been an exemption from copyright liability for audio home recording."); Joel L. McKuin, "Home Audio

Taping of Copyrighted Works and the Audio Home Recording Act of 1992: A Critical Analysis," *Hastings Communication and Entertainment Law Journal* 16 (Winter 1994): 317, 320; and Senate Committee on the Judiciary, *Audio Home Recording Act of 1991*, 102d Cong., 2d sess., 1992, S. Rep. 102–294, 31. On the injuries allegedly sustained by the record companies as a result of home taping, see Gary S. Lutzker, "DAT's All Folks: *Cahn v. Sony* and the Audio Home Recording Act of 1991—Merrie Melodies or Looney Tunes?" *Cardozo Arts & Entertainment Law Journal* 11 (1992): 145, 157–58.

4. See McKuin, "Home Audio Taping of Copyrighted Works," 329; Eric Fleischmann, "The Impact of Digital Technology on Copyright Law," *Journal of the Patent & Trademark Office Society* 70 (1988): 5, 6.

5. See McKuin, "Home Audio Taping of Copyrighted Works," 321–22; Senate Committee on Commerce, Science and Transportation, *The Digital Audio Tape Recording Act*, 101st Cong., 2d sess., 1991, S. 2358; and "Register of Copyrights Ralph Oman's Remarks to the ABA Conference," *BNA's Patent, Trademark & Copyright Journal* 38 (1989): 468, 471. The SCMS system prevents serial reproduction "via three sets of inaudible subcodes in the digital signals which track (1) whether copyright protection is asserted over the signal; (2) whether the signal emanates from an 'original' source . . . or a copy of such a source; and (3) what kind of device is sending the incoming signal." Lutzker, "DAT's All Folks," 162 (citing Seth D. Greenstein, "Contributory Infringement the Second Time Around: The Copyright Case Against Digital Audio Tape Recorders (pt. 1)," *Journal of Proprietary Rights* 3 (July 1991): 2. "When an SCMS-equipped device makes a copy from an original, it changes the information encoded with the track to tell other devices that no more copies are allowed." See *Audio Home Recording Act of 1991*, S. Rep. No. 102–294, 37.

6. See Lutzker, "DAT's All Folks," 164, 170.

7. 17 U.S.C. §§1002(a), 1004(a) and (b), 1006 (b) and (c), 1008. See also Don E. Tomlinson and Timothy Nielander, "Red Apples and Green Persimmons: A Comparative Analysis of Audio Home-Recording Royalty Laws in the United States and Abroad," *Mississippi College Law Review* 20 (Fall 1999): 5, 12; and Donald S. Passman, *All You Need to Know About the Music Business*, 3rd ed. (New York: Simon & Schuster, 2000), 251.

8. Varying explanations for the commercial failure of DAT technology can be found in Damon Luloff, "The Effects of the Compact Disc on the Recording Industry," Ellipsis.cx, http://www.ellipsis.cx/dcluloff/cd.html; and Recording Industry Association of America, "History of Recordings," http://www.riaa.com/issues/audio/history.asp#recording.

9. See Benton J. Gaffney, "Copyright Statutes that Regulate Technology: A Comparative Analysis of the Audio Home Recording Act and the Digital Millennium Copyright Act," *Washington Law Review* 75 (April 2000): 611, 631; *Recording Industry Association of America v. Diamond Multimedia System, Inc.*, 180 F.3d 1072 (9th Cir. 1999); and Alex Allemann, "Manifestation of an AHRA Malfunction: The Uncertain Status of MP3 under *Recording Industry Association of America v. Diamond Multimedia Systems, Inc.*," *Texas Law Review* 79 (November 2000): 189, 190, 200, 217.

10. Somewhat more specifically, the total amounts of royalties collected in each year since the implementation of the statute have been: in 1992, $118,227.42; in 1993, $520,162.84; in 1994, $521,999.64; in 1995, $473,592.20; in 1996, $397,152.52; in 1997, $969,178.06; in 1998, $1,978,457.93; in 1999, $3,551,030.86; in 2000, $5,427,095.15; in 2001, $3,948,568.87; in 2002, $3,449,269.03; and in the first three quarters of 2003, $2,288,654.61. *Source:* U.S. Register of Copyright, Licensing Division, Report of DART Receipts, December 9, 2003.

11. For an initially optimistic reading of the reach of the statute, see 137 Cong. Rec. S11, 852–53 (daily ed. August 1, 1991) (statement of Sen. DeConcini). For narrower readings, see Senate Committee on the Judiciary, *Audio Home Recording Act of 1991*, p. 52; and *A&M Records v. Napster*, Brief for the United States as *Amicus Curiae*, September 8, 2000.

12. See Peter S. Menell, "Envisioning Copyright Law's Digital Future," *New York Law School Law Review* 46 (2002): 63, 179, n.404; Colin Folawn, "Neighborhood Watch: The Negation of Rights Caused by the Notice Requirement in Copyright Enforcement Under the Digital Millennium Copyright Act," *Seattle University Law Review* 26 (2003): 979, 1002, n.153; Michelle Delio, "The Key to Encryption," *Wired News*, June 22, 2001, http://www.wired.com/news/ebiz/0,1272,44740,FF.html; and Pamela Samuelson, "The Digital Agenda of the World Intellectual Property Organization: Principal Paper: The U.S. Digital Agenda at WIPO," *Virginia Journal of International Law* 37 (1997): 369, 409–10. On the difficulty of designing an encryption system capable of defeating a sophisticated recipient of the encrypted data, see Martin F. Halstead, "The Regulated Become the Regulators—Problems and Pitfalls in the New World of Digital Copyright Legislation," *Tulsa Law Review* 38 (2002): 195, 225.

13. See Jeff Sharp, "Coming Soon to Pay-Per-View: How the Digital Millennium Copyright Act Enables Digital Content Owners to Circumvent Educational Fair Use," *American Business Law Journal* 40 (2002): 1, 25–28. On the fate of the aborted legislation, see Senate Committee on the Judiciary, "Competition, Innovation, and Public Policy in the Digital Age: Is the Marketplace Working to Protect Digital Creative Works?" 107th Cong., 2d sess., 2002, 95–96 (statement of Gary Shapiro, chairman of the Home Recording Rights Coalition). Information on DVD licenses is available from License Management International, http://www.lmicp.com/.

14. See David R. Johnstone, "The Pirates Are Always with Us: What Can and Cannot Be Done About Unauthorized Use of MP3 Files on the Internet," *Buffalo Intellectual Property Law Journal* 1 (2001): 122, 141–43; Cary Sherman, "SDMI and Metadata: Creating a Digital Marketplace" (presentation at "Names, Numbers, and Networks," a conference held as part of "the <indecs> project," Washington D.C., November 1999), http://www.indecs.org/washington/sdmi.pdf; the SDMI Homepage, http://www.sdmi.org/; and Edward Felten, Secure Internet Programming Laboratory, Princeton University, "SDMI Challenge FAQ," http://www.cs.princeton.edu/sip/sdmi/faq.html.

15. See *RealNetworks, Inc. v. Streambox, Inc.*, 2000 WL 127311 (W.D. Wash. 2000).

16. For the provisions affecting television services, see 47 U.S.C. §§553(a)(2) and 605(e)(4). For the provision pertaining to SCMS, see 17 U.S.C. §1002.

17. See 847 F.2d 255 (5th Cir. 1988); 977 F.2d 1510, 1527–28 (9th Cir. 1992); 911 F.2d 970 (4th Cir. 1990).

18. See Working Group on Intellectual Property Rights, "Information Technology and the National Information Infrastructure: A Preliminary Draft of the Report of the Working Group on Intellectual Property Rights" (Green Paper), July 1994, http://www.eff.org/GII_NII/Govt_docs/HTML/ipwg.html; and Working Group, "Intellectual Property and the National Information Infrastructure: The Report of the Working Group on Intellectual Property Rights" (White Paper), September 1995, http://www.uspto.gov/web/offices/com/doc/ipnii/ipnii.pdf. For studies of the evolution of the Green and White Papers, see Jessica Litman, *Digital Copyright* (Amherst, NY: Prometheus Books, 2001), 90–96; and Pamela Samuelson, "Digital Agenda," 369.

19. See Jeff Sharp, "Coming Soon," 30; and Samuelson, "Digital Agenda," 410.

20. See Samuelson, "Digital Agenda," 369–439; and "World Intellectual Property Organization: Copyright Treaty," December 20, 1996, *International Legal Materials*, 36 (1997): 71, http://www.wipo.int/clea/docs/en/wo/wo033en.htm.

21. See Pamela Samuelson, "Intellectual Property and the Digital Economy: Why the Anti-Circumvention Regulations Need to Be Revised," *Berkeley Technology Law Journal* 14 (1999): 519, 529; Calvin Van Ourkirk, "Fixing What Ain't Broke: The Digital Millennium Copyright Act (DMCA) Title I," *Intellectual Property Law Bulletin* 4(2): 1 (1999); and Julie Sheinblatt, "The WIPO Copyright Treaty," *Berkeley Technology Law Journal* 13 (1998): 535, 535–36.

22. See Samuelson, "Intellectual Property," 522–23 (internal citations omitted).

23. 17 U.S.C. §§1201(a)(1)(A), 1201(a)(2), 1201(b), 1203, 1204.

24. See 17 U.S.C. §§1201(a)(3)(A) and (B). See also Brian Bolinger, "Comment: Focusing on Infringement: Why Limitations on Decryption Technology Are Not the Solution to Policing Copyright," *Case Western Reserve Law Review* 52 (2002): 1091, 1094.

25. 17 U.S.C. §§1201(a)(2)(A-C), 1201(b)(1)(A-C), 1201(d), 1201(f), 1201(j), 1201(g), 1201(h), 1201(a)(1)(C), 1201(c)(1), 1201(c)(4). For detailed analysis of these intricate provisions, see Melville B. Nimmer and David Nimmer, *Nimmer on Copyright*, 3 §12A (release 062, December 2003); David Nimmer, "Appreciating Legislative History: The Sweet and Sour Spots of the DMCA's Commentary," *Cardozo Law Review* 23 (2002): 909, 935–42, 950–52, 979–89; Van Ourkirk, "Fixing What Ain't Broke," 1; and Bolinger, "Comment: Focusing on Infringement," 1091–1111.

26. *RealNetworks, Inc. v. Streambox, Inc.*, 2000 WL 127311 (W.D. Wash. 2000).

27. See *Universal City Studios, Inc. v. Reimerdes*, 2000 WL 48514 (S.D.N.Y. 2000); and *Universal City Studios Inc. vs. Reimerdes*, 111 F. Supp. 2d 294 (S.D.N.Y. 2000), judgment entered by 111 F. Supp. 2d 346.

28. See *Universal City Studios, Inc. v. Corley*, 273 F.3d 429 (2d Cir. 2001). In an analogous case decided by an intermediate appellate court in California, the First Amendment was given more weight, but the plaintiff in that suit had claimed that

posting copies of DeCSS on Websites violated state trade-secret law, not the DMCA. *DVD Copy Association v. Bunner*, 93 Cal. App. 4th 648, 113 Cal. Rptr. 2d 338 (2001). In any event, that decision was subsequently overturned by the California Supreme Court, *DVD Copy Control Association, Inc. v. Bunner*, 31 Cal. 4th 864 (2003).

29. Touretsky's "Gallery of CSS Descramblers" is still available at http://www-2 .cs.cmu.edu/dst/DeCSS/Gallery/. The T-shirts can be obtained from Copyleft's T-Shirt store at http://www.copyleft.net/category.phtml?page=category_apparel.phtml. For a few of the many other cease-and-desist letters sent by the MPAA to the operators of Websites offering DeCSS downloads, see the Chilling Effects Website: http://www.chillingeffects.org/anticircumvention/notice.cgi?NoticeID=383; http://www .chillingeffects.org/anticircumvention/notice.cgi?NoticeID=156; and http://www .chillingeffects.org/anticircumvention/notice.cgi?NoticeID=77.

30. Other successful invocations of the DMCA include *Sony Computer Entertainment America, Inc. v. Gamemasters*, 87 F.Supp.2d 976 (N.D.Cal. 1999) (granting a preliminary injunction against the sale of Game Enhancers, a product that bypassed encryption systems designed to prevent the playing of unauthorized games on Playstation consoles); *CSC Holdings, Inc. v. Greenleaf Electronics, Inc.*, 2000 WL 715601 (N.D.Ill. 2000) (granting a preliminary injunction against the sale of "black boxes" that descrambled encrypted cable-television signals); and *Directv, Inc. v. Hamilton*, 215 F.R.D. 460 (S.D.N.Y. 2003) (upholding a judgment, based on the DMCA, against two persons who purchased and used satellite TV descramblers). On the Felten fiasco, see "Future of Secure Digital Music Initiative Grim," *USA Today*, April 29, 2002, http://www.usatoday.com/tech/news/2002/04/29/sdmi.htm; "Click-Through Agreement for the SDMI Public Challenge," http://www.cs.princeton.edu/ sip/sdmi/clickthru.pdf; Felten, "SDMI Challenge FAQ"; and the materials made available by the Electronic Frontier Foundation at http://www.eff.org/IP/DMCA/ Felten_v_RIAA/.

31. See Joanna Glasner, "ElcomSoft Case in Juror's Hands," *Wired News*, December 12, 2002, http://www.wired.com/news/business/0,1367,56832,00.html; and the materials made available by the Electronic Frontier Foundation at http://www .eff.org/IP/DMCA/US_v_Elcomsoft/ and the corresponding "Frequently Asked Questions," February 19, 2002, http://www.eff.org/IP/DMCA/US_v_Elcomsoft/us_v _elcomsoft_faq.html.

32. For some recent cease-and-desist letters invoking the statute, see the Chilling Effects Website: http://www.chillingeffects.org/anticircumvention/notice.cgi ?NoticeID=24 (Sony alleges that Aibopet provides the means to circumvent the copy protection system of the "Memory Stick" of Sony's "Aibo" robotic dog. One of the purposes of the alleged circumvention was to enable purchasers to use Aibopet's own software [e.g., "Disco Aibo"] to train their robotic pets to dance.); and http://www .chillingeffects.org/anticircumvention/notice.cgi?NoticeID=83 (Live365 [the compendium of Webcasters discussed in Chapter 1] alleges that StreamRipper violated the DMCA in circumventing Live365's system designed to prevent users from downloading and storing the music being streamed via Webcast.).

33. See *Lexmark International, Inc. v. Static Control Components, Inc.*, 253 F.Supp.2d 943 (E.D. Ky. 2003); and Brian Bolinger, "Comment: Focusing on Infringement," 1101. For additional examples of troubling applications of the statute, see Electronic Frontier Foundation, "Unintended Consequences: Five Years Under the DMCA," October 3, 2003, http://www.eff.org/IP/DMCA/unintended_consequences .pdf.

34. On the development of MP3 technology and its rapid popularization, see MP3.com, "The History of MP3 and How Did It All Begin?," http://www.mp3-mac .com/Pages/History_of_MP3.html; Fraunhofer Institute for Integrated Circuits IIS, "Audio and Multimedia MPEG Audio Layer 3," http://www.iis.fraunhofer.de/amm/ techinf/layer3/index.html; and Gabriel Nijmeh, "Behind the Files: History of MP3," EncycloZine, http://www.kosmoi.com/computer/software/MP3.

35. See Christopher Jones, "Vaulting into Online Storage," *Wired News*, October 25, 1999, http://www.wired.com/news/technology/0,1282,32051,00.html; and Christopher Jones, "Dueling Over Digital Music," *Wired News*, February 22, 2000, http://www.wired.com/news/technology/0,1282,34114-3,00.html.

36. See Courtney Macavinta, "MP3.com's Move to Copy CDs Stirs Debate," *CNET News*, January 28, 2000, http://news.com.com/2100-1023-236237.html; Jim Hu, "MP3.com's New Features Get Mixed Reception," *CNET News*, January 12, 2000, http://news.com.com/2100-1023-235583.html; and Sara Steetle, "UMG Recordings, Inc. v. MP3.com, Inc.: Signaling the Need for a Deeper Analysis of Copyright Infringement of Digital Recordings," *Loyola of Los Angeles Entertainment Law Review* 21 (2000): 31, note 8 (indicating that, by March 2000, MP3.com's library contained over eighty thousand CDs and was growing at a rate of fifteen hundred CDs per day).

37. See Alexander G. Comis, "Copyright Killed the Internet Star: The Record Industry's Battle to Stop Copyright Infringement Online," *Southwestern University Law Review* 31 (2002): 753, 778; Jefferson Graham, "Upload CD, Keep It in Your Locker, Listen Anywhere," *USA Today*, September 12, 2000, 3D; and *UMG Recordings, Inc. v. MP3.com, Inc.*, 2000 WL 1262568, 2 (S.D.N.Y. 2000).

38. *UMG Recordings, Inc. v. MP3.com, Inc.*, 2000 WL 1262568, 2; and Macavinta, "MP3.com's Move to Copy CDs Stirs Debate."

39. *UMG Recordings, Inc. v. MP3.com, Inc.*, 92 F.Supp. 2d 349, 350 (S.D.N.Y. 2000).

40. On the initial round of settlements, see Jim Hu, "MP3.com Settles Copyright Dispute with Warner, BMG," *CNET News*, June 9, 2000, http://news.com .com/2100-1023-241677.html?legacy=cnet; and John Borland, "Time Running Out for MP3.com Settlement," *CNET News*, August 25, 2000, http://news.com.com/ 2100-1023-244942.html. Judge Rakoff's principal ruling on the issue of damages may be found at *UMG Recordings, Inc. v. MP3.com, Inc.*, 2000 WL 1262568, 4, 6. On MP3.com's final settlement with Universal, see Jim Hu, "MP3.com Pays $53.4 Million to End Copyright Suit," *CNET News*, November 15, 2000, http://news .com.com/2100-1023-248583.html.

41. See House Committee on the Judiciary, *Music Owners' Listening Rights Act*

of 2000, 106th Cong., 2d sess., 2000, H.R. 5275; John Borland, "Lawmakers Want to Legalize MP3.com Service," *CNET News*, September 26, 2000, http://news.com.com/2100-1023-246264.html; Rick Boucher, "Introduction of the Music Owners' Listening Rights Act of 2000," September 25, 2000, http://www.house.gov/boucher/docs/molra.htm; John Townley, "MP3.com Kicks Off Million Email March," *InternetNews.com*, September 28, 2000, http://www.internetnews.com/bus-news/article.php/471511; Stacey Fiene, "The Music Owners' Listening Rights Act of 2000: I Want My MP3," *DePaul-LCA Journal of Art & Entertaiment Law* 10 (Spring 2000): 515, 531-32; and Alexander Davie and Christine Soares, "The Music Online Competition Act of 2001: Moderate Change or Radical Reform?," *Duke Law & Technology Review* (2001): 31.

42. See Erich Luening, "MP3.com Reopens Service for Free, and For Fee," *CNET News*, December 5, 2000, http://news.com.com/2100-1023-249408.html; John Borland and Jim Hu, "MP3.com Buy: The Taming of a Generation," *CNET News*, May 21, 2001, http://news.com.com/2100–1023–257993.html; Jim Hu, "New Name, CEO Come to Duet Music Service," *CNET News*, June 11, 2001, http://news.com.com/2100-1023-268221.html?legacy=cnet&tag=cd_pr; Will Sturgeon, "Breaking News: Fat Lady Sings for MP3.com," *Silicon.com*, July 10, 2003, http://silicon.com/news/500019-500001/1/5088.html; Matt Hines and John Borland, "CNET to Buy, Retune MP3.com," *CNET News*, November 14, 2003, http://news.com.com/2100-1027-5107696.html?tag=nefd_hed; and MP3.com, "Important MP3.com Announcement: A Message from CNET Networks, Inc. (CNET)," email message to MP3.com subscribers, December 2, 2003.

43. The conversion or demise of several of the services can be traced in the following sources: *Wired News*, "Services, Online File Storage," October 2000, http://www.wired.com/wired/archive/8.10/p2p_pages.html?pg=26; IBackup, "Company Profile," http://ibackup.com/ibwin/newibackup/profile.htm; XDrive, "What Is XDrive?," http://xdrive.com/whatisxdrive; Anuvio Technologies, "Consumer Products," http://www.idrive.com; Rachel Konrad, "File Management Firm Nixes Popular Free Storage," *CNET News*, February 21, 2001, http://news.com.com/2100-1017_3-252912.html?tag=prntfr; Brad King, "Musicbank Calls It Quits," *Wired News*, April 11, 2001, http://www.wired.com/news/business/0,1367,42988,00.html; and Gwendolyn Mariano, "Online Storage Firm Shutters File Depot," *CNET News*, May 31, 2001, http://news.com.com/2102-1023_3-267654.html?tag=ni_print.

44. MP3.com, "Judgment Day for MP3.com," press release, April 28, 2000, http://pr.mp3.com/pr/81.html.

45. See House, *Digital Performance Right in Sound Recordings Act of 1995*, 104th Cong., 1st sess., 1995, H. Rept. 274, 5–9; Senate, *Digital Performance Right in Sound Recordings Act of 1995*, 104th Cong., 1st sess., 1995, S. Rept. 128, 10–13; Karen Fessler, "Webcasting Royalty Rates," *Berkeley Technology Law Journal* 18 (2003): 399, 401.

46. On the effort to establish, at this juncture, an unqualified public-performance right for sound recordings, see David Nimmer, "Ignoring the Public," *UCLA Entertainment Law Review* 7 (2000): 189, 190, and n.9.

47. The quotation comes from Senate, *Digital Performance Right in Sound Recordings Act of 1995*, 104th Cong., 1st sess., 1995, S. Rept. 128, 14; House, *Digital Performance Right in Sound Recordings Act of 1995*, 104th Cong., 1st sess., 1995, H. Rept. 274, 12. Discussions of the need to "protect" the revenues of copyright owners in the new technological environment may be found in House Committee on the Judiciary, *Digital Millennium Copyright Act*, 105th Cong., 2d sess., 1998, H. Rept. 796, 79; Senate, *Digital Performance Right in Sound Recordings Act of 1995*, 104th Cong., 1st sess., 1995, S. Rept. 128, 10, 12; and House, *Digital Performance Right in Sound Recordings Act of 1995*, 104th Cong., 1st sess., 1995, H. Rept. 274, 10.

48. See John Borland, "Ad Disputes Tune Web Radio Out," *CNET News*, April 11, 2001, http://news.com.com/2102-1023_3-255673.html; and Knowledge@Wharton, "Is Internet Radio Doomed?" *CNET News*, July 20, 2002, http://news.com.com/2009-1023-945156.html.

49. With respect to interactive Webcasting, see 17 U.S.C. §§114(j)(7) and (d)(3). With respect to noninteractive Webcasting, see 17 U.S.C. §§114(d)(2) and (f)(2). The primary regulations designed to reduce the likelihood of home copying were the following:

- A sound-recording "performance complement," which sharply limits the number of songs by the same artist that the service may transmit within a given period of time
- A prohibition upon announcing in advance the names of songs and the times at which they will be broadcast
- An obligation to include in broadcasted songs encoded copyright management information
- A prohibition upon making musical programming available in archival forms that would facilitate copying
- A duty imposed upon transmitters to cooperate to prevent recipients from "automatically scanning" their transmissions in order to select particular recordings
- A duty to employ available technological options that limit the ability of recipients to make copies of their transmissions

For an explanation of the function of these rules, see House Committee on the Judiciary, *Section-by-Section Analysis of H.R. 2281*, 105th Cong., 2d sess., 1998, Committee Print 6, 52.

50. See Edward Samuels, "Economic Justice: Copyright Owners, Performers, and Users," *New York Law School Law Review* 46 (2002): 749. The interactive Webcasters that have emerged are few and far between. One rare example is that of Streamwaves, http://www.streamwaves.com.

51. For the standards governing the acceptance or rejection of rates, see 17 U.S.C. §§802(f) and (g). For the criteria to apply in rate determinations, see 17 U.S.C §114(f)(2)(B). For the biannual review of rates, see 17 U.S.C. §114(f)(2)(C)(ii)(II).

The small set of existing subscription noninteractive services were governed by a different, more generous standard. See 17 U.S.C. §114(f)(1)(B). The Copyright Office did indeed construe the statute to reach simulcasting radio stations, and its construction was subsequently upheld by a federal court. See *Bonneville v. Register of Copyrights*, 153 F. Supp. 2d 763 (E.D. Pa. 2001).

52. For an overview and critique of the process, see Karen Fessler, "Webcasting Royalty Rates," 399. The process cost the parties a total of approximately $25 million in fees and produced approximately $15 million in initial revenues. See Philip S. Corwin, "Outlook for Copyright and Digital Media Legislation in the 108th Congress," *Spring Media Law and Policy* 11 (2003): 98, 113.

53. The Panel's decision, which set many compulsory rates in addition to the one discussed in the text, is available on the Copyright Office's Website, http://www.copyright.gov/carp/webcasting_rates.html.

54. See John Borland, "Webcasters Grumble Over Proposed Fees," *CNET News*, February 20, 2002, http://news.com.com/2100-1023-841612.html; John Borland, "Small Webcasters Campaign for Survival," *CNET News*, April 1, 2002, http://news.com.com/2100-1023-872765.html; Gwendolyn Mariano, "Webcasters' Silence Is Heard," *CNET News*, May 1, 2002, http://news.com.com/2100-1023-897076.html; Brad King, "Streaming Music Choked by Fees," *Wired News*, May 2, 2002, http://www.wired.com/news/mp3/0,1285,52245,00.html; and Gwendolyn Mariano, "Online Radio Heard in Congress," *CNET News*, May 15, 2002, http://news.com.com/2100-1023-914261.html.

55. See Copyright Office, "Rates and Terms for . . . Webcasting," http://www.copyright.gov/carp/webcasting_rates.html; Copyright Office, "Webcasting Determination," February 24, 2003, http://www.copyright.gov/carp/webcasting_rates_final.html; John Borland, "Feds Cut Webcasters a Break on Fees," *CNET News*, June 20, 2002, http://news.com.com/2100-1023-938037.html; Lisa M. Bowman, "Pioneer FM Station Shutters Webcasts," *CNET News*, July 19, 2002, http://news.com.com/2100-1023-945145.html; and BRS Media, "BRS Media's Web-Radio Reports a Steep Decline in the Number of Stations Webcasting," press release, September 12, 2002, http://www.brsmedia.fm/press020912.html. For indications of the decline in the number of Webcasters, see BRS Media's chart on the state of Internet radio at www.brsmedia.com; Dan Carnevale, "Radio Silence: Fees Force College Stations to Stop Webcasting," *Chronicle of Higher Education*, August 16, 2002, http://chronicle.com/free/v48/i49/49a03301.htm; John Borland, "Net Radio Raises a Pirate Flag," *CNET News*, July 3, 2002, http://news.com.com/2100-1023-941392.html; and John Borland, "Webcasters, Labels Appeal Net Radio Fees," *CNET News*, August 7, 2002, http://news.com.com/2102-1023_3-948834. html.

56. See Evan Hansen, "Bill Could Spare Webcasters from Silence," *CNET News*, September 26, 2002, http://news.com.com/2102-1023_3-959805.html; John Borland, "House Votes for Webcasters' Reprieve," *CNET News*, October 7, 2002, http://news.com.com/2102-1023-961100.html; John Borland and Jim Hu, "Senate Puts Webcasting Bill on Hold," *CNET News*, October 18, 2002, http://news.com

.com/2102-1023_3-962556.html; John Borland, "Deal Rescues Fee Break for Web-casters," *CNET News*, November 15, 2002, http://news.com.com/2102-1023_3-965985 .html; John Borland, "Webcasters Threaten to Sue RIAA," *CNET News*, July 9, 2003, http://news.com.com/2100-1027-1020614.html; and Allison Kidd, "Mending the Tear in the Internet Radio Community: A Call for a Legislative Band-Aid," *North Carolina Journal of Law and Technology* 4 (2003): 339. Somewhat more specifically, the final agreement reached between SoundExchange and the Voice of Webcasters (a consortium of small commercial Webcasters) provided that Web-casters with gross revenues of less than $1,000,000 for the period of November 1998 through June 2002 would pay the greater of 8 percent of their gross revenues or 5 percent of their expenses for the period of 1998 through 2002. Webcasters with gross revenues of less than $500,000 during 2003 would pay the greater of 10 per-cent of the first $250,000 in revenues plus 12 percent of revenues above that amount or 7 percent of expenses. Finally, Webcasters with gross revenues of less than $1,250,000 during 2004 (including third-party participation revenues and revenues from the operation of new subscription services) would again pay the greater of 10 percent of the first $250,000 in revenues plus 12 percent of revenues above that amount or 7 percent of expenses. All Webcasters were required to pay a minimum of $500 for 1998 and $2,000 for the years 1999–2002 (per year of operation). For 2003 and 2004, the minimum annual payment would be $2,000 for small Webcasters with gross revenues less than $50,000 and $5,000 otherwise. See Copyright Office, "No-tice of Agreement Under the Small Webcaster Settlement Act of 2002," *Federal Register* 67, no. 247 (December 24, 2002): 78510.

57. For a comprehensive critique of the CARP process, see House Committee on the Judiciary, Subcommittee on Courts, the Internet and Intellectual Property, *Copyright Arbitration Royalty Panel (CARP) Structure and Process*, 107th Cong., 2d sess., 2002, available at http://www.house.gov/judiciary/80194.pdf. See also Karen Fessler, "Webcasting Royalty Rates," 399. Fessler reviews a number of proposals to make the royalty determination process more stable and predictable by eliminating its ad-hoc nature. A bill proposing changing the CARP to a panel of expert judges was, in fact, proposed and is currently under consideration in the House Committee on the Judiciary as H.R. 1417. See Declan McCullagh, "Panel Delays Look at Web-casting Royalties," *CNET News*, March 27, 2003, http://news.com.com/2100 -1028-994272.html.

58. See Allison Kidd, "Mending the Tear," 339. The $300,000 per-participant figure is noted in James Turner, "Why Internet Radio May Fade," *Christian Science Monitor*, June 17, 2002, www.csmonitor.com/2002/0617/p16s02-wmgn.html; and Dan Carnevale, "Radio Silence: Fees Force College Stations to Stop Webcasting," *Chronicle of Higher Education*, August 16, 2002, http://chronicle.com/free/v48/i49/ 49a03301.htm.

59. See "Copyright Law: Congress Responds to Copyright Arbitration Royalty Panel's Webcasting Rates—Small Webcaster Settlement Act of 2002, Pub. L. No. 107–321, 116 Stat. 2780 (to be codified at 17 U.S.C. §114(f)-(g))," *Harvard Law Re-*

view 116 (2003): 1920, 1920–27; and Fessler, "Webcasting Royalty Rates," 420. References in the legislative history to the risk that the record companies would behave as a cartel and the importance of crafting the compulsory licensing system to avoid that danger include *Digital Performance Right in Sound Recordings*, S. 227, 104th Cong., 1st sess., *Congressional Record* 141 (August 8, 1995): S 11,961 (Statement of Sen. Leahy); *Digital Performance Right in Sound Recordings*, S. 227, 104th Cong., 1st sess., *Congressional Record* 141 (August 8, 1995): S 11,954 (Section-By-Section Description of DPRA); and *Digital Performance Right in Sound Recordings*, S. 227, 104th Cong., 1st sess., *Congressional Record* 141 (August 8, 1995): S 11, 962–63 (Letter from Assistant Attorney General Andrew Fois to Sen. Patrick Leahy, July 21, 1995).

60. Large Webcasters may also have been interested in killing off their smaller competitors. The Yahoo!-RIAA agreement appears to have been designed with a per-performance rather than a percentage-of-revenue rate in order to set a standard that competitors could not meet—partly in the hope that they would then join Yahoo!'s Broadcast.com aggregator service. See Paul Maloney and Kurt Hanson, "Cuban Says Yahoo!'s RIAA Deal Was Designed to Stifle Competition," *Radio and Internet Newsletter*, June 24, 2002, http://www.kurthanson.com/archive/news/062402/index.asp.

61. See Shawn Fanning, "Testimony of Shawn Fanning, Founder, Napster, Inc., Before the Senate Judiciary Committee," *United States Senate Committee on the Judiciary Online Library*, October 9, 2000, http://judiciary.senate.gov/oldsite/1092000_sf.htm.

62. See Paul Elias, "RIAA Turns Deaf Ear to Napster," *Red Herring*, October 4, 2000, http://www.redherring.com/Article.aspx?f=articles%2farchive%2findustries%2f2000%2f1004%2find-napster100400.xml; Gwendolyn Mariano, "Napster Fans Stretch Across the Border," *CNET News*, April 5, 2001, http://news.com.com/2100-1023-255378.html?legacy=cnet; Tom Mainelli, "Traffic Surges at Napster," *PCWorld.com*, July 14, 2000, http://www.pcworld.com/news/article/0,aid,17650,00.asp; BBC News Online, "Online Music-Swapping Rocks," *BBC News*, September 10, 2001, http://news.bbc.co.uk/2/hi/entertainment/1535789.stm; and Brad King, "Napster's Back, Almost," *Wired News*, January 10, 2002, http:// www.wired.com/news/mp3/0,1285,49624,00.html.

63. See Keith Regan, "Scour.com Wilts in Napster's Wake," *E-Commerce Times*, September 5, 2000, http://www.ecommercetimes.com/perl/story/4196.html.

64. See Alec Klein, "Going Napster One Better: Aimster Says Its File-Sharing Software Skirts Legal Quagmire," *The Washington Post*, February 25, 2001, http:// www.washingtonpost.com/ac2/wp-dyn?pagename=article&node=&contentId= A49314-2001Feb24&notFound=true; Richard D'Errico, "Aimster Software Maker Sues Recording Industry Association," *The Business Review*, May 3, 2001, http:// albany.bizjournals.com/albany/stories/2001/04/30/daily37.html; Richard D'Errico, "Aimster Changes Name to Resolve AOL Suit," *The Business Review*, January 25, 2002, http://albany.bizjournals.com/albany/stories/2002/01/21/daily58.html; and Jennifer Norman, "Staying Alive: Can the Recording Industry Survive Peer-to-Peer?," *Columbia Journal of Law & the Arts* 26 (2003): 384–87.

65. See *A&M Records, Inc. v. Napster, Inc.*, 2000 WL 573136, 10 (N.D. Cal. 2000); *A&M Records, Inc. v. Napster, Inc.*, 2000 WL 1009483, 8 (N.D. Cal. 2000); *A&M Records, Inc. v. Napster, Inc.*, 2000 WL 1055915 (9th Cir. 2000); *A&M Records, Inc. v. Napster, Inc.*, 114 F. Supp. 2d 896, 927 (N.D. Cal. 2000); *A&M Records, Inc. v. Napster, Inc.*, 239 F.3d 1004, 1027 (9th Cir. 2001); *A&M Records, Inc. v. Napster, Inc.*, 2001 WL 227083 (N.D. Cal. 2001); Reuters, "RIAA Sends Napster Music List," *Wired News*, March 12, 2001, http://www.wired.com/news/business/0,1367,42389,00.html; BBC News Online, "Napster Can Go Back Online," *BBC News*, July 19, 2001, http://news.bbc.co.uk/2/hi/entertainment/1446441.stm; *A&M Records, Inc. v. Napster, Inc.*, 284 F.3d 1091, 1099 (9th Cir. 2002); and Associated Press, "Swan Song: Bankruptcy For Napster," *CBSNews*, June 3, 2002, http://www.cbsnews.com/stories/2002/06/03/tech/main510891.shtml.

66. See Amy Doan, "Scour Says It's Not Into Dirty Work," *Forbes.com*, http://www.forbes.com/2000/08/05/feat2.html; Evan Hansen, "Scour Draws Big-Name Lawyers to Copyright Suit," *CNET News*, August 9, 2000, http://news.com.com/2100-1023-244292.html; Hane Lee, "It Ain't Over Till It's Over," *The Industry Standard*, August 7, 2000, http://articles.findarticles.com/p/articles/mi_mOHWW/is_29_3/ai_66675363; "Court Date a Disaster For Napster," *Red Herring*, http://www.redherring.com/Article.aspx?f=articles%2farchive%2findustries%2f2000%2f0727%2find-napster2072700.xml; Jim Hu, "Scour Files for Bankruptcy Protection," *CNET News*, October 13, 2000, http://news.com.com/2100-1023-247021.html?legacy=cnet; Evan Hansen, "Scour Scraps File-Swapping Service," *CNET News*, November 16, 2000, http://news. com.com/2100-1023_3-248753.html; and Brad King and Jeffrey Terraciano, "Scour: Going, Going, Gone," *Wired News*, December 12, 2000, http://www.wired.com/news/business/0,1367,40632,00.html.

67. See Erin Joyce, "Dueling Aimster Lawsuits: Who Trumps?," *Internetnews.com*, May 29, 2001, http://www.atnewyork.com/news/article.php/774881; "Aimster: Another Day, Another Lawsuit," *USA Today*, July 5, 2001, http://www.usatoday.com/tech/news/2001-07-05-aimster.htm; Will Sturgeon, "Aimster Follows Napster Through the Courts," *Silicon.com*, November 20, 2001, http://www.silicon.com/news/500022/1/1029284.html; Richard D'Errico, "Judge Grants Injunction Against Madster," *The Business Review*, September 5, 2002, http://albany.bizjournals.com/albany/stories/2002/09/02/daily26.html; Richard D'Errico, "Madster Ordered to Shut Down," *The Business Review*, December 4, 2002, http://albany.bizjournals.com/albany/stories/2002/12/02/daily46.html; *In re Aimster Copyright Litigation*, 334 F.3d 643, 653 (7th Cir. 2003); and Richard D'Errico, "Companies Founded by Deep File for Bankruptcy," *The Business Review*, March 19, 2002, http://albany.bizjournals.com/albany/stories/2002/03/18/daily15.html.

68. For a spectrum of views by artists concerning the merits of the Napster system, see "'Artists Against Piracy' Launches National Media Campaign," *Internetnews.com*, July 11, 2000, http://www.internetnews.com/ec-news/article.php/412001; Jennifer Vineyard, "Artists Sound Off On Digital Future," *Rolling Stone*, July 26, 2000, http://www.rollingstone.com/news/newsarticle.asp?nid=11355; Wade Beckett, "Artists Against Napster," *TechTV*, May 8, 2000, http://www.techtv.com/internettonight/

napster/jump/0,23009,2565051,00.html; and Napster, Inc., "Artists Sound Off," *Napster.com*, http://www.singsing.org/files/causacivile/napster/.

69. See Elias, "RIAA Turns Deaf Ear to Napster"; John Blau, "Napster Incites Another Lawsuit," *PCWorld.com*, February 20, 2003, http://www.pcworld.com/news/article/0,aid,109452,00.asp; and Nick Wingfield and Anna Wilde Mathews, "Music Publishers Sue Bertelsmann Over Napster Svc," *Yahoo! Finance*, http://sg.biz.yahoo.com/030220/72/3816h.html. I provided advice to the law firm representing Bertelsmann in the lawsuit filed against it by some of the other record companies after Bertelsmann's initiative failed and Napster went bankrupt. My sense of the merits of Bertelsmann's attempt to convert Napster into an authorized fee-based system contributed to my willingness to get involved in the litigation—but may also have been amplified by participation in the case. Again, therefore, the reader may wish to discount my comments on this issue.

70. See Cave, "Why Scour Is Not the New Napster."

71. See Brad King, "Multimedia 'Napster' Awaits Fate," *Wired News*, July 31, 2000; http://www.wired.com/news/culture/0,1284,37884,00.html.

72. For the Court of Appeals' persuasive analysis of these issues, see *Napster*, 239 F.3d at 1024–25.

73. The Supreme Court's analysis is reviewed in greater detail in Chapter 2. A tricky question is whether the Court's reasoning was applicable, not only to claims for contributory copyright infringement, but also to claims for vicarious infringement. The *Sony* decision does not resolve the question, because, for technical reasons, only the claims for contributory infringement were before the Court. The Court of Appeals in the *Napster* case, relying upon one commentator, took the position that the *Sony* doctrine did not extend to vicarious infringement claims (239 F.3d at 1022–23). This seems strained. The Supreme Court, although it noted that claims for vicarious infringement were not "nominally" before it, framed its analysis as a general discussion of the problem of third-party liability for copyright infringement. Judge Posner's view that the Supreme Court "treat[ed] vicarious and contributory infringement interchangeably," *In re Aimster*, 334 F.3d at 654, seems fairer than the Ninth Circuit's reading.

74. *Napster*, 239 F.3d at 1014. This argument would, of course, lose much of its force if Napster were capable of determining which of its subscribers were engaged in lawful activities and which were not—and then using that information either to cancel the subscriptions of the latter or to block their behavior. But with respect to sampling, at least, such differentiation is impossible. As the Court of Appeals emphasized in a separate section of its opinion, Napster probably was capable of distinguishing recordings whose copyright owners did not object to Internet distribution from recordings whose copyright owners did so object—and of taking steps to block exchanges of the latter (239 F.3d at 1020–22). But Napster could not know (and had no way of learning) what a given user did with the files he or she downloaded—and thus could not determine whether he or she was engaged in unlawful "librarying" or lawful sampling.

75. 239 F.3d at 1018.

76. 239 F.3d at 1018.

77. 239 F.3d at 1018.

78. *In re Aimster*, 334 F.3d at 648–52 (italics added).

79. See Damien A. Riehl, "Peer-to-Peer Distribution Systems: Will Napster, Gnutella, and Freenet Create a Copyright Nirvana or Gehenna?," *William Mitchell Law Review* 27 (2001): 1761, 1774.

80. LimeWire.com, "Understanding Peer-to-Peer Networking and File-Sharing," http://www.limewire.com/english/content/p2p.shtml. For additional information concerning Gnutella, see Timothy Ryan, "Infringement.com: RIAA v. Napster and the War Against Online Music Piracy," *Arizona Law Review* 44 (2002): 495, 518.

81. See Eoin Creedon et al., "P2P Networks: Gnutella," *Networks and Telecommunications Research Group*, http://ntrg.cs.tcd.ie/undergrad/4ba2.02–03/p5.html; and Ashlee Vance, "Music Swappers Called Takers, Not Givers," *InfoWorld*, August 21, 2000, http://archive.infoworld.com/articles/hn/xml/00/08/21/000821hngnutella.xml?0822tuam.

82. See Kelly Truelove, "Gnutella: Alive, Well, and Changing Fast," *O'Reilly Network*, January 25, 2001, http://www.openp2p.com/lpt/a/573; and Brad King, "Gnutella: File-Sharing Haven," *Wired News*, March 6, 2002, http://www.wired.com/news/mp3/0,1285,50858,00.html.

83. See Tim Wu, "When Code Isn't Law," *Virginia Law Review* 89 (2003): 679, 734–36. The licensing agreement between the developers of FastTrack and StreamCast Networks subsequently broke down, prompting the latter to begin using the Gnutella network instead. See John Borland, "Morpheus Looks to Gnutella for Help," *CNET News*, February 27, 2002, http://news.com.com/2100-1023-846944.html.

A somewhat more detailed description of the function of the "supernodes" follows: "One of the central features distinguishing FastTrack-based software from other peer-to-peer technology is the dynamic, or variable use of 'supernodes.' A 'node' is an end-point on the Internet, typically a user's computer. A 'supernode' is a node that has a heightened function, accumulating information from numerous other nodes. An individual node using FastTrack-based software automatically self-selects its own supernode status; a user's node may be a supernode one day and not on the following day, depending on resource needs and availability of the network. . . . This creates a two-tiered organizational structure, with groups of nodes clustered around a single supernode. When a user starts his/her software, the user's computer finds a supernode and accesses the network." *Metro-Goldwyn-Mayer Studios v. Grokster, Ltd.*, 259 F. Supp. 2d 1029, 1040 (C.D. Cal. 2003).

84. See Wu, "When Code Isn't Law," 734.

85. See Jasper Koning, "Dutch Court Cracks Down on Kazaa" *CNET News*, November 29, 2001, http://news.com.com/2100-1023-276409.html?legacy=cnet; Ben King, "KaZaA Comes Back to Life," *Silicon.com*, January 22, 2002, http://www.silicon.com/hardware/servers/0,39024647,11030611,00.htm; and *Buma & Stemra v. Kazaa*, Amsterdam Court of Appeal, March 28, 2002, http://www.eff.org/IP/P2P/BUMA_v_Kazaa/20020328_kazaa_appeal_judgment.html.

86. See *Metro-Goldwyn-Mayer Studios v. Grokster, Ltd.*, 259 F. Supp. 2d 1029

(C.D. Cal. 2003). KaZaA BV (the Dutch company) originally was also a defendant in these suits. However, after KaZaA BV sold its assets (including the KaZaA name) to Sharman Networks, it ceased defending the suit. Consequently, even though its legal status was essentially indistinguishable from those of Grokster and StreamCast, Judge Wilson entered a default judgment against it. Sharman Networks was not a party to the suit. Judge Wilson's ruling thus did not determine its potential liability.

87. See Jon Healey, "Record Labels Conduct Raid in Australia," *Los Angeles Times*, February 7, 2004, C1. The difficulty of predicting the final outcome of this round of litigation is enhanced by the fact that one of the defendants, KaZaA, has recently gone on the offensive, suing the plaintiffs for antitrust violations. See John Borland, "Kazaa Blasts Hollywood 'Conspiracy,'" *CNET News*, September 23, 2003, http://news.com.com/2100-1027-5081071.html.

88. See Declan McCullagh, "Piracy and Peer-to-Peer," *CNET News*, July 7, 2003, http://news.com.com/2010-1071-1023325.html.

89. For a description of the design and operation of the system, see Wikipedia .com, *Freenet*, http://en.wikipedia.org/wiki/Freenet. For accounts of its emergence, see Declan McCullagh, "P2P's Little Secret," *CNET News*, July 8, 2003, http://news. com.com/2100-1029-1023735.html; and John Borland, "Ian Clarke's Peer-to-Peer Debate," *CNET News*, May 6, 2002, http://news.com.com/2008-1082-899662.html.

90. The chart has been taken from http://www.pewinternet.org/reports/chart .asp?img=96_downdemos.jpg. For the full report, see Pew Internet & American Life Project, "Music Downloading, File-sharing, and Copyright," July 31, 2003, http:// www.pewinternet.org/reports/toc.asp?Report=96.

91. See Adam Liptak, "The Music Industry Reveals its Carrots and Sticks," *New York Times*, September 14, 2003, "The Week in Review," 1, 5, http://home.att .net/mrmorse/nytimes20030914lipt.html.

92. See Pew Internet and American Life Project, "Music Downloading, File-sharing, and Copyright."

93. See *In re Aimster*, 334 F.3d at 645; and Liane Cassavoy, "Music Labels Declare War on File Swappers," *PCWorld.com*, September 8, 2003, http://www.pcworld .com/news/article/0,aid,112364,00.asp.

94. See Seth Schiesel, "SBC Won't Name Names in File-Sharing Cases," *New York Times*, September 16, 2003, http://www.nytimes.com/2003/09/16/business/media/ 16SWAP.html?pagewanted=1&ei=5070&en=d9d4ec952e994a77&ex=1064894400.

95. See *In re Verizon Internet Services, Inc.*, 240 F. Supp. 2d 24 (D.D.C. 2003); and *In re Verizon Internet Services, Inc.*, 257 F. Supp. 2d 244 (D.D.C. 2003). For examples of the new style of freshman-orientation programs, see James Collins, "Some Colleges Warn Students on Sharing Music," *The Boston Globe*, August 1, 2003, http://www.uh.edu/ednews/2003/bglobe/200308/20030801riaa.htm; and Benny Evangelista, "Download Warning 101: Freshman Orientation This Fall to Include Record Industry Warnings Against File Sharing," *The San Francisco Chronicle*, August 11, 2003, http://www.sfgate.com/cgi-bin/article.cgi?file=/chronicle/archive/2003/08/11/ BU221002.DTL&type=tech.

96. See Frank Ahrens, "RIAA's Lawsuits Meet Surprised Targets," *Washington Post*, September 10, 2003, http://computercops.biz/article3066.html; and Jefferson Graham, "RIAA Lawsuits Bring Consternation, Chaos," *USA Today*, September 10, 2003, http://www.usatoday.com/tech/news/techpolicy/2003-09-10-riaa-suit-reax _x.htm.

97. See *Recording Industry Association of America v. Verizon Internet Services, Inc.*, 351 F.3d 1229 (D.C. Cir. 2003); Marcella Bombardieri, "Students Tune Out Industry Lawsuits," *Boston Globe*, September 14, 2003, A1; McCullagh, "P2P's Little Secret"; Earth Station Five, http://www.earthstation5.com; "Sex Lies, and Earth Station 5," *The Economist*, December, 20, 2003; and Amy Harmon, "New Parent-to-Child Chat: Do You Download Music?," *New York Times*, September 10, 2003, http://www.nytimes.com/2003/09/10/technology/10MUSI.html?ex=1064894400 &en=cbe47479e830be85&ei=5070. For a list of the currently available services, see www.download.com.

98. See Halstead, "The Regulated Become the Regulators"; and MySimon, "Samsung SW-252 CD-RW," http://www.mysimon.com/Samsung_SW_252_CD_RW/ 4505-3207_8-21007267.html?tag=pdtl-list.

99. See Halstead, "The Regulated Become the Regulators," 227; and U.S. Congress, Office of Technology Assessment, "Copyright and Home Copying: Technology Challenges the Law" (Washington, DC: GPO, 1989), 11–12, 271, 273–74 (describing the range of reasons for making copies of recordings in 1989).

100. See Bob Starrett, "Compact Disc Errors," *Roxio*, April 21, 2000, http:// www.roxio.com/en/support/cdr/cderrors.html; Ida Shum, "Getting 'Ripped' Off by Copy-Protected CDs," *Journal of Legislation* 29 (2002): 125, 131; and Rachel Gader-Shafran, "Confessions of a Serial Infringer: Can the Audio Home Recording Act of 1992 Protect the Consumer from Copy-Protected CDs?," *Intellectual Property Law Newsletter* 21 (2003): 10, 11. The recent acquisition of Midbar by Macrovision is likely soon to generate a hybrid of the Cactus Data Shield and SafeAudio systems.

101. The Shift-key maneuver was discovered by John Halderman, a Ph.D. student working under the supervision of Professor Felten at Princeton. It defeated a copy-protection system developed by SunnComm Technologies. When Halderman published a paper revealing the hole, SunnComm threatened him with a suit under the Digital Millennium Copyright Act. Negative publicity prompted the company to withdraw the threat. See John Borland, "Shift Key Breaks CD Copy Locks," *CNET News*, October 7, 2003, http://news.com.com/2100-1025-5087875.html; John Borland, "Student Faces Suit Over Key to CD Locks," *CNET News*, October 9, 2003, http://news.com.com/2100-1025-5089168.html; and Declan McCullagh, "SunnComm Won't Sue Grad Student," *CNET News*, October 10, 2003, http://news.com.com/ 2100-1027->5089448.html.

102. For examples of these problems, see Tom Spring, "Music Labels Target CD Ripping," *PCWorld.com*, November 5, 2001, http://www.pcworld.com/resource/ printable/article/0,aid,69504,00.asp; Gwendolyn Mariano, "Japanese Label Protects its CDs," *CNET News*, March 5, 2002, http://news.com.com/2100-1023-852540

.html; Evan Hansen, "Dion Disc Could Bring PCs to a Standstill," *CNET News*, April 4, 2002, http://news.com.com/2100-1023-876055.html; and John Borland, "Universal Copy-Protected CD Shuns Players," *CNET News*, December 18, 2001, http://news.com.com/news/0-1005-200-8225543.html.

103. Documentation of DeLise's suit may be found in Amy Harmon, "CD-Protection Complaint is Settled," *New York Times*, February 25, 2002, C8. Information concerning the pending class-action suit may be found at Milberg Weiss, http://www.milberg.com/pdf/audiocds/complaint.pdf.

104. See Aaron A. Hurowitz, "Copyright in the New Millennium: Is the Case Against ReplayTV a New Betamax for the Digital Age?" *CommLaw Conspectus* 11 (2003): 145, 153; "Time-Warner Cable Enters Digital Video-Recorder Fray in Orange County, Calif.," *The Orange County (Calif.) Register*, June 17, 2003; Farhad Manjoo, "Replay It Again Sam," *Salon.com Technology and Business Department*, December 9, 2002, http://www.salon.com/tech/feature/2002/12/09/pvr/print.html; and Powell Fraser, "Software Offers TiVo-Like Recording at Lower Price," *CNET News*, October 8, 2003, http://www.cnn.com/2003/TECH/ptech/10/08/tv.recording/index.html.

105. The prices set forth in the text are from *CNET Reviews*, http://reviews.cnet.com/Home_video/4502-6474_7-0.html?tag=dir and are current as of February 2004. For a discussion of the pricing strategies of the DVR manufacturers, see Michael Bartlett, "Personal TV Companies Should Cut Prices," *BizReport.com Entertainment Research*, February 28, 2001, http://www.bizreport.com//article.php?art_id=348. The quotations are from Diane Holloway, "Dawn of a View Era: Digital Video Recorders Are Changing Television Forever," *Austin American-Statesmen*, July 5, 2003, Lifestyle section. See also Christian Toto, "Gimme My DVR: VCRs Take a Back Seat to Digital Recorders," *The Washington Times*, June 26, 2003, Life section. The projections of DVR adoptions are from Josh Bernoff, "Will Ad-Skipping Kill Television?" *Forrester Research TechStrategy Report*, November 2002.

106. See *In re Aimster Copyright Litigation*, 334 F.3d 643, 649 (7th Cir. 2003).

107. See Hurowitz, "Copyright in the New Millennium," 153–57. The early models of ReplayTV offered a thirty-second skip feature, permitting consumers to skip through the advertisements. TiVo systems can also be programmed relatively easily to skip forward in thirty-second increments. (The requisite series of commands is Select, Play, Select, 30, Select.) However, with the new Commercial Advance feature offered in its 4000 and 5000 models, Replay enabled users to skip all advertisements automatically during playback and thus sharply increased the likelihood that consumers would view programming ad-free.

108. The four suits were *Paramount Pictures Corporation et al. v. ReplayTV, Inc.* (C.D. Cal. 2001) (Docket No.: 01-CV-9358); *Time Warner Entertainment Co. et al. v. ReplayTV, Inc. et al.* (C.D. Cal. 2001) (Docket No.: 01-CV-9693); *MGM et al. v. ReplayTV, Inc. et al.* (C.D. Cal. 2001) (Case No: 01-09801); and *Columbia Pictures et al. v. ReplayTV, Inc. et al.* (C.D. Cal. 2001) (Case No: 01-10221). The complaints are available from the Paramount v. ReplayTV case archive assembled by the

Electronic Frontier Foundation, http://www.eff.org/IP/Video/Paramount_v_ ReplayTV/. For evidence concerning the impact on advertisement revenues, see Tobi Elkin, "Impact of PVRs Dramatically Less Than Predicted," *AdAge.com Online Edition*, May 6, 2001, http://www.adage.com/news.cms?newsId=34640.

109. See Sandeep Junnarkar, "Japanese Firm Buys SonicBlue Units," *CNET News*, April 16, 2003, http://news.com.com/2100-1041-997128.html; Lisa M. Bowman, "ReplayTV Puts Ad Skipping on Pause," *CNET News*, June 10, 2003, http://news.com.com/2100-1041-1015121.html; and Dawn C. Chmielewski, "ReplayTV Undergoes Changes," *Pittsburgh Post-Gazette*, June 24, 2003, Arts and Entertainment section.

Chapter 4

1. Available at http://www.riaa.com/issues/piracy/default.asp. The Website of the Motion Picture Association of America contains equally forceful, although less lurid, denunciations of "piracy": http://www.mpaa.org/anti-piracy/.

2. The speech is available at http://www.house.gov/apps/list/speech/ca28_berman/ComputerCommunicationsIndustryAssosiation.html.

3. See Neil Netanel, "Impose a Noncommercial Use Levy To Allow Free Peer-to-Peer File Sharing," *Harvard Journal of Law & Technology* 17 (2003): 1, 22–24.

4. The metaphor of the bundle of sticks originated in Benjamin N. Cardozo, *The Paradoxes of Legal Science* (New York: Columbia University Press, 1928), 129. For another, influential use, see *Andrus v. Allard*, 444 U.S. 51, 65–66 (1979). For a survey of the main components of the bundle, see Charles Donahue, Jr., Thomas E. Kauper, and Peter W. Martin, *Cases and Materials on Property* (St. Paul, MN: West Pub. Co., 1993), 215–317.

5. See William Blackstone, *Commentaries on the Laws of England* (Chicago: University of Chicago Press, 1979)(facsimile of the 1st ed., 1765–69), Vol. 2, 2; Felix Cohen, "Dialogue on Private Property," *Rutgers Law Review* 9 (1954): 357, 374; Morris Cohen, "Property and Sovereignty," *Cornell Law Quarterly* 13 (1927): 8, 12; *Loretto v. Teleprompter Manhattan CATV Corp.*, 458 U.S. 419 (1982), on remand, 58 N.Y.2d 143 (1983); and Frank Michelman, "Property, Utility, and Fairness: Comments on the Ethical Foundations of 'Just Compensation' Law," *Harvard Law Review* 80 (1967): 1165.

6. Blackstone, *Commentaries*, Vol. 2, 18.

7. See *Edwards v. Sims*, 232 Ky. 791, 793–94 (1929).

8. Typical criminal-trespass statutes include Ky. Rev. Stat. §§511.070(1), 511.080, 511.090(4) (1975); and Me. Rev. Stat. Ann., Tit. 17A, §402(1)(C) (1964). Many of these laws have been influenced by section 221.2 of the Model Penal Code.

9. See, for example, *Harndon v. Stultz*, 124 Iowa 440, 442 (1904); *Diffendal v. Virginia*, 8 Va. App. 417, 421 (1989); and William L. Prosser & W. Page Keaton, *Torts* (St. Paul, MN: West Publishing, 1984), §21.

10. See 14 C.F.R. §91.119 (specifying current minimum safe altitudes); *Burn-*

ham v. Beverly Airways, 311 Mass. 628 (1942); *United States v. Causby*, 328 U.S. 256, 260–61 (1946); *Campbell v. Race*, 61 Mass. 408 (1852); *Proctor v. Adams*, 113 Mass. 376; and *State v. Shack*, 58 N.J. 297 (1971).

11. See, for example, section 13-1505 of the Arizona statutes ("A person commits possession of burglary tools by possessing any explosive, tool, instrument or other article adapted or commonly used for committing any form of burglary . . . *and intending to use or permit the use of such an item in the commission of a burglary.*"); and section 810.06 of the Florida statutes ("Whoever has in his or her possession any tool, machine, or implement *with intent to use the same, or allow the same to be used, to commit any burglary or trespass* shall be guilty of a felony of the third degree.") (emphasis added).

12. See, for example, *Katko v. Briney*, 183 N.W.2d 657 (Iowa 1971).

13. *Ploof v. Putnam*, 81 Vt. 471 (1908). The case that supports the suggestion that the plaintiff would have had to pay for any injury to the defendant's dock is *Vincent v. Lake Erie Transportation Co.*, 109 Minn. 456 (1910).

14. For evidence that the construction of the tower would not be permitted, see 14 C.F.R. §77.13(a)(2).

15. See Wesley Newcomb Hohfeld, "Some Fundamental Legal Conceptions as Applied in Judicial Reasoning," *Yale Law Journal* 23 (1913): 16, 34–36. (Hohfeld was disputing John Chipman Gray's previous discussion of legal rights in shrimp salad.)

16. The bulletin-board case was *United States v. LaMacchia*, 871 F. Supp. 535 (D. Mass. 1994). Indications that the Justice Department is increasing its attention to unauthorized distribution of copyrighted materials on the Internet may be found in Declan McCullagh, "DOJ to Swappers: Law's Not on Your Side," *CNET News*, August 20, 2002, http://news.com.com/2100-1023-954591.html.

17. See Michael Coblenz, "Intellectual Property Crimes," *Albany Law Journal of Science & Technology* 9 (1999): 235; Paul Goldstein, *Copyright: Principles, Law, and Practice* (Boston: Little Brown, 1989 and 1990 Pocket Part), §11.4.1.b; and *United States v. Moran*, 757 F. Supp. 1046 (D. Neb. 1991). Polls suggesting that, as of 2000, many Americans believed that downloading recordings was both morally and legally justified are discussed in the Introduction. The most recent polls suggest that the spate of lawsuits against individual file-sharers has raised public awareness of the illegality of this behavior. See Rick Carr, "Music Industry Ends a Down Year," *National Public Radio: All Things Considered*, December 30, 2003, http://www.npr.org/features/feature.php?wfId=1576789 (quoting Cary Sherman, president of the RIAA).

18. The text of the proposal can be found at http://cyber.law.harvard.edu/people/tfisher/CBDTPA.htm or http://www.politechbot.com/docs/cbdtpa/hollings.s2048.032102.html. Although the chances that the CBDTPA will make it through Congress in the near future are small, a much more modest version of this general approach was just adopted—not by Congress, but by the Federal Communications Commission. In a recent ruling, the Commission ordered consumer-electronics manufacturers by July 1, 2005, to ensure that all devices capable of receiving over-the-air digital signals (for example, digital televisions, DTV-compatible DVD recorders, and

computers equipped with DTV tuner cards) recognize and respect "broadcast flags" indicating that the programs in which they are embedded may only be copied using FCC-approved copy-control technology. That technology would permit consumers to make copies for their own use but not to redistribute them over the Internet. As even its strongest defenders concede, the FCC's ruling is a highly imperfect way of discouraging the redistribution of broadcast digital recordings. The reason: virtually all of the existing devices through which flagged programs can be freely played have analog outputs, to which a digital recorder may be connected. The resultant recordings—though slightly worse than digital recordings made directly from digital broadcasts—could be shared freely online. The record companies and film studios are currently looking for ways to plug this "analog hole." Among the options they are considering is legislation requiring any device that makes digital copies from analog signals to recognize and respect the flags. The accumulation of "surgical" reforms of this sort might eventually produce the equivalent of the CBDTPA. See *In re Digital Broadcast Content Protection*, MB Docket 02-230, 2003 *FCC Lexis* 6120 (November 4, 2003); "FCC Adopts Anti-Piracy Protection for Digital TV; Broadcast Flag Prevents Mass Internet Distribution; Consumer Copying Not Affected; No New Equipment Needed," 2003 *FCC Lexis* 6107 (November 4, 2003); Rob Pegoraro, "FCC Deserves a Digital Thanks for Nothing," *Washington Post*, November 9, 2003, F7; and "FCC Mandates DTV-capable DVD-Video Recorders Recognize Anti-Distribution 'Broadcast Flag,'" *DVD Report*, November 10, 2003.

19. See Andrew Russ Sorkin, "Software Bullet Is Sought to Kill Music Piracy," *New York Times*, May 4, 2003, Section 1, p. 1.

20. See Peter S. Menell, "Can Our Current Conception of Copyright Law Survive the Internet Age?: Envisioning Copyright Law's Digital Future," *New York Law School Law Review* 46 (2002): 63, 179; and Jeffrey L. Dodes, "Beyond Napster, Beyond the United States: The Technological and International Legal Barriers to On-Line Copyright Enforcement," *New York Law School Law Review* 46 (2002): 279, 313–15.

21. See Justin Oppelaar, "Hatch Backtracks on Destroying PCs," *Daily Variety*, June 19, 2003, 4. The text of Rep. Berman's bill is available at http://www.house .gov/berman/newsroom/p2p.pdf. The second quotation is taken from the speech in which Rep. Berman announced the legislative initiative, available at http://www .house.gov/apps/list/press/ca28_berman/piracy_prevention_act.html. See also the "Section by Section Analysis" that was drafted to accompany the bill, available at http://www.house.gov/berman/newsroom/p2p_analysis.html and http://www .politechbot.com/docs/berman.coble.p2p.analysis.072502.html. The provisions of the bill itself, unfortunately, did not embody this general principle well. But that level of detail need not detain us.

22. See Dan Burk and Julie Cohen, "Fair Use Infrastructure for Rights Management Systems," *Harvard Journal of Law and Technology* 15 (2001): 41.

23. See Burk and Cohen, "Fair Use Infrastructure."

24. Statistics (exaggerated but nevertheless suggestive) concerning rates of soft-

ware piracy in the United States and other countries can be found on the Website for the Business Software Alliance: http://www.bsa.org/usa/research/. For record and film companies' promises that, if shielded from the threat of piracy, they would make their materials available online, see WIPO Copyright Treaties Implementation Act, Hearing on H.R. 2281 Before the Subcommittee on Telecommunications, Trade, and Consumer Protection, House Committee on Commerce, 105th Cong. 42–46, 56–57 (1998) (statements of Hilary B. Rosen, president of the Recording Industry Association of America, and Steven J. Metalitz, representing the Motion Picture Association of America).

25. MusicNet may be found at http://www.musicnet.com/. The iTunes Music Store may be found at http://www.apple.com/itunes/store/. For a brief history of the service, see Wikipedia, "iTunes," http://en.wikipedia.org/wiki/Itunes. The new Napster may be found at http://www.napster.com/. For a good description of these services, see Amy Harmon, "What Price Music?," *New York Times*, October 12, 2003. For estimates of the relative popularity of legitimate and illegitimate downloading of sound recordings as of the end of 2002, see Dawn Chmielewski, "Fee-based Online Music Services Sing the Blues," *The Mercury News*, December 2, 2002. For indications that the gap is now beginning to close, see Tony Smith, "10m Americans Pay for Music Downloads in Q2," *The Register*, November 26, 2003, http://theregister .co.uk/content/6/34206.html (summarizing finding by the market research company Ipsos-Insight that, during the second quarter of 2003, 16 percent of Americans who downloaded music online had paid for at least some of it).

26. Wikipedia, "FairPlay," http://en.wikipedia.org/wiki/FairPlay. Apple's briefer description of the system may be found at http://www.apple.com/support/itunes/authorization.html.

27. On the cracking of FairPlay, see Andrew Orlowski, "DVD Jon Unlocks iTunes' Locked Music," *The Register*, updated version, December 22, 2003, http://www.theregister.co.uk/content/4/34141.html.

28. One of those antitrust lawsuits—a class-action suit brought against the five major record companies and three major retailers, alleging that they had conspired to set minimum prices for CDs—was recently settled. Although the defendants denied wrongdoing, they agreed to pay $13 to each of the hundred of thousands of individual plaintiffs and to give 5.6 million free CDs to the states. See Courtney Flynn, "Check in Mail for Some CD Buyers," *Chicago Tribune*, February 20, 2004, C5.

29. Robert P. Merges, "Contracting into Liability Rules: Intellectual Property Rights and Collective Rights Organizations," *California Law Review* 84 (1996): 1293, 1307–16, 1378–85.

30. Burk and Cohen, "Fair Use Infrastructure," 79–80.

31. The parody example is well explored in Robert P. Merges, "Are You Making Fun of Me? Notes on Market Failure and the Parody Defense in Copyright," *American Intellectual Property Law Association Quarterly Journal* 21 (1993): 305. The more general point is explored in the context of digital rights managements sys-

tems by Yochai Benkler, "An Unhurried View of Private Ordering in Information Transactions," *Vanderbilt Law Review* 53 (2000): 2063, 2077; and Julie E. Cohen, "Copyright and the Perfect Curve," *Vanderbilt Law Review* 53 (2000): 1799, 1812.

32. For general treatments of price discrimination, see Louis Phlips, *The Economics of Price Discrimination* (Cambridge: Cambridge University Press, 1983); and George Norman, ed., *The Economics of Price Discrimination* (Northampton, MA: Edward Elgar Publishing, 1999). The more precise of the two definitions is supplied by Michael J. Meurer, "Copyright Law and Price Discrimination," *Cardozo Law Review* 23 (2001): 55, 58.

33. See Norman, *Economics of Price Discrimination*, xii–xviii.

34. For essays exploring from different angles the price-discrimination opportunities that DRM systems create, see Benkler, "An Unhurried View," 2069–77; Tom W. Bell, "Fair Use vs. Fared Use: The Impact of Automated Rights Management on Copyright's Fair Use Doctrine," *North Carolina Law Review* 76 (1998): 557; James Boyle, "Cruel, Mean, or Lavish? Economic Analysis, Price Discrimination and Digital Intellectual Property," *Vanderbilt Law Review* 53 (2000): 2007; and Jonathan Zittrain, "What the Publisher Can Teach the Patient: Intellectual Property and Privacy in an Era of Trusted Privication," *Stanford Law Review* 52 (2000): 1201, 1213.

35. For a careful study of the risks of second-degree price discrimination, see Meurer, 71–80. The printer example comes from Boyle, "Cruel, Mean, or Lavish," 2024, who in turn relies upon Carl Shapiro and Hal R. Varian, *Information Rules: A Strategic Guide to the Network Economy* (Boston: Harvard Business School Press, 1999), 59.

36. See Wendy J. Gordon, "Intellectual Property," in Peter Can and Mark V. Tushnet, eds., *The Oxford Handbook of Legal Studies* (New York: Oxford, 2003), 617, 643–45; Wendy J. Gordon, "Rendering Copyright Unto Caesar: Free Speech, Locke, and the Gift of the Carob," *University of Chicago Law Review* (forthcoming 2004).

37. This danger is emphasized in Julie E. Cohen, "Copyright and the Perfect Curve," *Vanderbilt Law Review* 53 (2000): 1799, 1808–9. For a discussion of how compulsory terms and other copyright defenses (incorporating, for example, an expanded version of the fair-use doctrine) could be used to mitigate the risk, see William Fisher, "Property and Contract on the Internet," *Chicago-Kent Law Review* 73 (1998): 1203, 1240–55.

38. See Paul-Jon McNealy, "*Digital Consumers: Are They 'Fair Users' or Copyright Pirates?*" GartnerG2 Report Number: rpt-1002-0184 (2003).

39. See Mark A. Lemley and Lawrence Lessig, "The End of End-to-End: Preserving the Architecture of the Internet in the Broadband Ere," *UCLA Law Review* 48 (2001): 925, 930–31 (summarizing J. H. Saltzer, D. P. Reed, and D. D. Clark, "End-to-End Arguments in System Design," April 8, 1981, http://web.mit.edu/Saltzer/www/publications/endtoend/endtoend.pdf).

40. Timothy Wu, "Application-Centered Internet Analysis," *Virginia Law Review* 85 (1999): 1163, 1192–93.

Chapter 5

1. See Richard J. Pierce, Jr. and Ernest Gelhorn, *Regulated Industries*, 4th ed. (St. Paul, MN: West Group, 1999), 1.

2. On the spread of the railroads and the efforts to control their pricing practices, see Alfred D. Chandler Jr., ed., *The Railroads: The Nation's First Big Business* (New York: Harcourt, Brace & World, 1965), 185–212; Stephen Siegel, "Understanding the Lochner Era: Lessons from the Controversy over Railroad and Utility Rate Regulation," *Virginia Law Review* 70 (1984): 187; and Herbert Hovenkamp, "Regulatory Conflict in the Gilded Age: Federalism and the Railroad Problem," *Yale Law Journal* 97 (1988): 1017, 1035–54. Among other things, Hovencamp offers an intriguing theory of why secret "discounts," undercutting cartelization or "pooling" agreements among ostensibly competitive railroads, became so common.

3. See Joseph D. Kearney and Thomas W. Merrill, "The Great Transformation of Regulated Industries Law," *Columbia Law Review* 98 (1998): 1323.

4. See Kearney and Merrill, "The Great Transformation," 1329–64; and Richard J. Pierce, "Reconsidering the Roles of Regulation and Competition in the Natural Gas Industry," *Harvard Law Review* 97 (1983): 345.

5. Kearney and Merrill, "The Great Transformation," 1361.

6. The phrase, "affected with a public interest," was first used by Lord Chief Justice Hale in the seventeenth century. See Breck P. McAllister, "Lord Hale and Business Affected with a Public Interest," *Harvard Law Review* 43 (1930): 759, 760. Hale's notion that businesses so affected "cease[] to be *juris privati* only" was invoked by the United States Supreme Court in *Munn v. Illinois*, 94 U.S. 113, 126 (1876) to support the constitutionality of a state statute regulating the rates charged by grain warehouses.

7. *Chas. Wolff Packing Co. v. Court of Industrial Relations of Kansas*, 262 U.S. 522, 535–38 (1923).

8. See McAllister, "Lord Hale and Business"; and Walton H. Hamilton, "Affectation with Public Interest," *Yale Law Journal* 39 (1930): 1089, 1100–11.

9. For discussion of Title VIII of the Civil Rights Act of 1964—the primary vehicle for combating discrimination in the context of housing—see Jesse Dukeminier and James E. Krier, *Property*, 5th ed. (New York: Aspen, 2002), 460–77. For discussion of the conceptions of "discrimination" that dominated the railroad-regulation movement, see Hovencamp, "Regulatory Conflict in the Gilded Age," 1044–54. For the "universal service" ideal in the telecommunications context, see Kearney and Merrill, "The Great Transformation," 1346–49; and Eli M. Noam, "Will Universal Service and Common Carriage Survive the Telecommunications Act of 1996?," *Columbia Law Review* 97 (1997): 955, 957–63.

10. See Eyal Zamir, "The Efficiency of Paternalism," *Virginia Law Review* 84 (1998): 229, 254–75.

11. See Anthony T. Kronman, "Paternalism and the Law of Contracts," *Yale Law Journal* 92 (1983): 763; and Duncan Kennedy, "Distributive and Paternalist Motives in Contract and Tort Law, with Special Reference to Compulsory Terms and Unequal Bargaining Power," *Maryland Law Review* 41 (1982): 563, 624–38.

12. See Barry R. Litman, "Motion Picture Entertainment," in Walter Adams and James Brock, eds., *The Structure of American Industry*, 10th ed. (Upper Saddle River, NJ: Prentice Hall, 2001), 171–98; Rick Carr, "Music Industry Ends a Down Year," *National Public Radio: All Things Considered*, December 30, 2003, available at http://www.npr.org/features/feature.php?wfId=1576789; Harold L. Vogel, *Entertainment Industry Economics: A Guide for Financial Analysis*, 5th ed. (Cambridge: Cambridge University Press, 2001), 36–39; Benjamin M. Compaine and Douglas Gomery, *Who Owns the Media? Competition and Concentration in the Mass Media Industry* (Mahwah, NJ: Lawrence Erlbaum Associates, 2000), 285–435; Ronald V. Bettig and Jeann Lynn Hall, *Big Media, Big Money: Cultural Texts and Political Economics* (Lanham, MD: Bowman & Littlefield, 2003), 45–72; Geoffrey P. Hull, *The Recording Industry* (Boston: Allyn and Bacon, 1998), 158; "Universal Music Cuts Retail CD Prices Below $13," *Online Reporter*, September 6, 2003; and "UMG Cutting Prices on Its Top-Line CDs," *Hollywood Reporter*, September 4, 2003.

13. The numbers concerning the amounts of time Americans devote to media of different sorts were derived from U.S. Census Bureau, *Statistical Abstract of the United States: 2002*, No. 1102: "Media Usage and Consumer Spending: 1996–2005," http://www.census.gov/prod/2003pubs/02statab/infocom.pdf. Very similar projections can be found in MPAA, "U.S. Entertainment Industry: 2002 MPA Market Statistics," http://www.mpaa.org/useconomicreview/2002/2002_Economic_Review.pdf, 57. For another perspectives on the high rates with which Americans consume recorded entertainment, see *Trends in the Well-Being of America's Children and Youth* (U.S. Dept. of Health and Human Services, 1997), available at http://aspe.hhs.gov/hsp/97trends/intro-web.htm. The situation in other countries is not yet quite so extreme, but there are many troubling signs. The majority of even the poorest households in Brazil now have televisions. An especially chilling indicator comes from Thailand: "A recent survey in the northern provinces found that of the families who sold their daughters, two-thirds could afford not to do so but 'instead preferred to buy color televisions and video equipment.'" See Kevin Bales, "Because She Looks Like a Child," in Barbara Ehrenreich and Arlene Russell Hochschild, *Global Woman: Nannies, Maids, and Sex Workers in the New Economy* (New York: Henry Holt, 2002), 207–29, 211 (quoting "Caught in Modern Slavery: Tourism and Child Prostitution in Thailand," Country Report Summary prepared by Sudarat Sereewat-Srisang for the Ecumenical Consultation held in Chiang Mai in May 1990).

14. See *M. Witmark & Sons v. Fred Fisher Music Co.*, 125 F.2d 949, 955 (2d Cir. 1942) (dissenting opinion). For analysis of Frank's opinion, see Kent Greenawalt, "Variations on Some Themes of a 'Disporting Gazelle' and his Friend: Statutory Interpretation as Seen by Jerome Frank and Felix Frankfurter," *Columbia Law Review* 100 (2000): 176, 195–96. For illustrations of the many ways in which record companies take advantage of performers, see Chapter 2, pp. 54–58.

15. See Paul Goldstein, *Copyright: Principles, Law, and Practice* (Boston: Little Brown, 1989 and 1990 Pocket Part), Vol. I, 638–67; Chapter 2, pp. 41–42, 48–49, 51; and Chapter 3, pp. 102–10.

16. 17 U.S.C. §§203, 304(c). The extremely complex details of the "termination

right"—when may it be exercised, by whom, through what forms of notice, etc.—are summarized in M. William Krasilovsky and Sidney Shemel, *This Business of Music*, 8th ed. (New York: Billboard Books, 2000), 121–29. For the history of the sound recording–work for hire controversy, see Mary LaFrance, "Authorship and Termination Rights in Sound Recordings," *Southern California Law Review* 75 (2002): 375.

17. See 17 U.S.C. §114(g); and Copyright Law §18 (Greece), *available at* http://www.ifrro.org/laws/law_greece.html. Analogous provisions may be found in the copyright laws of Canada (see Copyright Act, R.S.C., ch. C-42, §19 [1985] [Can.], available at http://laws.justice.gc.ca/en/C-42/38355.html#rid-38485), and China (see 1-CHI International Copyright Law and Practice §8[2][e][iii]).

18. It should be emphasized that the iTunes Music Store does not currently limit its "shelves" to the products of the major record companies. On the contrary, its repertoire currently includes many recordings from independently distributed labels and freestanding imprints. See Berkman Center Digital Media Project, "iTunes: How Copyright, Contract, and Technology Shape the Business of Digital Media—A Case Study" (Green Paper, version 1.1, 2004), 87, http://cyber.law.harvard.edu/media/uploads/53/GreenPaperiTunes0304.pdf. The scenario sketched in the text represents an anxiety concerning the future, not a description of the present.

19. The same general strategy unlerlay one of the provisions of the Music Online Competition Act, proposed, unsuccessfully, by Congressmen Boucher and Cannon. See Statement of Congressman Rick Boucher, Introduction of Music Online Competition Act (August 3, 2001), http://www.house.gov/boucher/docs/moca-statement.htm.

20. See 47 C.F.R. §73.658(k) (PTAR); 47 C.F.R. § 73.658(j) (1990) (Fin/Syn). For justifications of these rules, see *Report and Order In re Amendment of Part 73 of the Commission's Rules and Regulations With Respect to Competition and Responsibility in Network Televisions Broadcasting*, 23 FCC 2d 382, 391, 395 (May 4, 1970). For analyses of them and studies of their evolution, see *Biennial Report, Review of the Commission's Broadcast Rules and Other Rules Adopted Pursuant to Section 202 of the Telecommunications Act of 1996*, 15 FCC Rcd. 11058 (2000); Stanley Besen et al., *Misregulating Television: Network Dominance and the FCC* (Chicago: University of Chicago Press, 1984); and Mara Einstein, *Media Diversity: Economics, Ownership, and the FCC* (Mahwah, NJ: Lawrence Erlbaum Associates, 2004), 40–111.

21. See the Telecommunications Act of 1996, Pub. L. No. 104-104 (1996); *In the Matter of Amendment of 47 CFR § 73.658(j)(1)(i) and (ii), the Syndication and Financial Interest Rules*, 94 FCC 2d 1019, 1066–67 (1993) (Fin/Syn Repeal); *In re Review of the Prime Time Access Rule, Section 73.658(k) of the Commission's Rules*, 11 FCC Rcd. 546, 547 and 551 (1995); 47 C.F.R. §§73.658(g), 73.3555(e)(1); *Broadcast Ownership Rules, Cross-Ownership of Broadcast Stations and Newspapers, Multiple Ownership of Radio Broadcast Stations in Local Markets, and Definition of Radio Markets*, 68 F.R. 46286, 46341 (2003); Stephen Labaton, "F.C.C. Plan to Ease Curbs on Big Media Hits Senate Snag," *New York Times*, September 17, 2003, A1; and Jacques Steinberg, "House Panel Adds Voice To Opponents Of Media Rule," *New York Times*, July 17, 2003, C1.

22. The Robinson-Patman Act itself is codified in 15 U.S.C. §§13, 13a, 13b, 21a (2003). For discussion of its frustrating intricacies, see Donald S. Clark, *The Robinson-Patman Act: General Principles, Commission Proceedings, and Selected Issues* (1995), available at http://www.ftc.gov/speeches/other/patman.htm; John C. Stedman, "Twenty-Four Years of the Robinson-Patman Act," *Wisconsin Law Review* (1960): 197; and Frederick M. Rowe, *Price Discrimination Under the Robinson-Patman Act* (Boston: Little, Brown, 1962). For documentation of the decline in the interest of the FTC and Justice Department in enforcing the statute, see Richard A. Posner, "A Statistical Study of Antitrust Enforcement," *Journal of Law and Economics* 13 (1970): 365, 369–70, 404–9; Andrew Jackson Holliday, *The Definition and Measurement of Antitrust Enforcement* (Greenwich, CT: JAI Press, 1998); and Timothy J. Muris, "Looking Forward: The Federal Trade Commission and the Future Development of U.S. Competition Policy," *Columbia Business Law Review* (2003): 359, 389.

23. For discussions of the hazards of price regulation in this context, see Robert Merges, "Contracting into Liability Rules: Intellectual Property and Collective Rights Organizations," *California Law Review* 84 (1996): 1293; and S. J. Liebowitz, "Alternative Copyright Systems: The Problems with a Compulsory License" (August 31, 2003), http://www.utdallas.edu/liebowit/intprop/complpff.pdf.

24. See Harry G. Henn, "The Compulsory License Provisions of the U.S. Copyright Law, reprinted in Copyright Law Revision," 86th Cong., 1st sess., *Studies Prepared for the Subcomm. on Patents, Trademarks and Copyrights of the Senate Comm. on the Judiciary* 53 (Comm. Print 1960); and Merges, "Contracting into Liability Rules," 1310–11.

25. See 17 U.S.C. 114(f)(2)(B). Had the arbitration panel followed the lead of the Court of Appeals for the Second Circuit (ruling, in a closely related context, that the "willing buyer/willing seller" criterion should be construed so as to correct for the market power wielded by ASCAP and BMI), its final determination would have been more palatable. See *ASCAP v. Showtime/The Movie Channel*, 912 F.2d 563 (2d Cir. 1990).

26. 17 U.S.C. §801(b)(1).

27. See Merges, "Contracting into Liability Rules," 1312–13.

28. The quoted language is drawn from the statute defining the authority of the Federal Communications Commission, 47 U.S.C. §303. Delegations of lawmaking power this broad were once considered unconstitutional, but more recently have been upheld by the Supreme Court. See *National Broadcasting Co. v. United States, Inc.*, 319 U.S. 190 (1943).

29. The evolution of these and other mechanisms for corralling administrative discretion (and of corresponding theories of administrative law) is documented in Richard Stewart, "The Reformation of American Administrative Law," *Harvard Law Review* 88 (1975): 1669; and Gerald Frug, "The Ideology of Bureaucracy in American Law," *Harvard Law Review* 97 (1984): 1277.

30. The rules establishing the structure of the FCC are set forth in 47 U.S.C. §154; 47 C.F.R. §0.1. For similar systems in place in the other "independent" federal

agencies, see 15 U.S.C. §78d(a) (SEC); 29 U.S.C. §153(a) (NLRB); 7 U.S.C. §2(a)(2) (CFTC); 42 U.S.C. §7171 (FERC); 42 U.S.C. §5841 (NRC); 15 U.S.C. §41 (FTC), 15 U.S.C. §2053 (CPSC); and 19 U.S.C. §1330 (USITC).

Chapter 6

1. Classic presentations of this argument can be found in Jeremy Bentham, *A Manual of Political Economy* (New York: G.P. Putnam, 1839); John Stuart Mill, *Principles of Political Economy*, 5th ed. (London: Longmans, Green & Co., 1909), 932–33; A. C. Pigou, *The Economics of Welfare*, 2d ed. (London: Macmillan & Co., 1924); and J. G. Head, "Public Goods and Public Policy," *Public Finance* 17 (1962): 197–221. Ronald Coase once argued that the parable of the lighthouse was misleading—that private parties had been able to construct lighthouses and operate them at a profit without state aid. See "The Lighthouse in Economics," *Journal of Law and Economics* 17 (1974): 357–76. It turns out, however, that Coase misinterpreted the relevant history. See David E. Van Zandt, "The Lessons of the Lighthouse: 'Government' or 'Private' Provision of Goods," *Journal of Legal Studies* 22 (1993): 47–72; and Steven Shavell, "The History of Lighthouses as Public Goods" (unpublished paper, February 1996).

2. See Paul A. David, "Intellectual Property Institutions and the Panda's Thumb: Patents, Copyrights, and Trade Secrets in Economic Theory and History," in Mitchel B. Wallerstein, Mary Ellen Mogee, and Roberta A. Schoen, eds, *Global Dimensions of Intellectual Property Rights in Science and Technology* (Washington: National Academy Press, 1993), 19, 27; and John M. Golden, "Biotechnology, Technology Policy, and Patentability: Natural Products and Invention in the American System, *Emory Law Journal* 50 (2001): 101–89.

3. The British example is described in Dava Sobel and William J. H. Andrewes, *The Illustrated Longitude* (New York: Walker, 1998), 63–73. The Soviet and Chinese systems are described in Haifeng Huang, "Reward System as an Alternative to Patent System: A Comparative Study of Chinese Experience" (unpublished paper, 2003). The treatment in the United States of inventions relating to atomic energy is described in Stefan A. Riesenfeld, "Patent Protection and Atomic Energy Legislation," *California Law Review* 46 (1958): 40–68. On Madison's initial proposal that the new American nation use governmental rewards rather than patents to foster innovation, see Edward C. Walterscheid, "To Promote the Progress of Science and Useful Arts: The Background And Origin of the Intellectual Property Clause of the United States Constitution," *Journal of Intellectual Property Law* 2 (1994): 1–56. The principal subsequent proposals for more extensive use of a reward system are: Robert Andrew Macfie, *The Patent Question under Free Trade: A Solution of Difficulties by Abolishing or Shortening the Inventors' Monopoly, and Instituting National Recompenses*, 2d ed. (London: W.J. Johnson, 1863); Robert Andrew Macfie, *The Patent Question in 1875: The Lord Chancellor's Bill, and the Exigencies of Foreign Competition* (London: Longmans, Green & Co., 1875); Michael Polanyi, "Patent Reform," *Review of Economic Studies* 11 (1944): 61–76; Michael Kremer,

"Patent Buy-Outs: A Mechanism for Encouraging Innovation," NBER Working Paper No. 6304 (1997), http://www.nber.org/papers/w6304; Steve Calandrillo, "An Economic Analysis of Property Rights: Justifications and Problems of Exclusive Rights, Incentives to Generate Information, and the Alternative of a Government-Run Reward System," *Fordham Intellectual Property, Media and Entertainment Law Journal* 9 (1998): 301–60; and Steven Shavell and Tanguy van Ypersele, "Rewards versus Intellectual Property Rights," *Journal of Law and Economics* 44 (2001): 525–47. Details of several of these recommendations will be considered later in this chapter.

4. The state boat-hull protection statutes were declared preempted by patent law in *Bonito Boats, Inc. v. Thunder Craft Boats, Inc.*, 489 U.S. 141 (1989). The resultant gap in the protections enjoyed by novel vessel designs has now been filled (in a different way) by 17 U.S.C. §§1301–1332.

5. On the defects of strategies one through three, see Mill, *Principles of Political Economy*, 933. On the defects of strategy four, see Kenneth J. Arrow, "Economic Welfare and the Allocation of Resources for Invention," in *The Rate and Direction of Inventive Activity: Economic and Social Factors*, Report of National Bureau of Economic Research, Special Conference Series 13 (Princeton: Princeton University Press, 1962), 609–25. On the defects of strategy five, see Robert G. Bone, "A New Look at Trade Secret Law: Doctrine in Search of Justification," *California Law Review* 86 (1998): 241–313. For an effort to assess the merits of the five strategies in different contexts, see Nancy Gallini and Suzanne Scotchmer, "Intellectual Property: When Is It the Best Incentive System?," in Adam Jaffe, Josh Lerner, and Scott Stern, eds., *Innovation Policy and the Economy* 2 (Cambridge: MIT Press, 2002), 51–77.

6. See Declan McCullagh, "RFID Tags: Big Brother in Small Packages," *CNET News*, January 13, 2003, http://news.com.com/2010-1069-980325.html.

7. A mechanism for making explicit one's intention to devote a recording to the public domain is available at http://www.creativecommons.org.

8. Remember, from Chapter 2, that one acquires a copyright nowadays merely by expressing in a tangible medium of expression a work having a minimal degree of originality. Registration of one's work with the Copyright Office is not a prerequisite—although one must do so before bringing suit against a copyist. Thus, the process of seeking an ordinary copyright registration from the Copyright Office and the process of registering one's work for the purposes of the compensation system described in this chapter could and probably should be independent of one another. A creator could do one without the other or one before the other. It would probably be simplest, however, to enable and encourage creators to do both simultaneously.

9. There are some potential complications. If a rap artist takes a small slice from another registered recording (say, a five-second bass riff) and then plays it twenty times in the background of his own recording, should he report inclusion of five seconds or one hundred seconds of material? If a filmmaker takes a thirty-second slice from another registered film but removes the audio track and adds a new one, should he report inclusion of thirty seconds of material or something less? Decent arguments could be made for either result in both cases. Rules governing these (and

many other unanticipated complications) could and should be developed by the Copyright Office. My own preliminary answers would be: providing appropriate stimuli and rewards for creativity would be best served by treating the first case as the incorporation of five seconds of material and the second case as the incorporation of thirty seconds of material.

10. Shavell and van Ypersele, "Rewards versus Intellectual Property Rights," 530.

11. Arnold Plant, "The Economic Theory Concerning Patents for Inventions," 1 *Economica* 30 (1934): 30–51; Glynn S. Lunney, Jr., "Reexamining Copyright's Incentive-Access Paradigm," *Vanderbilt Law Review* 49 (1996): 483–656.

12. The quotation from MacFie may be found in *The Patent Question under Free Trade*, 41. For the struggles of natural-law theorists to solve the problem of "proportionality," see Robert Nozick, *Anarchy, State, and Utopia* (New York: Basic Books, 1974), 175; Alan Ryan, *Property and Political Theory* (Oxford: Blackwell, 1984), 32–35; Wendy J. Gordon, "A Property Right in Self-Expression: Equality and Individualism in the Natural Law of Intellectual Property," *Yale Law Journal* 102 (1993): 1533, 1565–70; R. Anthony Reese, "Reflections on the Intellectual Commons: Two Perspectives on Copyright Duration and Reversion," *Stanford Law Review* 47 (1995): 707, 710–12; and Alfred Yen, "Restoring the Natural Law: Copyright as Labor and Possession," *Ohio State Law Journal* 51 (1990): 517, 546–57.

13. Fritz Machlup, "An Economic Review of the Patent System," Study No. 15 of Subcomm. on Patents, Trademarks, and Copyrights of the Senate Comm. on the Judiciary, 85th Cong., 2d sess. (1958), 80.

14. See RIAA, 2003 Yearend Statistics, http://www.riaa.com/news/newsletter/pdf/2003yearEnd.pdf. For the portion of total retail sales earned by the record companies, see the Appendix.

15. See Neil Netanel, "Impose a Noncommercial Use Levy To Allow Free Peer-to-Peer File Sharing," *Harvard Journal of Law & Technology* 17 (2003): 1, 48; Stan Liebowitz, "Will MP3 Downloads Annihilate the Record Industry? The Evidence So Far," in *Advances in the Study of Entrepreneurship, Innovation, and Economic Growth*, ed. Gary Libecap (Greenwich, CT: JAI Press, 2003), http://wwwpub.utdallas.edu/liebowit/knowledge_goods/records.pdf; and Stan Liebowitz, "Policing Pirates in the Networked Age," *Cato Policy Analysis* No. 438 (May 15, 2002), http://www.cato.org/pubs/pas/pa438.pdf. Recently, a continued decline in CD sales prompted Liebowitz to revise his estimates. See Drew Clark, "Research Alters Expert's View on Impact of File Sharing," *National Journal's Technology Daily*, January 31, 2003. He now predicts that file sharing "eventually could cost the recording industry up to 25 percent of its revenues." He has not, however, suggested that an injury of that magnitude is imminent. The data concerning the decline in album sales (CDs, cassettes, LP albums, and audio DVDs) between 2000 and 2003 were derived from RIAA, 2003 Yearend Statistics. Explanations for that decline other than the corrosive effect of unauthorized copying and distribution are presented in Liebowitz, "Will MP3 Downloads Annihilate the Record Industry?," 18–26.

16. For documentation of the estimate that 15 percent of the record companies revenues go toward manufacturing costs, see the Appendix. For May and Singer's

projections, see "Unchained Melody," *The McKinsey Quarterly*, 2001, Number 1, 128, 130.

17. The figure set forth in the text ($691 million as the total amount of American phono-mechanical license fees in 2000) is derived from National Music Publishers Association (NMPA), Eleventh Annual International Income Survey—2000, 7–8, Table 1, available at http://www.nmpa.org/nmpa/survey11/NMPA2002Survey11th Edition.pdf. (The appendix to that report [p. 37] indicates that that amount of money was actually "paid to copyright owners of musical compositions." Presumably, therefore, it excluded the fee of between 5 percent and 5.75 percent charged by the Harry Fox Agency for processing those payments. See http://www.harryfox.com/hfacommission.html.) Roughly the same number is generated by multiplying the gross revenues of the music companies ($7.35 billion) by 8 percent (the portion of those revenues that the Appendix estimates are typically paid to the assignees of the composers): $588 million. That these two numbers are reasonably close provides some independent support for the analysis in the Appendix. The first of the two figures—because it is supplied by the recipient of the funds—is undoubtedly the more accurate of the two, so we will use it when estimating the injuries that the publishers might sustain as a result of the establishment of the proposed regime.

18. See NMPA Report, 7, Table 1.

19. The data concerning retail sales and rentals of videotapes and DVDs come from Alexander and Associates, "Video Flash: Historical Data," http://www.alexassoc.com/video/videoflash/history02.shtml. A slightly lower estimate can be found in Veronis Suhler Stevenson, *Communications Industry Forecast*, 17th ed. (Media Merchant Bank, July 2003). Veronis Suhler Stevenson also provides the following projections of the growth of this figure through the present: $21.063 billion in 2000; $23.008 billion in 2001; $24.424 billion in 2002; $27.503 billion in 2003; and $29.882 billion in 2004. The estimate of $7.8 billion as the portion of the retail revenues that, in 2000, went to the studios is derived from Harold L. Vogel, *Entertainment Industry Economics: A Guide for Financial Analysis*, 5th ed. (Cambridge, MA: Cambridge University Press, 2001), 62 (Table 2.8). Vogel's estimate is reasonably consistent with Compaine and Gomery's contention that approximately 40 percent of home-video revenues ends up in the hands of the studios. Benjamin M. Compaine and Douglas Gomery, *Who Owns the Media? Competition and Concentration in the Mass Media Entertainment Industry*, 3rd ed. (Mahwah, NJ: Lawrence Erlbaum Associates, 2000), 412.

20. The first figure is provided by Veronis Suhler Stevenson, *Communications Industry Forecast*, 219, which goes on to estimate and predict premium-channel revenues for 2001 as $7.971 billion; for 2002 as $8.588 billion; for 2003 as $9.143 billion; for 2004 as $9.579 billion; for 2005 as $10.283 billion; and for 2006 as $11.040 billion. The rough division of the spoils is reported in Compaine and Gomery, *Who Owns the Media?*, 408–9.

21. A rough estimate of this figure may be found in Compaine and Gomery, *Who Owns the Media?*, 408–9. A more precise estimate, from which we derive the number used in the text, is provided by Veronis Suhler Stevenson, *Communications*

Industry Forecast, 224. Total payments in 2001 were $1.828 billion, and in 2002, were $2.1 billion. Veronis Suhler Stevenson predicts that the market will continue to grow, but that its increase will be curbed to some extent by the expansion of video-on-demand. Specifically, it projects total payments of $2.18 billion in 2003, $2.257 billion in 2004, $2.328 billion in 2005, and $2.44 billion in 2006. The estimates offered in the text of the percentages of premium-channel and pay-per-view revenues that eventually go to the studios are awfully slippery, but fortunately, we have some corroboration. Harold Vogel reports that, in 2000, the studios collected from all "pay cable" sources—presumably including both premium channels and pay-per-view services—$1.6 billion (*Entertainment Industry Economics*, 62, Table 2.8). Our own estimates produce a total of $1.818 billion. Because that figure is more conservative (i.e., higher) we will use it for the purposes of these calculations.

22. See M. William Krasilovsky and Sidney Shemel, *This Business of Music*, 8th ed. (New York: Billboard Books, 2000), 151, 153 (reporting the 16 percent overhead figure); Barry M. Massarsky, "The Operating Dynamics Behind ASCAP, BMI and SESAC," Coalition for Networked Information (July 3, 2002), http://www.cni.org/docs/ima.ip-workshop/Massarsky.html (reporting ASCAP's overhead charge as 18 percent); and Robert P. Merges, "Contracting into Liability Rules: Intellectual Property Rights and Collective Rights Organizations," *California Law Review* 84 (1996): 1293. The Department of Labor reports that inflation, measured by the Consumer Price Index, was 2.8 percent between 2000 and 2001, 1.6 percent between 2001 and 2002; and 1.3 percent in the first half of 2003. See http://www.bls.gov/cpi/cpido1av.pdf; http://www.bls.gov/cpi/cpido2av.pdf; and http://www.bls.gov/cpi/cpido3fv.pdf. For estimating inflation through the end of 2004, we'll assume that the CPI again rises 1.3 percent during the second half of 2003 and during the first and second halves of 2004. Total inflation for the period 2000–2004 would thus be 9.98 percent.

23. See National Aeronautics and Space Administration, President's FY2004 Budget Request, http://www.nasa.gov/pdf/2167main_04budget_sum_030227.pdf; National Science Foundation, FY2005 Budget Request, http://www.nsf.gov/home/budget/start.htm; James Glanz, "Loss of the Shuttle," *New York Times*, Section A, p. 1, Column 1; and Scott Nance, "Lawmaker Calls for More Aerospace Research," *Defense Week*, February 18, 2003.

24. For the data on the total number of households that file tax returns, see Peter Orszag and Matthew Hall, "Nonfilers and Filers with Modest Tax Liability," http://www.taxpolicycenter.org/research/Topic.cfm?PubID=1000548 (the total number of "tax units" minus the total number of "nonfilers" minus nontaxable filers is 87,284,000).

25. For a general analysis of the distortionary effects of income taxation, see Joseph E. Stiglitz, *Economics of the Public Sector*, 3rd ed. (New York: Norton, 2000), 535–48. The magnitude of those effects is controversial. For a survey (and reassessment) of the literature that regards them as modest, see Arthur Snow and Ronald S. Warren, Jr., "The Marginal Welfare Cost of Public Funds: Theory and Estimates," *Journal of Public Economics* 61 (1996): 289. For a sharply different view, contending

that, when one takes into account the effect of a tax on "education, occupational choice, effort, location, and all of the other aspects of behavior that affect the short-run and long-run productivity and income of the individual," deadweight losses may exceed in magnitude the amount of revenue raised by the tax itself, see Martin Feldstein, "How Big Should Government Be?," *National Tax Journal* 50 (1997): 197, 208–12. Louis Kaplow's demonstration that the distortionary effect, whether large or small, will not arise if the proceeds of the tax are devoted to the production of a public good, the benefits of which match the incidence of the tax itself, is set forth in "The Optimal Supply of Public Goods and the Distortionary Cost of Taxation," *National Tax Journal* 49 (1996): 513–33; "A Note on the Optimal Supply of Public Goods and the Distortionary Cost of Taxation," *National Tax Journal* 51 (1998): 117–25; and "On the (Ir)Relevance of Distribution and Labor Supply Distortion to Public Goods Provision and Regulation" (Working Paper 2004). The intuition that underlies Kaplow's formal argument is especially plausible in this particular context. For reasons explored more fully later in this chapter, under the proposed alternative compensation system most households would save through decreased expenditures on recorded entertainment more money than they would spend on increased taxes. In other words, the typical household would suffer no net diminution in its capacity to purchase goods and services. Thus, one would not expect its members to substitute leisure for work. (Unless, of course, the increased availability of good music and films made leisure relatively more attractive—but a substitution effect arising out of that circumstance should not necessarily be regarded as regrettable.)

The proposition that the benefits of the system considered in this chapter would vary with income might seem to be undermined by the recent Pew survey, which indicates that people with lower incomes are more likely than people with higher incomes to download music from the Internet. See Mary Madden and Amanda Lenhart, "Pew Internet Project Data Memo," *Pew Internet & American Life Project* (July 2003): 5, http://www.pewinternet.org/reports/pdfs/PIP_Copyright_Memo.pdf. However, that correlation probably has much to do with the fact that the activity in question is currently illegal—an hypothesis supported by the fact that downloading activity decreases with education level as well. If gaining access to entertainment over the Internet were legalized (as it would be under the new regime), the correlation suggested in the text would likely take hold.

26. See Netanel, "Impose a Noncommercial Use Levy." Netanel's article develops much more thoroughly ideas first suggested in Glynn S. Lunney Jr., "The Death of Copyright: Digital Technology, Private Copying, and the Digital Millennium Copyright Act," *Virginia Law Review* 87 (2001): 813, 851–58, 910–18; Raymond Shih Ray Ku, "The Creative Destruction of Copyright: Napster and the New Economics of Digital Technology," *University of Chicago Law Review* 69 (2002): 263, 312–15; and one of my own essays: "Digital Music: Problems and Possibilities" (2000), http://www.law.harvard.edu/Academic_Affairs/coursepages/tfisher/Music.html.

27. Devin Leonard, "This Is War," *Fortune*, May 27, 2002, 83; Newsline, *Billboard*, August 17, 2002, 73. Information concerning stand-alone versions can be found at http://www.ce.org/publications/books_references/digital_america/audio/

digital_recording.asp. Germany recently imposed a tax of 7.50 euros (approximately $7.30) on all PC-integrated CD burners. The taxes imposed under the scheme outlined in this chapter would likely be higher. But taxation of such devices is certainly not unprecedented.

28. Aditya Kishore, "The Death of the 30-Second Commercial," The Yankee Group: Media & Entertainment Strategies (August 2003), 6. For a summary and criticism of the earlier, more optimistic projections, see Phillip Swann, "Special Report: Is Bernoff 'Way Off'?," *TVPredictions.com*, http://www.tvpredictions.com/news2.html. For more conservative projections, see Veronis Suhler Stevenson, *Communications Industry Forecast*, 274. The estimates of the costs of purchasing a PVR and of the associated service were derived from the advertised prices for TiVo units. See http://www.tivo.com/2.0.asp.

29. See Phil Kloer, "Say You Want a Revolution?," *Atlanta Journal-Constitution*, August 3, 2003, 1M; and Lawrence B. Johnson, "Will Recordable DVDs Replace CD-ROMs?," *USA Today*, November 12, 2002. Cf. Mark Landler, "The Media Business: For Music Industry, U.S. Is Only the Tip of an Iceberg," *New York Times*, September 26, 2003, A1 (placing the figure at 1.8 billion).

30. See Paul Bond, "Economics Can't Keep Electronics from Selling Well," *The Hollywood Reporter*, January 13, 2003; Kirk Ladendorf, "Back on Its Feet, SigmaTel Is Aiming High," *Austin American Statesman*, January 13, 2003 (reporting a much higher estimate of 2002 sales—almost 8 million units); Henry Norr, "Rays of Hope for Technology," *San Francisco Chronicle*, January 16, 2003; and Amy Tsao, "Can Electronics Retailers Reconnect?," *Business Week Online*, January 22, 2003.

31. Phil Hardy, "New Products and Technologies Bring Online Music from the Computer to the Livingroom," *Music & Copyright*, December 25, 2002.

32. Veronis Suhler Stevenson, *Communications Industry Forecast*, 306–7. Similar estimates may be found in U.S. Department of Commerce, *A Nation Online: How Americans Are Expanding Their Use of the Internet*, National Telecommunications and Information Administration & Economics & Statistics Administration (February 2002), http://www.ntia.doc.gov/ntiahome/dn/anationonline2.pdf.

33. A subtle issue: Are wireless and satellite services fairly described as "broadband"? Probably. Even the satellite systems (the slower of the two) provide roughly twenty times the speed of dial-up modems. Although that's substantially slower than a cable or DSL connection, it seems fair to classify it as "broad." See https://www.ibuybroadband.com/ibb2/knowledge.asp.

34. Veronis Suhler Stevenson, *Communications Industry Forecast*, 306–7.

35. The estimate of StreamCast Networks' revenues during 2002 comes from "StreamCast Dream of Lucky Three (and a Move to LA)," *The Online Reporter*, May 3–9, 2003, http://www.onlinereporter.com/torbackissues/TOR346.htm.

36. Let's return now to the choice we considered a few pages ago: Should people who gain access to the Internet through dial-up modems be obliged to share in the tax burden? If we took the other fork in the road and decided yes, then the total tax base would increase by $7.699 billion—to a total of $27.947 billion. That substantial adjustment would, in turn, enable us to lower the tax rate to 8.5 percent.

Under this regime, each broadband subscriber would pay $3.88 per month in taxes (instead of $5.36) and persons with dial-up modem accounts would pay $1.57 per month in taxes.

37. See Stiglitz, *Economics of the Public Sector*, 563–66; William J. Baumol, "Ramsey Pricing," in John Eatwell, Murray Milgate, and Peter Newman, *The New Palgrave: A Dictionary of Economics* (London: Macmillan, 1987), Vol. 4, 49–51.

38. For studies of Americans' and Europeans' conceptions of distributive justice, see J. Stacy Adams and Sara Freedman, "Equity Theory Revisited: Comments and Annotated Bibliography," in *Advances in Experimental Social Psychology* 9 (Leonard Berkowitz and Elaine Walster eds., New York: Academic Press, 1976), 43, 47–49.

39. It would likely be most efficient if all parties obliged to gather and report this data used the same software to do so. One way to achieve such standardization would be for the Copyright Office to require all participants in the system to use a specific program. Though attractive on some levels, such a solution would forfeit the efficiencies associated with private software development (whether proprietary or open-source). On balance, therefore, a compromise on this issue seems best: the Copyright Office would develop a standard data-collection program—or, more likely, would commission a private firm to develop such a program—and would make it available, for free, to all participants in the Webcasting industry. But the office would also permit Webcasters to use other programs, provided that they were capable of transmitting the required information in a specified format. Such a system would not block innovation but would preserve consistency.

40. The data were kindly provided by Steve Crandall, one of the members of the AT&T team (now with Omenti Research).

41. For discussions of the danger that such a system would be "gamed," see S. J. Liebowitz, "Alternative Copyright Systems: The Problems with a Compulsory License," draft of August 31, 2003, http://www.utdallas.edu/liebowit/intprop/complpff.pdf; Aaron Swartz, "Privacy, Accuracy, Security: Pick Two," http://www.aaronsw.com/weblog/001016; and Eugene Volokh, "Download Tax," http://volokh.com/2003_09_07_volokh_archive.html#106314198323180349. Their worries are lent credence by the extent to which artists on the old MP3.com site strove to "game" that system. See Janelle Brown, "Whoring for Downloads," *Salon.com*, November 30, 2000, http://dir.salon.com/tech/feature/2000/11/30/download_trading/index.html?sid=999949.

42. For descriptions of the Nielsen system, see Suzanne Vranica and Charles Goldsmith, "Nielsen Adapts Its Methods as TV Evolves," *Wall Street Journal*, September 29, 2003, B1; James C. Raymondo, "Confessions of a Nielsen Household," *American Demographics*, March 1997, 21–24; and J. Ronald Milavsky, "How Good Is the A.C. Nielsen People-Meter System? A View of the Report by the Committee on Nationwide Television Audience Measurement," *Public Opinion Quarterly* 56 (1992): 102–15.

43. For a survey of studies documenting the overall accuracy of the system, see Hugh Malcolm Beville Jr., *Audience Ratings: Radio, Television, Cable* (1988), Appendix D. For analyses of the imperfections of the system, see Beville, *Audience Rat-*

ings, 232–33; Michelle Greppi, "Diaries and Youth an Unreliable Combo," *Electronic Media,* September 23, 2002, http://www.tvweek.com/topstorys/092302diaries.html; Robert J. Kent, "Second-by-Second Looks at the Television Commercial Audience," *Journal of Advertising Research* 42, No. 1 (2002), 71; Bill Carter, "NBC Faults Nielsen for Reduction in Viewers," *New York Times,* November 11, 2003, C1; Vranica and Goldsmith, "Nielsen Adapts"; and Erwin Ephron, "Why We Cannot Afford to Measure Viewers: The Case for VPVH (Viewers-Per-Viewing-Households) Modeling," *Canadian Advertising Research Foundation (CARF) Newsletter* #247, January 2001.

44. A variation on this theme that would be easier to administer but less effective in measuring actual consumption patterns would be to "sample," not listeners' and viewers' actual consumption patterns, but the contents of their hard drives. Software closely analogous to the programs now widely used by the file-sharing services would periodically report to the Copyright Office what registered recordings were stored on the computers of people who agreed to participate in such surveys. Assurances of privacy would be equally important under this regime. For the same reason, it would be crucial that the software only identified and reported registered recordings, not other material located on the participant's hard drives. A system of this sort would be reasonably effective in curbing the first and third of the kinds of distortion outlined above. It would do nothing to eliminate the second—but, then again, it would be no worse in this regard than the present system for distributing music. The main advantage of such a regime is that it would be relatively easy to implement and run.

45. James Love, "Artists Want to be Paid: The Blur/Banff Proposal," http://www.nsu.newschool.edu/blur/blur02/user_love.html, 7.

46. James Love, "Artists Want to be Paid," 7.

47. Peter Eckersley, "Virtual Markets for Virtual Goods: An Alternative Conception of Digital Copyright," http://www.cs.mu.oz.au/pde/writing/index.html, 12.

48. Volokh's example (designed to discredit a somewhat different system) appears in Volokh, "Download Tax."

49. A loosely analogous cut-off applied to shares in Native American land holdings was declared unconstitutional by the Supreme Court in *Hodel v. Irving,* 481 U.S. 704 (1987). Constitutional difficulty would not likely arise in this context, however, for reasons we will explore later in this chapter.

50. The estimate set forth in the text of the amount that the average household spends per year for access to recorded entertainment is based on the following figures. In 2000, the total retail value of sound recordings (including singles) sold in the United States was $14.042 billion; $21.856 billion was spent on video rentals and sales; $7.314 billion was spent on premium cable subscriptions; and $1.426 billion was spent on pay-per-view television, for a grand total of $44.638 billion. The average expenditure of each of the 105,480,101 households was thus $423. In 2003, the total retail value of sound recordings sold in the United States was $11.428 billion; $27.503 billion was spent on video rentals and sales; $9.143 billion was spent on premium cable subscriptions; and $2.18 billion was spent on pay-per-view television, for a grand total of $50.254 billion. The average expenditure of each of the 108,424,184

households was thus $463. In 2004, the number will surely be higher. (The continuing decline in total retail spending on sound recordings will be more than offset by the steady rise in spending for access to video recordings.) A conservative estimate of average per-household expenditures is thus $470. The sources for this data are *Households and Families: 2000*, Census 2000 brief, September 2001, http://www.census.gov/prod/2001pubs/c2kbr01-8.pdf; U.S. Census Bureau, "2002 American Community Survey Profile," Table 1: General Demographic Characteristics, http://www.census.gov/acs/www/Products/Profiles/Single/2002/ACS/Tabular/010/01000US1.htm; and the materials cited in notes 19–21. The amount that Americans "spend" to gain access to recorded entertainment intermingled with commercial advertising is suggested by the following figures: In 2004, each American will devote, on average, 1,521 hours watching broadcast or cable television (excluding premium channels) and another 995 hours listening to the radio. The overwhelming majority of the programming delivered through those channels consists of ad-supported, commercial material. Roughly ten minutes of each of those hours is devoted to advertisements. Thus, each American is exposed, on average, to 419 hours of advertisements per year. To be sure, they are able to avoid some of those ads—by leaving the room for a snack, by muting the television and engaging in conversation, by changing radio stations, etc. But even PVR users (many of whom buy their machines precisely to enable them to avoid advertisements) end up watching 45 percent of the ads embedded in the programs they record. Assuming then, conservatively, that the population as a whole watches 50 percent of the ads in the programming delivered to them, each person devotes, on average, 209 hours per year—the equivalent of twenty-six eight-hour days—to ad watching. For the data underlying these estimates, see U.S. Census Bureau, *Statistical Abstract of the United States: 2002*, No. 1102: "Media Usage and Consumer Spending: 1996–2005," http://www.census.gov/prod/2003pubs/02statab/infocom.pdf; and Kishore, "The Death of the 30-Second Commercial," 3, 7.

51. Would option C truly leave them no worse off? As the new system took hold, we would expect to see the retailers and lessors specializing in entertainment in the traditional formats (like Tower Records and Blockbuster) closing their doors at an accelerating rate. See Vanessa E. Jones, "They're Tuned in to Customers' Needs," *Boston Globe*, November 19, 2003, C12. However, large-scale intermediaries like Amazon.com and Netflicks, which deliver such products through the mail system, would likely survive and perhaps expand. So the adverse impact on consumers who stuck with the traditional formats would probably be modest at most.

52. On the defects of the fair-use doctrine, see William Fisher, "Reconstructing the Fair Use Doctrine," *Harvard Law Review* 101 (1988): 1659, 1667–95. On the clumsiness of other aspects of copyright law in dealing with improvements and the mild superiority of the analogous aspects of patent law, see Mark Lemley, "The Economics of Improvement in Intellectual Property Law," *Texas Law Review* 75 (1997): 989.

53. Filmmakers are especially likely to balk at this aspect of the proposed regime. In November of 2003, I discussed the proposed system in a meeting at Warner Bros. Entertainment, attended by lawyers for six of the seven major film studios. The attendees were troubled by many aspects of the plan—but the extent to

which it corroded the right of copyright owners to control the content of their works seemed to gall them the most.

54. On the limitations on architects' rights, see *Nimmer on Copyright*, §2.20.

55. For exploration of some of these complexities, see R. Anthony Reese, "Copyright and Internet Music Transmissions: Existing Law, Major Controversies, Possible Solutions," *University of Miami Law Review* 55 (2001): 237; and Hillel Parness, "Internet Radio: As RIAA and DiMA Prepare to Do Battle Over 'Interactivity,' Questions Resurface About ISP Liability," *Cyberspace Lawyer* 6 (2001): 2.

56. The numbers set forth in the text were derived from the most recent report on downloading activity: Pew Internet & American Life Project, "Sharp Decline in Music File Swapping: Data Memo from PIP and comScore Media Metrix," January 4, 2004, http://www.pewinternet.org/reports/toc.asp?Report=109.

57. For illustrations and analyses of the lobbying power of the major record companies and film studios, see Jessica D. Litman, "Copyright, Compromise, and Legislative History," *Cornell Law Review* 72 (1987): 857; Robert P. Merges, "One Hundred Years of Solicitude: Intellectual Property Law, 1900–2000," *California Law Review* 88 (2000): 2187, 2233–39; and William F. Patry, "Copyright and the Legislative Process: A Personal Perspective," *Cardozo Arts & Entertainment Law Journal* 14 (1996): 139.

58. Because this privilege would be limited to recordings that are registered pursuant to the new scheme, it would be possible to avoid the issue in section 107A—and instead deal with the matter through contract. In other words, the right to control the preparation of derivative works embodied in section 106(2) of the statute could be left unqualified, but copyright owners could be obliged, when registering recordings, to waive their rights in this respect. It seems more forthright, however, to make this aspect of the new regime explicit in the authorizing statute.

59. For the texts of the treaties, see http://www.wto.org/english/docs_e/legal_e/legal_e.htm#TRIPs; and http://www.law.cornell.edu/treaties/berne/overview.html.

60. See *New York Cent. R.R. Co. v. White*, 243 U.S. 188 (1917); Theodore F. Haas, "On Reintegrating Workers' Compensation and Employers' Liability," *Georgia Law Review* 21 (1987): 843. But cf. Martha S. Davis, "Worker's Compensation Systems and the Takings Problem," *South Dakota Law Review* 38 (1993): 234 (suggesting that the case might be decided differently today).

61. See Brett May and Marc Singer, "Unchained Melody," *The McKinsey Quarterly* (2001) Number 1, 128, http://mckinseyquarterly.com/article_page.asp?ar=978 &L2=17&L3=66 (registration required).

62. This figure was derived as follows: Using (conservatively) figures from the year 2000, the recording industry would suffer a decline in revenues of $7.35 billion, partially offset by a savings in manufacturing costs of $1.103 billion and in phono-mechanical license fees (plus commissions to the Harry Fox Agency) of $726 million, for a total loss of $5.521 billion. The music publishers would suffer a decline in phono-mechanical license fees of $691 million and (assuming, again conservatively, that the entire radio industry collapsed in the face of competition from Webcasters)

of $292 million in public-performance fees—for a total of $983 million. The movie studios would experience the elimination of their revenues from domestic videotape and DVD sales and rentals ($7.8 billion), cable and satellite services ($1.219 billion), and pay-per-view movies ($570 million)—for a total loss of $9.589 billion. The grand total: $16.093 billion. (The bases for all of these estimates are set forth on pages 210–12 and the accompanying footnotes. To repeat, most of these numbers are "soft," but most also are based on conservative assumptions.) Adjusting for inflation (which we've estimated at 9.98 percent between 2000 and 2004), this would be the equivalent of $17.699 billion in 2004 dollars. Finally, if we assumed (once again, conservatively) that 20 percent of funds raised would be diverted to administrative costs, we would need $22.124 billion to fund the system fully. Spread over the existing group of taxpayers (87 million households), this would generate an average tax burden of $254 per household.

63. This figure is derived by dividing the total tax burden of $22.124 billion by 109,508,425 households. (For the source of the latter figure, see Chapter 1, note 6.)

64. If the copyrights in the musical compositions performed in an audio recording were owned by persons or firms other than the registrant, then the registrant would have to obtain their permission to enter into such an agreement—presumably, by agreeing to share with them the revenues that he or she earned from the coop. Otherwise, for the reasons explained in Chapter 2, they would have a plausible claim against the coop for contributory copyright infringement.

65. Where would disk jockeys get the money necessary to launch and maintain such ventures? They might not need any at all. After all, they would not be paying any license fees, and their hardware costs would be modest. Thus, like the operators of many of the stations on Live365.com, they might do it for free. Alternatively, as suggested in the text, they could charge users modest fees. Finally, they might rely upon advertising revenues.

66. The Slashdot system itself may be found at http://slashdot.org/. Benkler's analysis comes from "Coase's Penguin, or Linux and the Nature of the Firm," *Yale Law Journal* 112 (2002): 369, 393–96.

67. Todd Larson's detailed development of this idea in the context of Webcasting may be found at "CommuniCast: Developing a Community-Programmed Webcasting Service" (May 10, 2003), http://cyber.law.harvard.edu/home/2004-01.

68. On the strengths and weaknesses of producer cooperatives, see Avner Ben-Ner, "Producer Cooperatives: Why Do They Exist in Capitalist Economies?," in Walter W. Powell, ed., *The Non-Profit Sector: A Research Handbook* (New Haven: Yale University Press, 1987), 434–46; Aver Ben-Ner, "Empirical Observations on Worker Owner and Capitalist Firms," *International Journal of Industrial Organization* 6 (1988): 7; Henry Hansmann, "When Does Worker Ownership Work? ESOPs, Law Firms, Codetermination, and Economic Democracy," *Yale Law Journal* 99 (1990): 1749; Henry M. Levin, "Employment and Productivity of Producer Cooperatives," in Robert Jackall and Henry Levin, eds., *Worker Cooperatives in America* (Berkeley, CA: University of California Press, 1984), 16–31; W. Bentley MacLeod,

"Equity, Efficiency, and Incentive in Cooperative Teams," *Advances in the Economic Analysis of Participatory and Labor-Managed Firms* 3 (1988): 5; Marco Marini, "Stable Producer Cooperatives in Competitive Markets," *Advances in the Economic Analysis of Participatory and Labor-Managed Firms* 6 (1998): 213; and Joyce Rothschild and J. Allen Whitt, *The Cooperative Workplace* (Cambridge: Cambridge University Press, 1986). On the history and structure of consumer cooperatives, see International Joint Project on Co-operative Democracy, *Making Membership Meaningful: Participatory Democracy in Co-operatives* (Saskatoon: Centre for the Study of Cooperatives, University of Saskatchewan, 1995); Robert Neptune, *California's Uncommon Markets: The Story of Consumers Cooperatives, 1935–1976* (Richmond, CA: Associated Cooperatives, 1977); *Co-operatives and Consumer Power Towards the Year 2000* (London: Co-operative Press, 1993); and the Website for the European Community of Consumer Cooperatives, http://www.eurocoop.org/cooperatives/en/default.asp.

69. On the tendency of the members of producer cooperatives to underinvest in improvements to the enterprise, see Rothschild and Whitt, *The Cooperative Workplace*, 161.

70. The progress of the Canto Livre project and the development of the associated alternative-compensation system can be observed on the following Website: www.direitorio.fgv.br/cts.

Appendix

1. The RIAA's Website states, "While the RIAA *does not collect information on the specific costs that make up the price of a CD*, there are many factors that go into the overall cost of a CD. . . ." Available at http://www.riaa.org/MD-US-7.cfm (emphasis added).

2. Brett May and Marc Singer, "Unchained Melody," *The McKinsey Quarterly* 2001 Number 1, 128, 130. May and Singer, in turn, rely in part on Harold Vogel, *Entertainment Industry Economics: A Guide for Financial Analysis*, 4th ed. (Cambridge, MA: Cambridge University Press, 1998) and *Next Magazine* (October 1996).

3. Ted Lathrop and Jim Pettigrew Jr., *This Business of Music Marketing and Promotion* (New York: Billboard Books, 1999), 123.

4. Neil Strauss, "Pennies That Add Up to $16.98: Why CD's Cost So Much," *New York Times*, July 5, 1995, Section C, p. 11, column 1. An older and less-well-documented breakdown is supplied by David Hinckley: "For a CD that retails at $15, Warners' price to distributors is $10–$11—from which, says Warners, the distributor gets 14 percent. The rest roughly breaks down, says Warners, to 40 percent for recording costs and royalties, 30 percent for manufacturing, and the rest for overhead and promotion—like videos, at $ 250,000 and up," in "Music Recordings Usually a Losing Proposition," *The Times Union*, Albany, NY, January 13, 1994, 9.

5. Benjamin M. Compaine and Douglas Gomery, *Who Owns the Media?*, 3rd ed. (Mahwah, NJ: Lawrence Erlbaum Associates, 2000), 326.

6. Chris Taylor, "Where the Money Goes: A Breakdown of the $19.95 [sale price of a CD]," *Canadian Musician*, December 1998. See also DaZZub at http://www.sandersontaylor.com/da_zzub_w2002.html#feature.

7. Phil Hardy, "Italian Soundcarrier Market Fell 9% in Local Currency Terms in 2001," *Music & Copyright*, June 19, 2002.

Index

"ABC's of Happiness" (film), 29
Acuff-Rose Music, 44–45, 47
administrative agencies, 195–96, 214, 244
Adobe Systems, 97
Advanced eBook Processor, 97
advertising: on decentralized file-sharing services, 220–21; fast-forwarding to avoid, 72, 74; personal video recorders excluding, 132, 296n107, 315n50; on radio, 23; radio as advertising recordings, 54, 103; for television broadcasts of films, 72, 74; in Webcasting, 103
Aeolian Company, 49
Agreement on Trade-Related Aspects of Intellectual Property Rights (TRIPS), 248
AHRA (Audio Home Recording Act), 85–87, 90, 99, 116, 129
Aibopet, 284n32
Aimster, 112, 114, 118–19, 151
air space, 137, 141, 143, 152
Albini, Steve, 30
albums, record. See record albums
alternative compensation system, 199–258; administrative costs of,

214, 243; advantages of, 203, 236–40, 243–46; Berne Convention modification for, 248–49; constitutional issues for, 249; copyright law revision for, 246–48; determining aggregate compensation levels, 205–15; digital rights management systems and, 247–48; disadvantages of, 240–42, 244–45, 246; Entertainment Coop for administering, 252–58; establishment of, 246–49; evolution of, 249–51; expanding to other forms of digital entertainment, 251; film industry revenue affected by, 212–14, 213; and foreign countries, 245, 246, 251; life cycle of, 246–51; logistics of, 203–36; measuring value of individual works, 223–34, 255; music industry revenue affected by, 209, 209–12; outline of, 202; registration, 203–5, 252; taxation needed for, 214; types of taxation to fund, 216–23
American popular culture, new technologies reinforcing, 4
American Society of Composers, Authors, and Publishers (ASCAP),

production (sound recording); record companies; Recording Industry Association of America; sound recordings
music lockers, 98–102; attempts to curtail, 7, 100–102; My.MP3.com, 100–102
MusicMatch, 253, 269n16
MusicNet, 155, 156, 188
Music Online Competition Act, 304n19
Music Owner's Licensing Rights Act, 101–2
music publishing companies: alternative compensation system affecting, 316n62; composers assigning rights to, 47–52, 103; declining CD and tape sales affecting, 211; and Digital Audio Tape Recorder Act, 85; Harry Fox Agency, 48, 50, 52, 60, 76, 211, 309n17; legal rights in music industry, 52; National Music Publishers Association, 48, 102; revenue streams in music industry, 60
My.MP3.com, 100–102
myMP3storage.com, 99
MyPlay, 99

Napster, 110–12; copyright-violation suit against, 1–4, 113–14, 116–20; and exposure effect, 33; fee-based "premium" service proposed, 111, 115, 292n69; forced to shut down, 4, 114; noninfringing uses of, 117–19, 292n74; resurrected, 120, 155, 257; scale of illegal behavior enabled by, 3–4; *Sony* case compared with that of, 71, 116–19, 292n73
National Endowment for the Arts, 217
National Music Publishers Association (NMPA), 48, 102
National Television Ownership Rules, 188, 189
natural-rights theory, 208
neighboring rights, 201
Netanel, Neil, 210, 217

network effects, 33, 34
new technologies, 11–37; American popular culture's power reinforced by, 4; artists benefiting from, 26; cost savings of, 18–25; creators' incomes eroded by, 31–35; cultural diversity promoted by, 26–28, 187; dangers of, 31–37; enabling large numbers of people to violate law, 2–4; entertainment industry destabilized by, 82–109; experience of entertainment altered by, 12–13; film industry business model threatened by, 5, 202; music industry business model threatened by, 1–2, 4–5, 158–59, 202; opportunities offered by, 18–31; semiotic democracy promoted by, 28–31, 184; social benefits of, 2, 6. *See also* digital files; Internet
niche markets, 26
Nichols, Mike, 28–29
Nielsen sampling approach, 226–29, 314n44
Nimmer, Melville B., 280n3
NMPA (National Music Publishers Association), 48, 102
No Electronic Theft Act, 147
noninteractive streaming: in cooperative alternative compensation system, 253; defined, 17–18; radio stations using, 17–18, 104; and Webcasting performance rights, 104–5, 109
Nozick, Robert, 208

"Oh, Pretty Woman" (Orbison and Dees), 44–45, 70
on-line credit card system, 21, 166–67
open range laws, 141
oral work, copyright in, 271n1
Orbison, Roy, 44–45
Ovitz, Michael, 112

Pagan Paradise Samhian, 26
Paramount Pictures, 63

276n45; production entities in, 60–64

production (sound recording): cost for record album, 54–55, 274n27; home studios, 23; Internet distribution savings on, 23, 159; record companies' role in, 22, 54–55, 56

promotion: under alternative compensation system, 242; in contract with music publisher, 47; independent promoters, 56, 59, 76; Internet distribution savings on, 23, 159; record companies' role in, 22, 55

property rights, 134–72; copyright and, 8, 42, 134–35, 143–54; effects of making copyright parallel to, 154–69; limitations, 140–43; rights, 136–40; sketch of property law, 135–49

property rules, 138–39, 144, 193

PROs. See performing rights organizations

P2P file-sharing systems. See decentralized (peer-to-peer) file sharing

public goods: deadweight losses and, 216, 311n25; government attempts to aid production of, 200–201; problem of, 199–200

public interest, 178–79, 181–82, 215

publicity, rights of, 63

public-performance rights. See performance rights

public utilities, 8–9, 174, 175

publishing companies, music. See music publishing companies

PVRs. See personal video recorders

quiet enjoyment, right to, 136, 140

Radar Station, 26

radio: as advertising sound recordings, 54, 103; alternative compensation system affecting, 211–12; blanket performance licenses for, 50, 52, 53–54, 60, 76, 103, 144; college stations, 108; digital broadcasting, 14; diversity sought in, 188–89; noninteractive streaming used by, 17–18, 104; number of hours Americans listen to, 182, 315n50; obtaining permission to play songs over the air, 50; payola, 58–59, 76, 158; simulcasting on Internet, 106, 288n51; Webcasting contrasted with, 23; and Webcasting royalty system, 104, 106. See also Webcasting

Radio Free Boonie, 26

radio frequency identification (RFID) tags, 203

railroads, 174

Ramsey pricing, 222–23

rap (Hip Hop) music, 30, 169, 205, 217, 234–36, 240, 307n9

rate court, 51, 185

RealAudio, 89

RealNetworks, Inc., 89–90, 94

RealPlayer, 89–90, 94

real property, 136

RealServer, 89

RealVideo, 89

record albums: defined, 274n29; global sales by format, 1973–2002, 32. See also cassette tapes (audio); CDs (compact discs); long-playing (LP) record albums

record companies: alternative compensation system affecting, 209, 209–12, 242, 316n62; artists taken advantage of by, 19–20, 55–56, 183–84; copy-protection schemes used by, 129–30; and home taping of music, 83–84; individual downloaders sued by, 124–28, 155, 243; inequality in music industry, 76; market power of, 181, 193; mechanical license to record composition, 48–49, 52, 60, 103; musicians becoming less dependent on, 24, 159, 238; music lockers opposed by, 100–102; Napster approaching